PSYCHOLOGY LIBRARY EDITIONS:
COGNITIVE SCIENCE

Volume 13

PHYSIOLOGICAL PSYCHOLOGY

Physiological Psychology
An introduction

Simon Green
Birkbeck College
University of London

Routledge & Kegan Paul
London and New York

First published in 1987 by
Routledge and Kegan Paul Ltd
11 New Fetter Lane, London EC4P 4EE

Published in the USA by
Routledge & Kegan Paul Inc.
in association with Methuen Inc.
29 West 35th Street, New York, NY 10001

Set in Baskerville
by Inforum Ltd, Portsmouth
Printed in Great Britain by
Butler & Tanner Ltd,
Frome and London

Library of Congress Cataloging in Publication Data

Green, Simon
Physiological psychology.

(Introductions to modern psychology)
Bibliography: p.
Includes index.
1. Psychology, Physiological.   I. Title.
II. Series. [DNLM: 1. Psychophysiology. WL 103 G798p]
QP360.G73   1987   612'.8   86–26081

British Library CIP data also available
ISBN 0–7100–9686–0 (c)
ISBN 0–7102–1128–7 (p)

To my Mother, to Elizabeth, Joseph, and Katie,
and to Daphné Joyce, who started all this . . .

Contents

Figures

Tables

Acknowledgments

Various people have contributed, sometimes unknowingly, to the writing of this book. In particular I would like to thank Steve Cooper and Steve Walker for reading and commenting in detail on various chapters, and many of my undergraduates who criticized, sometimes constructively, some of the middle chapters. Valerie Heap did the bulk of the typing, in her usual inimitable way, while Barbara Parnell and Sue Godfrey brought it to the finishing line. I thank them all.

Preface

This book has several aims. Physiological psychology covers the study of the relationships between the body's physiology and overt behaviour, and includes in particular the investigation of the behavioural aspects of brain function. This latter area has, over the last twenty years, been the fastest growing field of scientific research, and this has been reflected in the number of textbooks dedicated to physiological psychology, neuropsychology, psychobiology, behavioural neurology, or their equivalents.

A primary aim of this text is to sustain the *psychological* approach to brain function. Many of the most dramatic findings in brain research are made by neurologists, neurochemists, neuroanatomists, neuropharmacologists, and neurophysiologists. They have a natural tendency to assume that 'behaviour' is relatively simple to observe, measure, and analyse, in contrast to the complexity of brain structure and process. However, the contribution of the psychologist is crucial if a realistic picture is to evolve of the relationship between brain function and behaviour, as behaviour, even in the laboratory rat, is never simple; neither side of the brain/behaviour equation can be ignored. (For an extended discussion of this point, see Shuttleworth *et al.*, 1984.)

A second aim was to produce a volume of manageable size. Whereas in the 1960s a comprehensive textbook could be lifted by a reasonably fit student without external aids, its modern-day equivalent would come equipped with wheels. Each topic covered in this volume could be expanded to fill a book of its own, and most have been. My intention it to introduce the whole area, while giving some indications of advances made over the last two decades. To achieve this in the face of the available material has meant some ruthless selection and pruning which, while reflecting a degree of personal bias, maintains, I hope, the central core of physiological psychology. The subject matter is based upon an undergraduate course in physiological psychology. As such, it includes basic and traditional material, but also brings in, where I thought it relevant, more contemporary work and more complex ideas on the relations between brain and behaviour.

I have retained the traditional topic-by-topic approach as I feel this is most appropriate for an introductory text, but have also tried to emphasize the links within and between chapters that reflect the integrated nature of brain function. In addition I have included substantial accounts of brain chemistry in relation to behaviour, as benefits the most important area of brain research to emerge over the last twenty years. To allow for this and to keep the book to a reasonable size, some areas I consider to be of less psychological and more physiological interest are underrepresented. These include motor processes and basic neurophysiology.

Finally I hope, even in the face of the many imperfections in the following pages, that some of the excitement of contemporary physiological psychology gets across to the reader. If it does, I shall consider that the book has done its job.

1 The nervous system – basic principles of function and techniques of investigation

Physiological psychology is concerned with the links between the organism's physiology and its behaviour. Physiology incorporates the totality of physiological systems within the body – the nervous system, endocrine system (glands secreting within the body, such as thyroid, pituitary, adrenal glands), exocrine system (glands secreting via tubes, or ducts, such as sweat glands and tear ducts), skeletal muscles, the gastro-intestinal system, the circulatory system, etc. Although we shall be meeting some of these systems in later chapters, the predominant interest of the physiological psychologist lies in the brain and the rest of the nervous system. The basic unit of the nervous system is the neuron.

The neuron

All the cells of the body follow the same basic pattern, with a nucleus containing chromosomes, the genetic material consisting of strands of deoxyribosenucleic acid (DNA), which is surrounded by the jelly-like cytoplasm containing all the other cellular mechanisms, e.g. the mitochondria, for energy production, and the ribosomes, for protein synthesis. Every cell in the body contains an identical set of chromosomes. Besides embodying an organism's characteristics and controlling their transmission from generation to generation, the chromosomes and their DNA control the cell containing them. In some as yet unexplained fashion, they enable different cells to specialize in

1

different ways during development, despite having the same basic pattern. The muscle cells become specialized for contraction, gland cells for secretion, and neurons for the transmission of electrical impulses.

The particular functional specialization of the neuron leads to physical specializations which can be obvious or very subtle. Neurons are elongated (see Fig. 1.1), with the cell body ('soma') extending into a relatively long branching axon on one side and into a number of relatively short dendrites on the other. It is important to remember that the whole neuron is a single cell, with cytoplasm filling axons and dendrites.

Neurons come in a wide range of sizes and show an infinite variety of dendritic and axonal processes. The human brain contains of the order of fifteen billion neurons (15×10^9), most of which will have short dendrites and axons and be invisible to the naked eye. On the other hand, the axon transmitting

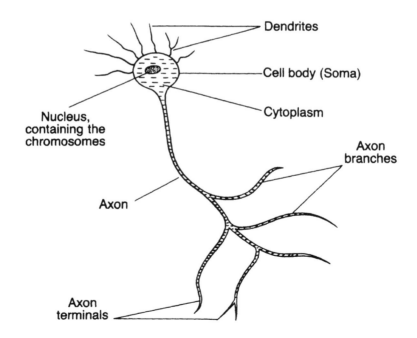

Figure 1.1   *The neuron*

electrical impulses from the spinal cord to the muscles of the toes belongs to a neuron which can be three to four feet long, depending on the length of your legs.

The subtle specialization all neurons have in common concerns the cell membrane, the outer barrier of the neuron. This is semi-permeable, allowing the passage of various electrically charged particles (ions) from inside to out and from outside to in. Usually there is a differential concentration of ions inside and out, leading to an electrical difference, or potential, of around − 70 millivolts across the membrane from inside to out. The situation can be altered by stimuli of various sorts, especially small electric currents. Any stimulus which shifts the membrane potential towards equilibrium (i.e. zero membrane potential) may provoke an *action potential* at that point on the membrane. As the potential across the membrane is decreased to around −50 millivolts, there is an explosive increase in membrane permeability, enabling sodium and chloride ions to rush into the neuron and potassium ions to pass out; this rapid exchange shifts the membrane potential from -50 to around +40 millivolts in about half a millisecond, and constitutes the action potential.

After the action potential has peaked at +40 millivolts, the membrane rapidly returns to its resting state of a − 70 millivolt potential. With a brief *refractory* period after the action potential during which the membrane is inactive, the whole sequence takes about four milliseconds, i.e. the temporal gap between action potentials must be at least four-thousandths of a second.

This gap becomes important when we consider what happens to the action potential. The structure of the neuronal membrane that enables action potentials to occur also enables them to travel along the neuron from the point at which they were first stimulated. Thus a wave of electrical activity (or 'depolarization', the explosive change in membrane potential from −70 to +40 millivolts) passes along the neuronal membrane. If a thin wire recording electrode is placed on the membrane, it will record this wave as a blip of electrical activity; this is the *nerve impulse*. If action potentials are successively stimulated, they will be recorded as sequences, or trains, of nerve impulses. Each part of the membrane traversed by an impulse will be inactive for around four milliseconds. Thus the maximum rate of impulse transmission, or frequency, is around 250/second. As one action potential is electrically identical to any other, each impulse is similarly indistinguishable from every other impulse. The crucial properties of impulse conduction are therefore the frequency and temporal patterning of trains of impulses.

Action potentials are usually initiated on the dendrites of the neuron and the nerve impulse is then propagated along the neuron in the direction dendrite → soma → axon → terminals of all axon branches. Before considering the initiation of the action potential in more detail, there is one fundamental point to be made. Information in any nervous system is embodied, or coded, entirely by the frequency and patterning of nerve impulses. Sensory and motor systems, perception, memory, cognition and thought, emotion, personality, etc., are all represented by patterns of nerve impulses in appropriate parts of the nervous system.

This can be simply demonstrated. Using thin wire stimulating electrodes, a tiny electric current can be applied to single neurons or groups of neurons in the brain. As the brain itself has no sensory receptors, this procedure can be performed in human patients using only a local anaesthetic for the area of the head and skull through which a hole will be drilled to allow entry of the electrode into the brain. Such techniques are normally part of a screening programme before major brain surgery.

If the stimulating currents are within the naturally occurring limits for nervous system electrical activity, then the normal function of an area of the brain can be mimicked. As the patient is conscious, he or she can report any subjective experiences. Over the years it has been shown that visual experience (flashes of light), auditory sensation, 'automatic' vocalization, feelings of unease and euphoria and outbursts of aggression, recall of memories, movement of limbs and of individual muscle groups, increases and decreases in heart-rate and blood pressure, can all be elicited by electrical stimulation of the appropriate part of the brain.

So we possess a brain of unimaginable complexity using a

fundamentally simple electrical code for the information represented within it. Every aspect of behaviour and physiology discussed in this volume has its essence in patterns of identical action potentials in the nervous system, i.e. if you want to be reductionist about it, our brains can be represented as machine-like. However, this machine has fifteen billion working units each, as we shall see, having several thousand interconnections with other units, and produces human behaviour and experience; it is only machine-like if we upgrade our concept of what machines are and what they can do, as even the most sophisticated computer can do little, apart from sums, that we would recognize as a truly human faculty.

The synapse

Neurons are not physically connected to one another. Otherwise, action potentials would simply travel haphazardly to all parts of the nervous system. Between an axon terminal and the next neuron is a gap, the synapse (see Fig. 1.2). Only visible under the electron microscope, the synapses are measured in angstroms (an angstrom is one-millionth of a metre), and present a barrier to the action potential travelling down the axon to the axon terminal (or pre-synaptic terminal); the action potential must be transmitted across the synapse to the post-synaptic membrane of the next neuron if it is not to be lost.

Transmission across the synapse is chemical. Quantities of the particular chemical ('synaptic neurotransmitter') are stored within the pre-synaptic terminal in spherical storage vesicles. When an action potential reaches the pre-synaptic region, it stimulates a number of vesicles to migrate to and merge with the actual neuronal cell membrane bordering the synapse, where they release their chemical contents into the synaptic cleft. The molecules of neurotransmitter diffuse across the synapse and combine with 'receptors' located on the post-synaptic membrane. This combination is most simply seen as a 'lock-and-key' affair. The molecule of transmitter has a certain spatial configuration which is assumed to match perfectly the spatial configuration of the receptor molecule.

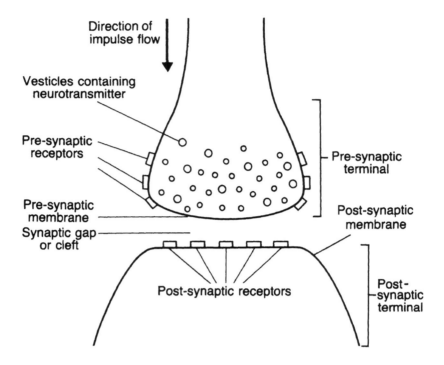

Direction of
impulse flow

Vesticles containing
neurotransmitter

Pre-synaptic
receptors

Pre-synaptic
terminal

Pre-synaptic
membrane

Post-synaptic
membrane

Synaptic gap
or cleft

Post-synaptic receptors

Post-
synaptic
terminal

Figure 1.2 *The synapse*

This interaction between transmitter and receptor is short-lived, but while it lasts produces a change in the permeability of the post-synaptic membrane. This change is along the lines described for the initiation and propagation of the action potential, but the combination of a single molecule of neurotransmitter with a single receptor is insufficient to fully depolarize the post-synaptic membrane. An action potential is based upon depolarization, and even the total amount of neurotransmitter released by a single action potential in the pre-synaptic terminal will not be sufficient to initiate an action potential in the post-synaptic neuron, i.e. the nerve impulse will not cross the synapse, and the information it represents will be lost.

For synaptic transmission to occur, sufficient nerve impulses must arrive within a short space of time at the pre-synaptic terminal to stimulate the release of a sufficient quantity of neurotransmitter into the synapse; when combining simultaneously with many post-synaptic receptors, this quantity will be enough to depolarize the post-synaptic membrane and so initiate an action potential which will in turn be transmitted along the post-synaptic neuron.

Thus the frequency of nerve impulses in the pre-synaptic neuron is unlikely to be matched by the frequency in the post-synaptic neuron. There is one obvious function for this mechanism, but also a further complication. The obvious function is the filtering out of irrelevant information. If touch receptors on the skin are momentarily activated by dust particles in the air, nerve impulses travel along sensory neurons towards the central nervous system. If the activation is momentary, the concentration of impulses will be insufficient to carry the first synapse in the chain leading to the brain and conscious awareness. Thus the information will be lost, or filtered out, a quite reasonable system for preventing the brain becoming overloaded with what is fundamentally irrelevant information.

The complication in the mechanism is that synaptic connections are not one-to-one, or even of the same type. As a very rough estimate, any central nervous system neuron makes contact via synapses with several thousand other neurons. Thus a nerve impulse in one neuron is the summated product of hundreds or thousands of inputs to that neuron; the nervous system does not operate along straight lines.

Neurotransmitters

Chapter 3 considers brain chemistry and behaviour in some detail. At this stage I want to make some general points regarding neurotransmitters in the brain.

Chemical neurotransmission was first demonstrated by Loewi in 1921 (following, incidentally, 'creative' dreaming!) using the neural connections to the frog's heart (Loewi and Navratil, 1926). Over the next thirty years work concentrated

upon the peripheral nervous system, particularly the synapses
between the axons of motor neurons and skeletal muscles (the
neuro-muscular junction), and it is still the case today that our
synaptic models are based upon the peripheral nervous system
or the accessible nervous systems of other animals. Technical
problems rendered the central nervous system (brain and
spinal cord) more or less impervious to pharmacological
investigation, and as late as 1950 it was still quite acceptable to
deny the existence of synapses in the brain, i.e. to believe that
transmission was entirely via electrical conduction along and
between neurons.

Chemical neurotransmission at a central nervous system
synapse was first demonstrated in the spinal cord (Eccles *et al.*,
1954), and rapidly became accepted as a fundamental means of
information transmission in the brain. (By 'demonstrated' I
mean that certain criteria were established, e.g. presence of
neurotransmitter in pre-synaptic terminals, its release in response to nerve impulses, presence of post-synaptic receptors
with which the neurotransmitter can combine, relevant electrophysiological changes, etc.).

By 1970 there were six established chemical neurotransmitters: noradrenaline, dopamine, and serotonin (all
monoamines), acetylcholine (tertiary amine), GABA (gamma-
amino butyric acid) and glutamate (both amino acids). It is a
basic principle, now under attack but still not fully disproved,
that a given neuron will secrete the same neurotransmitter at
all of its axonal terminals (Dale's principle), and that neurons
may therefore be characterized by their neurotransmitter.
Thus the brain contains noradrenergic, dopaminergic, serotonergic, cholinergic, GABA-ergic, and glutamatergic
neurons.

Added to this list by now are anywhere between twenty and
thirty possible neurotransmitters discovered over the last decade, some of which are discussed in Chapter 3 and whose
precise role in brain function has not yet been identified. Some
may be synaptic neurotransmitters in the classic sense, while
others may be 'neuromodulators', influencing neurotransmission in subtle ways. Regardless of the ultimate outcome, brain
chemistry has become the fastest-growing area of brain re-

search, partly because the existence of a chemical bridge between neurons provides a valuable means for influencing brain function using externally applied chemicals and for modelling drug effects on behaviour, and partly through a combination of sophisticated biochemical and pharmacological techniques which have only become available in the last fifteen years or so.

I mentioned earlier that synaptic receptors were specific to a given neurotransmitter. So, in line with the different transmitters there are dopamine, noradrenaline, acetylcholine, etc., receptors. I also pointed out that neurons receive many inputs via synapses, and so their dendritic and somatic membranes may possess many different types of receptor depending upon the types of input.

Two further complications. An axon terminal releases neurotransmitter into the synaptic cleft where it diffuses over to the post-synaptic membrane and combines with its specific receptors. It has been discovered that there are also receptors on the pre-synaptic terminal itself; some of the neurotransmitter diffuses to these receptors ('autoreceptors'), where the effect is to inhibit neurotransmitter release from the pre-synaptic terminal, i.e. a negative feedback system, as the more transmitter is released the less likely it is to be released.

Secondly, neurotransmitter receptors exist in several forms. There are muscarinic and nicotinic cholinergic receptors, alpha and beta noradrenergic receptors, D1, D2 and D3 dopaminergic receptors (with several more awaiting confirmation), and serotonin 1 and 2 receptors. The subtypes all combine with the neurotransmitter itself, but are distinguished by their ability to combine with (or bind to) other drugs. So the muscarinic cholinergic receptor is stimulated by acetylcholine and the drug muscarine, but not by nicotine, while the nicotinic cholinergic receptor is stimulated by acetylcholine and nicotine, but not by muscarine.

Receptor subtypes may also be distinguished by their synaptic or regional distribution. Thus noradrenergic pre-synaptic autoreceptors are of the alpha type, while all synapses at the skeletal neuromuscular junction are of the nicotinic cholinergic type. This amazing chemical heterogeneity makes the interpretation of drug effects extremely difficult, and while I have mentioned it here to illustrate the rapid pace of brain research, I do not intend to go into it more deeply than is necessary in subsequent chapters. There are some fine introductory texts (e.g. Iversen and Iversen, 1981)which cover the chemistry and pharmacology of brain function in impressive detail.

Techniques for investigating brain function

The two principles of information transmission in the nervous system – electrical and chemical – immediately provide two sets of investigatory techniques.

Electrical stimulation and recording

I have already mentioned the use of electrical stimulation to mimic the brain's natural activity. This necessarily involves localized stimulation using single wire electrodes, in some cases so small that individual neurons may be stimulated. For behavioural studies, stimulation usually involves larger electrodes activating many thousands if not millions of brain cells. The top rung of the electrical stimulation ladder is held by electro-convulsive shock, whereby large currents are passed through the brain to induce convulsive activity; this traumatic technique provides no insights into brain function, but is held by some to be a useful treatment for depressive disorders (see Chapter 12).

Electrodes may also be used to *record* the naturally occurring electrical activity of the brain. Recordings may be taken from single neurons (or single units), through populations of thousands of neurons, to the evoked potential and EEG recordings which may involve billions of cells. Evoked potentials, as their name implies, are electrical changes evoked by, or 'locked' onto, a stimulus in the environment, e.g. a flash of light or tone. They occur some milliseconds after the stimulus, the precise latency (delay) depending upon the exact location of the recording electrode. Single unit recording can show evoked activity (e.g. in studies of habituation, Chapter 7), but, more usually, evoked potentials are taken from the cortex using recording electrodes placed directly on the skull, i.e. this can be a 'non-invasive' technique. As the brain is constantly active, it is impossible to distinguish a single evoked potential from background electrical activity; repeated stimulus presentations are given, and a computer used to superimpose successive electrical recordings in the hope that the consistently elicited evoked potential will emerge as the random background activity is averaged out. Measuring evoked potentials is thus a complicated procedure, and although it is useful in checking whether stimuli are being registered in various parts of the brain, the precise functional significance of evoked potentials and their relation to cognitive processing remains a matter of debate.

Building on the pioneering work of Caton and Galvani in the nineteenth century on the electrical activity of the brain, Berger introduced in the 1930s (Berger, 1929) the idea that the gross electrical activity of the brain can reflect the subject's state of arousal, and he can be credited with introducing the EEG (electroencephalogram) into neurophysiology. The EEG as usually recorded from electrodes dotted over the skull surface reflects cortical activity, and is sometimes and pedantically referred to as the E.Cort.G. (electrocorticogram). It represents the continuous activity of billions of neurons, and occurs in two major variants; it can either be synchronized or desynchronized. A synchronized EEG has, after appropriate computer-based analysis of the raw signals, a characteristic repeated wave-form, which may be identified by the number of waves per second (Herz). Thus the alpha waves dominating the EEG of the drowsy subject have a frequency between 8 and 12/second (8–12 Herz), while delta waves found in the deep sleep EEG have a frequency of around 1/second. The desynchronized EEG, as its name implies, does not have a dominant and characteristic wave-form, but consists of irregular electrical activity. A fast desynchronized recording is typical of the waking, aroused state, and is also found in dreaming sleep (see Chapter 10).

EEG patterns may also be recorded from large subcortical structures using invasive implanted electrodes, usually in animals. Particularly prominent has been the hippocampal

EEG and its characteristic theta wave (4–7 Herz), whose functional significance has been a subject of lively discussion for many years (reviewed in Gray, 1982).

Chemical stimulation and recording
Since the earliest civilizations, drugs, often extracted from plants, have been used for their dramatic effects on perception, emotion, and cognition. Today mescaline (from the dried cactus, 'peyote'), psilocybin (from the so-called 'sacred mushroom' of Central America), opium and morphine (from the poppy), are still used for their hallucinogenic properties, while there is an enormous range of synthetic drugs used to alter behaviour and experience – anti-depressants, anti-anxiety drugs, anti-psychotic agents, pain-killers (analgesics), etc.

Most classes of synthetic drugs used in psychiatry were introduced before much was known about the chemistry of the brain, on the purely pragmatic basis of clinical effectiveness. As information accumulated during the 1960s and 1970s on synaptic neurotransmission in the brain, it became increasingly possible to relate the behavioural effects of drugs to interactions with synaptic transmitters. Thus 'Psychopharmacology' or 'Behavioural Pharmacology' evolved.

Psychopharmacology can be divided into two major areas. The first is concerned with the mechanisms of action of drugs used in the psychiatric clinic, and is dealt with in Chapter 12. The second is concerned with the use of drugs as tools to investigate brain function in relation to behaviour. Obviously the two areas interconnect and overlap, as we assume that all drugs, as chemicals, exert effects on the chemistry of the brain and hence on behaviour. The difference lies in the relative objectives. An effective antianxiety drug such as chlordiazepoxide (Librium) has become established via its therapeutic action in anxious patients. It is the *subject* of analysis, as a determination of its pharmacological action in the brain may help unravel the brain mechanisms of 'anxiety' and suggest more effective drugs.

On the other hand one may be interested in the behavioural functions of cholinergic neurons in the brain. The need then is for drugs with a specific pharmacological action on cholinergic synapses, drugs which may also have clinical utility but more often do not. It is their pharmacology, rather than their clinical/behavioural actions, which is important.

Over the last twenty years many drugs have been identified as having specific pharmacological effects at nervous system synapses. Given the complexity of synaptic neurotransmission, there are several ways in which it may be influenced, often involving the injection of drugs through permanently implanted intra-cranial cannulae (tiny steel tubes inserted through the skull into the brain) onto specific sites within the brain. Amongst these ways are the following:

1   Drugs which are similar in structure to natural transmitters may act directly upon synaptic receptors, either to stimulate them ('agonists') or to block them ('antagonists'). Thus apomorphine is a dopamine agonist, scopolamine a cholinergic antagonist.

2   Drugs may influence the release of the neurotransmitter from the pre-synaptic terminal. Amphetamine increases the release of dopamine and noradrenaline from their terminals, and is therefore an *indirectly acting* agonist.

3   Drugs may interfere with the metabolic pathway of a given neurotransmitter. Neurotransmitters are synthesized within neurons from raw materials transported in the bloodstream. Specific enzymes are essential for each stage of the synthetic process, and specific enzymes inactivate the neurotransmitter after its action at the post-synaptic receptor (otherwise post-synaptic stimulation would be continuous). In general we can say that interference at any point can have profound effects upon synaptic transmission. As examples, α-methyl-p-tyrosine inhibits the enzyme tyrosine hydroxylase, which is crucial to the synthesis of dopamine and noradrenaline. As a consequence, brain levels of these two neurotransmitters rapidly fall. (It is a general point that the total brain content of any transmitter will be released, broken down, and resynthesized within a matter of hours or days. Normal levels are sustained only by constant synthesis.)

There is a group of anti-depressant drugs known as the

monoamine oxidase inhibitors (MAOIs). Monoamine oxidase is an enzyme involved in the breakdown and removal of noradrenaline, dopamine, and serotonin from the synapse after they have combined with their respective receptors. Inhibition of this enzyme prevents the breakdown, and allows high levels of neurotransmitter to be maintained at and around the synapse with consequent high levels of synaptic transmission.

4   Drugs may have less specific actions. Anaesthetics seem in general to act upon the neuronal membrane, reducing its excitability, rather than upon the synapse.

5   Drugs may be used to produce specific chemical 'lesions', i.e. localized areas of damage after injection directly into the brain. These drugs are known as neurotoxins, and include 6-hydroxydopamine (6-OHDA) which is taken up by and destroys dopaminergic and noradrenergic nerve terminals, and 5,7 dihydroxytryptamine (5,7–DHT) which does the same to serotonergic terminals.

For all the classical neurotransmitter systems, and for some of the newer candidates, we have comprehensive batteries of drugs to stimulate, block, increase levels of, or decrease levels of the neurotransmitter. We can also measure levels of brain neurotransmitters at post-mortem (see Chapter 12 in relation to brain chemistry and schizophrenia). In the living patient, our most direct insight into the brain's chemical working comes from analyses of cerebro-spinal fluid (CSF).

In the centre of the spinal cord lies the narrow spinal canal. This continues up into the brain where it expands to form the ventricular system, consisting of fluid-filled chambers which provide a means for the disposal of the waste products of brain metabolism. The CSF constantly circulates between brain and spinal cord, and a sample can be extracted via a hypodermic inserted between the lower vertebrae and into the spinal canal – the lumbar puncture. Analysis of CSF can reveal various aspects of the brain's metabolic activity. Presence of virus particles can confirm a diagnosis of meningitis (inflammation of the protective membranes covering the brain), while fragments of red blood corpuscles confirm that a cerebral haemorrhage has occurred. The CSF also contains the metabolic breakdown products of synaptic neurotransmitters, and some workers suggest a direct relationship between, e.g., levels of brain dopamine and levels of CSF homovanillic acid (HVA), its major breakdown product. Chapter 12 covers this approach in more detail.

Lesions: physical destruction of brain tissue

The neurotoxin technique mentioned above is relatively recent. Until then, and still massively popular, a range of lesioning techniques dominated physiological psychology. Brain tissue has been damaged or removed by knife cuts, suction (especially the cerebral cortex in rats), injection of pure alcohol (the early frontal lobotomy of Moniz: see Chapter 8), focal (localized) cooling of specific sites, implantation of radio-active pellets, coagulation and, most frequently, by electrolytic lesions. These latter involve thin wire electrodes implanted in the brain through which relatively high currents are passed. The heat generated by the current coagulates ('electro-coagulation') the tissue in the immediate vicinity of the exposed tip of the electrode, effectively producing a small sphere of destruction.

A 'lesion' usually refers to damage to a localized and small amount of brain tissue. An 'ablation' – less common now as techniques and data focus upon smaller units of brain structure – refers more to the destruction/removal of whole brain regions, e.g. the cortex, hippocampus, etc. The very rare 'lobotomy' refers to the physical destruction of a lobe of the cerebral hemisphere, while 'leucotomy' refers to the cutting of pathways connecting various parts of the brain.

Recent developments in non-invasive procedures

An invasive procedure involves the penetration of the skull and brain for recording, lesioning, electrical and chemical stimulation, etc. It will, for practical and ethical reasons, often involve non-human animals. Non-invasive procedures do not involve direct contact with brain tissue. Some, such as the electro-encephalogram, have been around for many years. Others have only recently been introduced, and have led to a rapid increase in studies on the living brains of human subjects.

The CAT scanner (computed axial tomography) takes X-rays of the brain from all angles; a computer reconstructs these two-dimensional slices and then produces a three-dimensional overall view of the brain. Resolution is not yet high, so this technique is best for identifying large structures such as the ventricles, and for localizing large tumours and areas of haemorrhage, etc. Sometimes the CAT scanner is combined with an injection of radio-actively labelled glucose; this glucose concentrates in areas of high metabolic activity, and the emitted radio-active particles show up as lighter zones on the CAT scan. This technique is known as positron emission tomography (PET), and has been used to confirm brain regions involved in speech and other cognitive functions.

An even more recent technique is nuclear magnetic resonance (NMR). A powerful magnet is used to create a magnetic field around the head which aligns all the protons in the hydrogen atoms in neurons in the same orientation (it is apparently perfectly safe!). These are then bombarded with radio waves, and begin to resonate, producing radio waves of their own. These are recorded, computerized, and a three-dimensional picture of the brain emerges. The resolution and detail is on the whole better than with the CAT scanner.

Other techniques can be used to measure blood-flow to various brain regions (cerebral angiography), and at least one paper has reported the visualization of brain dopamine neurons in the living human subject, using a variation of the PET technique. Doubtless progress will continue until we can measure detailed brain function during all aspects of behaviour. This will perhaps reduce the dependence of brain research on animal subjects.

The use of non-human animals in physiological psychology

Much of the experimental work described and referred to in this book has been done on non-human animals: rats, cats, monkeys, great apes (chimpanzees and gorillas), mice, reptiles, fish, birds, and invertebrates such as the octopus, flatworms, and marine molluscs. Many of the experimental procedures involve chronic (long-lasting) implantations of electrodes for lesioning, stimulating, and recording, implantation of cannulae for chemical stimulation, destruction of brain tissue using the sorts of procedures outlined in the previous section, acute (short-term) drug administration using hypodermic injections into the peripheral circulation (intra-venous, i.v.) or into the abdominal cavity (intra-peritoneal, i.p.), etc. If lesion or injection sites within the brain need to be localized, animals are sacrificed at the end of the experiment so that the brain can be dissected and the sites identified.

Behavioural tests used are often benign, as in the case of exploration, discrimination learning, appetitive operant tasks, etc. However, mild footshock is frequently used in avoidance learning, while some procedures such as sleep deprivation and lesion-induced changes in primate dominance hierarchies are inherently stressful.

Animal experimentation in Great Britain is controlled by the Home Office, and all workers using animals, whether pharmacologists, psychologists, biochemists, neurologists, etc., have to be licensed. The essence of the control is that whatever procedures are involved, the animal is not subjected to undue stress or pain. Thus brain stimulation and lesioning involve the implantation of electrodes and cannulae under authentic surgical conditions of anaesthesia and monitored post-operative recovery. Animals showing pain or distress in recovery are euthanased. Behavioural techniques are also controlled, such that only limited periods of food and water deprivation and only mild levels of stressors such as footshocks and noise can be used.

In other countries the control of animal experimentation may be less rigorous, but even so it is probable that the key issue is not how well regulated is the use of animals, but whether they should be used in the first place.

Historically rats have been used in psychology in general and by physiological psychologists in particular because they are available in large numbers and at low cost. Cats and primates have been used less often, as they are relatively less available and more expensive, although closer to Homo sapiens sapiens on the evolutionary ladder. Even though cats and monkeys have a more sympathetic public image, any moral arguments obviously apply to all experimental animals, while a scientific debate may hinge on the practical relevance of the species used, i.e. do results from rat studies have any bearing on human brain function? The answer to this latter question is yes. Even if the rat brain and rat behaviour prove to be quantitatively entirely distinct from the human brain and human behaviour (and there is much evidence to the contrary), consistent evolutionary trends have emerged (see Chapter 2) which justify the field of comparative neuropsychology; we would know more about human brain function if we knew the evolutionary stepladder it had emerged from. Primate studies have a much more direct relevance to modelling the human brain, as we can assume that primate and human functional brain circuits will have much in common; in terms of the fundamental genetic material in the chromosomes, humans are much more closely related to chimpanzees than, for instance, mice are to rats.

Thus one can justify on scientific grounds the study of the animal brain in relation to behaviour. An even stronger case can be made where animals are used to help develop treatments for human neurological and psychiatric disorders (see, e.g. Chapters 3 and 12), and at an extreme one could say that any study of animals will at some point contribute to the alleviation of human distress, as the more we know of brain and behaviour the better able we are to cope with their disorders.

That is the positive side. On the negative side there are studies within physiological psychology which seem to me unjustified on any grounds, as the results are out of all proportion to the distress caused to the subjects. There is a moral position that rejects the use of any animals in any research, and which, if you hold it, eliminates any dilemmas. The pressure from holders of this position has had the beneficial effect of at least making anyone working with animals justify, however flimsily (e.g. the cosmetics industry), the work they do. Within physiological psychology it has produced a trend towards experimental work directly related to human behaviour, often with a clinical angle, e.g. the development of new drug therapies. It is, in my opinion, incontrovertible that drugs have been a major factor in alleviating physical and psychological distress, and equally incontrovertible that animal research in the medical sciences and in physiological psychology has been essential to their development. Thus, it appears to me that some animal research can be justified. Tighter control of procedures as related to aims would reduce the number of unnecessary experiments, but whether this will come about through the new Home Office regulations currently being processed or via the continuing public debate on the use of animals is a matter for conjecture. Unlike some of my fellow researchers, I do not feel that the debate is best left to the professionals.

2 The nervous system – organization and functions

Evolutionary considerations

Physiological psychology is primarily concerned with the advanced nervous system found in vertebrates – fish, amphibians, reptiles, birds, and mammals (see Table 2.1 for a simplified phylogenetic scale). This consists of a brain at the head of a spinal cord, with nerves distributed throughout the body. The vertebrate nervous system evolved from the 'nerve-net', a network of neurons and axons without any apparent organization, and able only to mediate simple behavioural responses such as whole body contraction. This type of nervous system is found in primitive invertebrates such as the protozoan 'hydra', and is of interest to us only in that the elements – the neurons – function on exactly the same principles as those in our own brain, even down to the synaptic neurotransmitters involved.

A further stage in the evolution of the nervous system is reached with the insects and molluscs. Here we see some organization appearing. Neuronal cell bodies cluster together, and are surrounded by protective connective tissue to form 'ganglia' (singular 'ganglion'), a term still applied to clusters of neuronal cell bodies wherever they occur. In addition the axons leaving the cell bodies in the ganglia to innervate the body tissues in part travel in bundles, again surrounded by a tough connective coat. Bundles of axons (occasionally dendrites) so bound together constitute 'nerves'; in higher vertebrates, the nerves travelling around the body will contain some hundreds of thousands of neuronal fibres.

Table 2.1   Phylogenetic scale – simplified

	Invertebrates
e.g. Annelida	(segmented worms)
Mollusca	(e.g. snails, Aplysia californica)
Arthropoda	(e.g. Insects, spiders)
	Vertebrates
e.g. *Agnatha*	(jawless fish – lamprey, hagfish)

Gnathostomata – Classes

Elasmobranchii (cartilaginous fish – dogfish, skates, rays, etc.)
Actinopterygii (bony fish)
Amphibia (e.g. frogs, toads, newts, salamanders)
Reptilia (e.g. tortoises, lizards, snakes, crocodiles)
Aves (birds)
Mammalia

Class *Mammalia – Orders*

e.g. Monotremata	(platypus, spiny anteaters)
Marsupialia	(kangaroos, wombats, koalas)
Insectivora	(hedgehogs, moles, shrews)
Chiroptera	(bats)
Edentata	(anteaters, sloths, armadillos)
Rodentia	(squirrels, voles, mice, rats)
Lagomorphs	(hares, rabbits)
Cetacea	(whales, dolphins, porpoises)
Carnivora	(dogs, wolves, weasels, bears, cats)
Sirenia	(sea cows)
Perissodactyla	(horses, zebra, rhinoceros)
Artiodactyla	(pigs, hippopotamus, camels, deer, giraffes)
Primates	

Order *Primates – suborders*

Prosimians (lemurs, aye-aye, loris, tarsier)
Anthropoidea – superfamilies
Ceboidea (New World Monkeys – marmoset, capuchin, spider, howler monkeys)
Cercopithecoidea (Old World Monkeys – rhesus, macaques, baboons, mandrills)
Hominoidea – families
Pongidae (Apes, gorillas, orang-utans, chimpanzees)
Hylobatidae (Gibbons)
Hominidae (Humans – Homo sapiens)

This scale is based on a traditional classification. Taxonomy – the classification of animals – is in a particularly dynamic state at present, with serious challenges to established views. However, general relationships still hold. Primates are evolutionarily more advanced than rodents, and rodents more advanced than insectivora. The long-held view that mammals and birds evolved from reptiles, and reptiles from amphibia, is still widely accepted, although alternative approaches to this traditional Darwinian view are emerging.

In the ganglionic nervous system some regional organization is apparent, e.g. a head ganglion is usually identifiable. However, the internal structure of any one ganglion is comparable to that of any other, and the head ganglion of an insect is not directly comparable to the vertebrate brain.

The evolutionary pressures leading to the development of a brain are discussed by Jerison (1973) in a stimulating book. He argues convincingly that many of these pressures were essentially sensory. It is still the case with present-day lower vertebrates that much of the nervous system is devoted to sensory and motor processes; analysing input from sensory receptors and producing motor responses (via control of skeletal muscles and internal response systems such as smooth muscle and glands). Even with mammals there is a high correlation between brain weight and body size – the larger the body, the greater the number of sensory receptors and response systems, and the larger the amount of neural tissue necessary to cope with them. Thus large animals have bigger brains than smaller animals.

As invertebrates such as the squid and the octopus evolved complex sensory systems such as eyes and ears (or their aquatic equivalent, the lateral line system), and as these sophisticated receptors concentrated where they were most needed – the front or anterior end of the body which entered a new and possibly hostile environment first – the increase in neural tissue needed to process the vast increase in sensory input occurred close to the receptors, i.e. at the anterior end of the nervous system. Similarly, it can be argued (Jerison, 1973) that the significant increase in brain size found in mammals as compared to reptiles occurred as a result of our 'mammal-like' reptilian ancestor occupying a nocturnal niche, where competition from the dominant but daylight-dependent large reptiles was minimal. Successful adaptation to a nocturnal habitat requires the development of sensitive olfactory (smell) and auditory systems to handle distant stimuli when vision is impaired; the neural tissue that evolved in parallel with these senses contributed to the markedly larger brain characteristic of mammals.

Jerison introduced a statistical technique to help identify

major shifts in brain evolution. Within a related group of animals, e.g. fish, reptiles, or primates, a plot of body weights against brain weights produces a series of points lying around a straight line, the regression line. Assuming that the regression line is characteristic of that group of animals, the relative brain development in any single species can be assessed. Thus, for instance, despite their large (in absolute terms) brains, whales and elephants lie on or around the higher vertebrate regression line, rats and moles a little below, and modern humans (Homo sapiens sapiens) and dolphins well above.

In more detail, human brains can also be evaluated against our closest relatives, the primates – monkeys and the great apes such as the chimpanzee and the gorilla. A plot of brain weight against body weight in primates produces an orderly straight line relationship, from which we can estimate the brain size of a primate with our own body size; it appears that humans possess a brain about three times as large as we would expect for such a primate (before we get too excited, we should note that the dolphin outperforms us when it comes to having a much larger brain than expected from its body size and classification). This increase is concentrated in the hippocampus of the limbic system, the cerebellum of the hindbrain, and the neocortex (see p.39). The neocortex is the most recently evolved area of the brain, and, involved as it is in many higher cognitive functions which underly our position as top species, might be expected to reflect this by showing extremely rapid evolutionary development.

However, it is the case that the volume of neocortex as a proportion of brain volume increases steadily throughout the primate series; large primates possess more neocortex than small primates, and we have no more than we can expect for a primate of our brain size. In addition, the type of neurons and their arrangement in the neocortex does not especially distinguish us, and the overall picture is of a large brain, but one that closely follows the primate pattern. It should also be emphasized that all the structures found in the human brain can be identified, even if only in a primordial form, in the brain of the lowliest vertebrate swimming about in the sea. For a more detailed discussion of these issues see Walker (1983) and Passingham (1982).

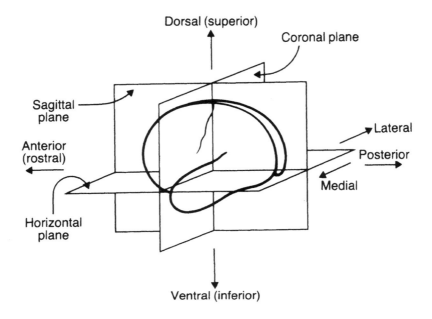

Figure 2.1   *Planes of orientation in the brain*

Organization of the nervous system

The vertebrate nervous system is, like the rest of the body, bilaterally symmetrical, i.e. if sliced through lengthways (the sagittal plane – see Fig. 2.1), two identical mirror halves result. Vertebrates are also segmented organisms; although it is not immediately obvious, studies on the developing embryo show that we are fundamentally segmented in an analogous fashion to the earthworm, and in the adult one of the most obviously segmented systems is the nervous system. In the earthworm, the nervous system (Fig. 2.2) is organized into a ventral nerve cord with paired nerves innervating (supplying) each segment. In vertebrates the nervous system consists of a brain at the head

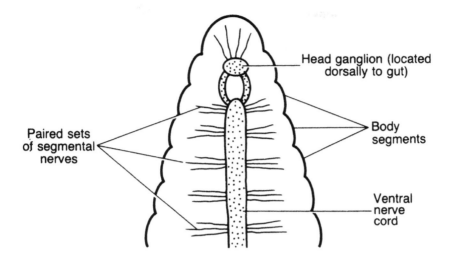

Figure 2.2   *Outline of earthworm nervous system – anterior end of body. Compare segmental arrangement with vertebrate peripheral nervous system (Fig. 2.3)*

of a spinal cord, with paired spinal nerves leaving the cord to innervate the body. Thus an initial classification of the nervous system divides it into the central nervous system (CNS: the brain and the spinal cord) and the peripheral nervous system (PNS: the spinal nerves).

The peripheral nervous system

In primates, the thirty-one pairs of spinal nerves carry hundreds of thousands of neuronal fibres, mainly axons. They can be carrying information from sensory receptors into the CNS (sensory or afferent), or carrying commands from the CNS out to response systems, or effector organs, such as muscles and glands (motor or efferent) (Fig. 2.3). The location and type of receptors and effectors is used to subdivide the PNS into two major systems. The somatic nervous system (SNS) includes

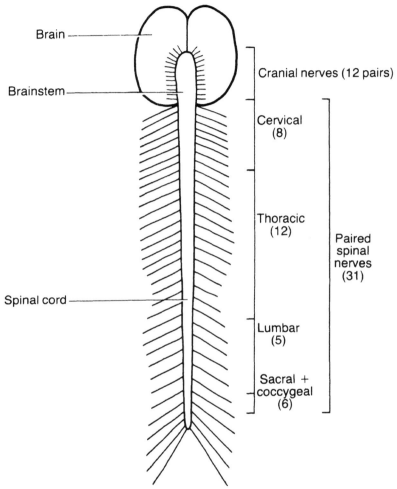

Figure 2.3 *Outline organization of vertebrate peripheral nervous system.*
Each spinal nerve contains thousands of neuronal fibres — motor axons of
the autonomic nervous system, innervating the heart, smooth muscle of
intestine and blood vessels, and glands; motor axons of the somatic nervous
system travelling to skeletal muscle, and sensory fibres of the somatic nervous
system carrying information from sensory receptors on the skin and in
muscles and joints. The cranial nerves handle the sensory and motor
functions of the head and anterior end of the body

those afferent pathways from touch, pain, pressure, and temperature receptors on the surface of the body and in muscles and joints, etc., and efferent motor pathways to the striped muscle of the skeleton. Sensory input from the complex sensory structures of the head (eyes, ears, the vestibular balance system of the inner ear) may also be seen as part of the SNS, whose overall role, in a simplified way, can be seen as enabling the regulation of the organism's interactions with the external environment, i.e. it passes information from the outside world into the CNS and carries commands out from the CNS to skeletal muscle, providing movement.

The second division of the PNS, the autonomic nervous system (ANS), is, in a superficially analogous fashion, concerned with the internal environment of the body. It is a purely motor system, with fibres innervating the smooth muscle of the digestive tract and blood systems, the musculature of the heart, and various glands (e.g. adrenal medulla, pancreas, salivary glands, etc.). It is vital to homeostasis, the regulation of a constant internal environment, as expressed, for instance, in the modulation of heart-rate and blood-pressure in response to physical demands, in the smooth running of the digestive system, or in the maintenance of body temperature. As its name implies, this regulation is usually unconscious – you do not consciously ask your heart to speed up when you run – and to enable it to perform its functions the ANS has two branches. The fibres of the sympathetic branch tend to increase heart-rate and blood-flow to the skeletal muscles, open the respiratory passages, increase the release of adrenaline and noradrenaline from the adrenal gland, and in general prepare the animal for action; a state of peripheral or sympathetic arousal.

The fibres of the parasympathetic branch of the ANS innervate the same target organs as the sympathetic branch, but tend to have the opposite effects, i.e. slowing down heart-rate and blood-pressure, diverting blood to the digestive system, and in general calming things down and conserving energy. A dynamic balance is maintained between the two branches, shifting towards one or the other in response to the body's demands, and moving back to equilibrium when the immediate demand is accommodated. We deal with the ANS in relation to emotion and peripheral arousal in Chapter 9, while Van Toller (1979) presents a clear and comprehensive account of ANS functions.

There is also a sensory system involved with the internal tissues. The visceral afferent network relays information from receptors in the smooth muscle of the gut and circulatory system to the CNS. Although not classified with the ANS, it can be seen as a less-developed sensory partner to the motor output of the ANS.

Apart from the somatic and autonomic nervous system fibres distributed via the spinal nerves, SNS and ANS fibres also make up the cranial nerves. The twelve pairs of cranial nerves emerge from the brainstem rather than from the spinal cord, and supply the specialized senses (vision, hearing, balance, etc.) and musculature (e.g. those involved in speech and facial expression) of the head and anterior end of the body. Autonomic fibres, particularly in the vagus cranial nerve, supply visceral organs in the chest and abdominal cavities.

The central nervous system
The CNS is comprised of the brain and the spinal cord. The spinal cord is continuous with the hindmost part of the brain, the medulla. In cross-section the cord is seen to consist of a central area of grey matter – the cell bodies of neurons – surrounded by areas of white matter-neural fibres coursing up and down the cord. A major function of the spinal cord is to connect the afferent and efferent fibres of the spinal nerves with the brain. Thus the white matter can be divided into various pathways, or tracts, named after the zones they interconnect: e.g. corticospinal (cortex to spinal cord), spinothalamic (spinal cord to thalamus), spinocerebellar (spinal cord to cerebellum), etc. These tracts carry specific information; of the three examples, the first conveys motor control of posture and fine movement, the second sensory input relating to pain, touch, and temperature, and the third sensory information from muscles and joints. There are also spinal-spinal tracts interconnecting zones within the spinal cord.

Damage to the spinal cord disrupts the ascending and

descending flow of information. Clearly, the higher up the damage occurs, the more severe the outcome, with motor paralysis and loss of bodily sensation resulting from a complete transection of the cord. However, even in cases of severe paraplegia (paralysis), some responses may still exist. As the cord is severely damaged, there is no voluntary muscular movement because the commands, formulated in the motor cortex of the brain, cannot reach the executive muscles via the spinal nerves; damage to neurons is usually permanent, although recent work on brain grafts and stimulation of axonal branching gives some hope for eventually repairing damaged pathways. But below the point of cord transection spinal nerves themselves are intact. Thus sensory information from, e.g., pressure receptors in the knee joint is still transmitted into the spinal cord, and the final limb of the motor pathway out from the cord via the spinal nerve to the muscles of the leg may still be functional. (It would certainly exist anatomically, but the functioning of neurons depends upon a minimal level of continuous impulse conduction. Otherwise degeneration occurs.) If the sensory input pathway is directly connected to the motor outflow via spinal-spinal neurons, then a stimulus applied to the knee may still elicit the knee jerk reflex; obviously the subject is unaware of the stimulus, as the pathway ascending the spinal cord to the brain is broken. Even in intact subjects the knee jerk reflex is not subject to voluntary control, although they would feel the stimulus. The difference is that the intact subject can mimic the leg movement voluntarily, whereas the spinally damaged subject cannot.

Usually, autonomic regulation in paraplegic patients is not badly affected – if it were, they would not survive. This is because a major component of the ANS leaves the CNS via the cranial nerves of the brainstem, within the skull, and is therefore unaffected by damage to the spine lower down.

The brain is the major concern of the physiological psychologist, and most of this book is devoted to it, in one way or another. In this section I give an overview of some of its major components and their role in behaviour. The remainder of the book fleshes out this skeleton in more detail, particularly in regard to behaviour. Neuroanatomical detail can be found in any one of several excellent texts, e.g. Carpenter (1978).

The brain can be divided into some hundreds of separate structures, zones, nuclei (clusters of neuronal cell bodies), etc. Partly to simplify, and partly because data on the precise behavioural significance of many of them is lacking, the physiological psychologist usually deals with the more major elements. A typical classification of the brain and its components is given below:

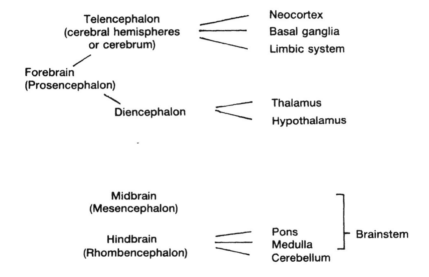

Hindbrain and midbrain

The pons, medulla, and midbrain make up the brainstem (which in some systems also includes the diencephalon). The medulla is a transition area between the spinal cord and the brain, and both pons and the midbrain also resemble the cord in containing large bundles of ascending and descending fibres. In addition the cranial nerves join the brain at intervals along the brainstem, while the nuclei (meaning a close aggregation of neuronal cell bodies) of a large autonomic outflow lie in the brainstem, with axons leaving via the cranial nerves. Occupying the central core of the brainstem is the reticular formation, resembling, as its name implies, an apparently undifferentiated network of some millions of neurons. The reticular formation (RF) is central to the regulation of the brain's general level of activation. It receives direct information on the amount of sensory information entering the brain (via branches from afferent sensory pathways ascending the brainstem), and the consequent level of activity in the RF has a modulatory effect on the activity of higher brain structures such as the cortex. The RF is dealt with in detail in Chapter 10 in relation to sleep and waking, but it should be noticed here that although it does resemble a reticulum (network), identifiable nuclei do exist with specific functions in relation to activation, e.g. the raphé nuclei of the pons and medulla.

Besides any other functions, the concentration in the brainstem of the cranial nerve nuclei, involved in the sensory and motor regulation of the anterior end of the body and the head, and in the autonomic regulation of visceral processes such as heart-rate and blood pressure, make the brainstem vital for the animal's existence. So essential is this area that the concept of 'brainstem death' is used by neurologists as an index of brain death. If various reflexes and responses indicative of brainstem function are absent, then the patient is defined as dead regardless of any residual spasmodic electrical activity higher up the brain. Experimental separation of the forebrain from the brainstem in animals has also been used to demonstrate the ability of the brainstem to independently regulate the body's vital functions within acceptable limits. In humans there is a rare condition called anencephaly, often associated with spina bifida, in which much of the forebrain fails to develop; the baby is severely impaired, but can still live as long as the brainstem regulatory centres are intact. Thus the brainstem can be seen as the site of 'essential' functions, even if many of them are not central to physiological psychology.

The midbrain contains other structures of interest. The superior ('above') and inferior ('below') colliculi are concerned with eye movement control and with relaying auditory information onwards to the thalamus respectively. The substantia nigra ('black stuff', an example of less romantic neuro-

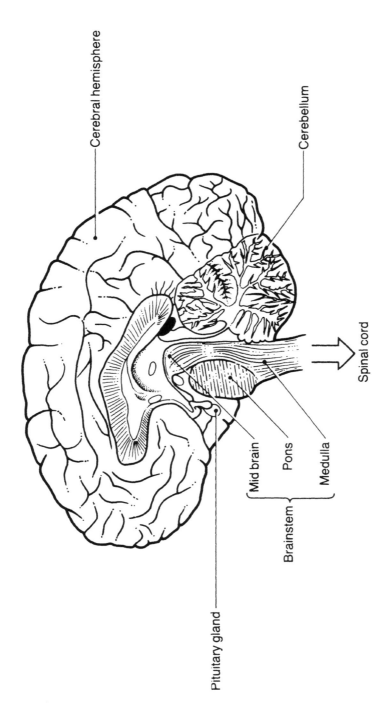

Cerebral hemisphere

Cerebellum

Spinal cord

Pituitary gland

Mid brain
Pons
Medulla

Brainstem

Figure 2.4   *Midline (sagittal) section through the brain*

anatomical terminology) is a large nucleus powerfully connected to the basal ganglia of the forebrain and concerned with motor functions. This would also be an appropriate time to emphasize that, in line with the vertebrate bilaterally symmetrical body, the brain is bilaterally symmetrical, and that any structure not actually in the midline therefore has a pair in the opposite (contralateral) half. Thus the colliculi and the substantia nigra are paired structures, along with virtually all the structures that go to make up the forebrain.

The cerebellum (Fig. 2.4) is classified with the pons and medulla as the hindbrain, but has a distinctive appearance and structure that distinguishes it from the brainstem. After the neocortex, it is the largest brain structure in terms both of volume and of number of neurons. Indeed, some estimates (Blinkov and Glezer, 1968) give it as many neurons as are found in the neocortex, or even more, somewhere between 10 and 100 billion. The functions of the cerebellum principally relate to the coordination of bodily movement and the maintenance of (physical) equilibrium. Lesions may produce tremor, impairments of skilled voluntary movements, unsteadiness, jerky uncoordinated locomotion, and even speech disturbances via disrupted control of the muscles of larynx, pharynx, and lips.

Forebrain

Diencephalon
The thalamus and hypothalamus, although occupying only around 2 per cent of brain volume, between them are involved in many complex behavioural and physiological functions. The hypothalamus on each side is about the size of the tip of your little finger, and consists of some hundreds of thousands of neurons, i.e. a small number in comparison with the billions of neurons in cerebellum and neocortex. It is therefore an excellent example of the processing power of brain tissue. It lies on the ventral (lower) surface of the brain, immediately above the pituitary gland (Fig. 2.4) to which it is connected via the pituitary stalk or infundibulum. Via a combination of direct

neural connections and chemicals carried down the infundibulum in the blood supply, the hypothalamus controls the secretion of the pituitary hormones. These hormones, including growth hormone, hormones to stimulate the adrenal and thyroid glands, gonadotrophic hormones such as luteinizing hormone, follicle-stimulating hormone and prolactin, and hormones concerned with the body's fluid balance such as vasopressin, are crucial to bodily function. In addition the hypothalamus, via direct neural connections travelling down the brainstem, regulates the activity of the autonomic nervous system. Given its control over the pituitary gland and ANS the hypothalamus can be seen as a higher-order controlling centre for functions related to homeostasis. As we shall see later, through its involvement in physiological regulation it is concerned in basic motivational drives such as hunger and thirst, in the control of peripheral arousal, especially in states of emotion and stress, and in the phasing of sleep/waking cycles.

The thalamus is a large structure lying above the hypothalamus. It is divided into around seventeen distinct nuclei, but these can be classified into three major groups on the basis of their afferent (incoming) and efferent (outgoing) connections and their consequent role in brain functions. *Specific relay nuclei* such as the anteroventral and the medial and lateral geniculate project to and receive fibres from specific cortical areas concerned with sensation and perception. Thus a major function of the thalamus is to relay ascending sensory information on to the cortex, and it is notable that with the sole exception of olfaction (smell), all sensory systems project directly to the thalamus. This 'relaying' is not a passive transfer across one synapse; a significant amount of sensory processing occurs in the thalamus, as we shall see in relation to the visual system (Chapter 4), while the reciprocal cortico-thalamic fibres again emphasize that sensory processing involves complex feedback loops and is a parallel rather than a sequential phenomenon.

Association nuclei such as the pulvinar and parts of the dorsomedial nucleus project to and receive fibres from the association (i.e. non-sensory/motor – see p.45) cortex. They do not receive inputs from the ascending sensory pathways, but are interconnected with other thalamic nuclei and receive some afferents from other subcortical structures. Their role in behaviour is as yet unclear, but is obviously related to the areas of association cortex they interconnect with; thus the dorsomedial nucleus may be involved in the emotional and cognitive behaviours thought to be mediated by the cortex of the frontal lobe, with which it is reciprocally connected.

The *intralaminar and midline* nuclei of the thalamus are in evolutionary terms ('phylogenetically') older than the rest. They receive inputs from brainstem regions, including the reticular formation, the cerebellum, and other subcortical structures. Projections are sent downstream to the brainstem, to forebrain structures such as the basal ganglia, and there are interconnections with other thalamic nuclei. From the functional point of view, the most important projection system of these nuclei is a diffuse network of pathways innervating large areas of the cortex, i.e. a nonspecific system in comparison with the specific projections of the relay nuclei. The diffuse thalamic-cortical projection is thought to relay on to the cortex ascending impulses from the brainstem reticular formation, and therefore to mediate the cortical activation produced by reticular activation or stimulation (see Chapter 10).

Telencephalon (the cerebral hemispheres)
Limbic system The limbic system consists of a number of related structures (Fig. 2.5). Each has substantial connections with the cortex and with diencephalic, midbrain, and hindbrain areas. They are thus in a position to influence many types of behaviour, and their study has in some ways been the major concern of the physiological psychologist, as this book demonstrates. Experimental studies have shown that the limbic system is involved in cognitive behaviours such as learning and memory, in the modulation of peripheral arousal as related to emotion and stress, in the control of aggressive behaviour, and in the modulation of the hypothalamus and all the systems that structure controls. Given the number of structures and pathways, it is difficult to see the limbic system as a unified whole, but its position between cortex and brainstem means that neural pathways mediating many different functions come together in this particular brain region.

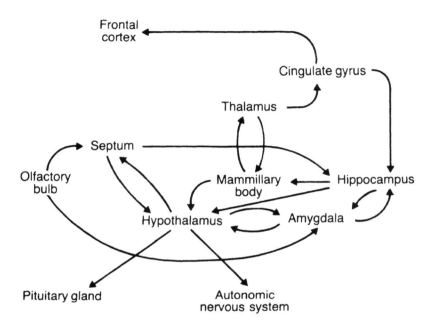

Figure 2.5   *Some interconnections of the limbic system*

The concept of 'modulation' is crucial to understanding the role of forebrain structures, especially the limbic system. A milder version of 'regulate', 'modulate' implies a biasing of systems in one direction or another. Thus an amygdala lesion can produce placidity in monkeys, while septal lesions lead to a hyper-aggressive response. However, complete removal of the telecephalon does not prevent the production of integrated aggressive behaviour (see Chapter 8), i.e. the behaviour is organized at diencephalic and brainstem levels, but its appropriate display is modulated by higher brain centres. Similarly stimulation of various points in the limbic system and in the cortex can lead to autonomic sympathetic arousal and the release of pituitary hormones. However, we know that effective control of these systems resides in the hypothalamus, and the modulatory effects are therefore mediated via pathways from higher brain centres to the hypothalamus and brainstem.

Given their involvement in most aspects of behaviour, limbic system structures are referred to repeatedly in later chapters. They illustrate one of the principles behind brain-behaviour relationships; although it is usual to consider one structure or one element of behaviour at a time, realistically no one structure is involved in only one behaviour, and no single behavioural component is the sole responsibility of any single structure. As an example, the hippocampus has been implicated in different aspects of memory, in behavioural inhibition, in emotional behaviour such as anxiety, and in feedback regulation of the hypothalamic-pituitary-adrenal gland system. Even though some of these hypotheses may be incorrect, there is no reason, given the established processing power of a much smaller structure such as the hypothalamus, why the hippocampus should not be involved in many aspects of behaviour. Conversely, a cognitive behaviour such as 'memory' is not a unitary concept; there are sensory input pathways, brief sensory stores, short-term memory stores, long-term memory stores, and retrieval systems to enable recall and recognition. Obviously many brain structures will be involved in 'memory', and it is no surprise that a wide range of brainstem, limbic, and cortical manipulations have been shown to influence memorial processes (see Chapter 6). It is also technically difficult to localize the behavioural effect of a given lesion or stimulation to the structure directly affected, as no brain structure is entirely isolated; the extensive neuronal pathways interconnecting brain structures mean that a change in any one has effects 'at a distance' on the functioning of any others it is connected with.

Despite all these problems, later chapters will, I hope, demonstrate how our knowledge of brain and behaviour has increased exponentially over the last twenty years, particularly in regard to the limbic system.

Basal ganglia These are a group of relatively large nuclei, including the globus pallidus and the neostriatum, usually shortened to striatum. The striatum is in turn made up of the caudate nucleus and the putamen. Phylogenetically the amygdala is closely related to the basal ganglia, and if it is discussed in that context, the striatum and globus pallidus are together referred to as the corpus striatum to distinguish them from the amygdala. However, it is now accepted that functionally the amygdala is much more closely related to the limbic system, and is usually discussed under that heading.

The striatum receives afferent (incoming) input from virtually all areas of the cortex. The major subcortical inputs are from the intralaminar nuclei of the thalamus and from the substantia nigra of the midbrain, while striatal efferent output pathways include a reciprocal one to the substantia nigra. The other major output pathway leads to the globus pallidus, and thence to various ventral thalamic nuclei and from there on to the motor cortex.

Although there is increasing interest in the cognitive aspects of striatal function (especially the caudate nucleus, with its massive input from the cortex), the basal ganglia in general are considered as motor structures. The progressive motor disorder known as Parkinsonism, characterized initially by tremors of the extremities, has for some decades been linked with an irreversible degeneration of pathways between the striatum and the substantia nigra (striato-nigral and nigro-striatal tracts; see Chapter 3). Other motor disorders (or dyskinesias), such as Huntington's chorea, have also been attributed to basal ganglia impairment. This involvement in motor control has led to the corpus striatum and related structures being referred to as the 'extrapyramidal motor system'. Direct cortical control of voluntary movement is mediated by the pyramidal tract running from the pyramidal (pyramid-shaped!) neurons of the motor cortex down to the spinal cord. The basal ganglia are seen as in some ways accessory to this major system, helping in the fine control of motor activity but not essential for it. However, the basal ganglia do not constitute an independent motor system, as their effects are mediated ultimately by the same motor cortex that gives rise to the pyramidal tract (via the globus pallidus → thalamus → motor cortex output pathway).

Neocortex – organization and functions

The final telencephalic structure is the neocortex, which represents the present peak of brain evolution. Rudimentary in birds and reptiles, it is represented in its most elaborate form in the human brain, and clear differences can be seen even between primates and more primitive mammals such as the insectivores (e.g. hedgehog). The neocortex is a layer of tissue covering the cerebral hemispheres, with an average thickness of 3.00 mm, varying between 1.5 and 4.5 mm. The layer of tissue is in turn made up of six layers of neurons, differentiated on the basis of cell shape, dendritic and axonal characteristics, and input/output pathways.

This six-layered arrangement seems fundamental to the neocortex, and therefore presents a logistical problem for brain evolution as the neocortex cannot increase its size by becoming thicker. It can only increase via an expansion of its surface area, and as it is inextricably attached to the cerebral hemispheres, this can only happen with an expansion of hemisphere surface area. However, this would imply an increase in brain volume, which has happened up to a point. Beyond that point, mechanical problems intervene; the brain is protected by the bony skull, which is supported by the skeleton and moved around by a sophisticated muscle system. As the skull enlarges, the support and movement demands become excessive. Therefore the brain has evolved an alternative method for increasing its surface area. The surface has invaginated ('infolded') upon itself with deep clefts visible on the surface only as a patterning of lines (see Fig. 2.6). This has the effect of increasing the surface area, and therefore neocortical area, without significant increases in brain volume. It also means that in the human brain only about a third of the two square metres of neocortex is visible on the surface, with the remainder buried in the clefts ('fissures' or 'sulci', singular 'sulcus'). The visible surface neocortex between two fissures is known as a 'gyrus' (plural 'gyri').

The patterning of fissuration on the mammalian brain is a crude index of evolutionary status; the most intensive infoldings are found in the higher primates and humans, while the

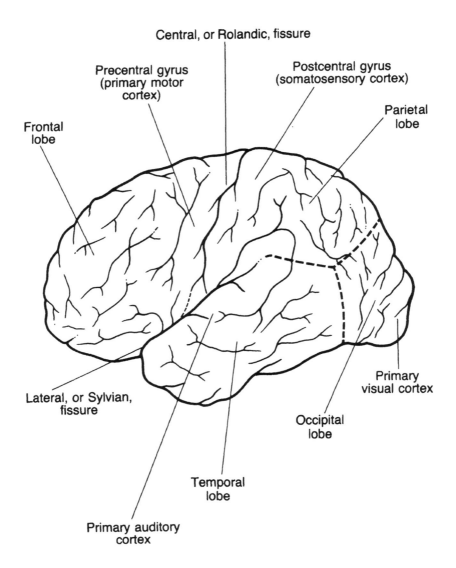

Central, or Rolandic, fissure

Precentral gyrus
(primary motor
cortex)

Postcentral gyrus
(somatosensory cortex)

Parietal
lobe

Frontal
lobe

Lateral, or Sylvian,
fissure

Primary
visual cortex

Occipital
lobe

Temporal
lobe

Primary auditory
cortex

Figure 2.6   *Side-view of brain, showing cortical infolding, lobes of the
hemispheres, and primary sensory and motor areas*

surface of the rat brain is virtually smooth. Within a species the patterning is not consistent from one individual to the next, with only two major landmarks (the central or Rolandic fissure and the lateral or Sylvian fissure – see Fig. 2.6) being readily identifiable.

The term 'cerebral cortex' technically refers to both the recently evolved neocortex and earlier forms of cortex found in the brain. 'Cortex' is purely a descriptive term for a layered covering – a tree, the adrenal gland, and the cerebellum all have a cortex – and other cortical structures in the forebrain include the amygdala ('palaeocortex') and the hippocampus ('archicortex'). These have three to five cell layers, and can be seen as intermediate forms on the evolutionary stepladder leading to the neocortex. As around 96 per cent of cerebral cortex is made up of the neocortex, the two terms have become effectively synomymous, which is how I will usually treat them.

The cerebral cortex contains around 15 billion (15×10^9) neurons, well over 90 per cent of all the neurons in the forebrain. Neuronal cell bodies appear grey under the light microscope, and the cortex is therefore accurately described as grey matter. A substantial part of the interior of the forebrain consists of axonal pathways interconnecting various structures, with nuclear masses such as the thalamus and limbic system distributed amongst them; the term 'white matter' is given to these subcortical areas, taken from the microscopic appearance of densely packed axons.

The functions of the human cerebral cortex are in many ways the final frontier in physiological psychology, but, although we tend to deal with structures in isolation, it is important to remember that the cortex is not independent of subcortical structures. It is not a layer mediating brand new functions superimposed on a phylogenetically older brain. The visual cortex is vital to the primate visual system, i.e. seeing. However, birds, reptiles, and fish have perfectly efficient visual systems without the benefit of a visual cortex. Obviously the cortex enables more sophisticated cognitive functions to develop, but even with these the afferent pathways to the cortex and the efferent pathways transmitting the results of its deliberations can receive additional processing at subcortical waystations. Even the uniquely human ability of language can, as we shall see, be affected by damage to subcortical structures.

Organization of the cerebral cortex

The cerebrum or telencephalon can be divided in various ways. First there is a left and a right cerebral hemisphere, and then each hemisphere can be divided into lobes (see Fig. 2.6). These lobes are three-dimensional, consisting of the surface cortical layer and various subcortical pathways and structures. Thus the temporal lobe has buried within it the hippocampus and amygdala, while the basal ganglia lie more in the frontal lobe. The cortical surface of the hemispheres has, at various times throughout the last century, been subdivided in different ways. One of the more popular is the division by Brodmann (1909) into forty-seven distinct areas, differentiated by the precise type and arrangement of neurons within the six basic layers, i.e. not a functional but a neuroanatomical analysis.

A functional analysis of the cortex may be approached by dividing it initially into three types. Primary sensory cortex receives afferent inputs from the sensory relay nuclei of the thalamus, and is modality-specific, i.e. it deals only with one type of sensory input. Thus stimulation of cells in the primary visual cortex of the occipital lobe evokes the sensation of light in awake subjects, and these same cells are activated by visual stimuli but not by sounds. Conversely stimulation of neurons in the primary auditory cortex of the temporal lobe (see Fig. 2.6) evokes the sensation of sound, and they respond to auditory input but not to visual stimuli. Just behind the central fissure in the parietal lobe lies an area of cortex known from its location as the post-central gyrus. This is also a primary sensory region, responding to touch, pain, and pressure stimuli from the skin, muscle, and joints; from its association with the general body senses this region is known as somaesthetic or somatosensory cortex. Stimulation produces a sensation of numbness or tingling, and also reveals that the representation of the body on this area of the cortex is topographic, i.e. there is a point-for-point representation of the body surface in the somatosensory cortex. The representation is inverted, with feet and legs at the top and neck and face at the bottom. Parts more richly endowed with

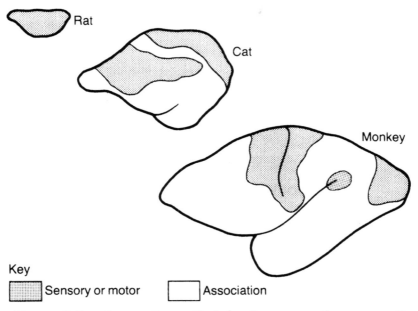

Rat

Cat

Monkey

Key

Sensory or motor   Association

Figure 2.7   *Comparative cortical functions across three mammalian brains*

sensory receptors, such as the hands and face, take up proportionally more cortex.

These three major sensory zones are each surrounded by secondary cortical areas also dedicated to the given sensory modality (visual, auditory, somaesthetic), and in the cases of visual and auditory zones, by tertiary modality-specific areas. As we see in Chapter 4 in relation to vision, primary, secondary, and tertiary sensory reception areas represent progressively more elaborate processing of sensory input, i.e. a transition between sensation and perception. While damage to primary reception cortex can produce complete loss of sensation (i.e. blindness, deafness, anaesthesia), damage to secondary and tertiary zones leads to higher-level loss, where

physical sensation is retained but complex perceptual processes may be impaired.

Neurons in some other cortical areas also respond to sensory
stimulation, but without discriminating between types, i.e.
they are independent of the sensory modality, or supramodal.
The best example of this type of cortex is the zone where
parietal, occipital, and temporal lobes meet in the region of the
inferior parietal lobule (IPL). These areas presumably integrate the products of sensory/perceptual processing from each
of the modality-specific cortical zones, and would be crucial in
the animal's 'world-view' and interactions with the environment. The IPL is discussed in Chapter 5 in relation to the
evolution of language.

The primary motor cortex lies in the gyrus anterior to the
central (Rolandic) fissure, the pre-central gyrus (see Fig. 2.6).
As with the post-central somatosensory cortex, representation
is topographic, i.e. a point-for-point representation of the body
on the cortical surface. Stimulation of the motor cortex results
in isolated movements of individual muscles or muscle groups.
Damage to this area produces paralysis, with a variable degree
of recovery; the higher up the phylogenetic scale, the more
severe and permanent the effects, with the cat being able to
walk after ablation of the motor cortex, while primates, including humans, suffer permanent or semi-permanent paralysis.

In front of the primary motor cortex is an area of premotor
cortex. Electrical stimulation here also results in muscular
activity, probably via pathways running from the premotor
zone to primary motor cortex, so connecting with the major
cortex → spinal cord → spinal nerves → skeletal muscles
pathway (the pyramidal tract). Damage to the premotor cortex
has far less drastic effects than damage to primary motor
cortex. Additionally there is a supplementary motor area lying
anterior (in front of) the primary motor cortex and mostly
hidden in the cleft between the hemispheres. This zone appears
to be concerned with control of body posture.

Finally, in front of the premotor cortex lies a small cortical
area devoted to the control of voluntary eye movements, and
referred to as the frontal cortical eye field. Stimulation here
produces movement of the eyes to left or right, and in general

this area is thought to mediate eye movements which are independent of visual stimuli. In the occipital visual cortex are other cortical zones from which eye movements can be elicited; it is thought that the occipital eye field controls movements related to visual stimuli, i.e. pursuit or tracking. Both frontal and occipital eye fields have substantial connections with the superior colliculus of the midbrain, which probably relays their instructions to the eye muscles.

Association cortex

In lower mammals most of the cortex is dedicated to the sensory and motor functions outlined above, which are shown in Fig. 2.7. Throughout mammalian evolution there is a trend towards an increase in the amount of non-sensory/motor cortex, and most of the cortical advantage seen in the human brain over other primates lies in these zones. Assuming that the overall function of non-sensory/motor cortex is to mediate increasingly complicated interactions between sensory input and motor output (stimulus and response), it is given the generic name 'association cortex'. In a simplistic fashion, it can be seen as the current end-product of a process that began with the purely reflexive behaviour (i.e. a perfectly predictable relationship between stimulus and response) seen in organisms with primitive nervous systems, i.e. with very few neurons interposed between the sensory neuron and the motor neuron.

Most of the human cerebral cortex is association cortex. Within it lie controlling centres for higher cognitive functions such as speech and reading and for psychological constructs such as personality and self-awareness. The psychological complexity of these processes had produced correspondingly slow progress in mapping them onto the brain, especially in comparison to the detailed maps of sensory and motor functions. However, there is a great deal of clinical and experimental evidence, particularly from brain-damaged patients, which allows tentative and not-so-tentative attempts at functional localization within human association cortex. Before briefly reviewing these, some general principles of cerebral hemisphere organization should be considered.

Modular organization

The six layers of neurons which make up the neocortex consist of cell bodies of different shapes and sizes. A system such as Brodmann's divides the cortex into areas on the basis of variations in the density of cells within the six layers, although the layers themselves are identifiable across all cortical zones. However, the cortex has a depth dimension as well as a surface or areal dimension. In 1959 Hubel and Wiesel (see Chapter 4) demonstrated that the *functional* unit within the occipital lobe visual cortex was a *column* of neurons at right angles to the cortical surface, i.e. there was a regular and predictable relationship between the visual stimuli triggering each neuron as the recording electrode penetrated down through the six layers. They established that this columnar organization was basic to the functions of the visual cortex. Since then functional columns have been identified in most cortical areas studied. For association cortex it can be difficult to find an appropriate stimulus with which to test a 'functional' arrangement, as cognitive functions do not break down in small units in as simple a way as visual stimuli may. However, Rockel *et al.* (1980) have demonstrated an impressive uniformity in the vertical structure of the cerebral cortex. They looked at mice, rats, cats, monkeys, and humans, and sensory, motor, and association cortex. Across all species and all areas, the number of neuronal cell bodies in a narrow strip through the depth of the neocortex was remarkably consistent – around 110, regardless of the relative width and density of the six cell layers. They concluded that the intrinsic structure of neocortex is uniform, regardless of functional considerations, and that these cell columns may well provide the neuroanatomical basis of the functional columns which have been and remain to be identified.

Despite this basic uniformity, it would still be possible for *functionally* distinct areas to emerge. The neocortex is not isolated from the rest of the brain, and it is the pattern of connections that determine what functions a particular cortical area will be concerned with.

Cortical connections

Projection pathways

Several of these have already been mentioned. They are pathways carrying information to the cortex from deeper structures such as the thalamus (afferent), and those carrying information from the cortex to deeper structures (efferent).

Association pathways

There are bundles of neuronal fibres interconnecting cortical zones within one hemisphere. The arcuate fasciculus, for instance, runs from the temporal lobe to the frontal lobe on the same side.

Commissural pathways

Commissures run transversely across the brain interconnecting homologous ('the same') areas in the two hemispheres. The major cerebral commissure is the corpus callosum, interconnecting most cortical zones in the two hemispheres via a vast bundle of some 250 million axons. The other commissures are the anterior and the hippocampal, each containing, in primates, just a few million fibres. This pattern is not typical of all mammals. Marsupials such as the wombat and kangaroo have no corpus callosum, but a relatively large anterior commissure. The corpus callosum is discussed in more detail in Chapter 5.

Functional lateralization

Mammals are bilaterally symmetrical animals, with a body divisible into two mirror-image halves, and a forebrain composed of two cerebral hemispheres. It is a feature of the brain's organization that the pathways serving sensory and motor control are predominantly lateralized, i.e. connecting one side of the brain with one side of the body. These pathways are usually crossed, running from the left side of the brain to the right side of the body, and *vice versa*, and known as crossed-lateral or 'contralateral' pathways. Some pathways do exist connecting the same sides of the brain and body; such pathways are referred to as 'ipsilateral'. The reasons for the evolution of this 'crossed' primary pattern of pathways is unknown.

When motor cortex or somatosensory cortex is stimulated, the resulting muscular activity or sensation occurs on the opposite side of the body. Damage to the motor cortex of the left hemisphere produces a unilateral ('one-sided') right-sided motor paralysis, while damage to the somatosensory cortex of the right hemisphere would produce a left-sided anaesthesia. The auditory system is also predominantly lateralized, with signals entering the left ear being transmitted to the right hemisphere, while the right ear projects to the left hemisphere. However, functional ipsilateral pathways do exist, and so unilateral damage to the temporal lobe primary auditory cortex leads to profound deafness in the contralateral ear and mild hearing loss in the ipsilateral ear; complete deafness from cortical damage requires that both auditory areas be affected, i.e. damage must be bilateral ('both-sides'). The visual system is the most complicated of our sensory systems, and is discussed in detail in Chapter 4. Briefly, the visual pathways leading from the retina of one eye to visual cortex are partially crossed. Half of the fibres are contralateral, and half ipsilateral. Thus the input to the visual cortex of one hemisphere consists of contralateral fibres from the eye on the opposite side of the body, and ipsilateral fibres from the eye on the same side, and severe damage restricted to one hemisphere produces a loss of half the visual field (field of view) in each eye (hemianopia – see Chapter 4).

Although ipsilateral, contralateral, and partially crossed pathways exist, the organization of sensory and motor systems is essentially symmetrical. At the cortical level, left and right hemispheres are mirror images, and a description of sensory and motor representation applies equally well to both. However, this functional symmetry does not apply to association cortex, where we can find different effects of brain damage depending on the precise parts of the cerebral hemisphere involved *and* on the side to which the damage occurs. This functional asymmetry is discussed in detail in Chapter 5, and will be referred to in the following section.

Functions of association cortex

The cerebral hemispheres (telencephalon) are made up of neocortex and the subcortical structures of the basal ganglia and limbic system. They are divided up into four *lobes*, the temporal, frontal, parietal, and occipital (Fig. 2.6). Each lobe therefore possesses a surface neocortical mantle plus subcortical structures and white matter. Damage to a lobe of the cerebral hemispheres via stroke, accident, trauma, etc., usually, therefore, involves tissue beyond the surface neocortex, and so inferences from brain-damaged patients as to brain function cannot necessarily be restricted to the cortex. Sensory and motor cortex, which are comparable across primate groups, have been carefully mapped using microelectrode recording and stimulation techniques in animals, backed up by clinical data from brain-damaged human patients; we can be reasonably sure that here we are dealing specifically with cortical function.

As the functions linked with assocation cortex are not directly comparable across primate groups, there is a greater emphasis on the human clinical data. As brain damage is not systematically localized, any discussion of the functions of association cortex is usually included in a broader analysis of the functions of the *lobes* of the hemispheres. Recent technological advances such as the CAT scanner have helped dissociate specifically cortical involvement from joint cortical/ subcortical contributions to the effects of brain damage, but this is the exception rather than the rule. Where possible, the following discussion will mention where behavioural impairment is due specifically to association cortex damage rather than to the additional involvement of subcortical structures.

Occipital lobe

Although consisting mainly of visual sensory cortex, the tertiary visual areas of the occipital lobe can be regarded as association cortex where damage produces perceptual deficits which are independent of primary visual processes such as sensitivity and acuity. These deficits are usually agnosias ('without knowledge'), a general term referring to perceptual loss. Thus damage to the left occipital lobe may produce *visual object agnosia*, an inability to recognize familiar objects or pictures, although they may be recognized by touch, i.e. it is a modality-specific impairment. Damage to the right occipital lobe tertiary zones may lead to *prosopagnosia*, an inability to recognize familiar faces, while damage to either side may produce *colour agnosia*, a failure to recognize colours even when discrimination is intact (i.e. a colour agnosic can tell that different colours are present), and *simultanagnosia*, an inability to handle more than one aspect of a stimulus at a time (i.e. given a picture of an elephant, the patient may list each feature and then realize what the whole thing is).

Visual cortex damage also plays a role in language impairments such as alexia (inability to read words). These are considered on page 54.

Parietal lobe

It is generally recognized that the parietal lobe is the most difficult to demarcate, especially in the postero-ventral areas where occipital, temporal, and parietal lobes meet. The relevant parietal zones in this area include the supramarginal and angular gyri which represent integrative zones for visual, auditory, and somatosensory information, i.e. they are supramodal, and damage to them has consequently severe effects related to the impairment in integrating sensory inputs.

Besides visual object agnosia and prosopagnosia, these may include deficits in cross-modal matching (e.g. matching an object seen with the same object felt), tactile agnosia (inability to recognize objects through touch), and *apraxias*. Apraxia is an inability to perform purposive or skilled acts in the presence of intact sensory, motor, and intellectual function. Posterior parietal damage may produce constructional apraxia, where the patient cannot assemble the parts to make a whole, and left parietal damage ideomotor apraxia, where the patient cannot follow instructions but may perform the task spontaneously. Drawing ability is often severely impaired.

Another range of behavioural disabilities produced by parietal injury involves the subject's relationships with the surrounding space. The most extreme example is the *unilateral neglect* seen after parietal lesions; this, as its name implies, involves an apparent unawareness of the space to one side of the patient (i.e. a contralateral neglect), and is much more common after right-sided damage. The patient may draw only one side of a clock face (with all the numbers crowded together), dress only one side of their body, and (if male) shave only one half of their face. Often they deny that any disability exists (anosognosia). Right–left confusion is also found, more commonly after left parietal injury, often associated with disorders of the body scheme such as finger agnosia, where the patients seem unaware of their own fingers.

A peculiar symptom sometimes found after left parietal damage is acalculia or dyscalculia, an inability to handle numbers and do simple arithmetic. This occurs often enough in combination with finger agnosia, right–left disorientation, and *dysgraphia* (inability to write in the presence of otherwise normal language functions) for the combined pattern of symptoms to be given a name – Gerstmann's syndrome.

These symptoms of parietal lobe injury are not mutually exclusive, and neuropsychological diagnosis is often a case of probabilities and overlapping categories. Many of the symptoms seem to involve the patients' ability to internally represent external space and their relationships with it, a function which involves integrating across sensory modalities and for which the parietal lobe is ideally placed. More specific symptoms of parietal damage have been identified. One patient had an impairment of auditory short-term memory after left parietal damage (see Chapter 6), while the angular gyrus has a particular role in language, discussed on page 57.

Temporal lobe

The neocortex covering the temporal lobe contains primary, secondary, and tertiary auditory projection areas, and damage to the secondary and tertiary areas produces high-level perceptual disturbances in hearing. Left-sided involvement produces problems in language comprehension (see p.55), while right-sided damage may lead to *auditory agnosia* − a failure to recognize common non-verbal sounds.

Besides its major role in auditory processes, especially as related to the perception of speech, the temporal lobe also contains within it deeper lying structures belonging to the limbic system. These structures, notably the hippocampus and the amygdala, are involved in cognitive and affective ('emotional') functions. When they are damaged, either by accidental penetrating damage to the brain, subcortical trauma such as haemorrhage, tumour, or infection, or by surgical intervention in cases of temporal lobe epilepsy (see Chapter 6), the consequences can be severe. Unilateral hippocampal damage can lead to memory impairment (specific to verbal material if left-sided, non-verbal if right-sided), while bilateral involvement produces severe global anterograde amnesia (Chapter 6). Amygdala damage can, at least in non-human animals, lead to significant changes in emotional behaviour, particularly aggression (Chapter 8).

Frontal lobe

The neocortical and subcortical components of the frontal lobes make up around a third of the cerebral hemisphere. Discounting the motor and premotor cortical zones, the frontal lobes contain the largest amount of association cortex in the brain, and consequently have been and remain a stimulating problem for the neuropsychologist.

A simple subdivision of frontal cortex produces three major zones − motor, premotor, and prefrontal cortex − with the latter being synonymous with frontal association cortex. An alternative and quite popular approach is based on the relative densities of neuronal cell bodies in various of the six cortical layers. Motor cortex, due to a scarcity in layers II and IV, has an *agranular* appearance under the microscope, while prefrontal cortex in contrast presents a *granular* appearance. Hence the terms frontal agranular (motor) and frontal granular (association) cortex.

Prefrontal cortex is directly connected to most other forebrain regions and structures. There are reciprocal connections with the sensory regions of parietal, occipital, and temporal cortex on the same side. Afferent ('to' the prefrontal cortex) pathways include a contribution from the non-specific thalamo-cortical radiation, connections with limbic system structures such as the amygdala, and ascending pathways from basal ganglia structures such as the substantia nigra. Efferent ('from' the prefrontal cortex) pathways link the prefrontal cortex with the thalamic nuclei, the caudate nucleus of the basal ganglia, amygdala, hypothalamus, and midbrain and brainstem regions.

This extensive and often two-way pattern of connections between prefrontal cortex and the rest of the brain implies that it will be involved in most aspects of behaviour, from perception through complex information processing to motor output. Despite this wide range of potential effects, damage to the frontal lobes has been observed, over the years, to produce behavioural changes consistent enough to be referred to as the 'frontal lobe syndrome'.

Evidence comes traditionally from two major areas: injury through accident or disease (beginning with the classic case of Phineas Gage, a railway worker whose frontal lobes were effectively obliterated when, in 1848, a tamping iron was blown through them), and from the use of psychosurgical treatment for psychiatric disorders. The frontal lobotomy, or prefrontal leucotomy, is discussed in detail in Chapter 8.

It was pointed out earlier that severe damage to the forebrain need not be fatal, and, in the case of prefrontal cortex, may produce significant but surprisingly mild changes in personality and behaviour. The frontal lobe syndrome has several components (reviewed in detail in Walsh, 1978). There is a loss of initiative and a diminution of abstract and creative thought.

There is some loss of social inhibition, leading to irreverent and profane behaviour, coupled with a decrease in general anxiety and concern for the future. Although impulsivity is increased, there is a profound loss of the ability to plan ahead, to organize behaviour across time and space to fulfil goals and intentions. In its place may be a tendency to perseverate in a given task, i.e. to fail to shift from an unsuccessful to a successful strategy, or to move on to the next component of a sequential problem. On a more general level the patient may vacillate between several action plans, never following one through to fruition.

Over the last twenty years there has been an effort to pin down the effects of prefrontal damage more precisely, and to assess the relative contributions of the various afferent/efferent pathways. For instance, a major output target is the caudate nucleus of the basal ganglia extra-pyramidal motor system, and it is the view of many investigators that the prefrontal cortex and basal ganglia are jointly concerned in the regulation of all voluntary motor activity, which is finally expressed via the frontal motor cortex.

Using recent techniques of PET scans and blood flow studies, attempts have been made to localize functionally distinct zones within prefrontal cortex. Given its extensive connections, it is no surprise that Roland (1984) should identify seventeen such zones, although I, for one, find his general conclusion easier to grasp: *'in man one or more prefrontal areas participate in any structured treatment of information by the brain in the awake state'*.

Recent models of prefrontal cortex involvement in sensation, perception, cognition (including memory), and motor functions are presented in the journal *Trends in Neurosciences*, November 1984.

Language and the brain

I have mentioned previously how, in some cases, the behavioural effects of brain damage depend upon which side of the brain is affected. The clearest evidence for hemisphere asymmetries of function, or, to put it another way, *functional lateralization* in the brain, comes from studies of language.

In the early years of the nineteenth century, several

neurologists, including Bouillard, Dax, and Bouillard's son-in-law Auburtin, studied patients with unilateral brain damage and suggested a consistent association between left hemisphere damage and disorders of language (speech production, speech perception, reading, and writing). Building on this work and using his own studies Paul Broca presented in the 1860s a hypothesis that an area in the posterior and ventral zone of the frontal lobe of the left hemisphere (now referred to as 'Broca's area') was the site of damage which led to speech problems (aphasias). Carl Wernicke elaborated the model in the 1870s when he identified a region in the temporal lobe which, when damaged, again produced language difficulties: this area is now known as 'Wernicke's area'. (See Fig. 2.8.)

The two syndromes were qualitatively distinct. Injury to Broca's area produced a severe impairment of expressive speech, while speech comprehension (e.g. following verbal commands) could be more or less intact. Damage to Wernicke's area produced a loss of speech comprehension, while speech production could be fluent, though confused, as the patients would not monitor what they were saying.

Wernicke suggested that sound images of words and objects were stored in the temporal lobe, and transmitted to Broca's area which held the representations of speech movements. Loss of Wernicke's area preserved speech movements in the absence of speech comprehension (Wernicke's, receptive, or fluent aphasia), while loss of Broca's area preserved speech comprehension in the absence of fluent speech production (Broca's, expressive, non-fluent, or motor aphasia). The emphasis on Broca's area and speech production and on Wernicke's area and speech comprehension fits in well with the proximity of the former to the primary motor cortex of the precentral gyrus and of the latter to the primary auditory reception cortex in the temporal lobe. It should be emphasized that primary motor cortex is crucial to all motor activity including speech, and similarly auditory cortex is essential to the reception and analysis of all sounds, including speech. Damage to either will obviously affect speech production and comprehension, although specific deficits will usually be lost in the general patterns of motor paralysis and deafness respectively. Aphasias

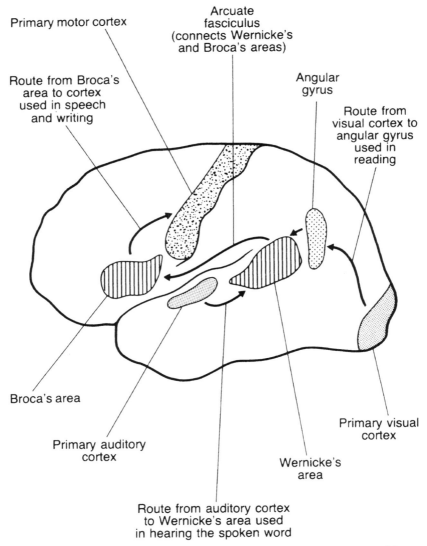

Primary motor cortex

Arcuate
fasciculus
(connects Wernicke's
and Broca's areas)

Route from Broca's
area to cortex
used in speech
and writing

Angular
gyrus

Route from
visual cortex to
angular gyrus
used in
reading

Broca's area

Primary visual
cortex

Primary auditory
cortex

Wernicke's
area

Route from auditory cortex
to Wernicke's area used
in hearing the spoken word

Figure 2.8   *Components of the left hemisphere language system. Note
how separation of the angular gyrus/visual cortex system from Wernicke's
area prevents reading but leaves speech and writing intact, while damage
to the arcuate fasciculus leaves language comprehension and production
systems intact but desynchronized*

and other language disorders are, like other disruptions linked with the functions of association cortex, defined as occurring in the presence of intact sensory and motor processes.

Given the simple basic model of two major language centres in the left hemisphere, other forms of aphasia could be predicted, observed, and explained. Destruction of both Broca's and Wernicke's area results in a loss of both speech production and speech comprehension, termed *global* aphasia. Damage to the pathway connecting the two centres (the arcuate fasciculus) leaves both production and comprehension intact, but out of synchrony. Speech is fluent and spontaneous, while comprehension of speech and the written word is good, but the two are disconnected. This is best seen in the failure of the patient to repeat aloud a passage spoken to him; normally speech comes into the temporal lobe auditory reception area, is interpreted in and around Wernicke's area, and, for repetition, passed immediately through the arcuate fasciculus to Broca's area where the motor output (speech) is prepared. Without the arcuate fasciculus, this cannot happen. The syndrome as a whole is termed *conduction* aphasia, and is one of a number of *disconnection* syndromes, so called as they appear to represent a separation of intact functions normally interconnected and coordinated.

The other major area of language investigated has been reading. Disorders of reading are *dyslexias*, while total loss is *alexia*. Crucial to, for instance, reading aloud, is the conversion of the visual input to the internal linguistic code which is then conveyed to Broca's area where the motor response – reading aloud – is organized. Therefore damage to pathways connecting the occipital lobe visual reception areas to visual conversion centres in the angular gyrus of the parietal lobe can affect reading while leaving visual perception otherwise intact. As the angular gyrus is unaffected and still connected to Broca's area in the frontal lobe, writing is fluent. This can produce the bizarre syndrome of a patient who can write a page of coherent prose but cannot then read it back, and is known as *pure alexia* or alexia without *agraphia* (meaning loss of writing ability). We have two occipital lobes, and although the right hemisphere normally lacks language centres (for variations on the 'left hemisphere language' plan, see Chapter 5), the right visual cortex is connected to the left hemisphere angular gyrus via commissural fibres travelling in the corpus callosum. So, even in the presence of left visual cortex damage, reading can still be handled by eye movements which allow the words to be transmitted to the right visual cortex and thence via the corpus callosum to the left hemisphere language centres. Pure alexia therefore normally requires two lesions to separate the angular gyrus from both visual cortices – one in the left occipital lobe, and one in that part of corpus callosum carrying information from the right visual cortex to the left angular gyrus, known as the splenium.

As both these areas are supplied by the left posterior cerebral artery, haemorrhage or stroke involving this vessel could produce the necessary damage and a number of cases are known. Less common is brain damage that eliminates the angular gyrus – either directly, or by severing the pathways connecting it to other brain regions. The effects of such damage are severe. The angular gyrus appears to be crucial as a store of the internal representations of words that are essential for reading and for writing, and its loss results in a syndrome of *alexia* with *agraphia* – the inability to read or write.

Table 2.2   Western aphasia battery – scaled   0 = Absent, 10 = Normal

Type of aphasia	Speech fluency	Speech comprehension	Naming	Repetition
Global	0–4	0–4	0–5	0–6
Broca's	0–4	5–10	0–8	0–8
Wernicke's	5–10	0–7	0–8	0–7
Conduction	5–10	7–10	0–7	0–9

This has been a simplified description of the role of Wernicke's and Broca's areas in aphasias and the role of the visual cortex and the angular gyrus in dyslexias and agraphias. The neuropsychology of language is a large and rapidly expanding field, and many of the old assumptions have been questioned.

The functional localization approach itself is probably an oversimplification. It appears, for instance, using the modern techniques outlined in Chapter 1, that damage to Broca's area is not essential for the syndrome of Broca's aphasia, but crucial is damage extending to both prefrontal cortex and to the basal ganglia (for a review of recent neuropsychological approaches to language, see Kertesz, 1983). A more general problem is that these syndromes hardly ever occur in their 'pure' form; classification is a matter of which symptoms predominate in the clinical picture, as shown in a standard aphasia test battery as outlined in Table 2.2.

It may be that the various subprocesses involved in language are perfectly localized, but that brain damage invariably affects several functional areas and consequently produces mixed aphasias or dyslexias. Alternatively, given the processing power of even small units of neural tissue, it may be that no cognitive functions are perfectly localized, and that the gross division of impairments into exclusive categories is unjustified. This is the approach taken by Ojemann (1983), who, on the basis of experiments studying the effects of electrical stimulation of the brain on language functions, suggests that a division into an anterior speech production zone (Broca's) and a posterior speech comprehension zone (Wernicke's) is not supported by the evidence. Effects on production and comprehension were found equally in anterior and posterior cortical areas.

The neuropsychology of language is thus in a dynamic phase. What is undoubted is the contribution of the psychological analysis of brain-damaged patients to the cognitive modelling of normal language functions. This area is considered in detail in the companion volume by Harris and Coltheart (1986).

Finally, it should be remembered that the commonest language disorder – development dyslexia in children – occurs in the absence of gross organic damage, and almost certainly represents a high-level problem in the organization and integration of functions within and across hemispheres. We consider hemisphere function in detail in Chapter 5.

3 Brain chemistry

Introduction

For the physiological psychologist, the most radical of the various advances in brain research has been the increasing emphasis upon neurotransmitter pathways as functional units in the modelling of behaviour. Chapter 12 discusses in detail the role of drug therapy for human psychopathologies in drawing attention to brain chemistry, while advances in histochemistry have enabled neurotransmitter pathways to be precisely located in the brain.

The traditional use of 'structures' as functional units has not been replaced, but we are entering an era when the same behaviour is likely to be correlated with both an anatomical and a neurochemical substrate. Given that the brain consists of both neurons and neurotransmitters, all behaviour mediated by it will have both anatomical and neurochemical correlates; it will involve neurons and synapses, physiological and neurochemical processes. What is new is the conceptualization of the brain as a set of interacting pathways defined by their synaptic transmitters, rather than as a set of interconnecting but anatomically discrete structures. Thus the hypothalamus does not disappear, but is seen as containing the terminal sites of, for instance, noradrenergic fibres, and also various fibres of passage coursing through the hypothalamus *en route* to the forebrain. Behavioural changes after hypothalamic lesions may therefore be due entirely to intra-hypothalamic damage, or, more likely, to a combination of intra-hypothalamic and extra-hypothalamic damage via the interruption of these fibres of passage (see the section on ventro-medial hypothalamic obesity in Chapter 11).

Interest in brain pathways began with the discovery of rewarding electrical stimulation of the brain (ESB) by Olds and Milner in 1954. They were using electrodes to stimulate various brain structures. One electrode missed its target, and ended up, as they eventually discovered, in the septum. What they immediately noticed was that the rat spent more and more time in that part of the cage in which it received stimulation through the electrode, i.e. it appeared to like the effect. Eventually Olds and Milner set up an operant procedure in a Skinner box, such that a rat could receive brief electrical stimulation via an implanted electrode whenever it pressed the bar. In this way they demonstrated that certain sites in the brain supported high rates of bar-pressing, presumably because the stimulation was experienced by the rat as rewarding. Analogously, there were sites within the brain which were aversive or punishing, in that rats would press a bar to terminate electrical stimulation of that area. Motivational aspects of electrical self-stimulation of the brain (ESB) are considered in Chapter 11.

Classic mapping work by Olds and others identified a network of rewarding ESB sites in the brain, which appeared to correlate precisely with the route of the median forebrain bundle (MFB) passing from hindbrain to forebrain. Stein (1968) additionally identified a network of punishing ESB sites, and located them along the ascending periventricular system of fibres. Thus there were anatomically defined a 'reward' and a 'punishment' pathway.

Now, since the early years of the century and the work of Thorndike and Watson, 'reinforcement' has had a major role in explaining the motivation, or the 'why', of behaviour. This culminated in Hull's (1943) specific explanation of all learning in terms of drive-reduction: animals behave in order to reduce drives via reinforcing stimuli, and learn responses to stimuli on the basis of reinforcement. Despite the subsequent rejection of this rather megalomaniacal approach to behaviour in favour of more specific and testable hypotheses, it is clear that reward and punishment are important determinants of behaviour, and

Olds, Stein, and others appeared to have established their anatomical bases.

Not, however, content with anatomy, Stein then combined ESB with simultaneous chemical stimulation via intra-cranial cannulae. By using drugs known to have specific stimulating (agonist) or blocking (antagonist) actions on brain neurotransmitters, Stein was able to associate rewarding ESB with an increase in activity in noradrenergic pathways, and punishing ESB with activity in acetylcholine (cholinergic) pathways. He concluded that any rewarding stimulus activates the noradrenegic reward system, and any punishing stimulus the cholinergic system, and that these effects could be mimicked by suitable drugs; thus a drug inducing pleasurable sensations in humans, such as amphetamine, would do so via brain noradrenaline. Further, by defining a major psychopathology in schizophrenia as a loss of responsiveness to rewarding stimuli, Stein could hypothesize that the underlying physiological pathology involved the noradrenergic reward system (Stein and Wise, 1971; see also Chapter 12). So the chemical pathway concept had immediate practical value.

The straightforward mapping, using histochemical techniques, of neurotransmitter pathways also began in the 1960s. The cholinergic system had been traced by Shute and Lewis (1967; Lewis and Shute, 1967), and the extensive investigations into monoamine pathways (i.e. the catecholamines noradrenaline and dopamine, and the indoleamine serotonin) at the Karolinska Institute in Stockholm culminated in a classic paper by Ungerstedt in 1971 (Ungerstedt, 1971c). It is now possible, using the results of these and subsequent studies (e.g. Lindvall and Bjorklund, 1974), to outline the principal features of the 'long-axon' neurotransmitter systems.

There are of the order of 15×10^9 neurons in the brain. Each has identifiable dendritic and axonal processes, but the range of sizes, lengths, and spatial configurations is immense. When considering neurotransmitter pathways, we are concerned with subsets of brain cells which conform to a consistent pattern. The neurons will have their cell bodies clumped together somewhere in the brainstem (i.e. in the midbrain, pons, or medulla), and each neuron will contribute its axon to the pathway, which therefore consists of thousands of axons travelling together from hindbrain regions towards forebrain regions. As the pathway courses through various structures on its journey to the forebrain, axons within it may send off branches to innervate these structures. Branching and a general ramification of the pathway become more noticeable as it approaches the points of final termination, usually in basal ganglia, limbic system, or cerebral cortex. If the axon of one neuron is traced, we would be able to identify its passage from the cell body in the brainstem up to its synaptic terminals (perhaps a hundred or more) in the forebrain; that neuron is a single unit, and it is a basic pharmacological principle (Dale's Principle) that it will release the same neurotransmitter at each of its synaptic terminals. The crucial finding of the histochemists was that *all* the neurons whose cell bodies clumped together in the brainstem and whose axons made up a given pathway utilized the same neurotransmitter.

It was therefore possible to identify a number of pathways conforming to this basic pattern: long axons, ascending through the brain from brainstem sites of origin, to innervate forebrain areas. The differentiation of the various pathways then relies on the identification of precisely where they begin and where they end, and what neurotransmitter they use. The next section summarizes this information, and briefly reviews some ideas on their behavioural functions.

Chemical pathways in the brain

Acetylcholine (ACh)

Lewis and Shute (1967; Shute and Lewis, 1967) have identified two major cholinergic systems in the brain: an ascending cholinergic reticular system seen as a continuation of the brainstem reticular formation, and a cholinergic limbic system centring on the hippocampus (see Fig. 3.1).

The ascending cholinergic reticular system consists of two separable pathways, a dorsal tegmental and a ventral tegmental pathway. The dorsal path originates in the nucleus cuneiformis in the midbrain, and supplies the lateral geniculate nucleus

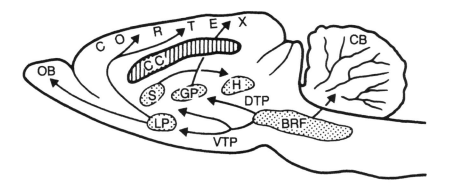

Key

DTP=Dorsal tegmental pathway; VTP =Ventral tegmental pathway;
BRF=Brainstem Recticular Formation; CB=Cerebellum; CC=Corpus
Callosum; GP=Globus Pallidus; H=Hippocampus; LP=Lateral Preoptic
Area of Hypothalamus; OB=Olfactory Bulb; S =Septum

Figure 3.1   *Outline of ascending acetylcholine (ACh) pathways*

of the thalamus and the globus pallidus of the basal ganglia; the
ventral pathway originates in the ventral tegmental regions of
the anterior midbrain, and innervates the hypothalamus in the
diencephalon, the mammillary bodies, and the globus pallidus.
Fibres from the hypothalamus pass to the corpus striatum (i.e.
the caudate nucleus and putamen of the basal ganglia), various
neocortical regions, and the septum.

The cholinergic limbic system is a pathway with cell bodies
in the septum whose axons run via the fornix to the hippocampus; from the hippocampus subsequent projections distribute
to a wide range of forebrain and midbrain areas.

The behavioural correlates of central cholinergic activity
focus on cortical arousal and hippocampal activity. Moruzzi
and Magoun (1949) demonstrated the controlling influence of

the brainstem reticular formation upon cortical and behavioural arousal; electrical stimulation of the reticular formation awakens a sleeping cat, and converts a drowsy EEG into a desynchronized aroused EEG (see Chapter 10). The cortical desynchronization is produced by the liberation of acetylcholine at the cortical surface – reticular stimulation increases activity in the ascending cholinergic pathways, resulting in increased ACh release where the pathways synapse in the cortex. The amount of ACh produced is proportional to the degree of EEG desynchronization (Kanai and Szerb, 1965), and lesions of the reticular formation reduce the resting output of ACh at the cortex (Pepeu, 1972). It seems that acetylcholine plays a central role in the regulation of cortical activity, and there are implications of this role for the processing of stimulus input. Warburton (1977) has studied the effects of cholinergic agonists and antagonists on various aspects of behaviour in rats. Using a signal detection analysis, he has shown that antagonists such as atropine and scopolamine (incidentally, these drugs occur naturally in various plants such as atropa belladonna and thorn apple) impair the animal's ability to discriminate lights and tones by reducing the signal-to-noise ratio. This would suggest that the normal function of the ascending cholinergic reticular pathways is to modulate general cortical arousal so that specific inputs or signals can be registered; if the system is blocked, signals are undetectable against the general level of background 'noise'.

The septo-hippocampal cholinergic limbic pathway implies that ACh is also involved with hippocampal function – both neurophysiological and behavioural – and the effects of cholinergic drugs confirm this. The characteristic 'theta waves' recorded from the hippocampus can be induced by cholinergic agonists and blocked by antagonists such as scopolamine. Indeed, Douglas (1975) suggests that the behavioural effects of hippocampal lesions and of cholinergic blocking drugs are in fact identical, and are related to the control of behavioural inhibition. This accords with Stein's idea of a cholinergic pathway mediating the inhibitory consequences of punishment; although Stein has changed his position somewhat (see later in this chapter) and the precise behavioural functions of the hippocampus are still in dispute (see Chapter 6), the association of central cholinergic pathways with the mediation of inhibition has been popular for many years.

Although the cholinergic reticular system and the cholinergic septo-hippocampal circuit may well be involved in different behaviours, it should be noted that if acetylcholine activity is central to the registration of stimulus input, as discussed above, then it will anyway affect behaviours dependent upon adequate processing of stimuli, i.e. virtually everything, including behavioural inhibition and memory.

Over the last few years there has been much interest in relations between brain acetylcholine and senile dementia. A key symptom of senile dementia is a profound amnesia, while post-mortem studies show that a significant loss of brain acetylcholine occurs in dementia. However, there is a greater loss of brain GABA (see later), and attempts to improve memory performance in senile dements by giving cholinergic agonists have had unspectacular results. More positively, it is possible to see an association between the septo-hippocampal cholinergic system, behavioural inhibition, and memory processes. Behaviour is inhibited in response to environmental stimuli signalling, for instance, punishment or non-reward. So current input has to be assessed in the light of experience, or memory, and it may be that the hippocampus plays a key role in these interdependent processes. These ideas are further developed in Chapters 6 and 12.

Noradrenaline (NA)

There are two major ascending NA pathways in the brain (see Fig. 3.2). The ventral pathway arises from cell groups in the medulla oblongata and the pons of the hindbrain. As it ascends through the brain, branches are given off to innervate midbrain regions, including components of the reticular formation, while the major terminus for this pathway is the hypothalamus in the diencephalon; all hypothalamic nuclei receive an NA innervation from the ventral tract.

The dorsal NA pathway (or 'bundle') originates in the locus coeruleus in the lower pons of the hindbrain. As it passes through the diencephalon branches are given off to thalamus

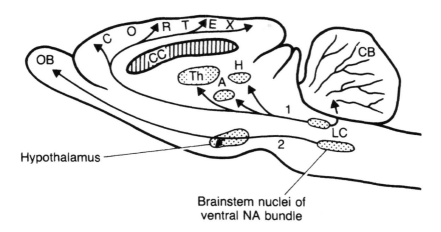

Key

1 = Dorsal NA bundle (pathway)
2 = Ventral NA bundle (pathway)
A = Amygdala; CB = Cerebellum; CC = Corpus Callosum;
H = Hippocampus; LC = Locus Coeruleus; OB = Olfactory Bulb;
Th = Thalamus

Figure 3.2 *Outline of ascending noradrenergic (NA) pathways*

and to hypothalamus, and major terminal sites for the pathway
are in the hippocampus and amygdala of the limbic system and
the cerebral cortex. Most, if not all, forebrain structures receive
an input from the dorsal NA pathway, and as the locus
coeruleus also sends *descending* fibres to innervate lower brainstem nuclei and the cerebellum, it appears that this NA nucleus
is in a position to influence virtually the whole of the brain.

With the ventral NA pathway concerned with hypothalamic
function and the dorsal pathway innervating the limbic system
and cortex, brain noradrenaline could be involved in the
regulation of cognitive (via the cortex), affective (via the limbic
system control of emotional expression), endocrinological and
autonomic (via the hypothalamus) functions. Stein attempted
to conceptualize on a more integrative level by associating NA

with rewarding ESB. As reinforcement is congruent with behavioural excitation, Stein suggested that brain noradrenaline mediated excitation, and this was supported by the stimulant effects of noradrenergic agonists such as amphetamine.

As the NA pathways have such tightly organized points of origin (the rat locus coeruleus contains only around 1,500 neurons: Swanson, 1976), lesions to effectively remove one, or both, are relatively simple. Using this technique, various workers have investigated the involvement of noradrenaline in specific behaviours.

A general conclusion is that a severe (70–80 per cent) depletion of brain NA does not prevent acquisition of even complex motor tasks (Mason and Iversen, 1977). (For a review of the area, see Clark, 1979; Gray, 1982.) Simple motor tasks, active and passive avoidance, and various operant responses are also acquired by the NA-depleted animal, which, if NA pathways mediated the reinforcement upon which learning is based, would not be possible.

There are various effects. Animals with dorsal NA bundle lesions show a resistance to extinction, maintaining high levels of responding in the absence of reinforcement (Mason and Iversen, 1977; Mason and Fibiger, 1978). It has been suggested that the basis of this effect is that NA-depletion leads to increased distractibility or stimulus-sampling; this allows more stimuli to become associated with the response during learning, and prolongs responding during extinction (Mason and Fibiger, 1978). This attentional hypothesis of dorsal NA bundle function is disputed by Gray (1982), whose alternative idea is that it tags stimuli as important and worthy of further analysis. (Gray's proposal is discussed in more detail in Chapter 12).

The most influential hypothesis in regard to brain NA has been that it mediates reinforcement or reward. The evidence, as already described, comes from studies of electrical self-stimulation of the brain (ESB), which suggest that, specifically, the dorsal NA pathway from the locus coeruleus is the anatomical substrate of rewarding ESB. As lesioning this pathway does not necessarily impair learning, doubt is cast upon the hypothesis – perhaps ESB is not akin to natural rewards (see Chapter 11). Doubt has also been cast upon the dependence of

ESB on noradrenaline at all (Wise, 1978), although several influential authors accept the relationship (Crow, 1973; German and Bowden, 1974).

Less controversial is the involvement of the ventral NA pathway in hypothalamic functions. Some aspects of feeding behaviour, for instance, appear to be under direct noradrenergic control (see Chapter 11).

The wide distribution of NA fibres and terminals suggests a broad involvement in many aspects of behaviour. Two reviews (Clark, 1979; Amaral and Sinnamon, 1977) both conclude that highly organized regulation of specific behaviours is unlikely, particularly for the dorsal locus coeruleus pathway; even the traditional role in the control of REM sleep (see Chapter 10) has come under attack (Ramm, 1979).

Dopamine (DA)

Dopamine has been the neurotransmitter of the 1970s. Stimulated by the involvement of DA pathways in schizophrenia (see Chapter 12), a neurotransmitter virtually unknown in 1970 now plays a major role in our models of the brain and behaviour.

There are three major dopamine pathways. The first runs from the substantia nigra in the midbrain to the corpus striatum of the basal ganglia (the corpus striatum consists of the caudate nucleus and the putamen – see Chapter 2); extensions of this pathway innervate the amygdaloid nucleus. The second tract arises from cell bodies close to the substantia nigra, and terminates in the nucleus accumbens and olfactory tubercle of the limbic system; DA terminals in the cortex are probably extensions of this meso- (referring to the midbrain) limbic pathway (see Fig. 3.3).

Finally, a dense collection of DA cell bodies is found in the hypothalamus, where they are involved in controlling secretions from the pituitary gland; this tubero-infundibular system seems to be entirely independent of the two major pathways. It normally inhibits the release of the hormone prolactin from the anterior lobe of the pituitary, so that DA agonists such as amphetamine and apomorphine further reduce resting blood levels of prolactin: conversely, DA blocking drugs, such as the anti-schizophrenic agent chlorpromazine, produce an im-

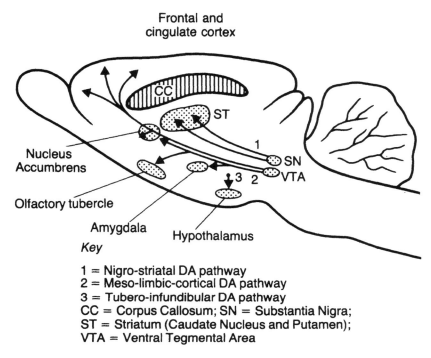

Figure 3.3   *Outline of ascending dopamine (DA) pathways*

mediate increase in prolactin levels.

The nigro-striatal and meso-limbic-cortical pathways have more complex behavioural and physiological functions. The nigro-striatal DA system is identical with a neuroanatomically defined tract running from the substantia nigra to the striatum, and known for many years to be involved in the Parkinsonian syndrome. This is a disorder of what is called the extra-pyramidal motor system (so called because it lies outside the main motor output pathways, which run from the pyramidal cells in the motor cortex), with symptoms of akinesia (failure to initiate movements), rigidity, and tremor of the extremities. Patients who die from this progressive neurological disease show substantial degeneration of the substantia nigra and striatum, and a subsequent loss of dopamine. The most effective therapy consists of injections of drugs such as L-DOPA, a precursor of dopamine which acts to increase functional levels of the neurotransmitter in the brain.

The presence of localized damage in the human brain, whose neuroanatomical and neurochemical correlates are known and whose behavioural effects have been described, has stimulated great interest in the nigro-striatal DA pathway in animals. One of the earliest and most dramatic findings was the 'rotating rodent' (Ungerstedt, 1971b).

In common with virtually all brain structures, the nigro-striatal tract is represented bilaterally – there is one pathway on each side of the brain. If one of them is lesioned, i.e. destroyed, and a dopamine agonist injected, the animal rotates for the duration of the drug's action. Intriguingly, amphetamine produces circling towards the lesioned side, while apomorphine-injected rats circle away from the lesioned side.

The explanation lies in the respective modes of action of the two drugs. After the lesion, there is an intact pathway from substantia nigra to striatum on one side, while on the other only the post-synaptic receptors in the striatum are left (see Fig. 3.4).

These receptors, attempting to compensate for the loss of pre-synaptic dopamine, become supersensitive to any of the neurotransmitter that may be available. Apomorphine acts directly on DA receptors, and has a more potent action on the supersensitive receptors of the lesioned side; this imbalance produces circling towards the opposite, intact, side. Amphetamine is an indirectly acting DA agonist, releasing endogenous (naturally occurring in the brain) neurotransmitter from pre-synaptic terminals; it can therefore only release DA from the intact pathway, and this imbalance produces rotation towards the opposite, lesioned, side.

The rotating rodent is a pure example of brain dopamine activity, and as such can be used to test drugs for the ability to stimulate or to block DA receptors. Almost all anti-schizophrenic drugs (also known as anti-psychotics, neuroleptics, or major tranquillizers) are DA antagonists, and block amphetamine-induced rotation in the unilateral nigro-striatal lesioned rat. Given the association between the loss of nigro-

72   *Brain chemistry*

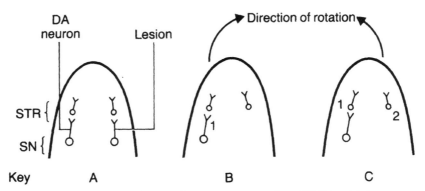

Key   A   B   C

A   Intact dopamine pathways from substantia nigra (SN) to striatum (STR), showing site of unilateral lesion (diagrammatic view from dorsal surface).

B   In unilateral nigro-striatal lesioned rat, *AMPHETAMINE* acts at (1) to release dopamine from *intact* DA terminal, producing left-sided activation and rotation towards the lesioned side.

C   *APOMORPHINE* acts at (1) and also at supersensitive DA receptors on striatal neuron (2), producing relatively more right-sided activation and rotation away from the lesioned side.

Figure 3.4   *The rotating rat – effects of indirect agonist, amphetamine, and direct agonist, apomorphine*

striatal dopamine and Parkinsonism, it might also be expected that DA blockers would produce Parkinsonian symptoms in humans; and this is what is found. Prolonged treatment with neuroleptic drugs in schizophrenia consistently produces Parkinsonian, or 'extra-pyramidal', side-effects.

These side-effects are not seen with all neuroleptics; e.g. thioridazine has a very low incidence of extra-pyramidal symptoms, and also fails to antagonize amphetamine-induced rotation. These phenomena have been attributed to the potent anticholinergic properties possessed by thioridazine, and the side-effects of other neuroleptics may be controlled by combining them with an anticholinergic drug.

The explanation for this dopamine/acetylcholine interaction

lies in the circuitry of the extra-pyramidal system. Dopamine axons ascending from the substantia nigra synapse in the striatum on to cholinergic neurons. DA released from the pre-synaptic terminal normally acts to inhibit this cholinergic neuron; however, in Parkinsonism or after a blockade of DA receptors by neuroleptic drugs, activity in the nigro-striatal pathway is reduced and the cholinergic neuron is released from inhibition. Extra-pyramidal symptoms are therefore produced by overactive cholinergic neurons in the striatum (specifically, in the caudate nucleus).

To restore the DA/ACh balance in the striatum, one can either beef up the reduced DA by using a drug such as L-DOPA, or reduce the overactive ACh by using an anticholinergic. Thus thioridazine does not produce extra-pyramidal side-effects as it simultaneously blocks both DA and ACh, so maintaining the DA/ACh balance in the striatum. (See Fig. 3.5.)

The involvement of the nigro-striatal pathway in extra-pyramidal motor functions is now well established. It is also implicated in other specific aspects of behaviour such as eating and drinking, as will be seen in Chapter 11. For the moment, however, we can consider the implications of the nigro-striatal/ DA/Parkinsonism/neuroleptic drug story for the possible physiological bases of schizophrenia. The DA-blocking action of neuroleptics in the striatum produces side-effects, which may be alleviated by anticholinergic drugs or L-DOPA. However, their anti-psychotic action is unaffected. If the anti-psychotic action depends upon DA-blockade (see Chapter 12), then it cannot be a DA-blockade in the striatum as this can be nullified without affecting the drug's anti-psychotic action. We must look elsewhere for the probable sites of action.

By a process of elimination, the most likely candidates lie in the meso-limbic-cortical DA pathway. The cortex and limbic system regulate, between them, cognition, learning, memory, and emotion, and so damage to these areas could easily give rise to the symptoms of a schizophrenic breakdown. Although this DA model of schizophrenia occupies the foreground and is discussed in detail in Chapter 12, it has given rise, in the background, to hypotheses on the role of dopamine pathways in normal behavioural regulation.

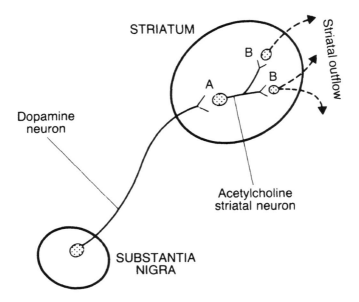

Figure 3.5   *Dopamine/acetylcholine balance in striatum. DA released from the nigro-striatal DA neuron acts at synapse A to inhibit the ACh interneuron. Neuroleptic drugs block synapse A, release the ACh neuron from inhibition, and increase ACh transmission at synapses B. The unbalanced striatal outflow can lead to Parkinsonian symptoms. An anticholinergic drug given with the neuroleptic blocks the increased ACh transmission at synapses B and restores the DA/ACh equilibrium*

One of the more interesting of these (Matthysse, 1974) assumes that the two main DA pathways operate in analogous fashion, but in two different spheres of behaviour. The nigro-striatal system regulates the responsiveness of the basal ganglia (including the striatum) to motor commands originating in the cortex; the function of the basal ganglia is to convert motor commands into action, so the ascending dopamine pathway controls the emergence of motor 'plans' into observed action by modulating the responsiveness of the basal ganglia. The meso-limbic-cortical pathway does the same thing, only for preconscious thoughts and fantasies. At any one time our behaviour is to a large extent consciously dominated by one idea or intention, and it is the ascending dopamine pathway that controls the emergence of a given idea into consciousness. An alternative way of looking at it is to see the two dopamine pathways as inhibiting motor response patterns and thoughts respectively; a loss of nigro-striatal DA leads to a loss of motor response inhibition and the occurrence of extra-pyramidal motor disorders, while a loss of meso-limbic DA leads to a loss of 'thought-inhibition', and the dominance of conscious experience by an uncontrolled stream of ideas and fantasies. As this latter phenomenon can be likened to some forms of schizophrenic thought disorder, the link between dopamine and schizophrenia is explained.

Although such hypotheses are very difficult to text experimentally (particularly, if using animals, the control of conscious thought processes), others have presented similar ideas (e.g. Stevens, 1977), and their very complexity makes them intuitively plausible. Profound behavioural breakdowns such as schizophrenia must represent an equally profound breakdown in the activity of the brain.

Before leaving dopamine, mention should be made of its possible role in electrical self-stimulation (ESB). Over the last decade there has been a lively dispute on the relative involvements of dopamine and noradrenaline in ESB; the debate is important if we follow the progression, 'rewarding ESB is equivalent to natural rewards, and therefore the neurotransmitter involved in ESB is the neurochemical basis of natural reward'. Stein and his group have consistently favoured an exclusive role for noradrenaline, but German and Bowden (1974) and Crow (1973) suggest that both neurotransmitters may be involved. Crow showed that rats would self-stimulate with electrodes in either the dorsal NA pathway or in the meso-limbic DA pathway. The dorsal NA animals were quite lethargic, though persistent, in pressing the bar for ESB, while the meso-limbic DA group were manically overaroused, leaping on to the bar with all four feet. He therefore suggests that, while both pathways can support ESB, they do so via different mechanisms: the dorsal NA tract via its control of 'reinforcement' (*à la* Stein), and the meso-limbic DA pathway via its control of 'drive' or 'incentive'.

This distinction between reinforcement and the drive that leads to the search for reinforcement is supported by Herberg *et al.* (1976), who, again using ESB, associate noradrenaline with reinforcement and dopamine with motivation. Remember, however, the ability of animals depleted of 80 per cent of brain noradrenaline to acquire new responses on the basis of reinforcement, and it seems that the picture is still unclear.

A major technical problem in this area is that the various ascending neurotransmitter pathways are extremely close to each other. My presentation has emphasized their distinctiveness, but as they all arise in the brainstem and funnel through narrow regions such as the midbrain, they do come into close contact. For example, the median forebrain bundle, a large assembly of fibres connecting hindbrain and forebrain, in fact contains within it several of the pathways I have described, travelling together for the sake of neuroanatomical convenience. Of course, they have different origins and termini and utilize different neurotransmitters, but it is difficult to be sure that a small lesion or self-stimulation electrode is exactly where you think it is.

Given these reservations, it still seems likely that both the catecholamines, noradrenaline and dopamine, play a part in ESB, but that ESB may not be as closely related to the natural experience of reward as we would wish. This point is taken up in Chapter 11.

Serotonin (5-HT)

Serotonin is an indoleamine, one of the subgroups of monoamines (another subgroup is the catecholamines, noradrenaline and dopamine). The full chemical name is 5-hydroxytryptamine, and it is usually referred to as 5-HT.

The ascending serotonin system originates in the raphé nuclei, a large group of cell bodies extending from the medulla in the hindbrain to the edge of the midbrain. Early branches from the pathway innervate the midbrain reticular formation, while later target zones include the hypothalamus, striatum, amygdala, hippocampus, septum, and cerebral cortex. (See Fig. 3.6.)

The distribution of the serotonin system is roughly similar to that of the ventral noradrenergic pathway.

The behavioural correlates of the central serotonin system have been less studied than those of other neurotransmitter pathways. A reason for this is the general lack of suitably specific drugs for stimulating and blocking the system, so that much of the work has been done using drugs or lesions which produce enormous increases or decreases in overall brain serotonin content.

One of the earliest and most reliable findings was Jouvet's demonstration of the controlling part played by serotonin in

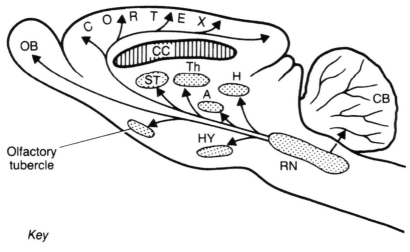

Key

CB = Cerebellum; CC = Corpus Callosum; A = Amygdala;
H = Hippocampus; HY = Hypothalamus; RN = Raphé Nuclei;
ST = Striatum (Caudate Nucleus and Putamen); Th = Thalamus

Figure 3.6   *Outline of ascending serotonin (5-HT) pathways*

slow-wave sleep (Jouvet, 1969 – see Chapter 10, below). Using either PCPA (para-chloro-phenylalanine, a drug which depletes the brain of serotonin) or lesions of the raphé nuclei which can deplete brain 5-HT by 90 per cent or more, he showed that rats become insomniac in the absence of the neurotransmitter; the degree of insomnia was roughly proportional to the loss of forebrain serotonin. The effect could be prevented by injections of 5-HTP (5-hydroxytryptophan), a serotonin precursor (i.e. increases brain levels of 5-HT). (For a fuller discussion, see Chapter 10.)

Raphé lesions or injections of PCPA also make rats more exploratory, hyper-reactive, and occasionally hyper-aggressive (Geyer *et al.*, 1976; Aprison and Hingtgen, 1972), and it has been suggested (Wise *et al.*, 1973) that the central serotonin system mediates behavioural inhibition, so that decreases in brain 5-HT lead to increases in behavioural output. Chapter 12 describes the postulated involvement of serotonin in the disinhibitory effects of anti-anxiety drugs such as Librium and Valium. Injections of PCPA can mimic the actions of anti-anxiety drugs in animal models of anxiety (Hodges and Green, 1984), and Gray (1982) suggests that ascending serotonin pathways play a major role in the experience of fear or anxiety, by labelling incoming stimuli as being associated with punishment, and so enhancing behavioural inhibition.

The consequences of increasing serotonin levels are less clear. Minor variations have little effect, while more dramatic increases induced by 5-HTP or by direct stimulation of receptors (using recently developed drugs such as 5-methoxy-N, N-dimethyltryptamine) produce a specific but very abnormal behavioural syndrome. This consists of a resting tremor of head and forelimbs, rigidity of the torso, splaying of the hindlimbs, and slow side-to-side head movements (Jacobs, 1976; Sloviter *et al.*, 1978). It bears some resemblance to the 'stereotypy' model of dopamine overstimulation (see Chapter 12), and, like that model, serves as a test-bed for drugs, i.e. if you suspect that a drug may affect serotonin pathways, high doses should either induce the syndrome (if it is a serotonin agonist), or block the syndrome induced by known serotonin agonists (if it is an antagonist). The syndrome is less helpful to the physiological psychologist. In that state the animal cannot be tested for locomotor activity, learning, memory, attentional processes, etc.; it is a pharmacological model rather than a behavioural one.

One effect of elevating serotonin levels specifically in the hypothalamus may be to decrease eating. Hypothalamic centres are crucial to feeding and satiety (inhibition of feeding when full – see Chapter 11), and it is thought that the two most popular 'slimmer's drugs', amphetamine (Benzedrine) and fenfluramine (Ponderax), both act through hypothalamic mechanisms. Amphetamine, as mentioned earlier, liberates dopamine and noradrenaline from pre-synaptic terminals, while fenfluramine similarly releases serotonin; this would suggest an intra-hypothalamic serotonin system normally involved in the inhibition of eating.

Cholinergic, noradrenergic, dopaminergic, and serotonergic pathways together represent the major long-axon neurotransmitter systems in the brain. There is a reasonable consistency in the pattern from species to species (rat, monkey, cat, humans) insofar as they have been compared, and we would anticipate behavioural similarities as well.

While we have to remember that a full description of all these pathways still only accounts for around 30 per cent of neurotransmitter activity in the brain, the justification for emphasizing these long-axon systems is precisely the fact that they are so organized. Originating from compact nuclei in the brainstem and ascending as identifiable bundles of fibres to target zones in the forebrain, the various systems are well placed to have profound and systematic effects on the rest of the brain and on behaviour. It is the aim of the psychopharmacologist to clarify these effects, whether they involve the general modulation of overall arousal states or the specific control of limited behavioural 'units' such as attention or hunger.

Other neurotransmitters

The models we have of synaptic structure and function in the brain are based very much on our knowledge of the peripheral nervous system. The pioneering work of people such as Dale and Feldberg in the early years of the century described synaptic transmission in the autonomic nervous system and at the neuro-muscular junction in the somatic nervous system. The traditional picture of the synapse, with vesicles being extruded into the cleft in response to action potentials in the pre-synaptic terminal, is based absolutely upon these studies of peripheral transmission; no single central nervous system synapse has been analysed in such convincing detail, and even the positive identification of a CNS synapse using chemical neuro-transmission was delayed until the 1950s (Eccles *et al.*, 1954).

One simple reason for this is that the criteria for positive identification of synaptic transmission are severe, and technically very difficult to fulfil within the brain; to isolate pre-synaptic vesicles and identify the chemical they contain is but the start of the process.

Some neurochemicals are very probably neurotransmitters in the brain, particularly the ones we have already considered. Others, such as GABA, glutamate, and glycine, are equally as well-established on pharmacological grounds, but are not, on the whole, organized into long-axon pathways; drugs influencing them tend to produce bizarre behavioural effects or to have no effect at all.

GABA (gamma-amino-butyric-acid), glutamate, and glycine are widespread in the central nervous system. GABA and glycine are inhibitory neurotransmitters (inhibitory in the pharmacological sense of making the post-synaptic membrane less responsive), while glutamate is excitatory. From their distribution and pharmacological actions, one would predict that their most likely function would be to modulate activity in other neurons, e.g. in the long-axon pathways already discussed. Interference with them tends to have an all-or-none flavour; a GABA antagonist such as picrotoxin has no apparent effect in low doses, but induces generalized convulsions in higher doses. As GABA may be the transmitter at up to 40 per cent of CNS synapses (McGeer *et al.*, 1978), it cannot be ignored; however, until less dramatic techniques are found for influencing these widespread and apparently non-specific systems, their precise role in behaviour will remain elusive. In recent years, it has become apparent that some of these apparently non-specific systems may mediate drug effects on behaviour. If GABA has a general inhibitory role in the brain,

Table 3.1   Neurotransmitters in the central nervous system

(a) *Established neurotransmitters*

Acetylcholine (Ach)	Tertiary Amine	
Dopamine (DA)	} Catecholamines }	Monoamines
Noradrenaline (USA: Norepinephrine. NA or NE)		
Serotonin (5-hydroxytryptamine: 5-HT)	Indoleamine	
GABA (Gamma-aminobutyric acid)		
Glycine (GLY)	} Amino Acids	
Glutamate (GLU)		

(b) *Examples of neuropeptide candidates for neurotransmitters or neuromodulators*

Carnosine	Substance P
Cholecystokinin	Neurotensin
β-Endorphin	Vasoactive intestinal peptide
Leucine-Enkephalin	Vasopressin
Met-Enkephalin	

(c) *Synthesis of major neurotransmitters*

Acetylcholine neuron

$$\text{CHOLINE} + \text{ACETYL-COENZYME A} \xrightarrow[\text{choline acetyltransferase}]{\text{catalysed by enzyme}} \text{ACh}$$

Dopamine neuron

$$\text{PHENYLALANINE} \xrightarrow[\text{hydroxylase}]{\text{tyrosine}} \text{TYROSINE} \xrightarrow[\text{hydroxylase}]{\text{tyrosine}} \text{DOPA}$$

aromatic amino acid decarboxylase

↓

DOPAMINE

Noradrenaline neuron
As for Dopamine. Then

$$\text{DOPAMINE} \xrightarrow[\text{hydroxylase}]{\text{dopamine-B}} \text{NORADRENALINE}$$

Serotonin neuron

$$\text{TRYPTOPHAN} \xrightarrow[\text{hydroxylase}]{\text{tryptophan}} \text{5-HYDROXYTRYPTOPHAN}$$

aromatic amino acid decarboxylase ↓

5-HYDROXYTRYPTAMINE
(SEROTONIN)

After synaptic action, a proportion of released neurotransmitter is re-absorbed by the pre-synaptic neuron for re-use, and a proportion is broken down by enzymatic action: ACh by acetylcholinesterase, 5-HT by monoamine oxidase, and DA and NA by monoamine oxidase and by catechol-0-methyltransferase.

then variations in GABA activity will produce variations in the level of inhibition, and a correlated variation in the activity of the neurons being inhibited by GABA. There is now convincing evidence, discussed in more detail in Chapter 12, that the benzodiazepine anti-anxiety drugs, such as Librium and Valium, have as one of their main actions a facilitation of GABA transmission, i.e. they act to increase GABA-mediated inhibition of various neuronal populations, particularly serotonergic pathways. If, as Stein originally suggested, serotonin is involved in *behavioural* inhibition, increased *pharmacological* inhibition of serotonin activity via GABA synapses will result in *decreased behavioural* inhibition. This, as reviewed in Chapter 12, is a feature of benzodiazepine effects on behaviour.

There are a number of potential neurotransmitters (see Table 3.1), and the list is growing almost monthly. This book is not the place for a detailed review of the field (see McGeer *et al.*, 1978; Iversen and Iversen, 1981), but to give the flavour of contemporary research into brain chemistry, the next section describes the discovery and behavioural implications of the brain's endogenous opiate system.

The opiate receptor and pain perception

One of the enduring quests within clinical pharmacology is for a pain-relieving drug (i.e. an analgesic) without the powerful physical addictive properties of the opiate narcotic analgesics. Of the latter, morphine is the best-known and most widely used. It has potent analgesic properties, and may also induce states of relaxation and mild euphoria. The ability to produce euphoria has led to some opiates becoming drugs of abuse, while their addictive qualities have made a drug such as heroin the single most intractable problem in the whole field of drug dependence.

The increase in the use of direct intra-cranial injections during the 1960s revealed that opiate analgesics showed a regional specificity in their actions in animals; injections into the central grey of the midbrain were much more effective than injections into, for example, the cerebral cortex. The potency and specificity of morphine's action suggested an interaction with a specialized synaptic receptor in the brain, and the so-called 'opiate receptor' was identified and isolated in the early 1970s; the overall distribution of these receptors in the brain could be mapped, and, as expected, paralleled exactly the regional specificity of morphine's action. (See Simon, 1976, for a review of the discovery and properties of the opiate receptor.)

We had fortuitously hit upon an extract of the poppy, morphine, which was chemically a perfect match for the endogenous (naturally occurring) receptor. Assuming that the receptors were around before morphine, and that brain mechanisms evolve for some sort of specific function, it is then a simple step to suggest that there must exist an endogenous neurotransmitter akin to morphine which would act at the endogenous receptor. The classical role for receptors in the nervous system is to enable transmission of information across the synapse – they are situated on the post-synaptic membrane, and bind a specific neurotransmitter released from the pre-synaptic terminal. Once opiate receptors were identified it was assumed that their most likely location was on a post-synaptic membrane, and the search began for an endogenous 'opiate' to be released from the terminal of an 'opiate' neuron to act on the receptors.

It was in 1975 that Hughes reported the isolation and identification of an opiate-like endogenous chemical in the pig brain (Hughes, 1975; a readable review of the discovery is contained in Kosterlitz and Hughes, 1977). The name 'enkephalin' was given to this chemical, and two basically similar forms were described: methionine-enkephalin and leucine-enkephalin. The enkephalins resemble morphine in their specific affinity for the opiate receptor, but their analgesic effects have been difficult to assess as they are rapidly broken down by enzymes after intra-cranial injection.

Then closely related chemical fragments were identified in extracts of the pituitary gland, given the generic name 'endorphins', and shown to be potent analgesics, in the case of β-endorphin many times stronger than morphine. Further studies have shown that both enkephalins and endorphins have analgesic properties, but that prolonged exposure still induces tolerance and physical dependence in an analogous fashion to morphine. Their behavioural effects are antagonized by the highly specific opiate receptor antagonist drug naloxone, and the distribution of enkephalin in the calf brain matches impressively the distribution of opiate receptors (Simantov *et al.*, 1976). The evidence in general forces the conclusion that enkephalin (specifically leucine-enkephalin) is the endogenous opiate neurotransmitter.

Using the known effects of morphine as a model, it is possible to speculate on the normal functions of an endogenous opiate system. Enkephalin is stored in the pre-synaptic terminal; under appropriate circumstances it is released into the synapse and acts upon the post-synaptic opiate receptors; this would be the basis of normally occurring analgesia. That the system can be overactive when occasion demands is shown by the reports of soldiers fighting on in the presence of grotesque physical injury. More prosaically, individual differences in suscept- ibility to pain may involve fundamental neurochemical varia- tion in the respective opiate pathways. More interestingly, slightly bizarre techniques such as acupuncture may involve stimulation of the endogenous opiate system, while there is some evidence that naloxone can block hypnosis-induced analgesia. In addition, endogenous opiates may help explain 'placebo' effects, in which subjects respond to an inert chemical they believe is a potent drug.

If the endogenous opiate system is conceived of as a set of neurons, axons, dendrites, etc., in the manner of the neuro- transmitters already described, then questions concerning a more general role in behaviour can be asked. There is specu- lation that obesity in humans may involve enkephalin, but rather more soundly based is the suggestion by Belluzzi and Stein (1977) that enkephalin may play a part in the normal functioning of reward pathways in the brain. They have shown that rats will happily self-administer enkephalin via intra- cranial cannulae, in the same way as they will do for morphine. They then implanted electrical self-stimulation electrodes in the midbrain, and demonstrated that rates of self-stimulation were significantly reduced by the opiate antagonist naloxone; this would suggest that self-stimulation depends upon the release of enkephalin to act upon opiate receptors. In the same animals, a drug depleting brain noradrenaline had the same effect, and Belluzzi and Stein conclude that 'reward' or 'rein- forcement' is regulated by both noradrenaline and enkephalin.

The discovery of enkephalin has been one of the more dramatic breakthroughs of the past few years. It reflected the systematic application of our knowledge of synaptic structure and function, and serves as a convincing justification for the technically sophisticated micro-physiological approach. There will be other major discoveries, but each one in turn should be analysed at the behavioural as well as the micro-physiological level. Pain perception clearly reflects social and cultural factors as well as any inbuilt system, and the full description and explanation of how and why we feel pain demands a multi-level approach.

As a pointer to the lateral thinking approach to speculation, one can quote the work of Simantov *et al.*, (1976) who studied the distribution of enkephalin across different animal species. They report that the endogenous opiate is found in all the vertebrate species studied, but in none of the invertebrates. This implies a relatively late evolution of this system, and one can speculate as to how pain perception is mediated in invertebrates. The vertebrate/invertebrate distinction is also found with respect to the distribution of the endogenous benzodiazepine receptor (see Chapter 12); there is clearly something about being a vertebrate that involves a lot of pain and anxiety. Other neurotransmitters, including the well-established ones already described in some detail, are present in all animal species possessing even a rudimentary neuronal nervous system, and are therefore archaic compared with enkephalin.

This chapter has reviewed in general terms the associations between brain chemistry and behaviour. The picture presented has been necessarily simplified. No single transmitter system exists in isolation, and effects on one must involve indirect effects on others. There is no reason in principle why several neurochemicals should not be involved in the same specific behaviour. This is particularly the case when we consider the possible roles of the neurotransmitter candidates in Table 3.1. It is likely that several of these will prove not to be classical neurotransmitters, but to have a 'modulatory' role on neural activity. It has recently been discovered that some of them, such as cholecystokinin (CCK), are found co-existing with classical transmitters; mesolimbic dopamine neurons also contain CCK, which appears to influence directly neural activity in these dopaminergic pathways. Unravelling the chemical spaghetti of the brain has hardly begun.

4 Sensory systems

Introduction

The world that we are aware of is a construction of our central
nervous system. The building blocks are nerve impulses,
travelling into the CNS along sensory pathways, produced by
the various stimuli which surround us. Therefore the only
stimuli which we can be aware of are those which produce
neural activity – action potentials or nerve impulses – in those
sensory pathways.

The stimuli in the environment around us exist in various
forms. Vision depends upon electro-magnetic radiation from
the object, hearing relies upon mechanical pressure waves
transmitted via the molecules in the air, touch is a direct
mechanical deformation of the skin, while taste and smell
represent information coded as chemical structure. The crucial
stage leading to our being able to sense and perceive these
stimuli is the conversion of the various forms of energy into a
neural code; i.e. whatever the stimulus, it is eventually coded as
trains of nerve impulses travelling along sensory nerve fibres.

The conversion of stimulus energy into a neural code is
known as transduction, and involves sensory receptors. These
range in complexity from the highly specialized visual and
auditory receptor cells found in the eye and ear, to the free
nerve endings found in the skin which, even though barely
modified from straightforward axons, are sensitive to painful
stimuli and to heat and cold. Whatever their nature, the
purpose of sensory receptors is to react to an appropriate
stimulus by triggering action potentials in sensory afferent
neurons.

The absolute dependence of our experiential world upon the nature and distribution of sensory receptors can be easily demonstrated. The first two chapters described various intentional and accidental manipulations of the brain in the conscious human subject. Electrodes can be implanted to stimulate or record sites within the brain, with the patient able to provide a running commentary. Devastating damage can occur to whole regions such as the frontal lobes (p.53), with the victim aware that something has happened, but unaware of the extent of the injury.

The brain can therefore suffer physical insult and yet the patient feels little or no pain. This is because brain tissue itself does not contain sensory receptors which respond to painful stimuli. In a pure sense, damage to the brain does not 'exist' as a painful stimulus for the brain, because it cannot be transduced into a neural code that the brain can operate upon. Obviously any other effects of the damage – on sensory, cognitive, affective, or motor systems – will be noticed, and there are regions of the brain devoted to the perception of painful stimuli encoded in pain pathways by sensory receptors in the body (see later). Stimulation in these latter areas can produce the experience of pain, just as stimulation of the visual cortex can produce the experience of vision. Even the 'headache' represents changes in fluid volumes encoded by sensory pressure receptors in cranial blood vessels, and only then passed to the pain centres of the brain for interpretation.

With each of our senses, or modalities, we respond to (or are aware of) a range of stimuli; we see bright and dark objects, hear high-pitched and low-pitched sounds, taste sweet and sour foods. The range we respond to represents only a proportion of the available range, and for every sensory modality we could find another species with a different battery of sensory receptors and which therefore responded to a different range of stimuli. So, to return to my opening point, each species constructs its own view of the world, based upon the surrounding stimuli it can transduce into the sensory information which serves as the basis of perception; but although each species occupies a unique perceptual niche, related species such as the higher mammals usually show substantial similarity in the structure and organization of sensory systems.

Our sensory systems may be readily divided into the five traditional modalities – vision, hearing, touch, smell, taste – plus pain and *proprioception*, which concerns the awareness of bodily movement and position in space. They may be further classified into functional groups: e.g. exteroceptive senses, covering those modalities dealing with the outside world such as vision, hearing, touch, taste, and smell; proprioceptive senses (as above); and interoceptive senses, covering those sensory receptors handling information from internal structures, such as pressure receptors and glucose receptors in the walls of blood vessels. However, the most straightforward approach is to consider the various sensory modalities one by one. I shall outline the organization of sensory systems dealing with touch, taste, and smell, cover pain and hearing in more detail, and then discuss the visual system at length. Although this matches relative importance as assessed by the amount of research devoted to each, it should be emphasized that the hearing or auditory system in particular is as relevant to the psychologist as the visual system.

Touch

The sensation of touch comes in various forms, all involving stimulus contact with a variety of touch receptors in the skin. The sensations include light and heavy touch pressure, tickling and movement of a stimulus across the skin, cold and warmth, and pain. Categories overlap – a cold stimulus applied with heavy pressure can result in pain.

The receptors involved (mechanoreceptors, as they respond to mechanical or physical contact) number some hundreds in every square millimetre of skin surface, although some regions are relatively well-endowed (e.g. the fingertips) and others relatively insensitive (e.g. the ear lobes). There are several receptor subtypes, with a degree of stimulus specificity in their responsiveness. The most basic are the free nerve endings mentioned earlier, responding particularly to cold, warmth, and painful stimuli. Modified hair follicles respond to movement of hairs on the body surface, while Meissner corpuscles and Pacinian corpuscles are particularly sensitive to a stimulus moving across the skin and to a vibratory stimulus respectively. Krause end-bulbs and Ruffini endings are also found, although their specific functions are unclear. In fact the whole question of receptor specificity is unsettled, as there is some evidence that the whole range of touch sensations can be elicited from areas of the body innervated only by free nerve endings. In addition, given the concentration of receptors in the skin, any stimulus is almost certain to contact, if not activate, many receptors.

What is certain is that afferent sensory impulses from touch receptors on the body surface travel along sensory fibres in the spinal nerves (see p.25) to the spinal cord. After synapsing in the spinal cord grey matter, tactile touch information (i.e. not thermal or pain information) ascends the spinal cord in the dorsal column pathway, entering the medulla of the hindbrain as the medial lemniscus. This tract crosses sides and travels to the thalamus. After synapsing in the thalamus, this somatosensory pathway projects to the somatosensory cortex of the post-central gyrus in the parietal lobe (p.42).

Pain and thermal information ascend the spinal cord along the various pathways in antero-lateral zones. After entering the brain, pain pathways in particular radiate and synapse extensively in the midbrain and the thalamus, before a continuation of the spino-thalamic tract projects to the somatosensory cortex. (For further discussion of pain, see p.93.)

Throughout the somatosensory system, from afferent sensory fibres in spinal nerves to terminal zones in post-central somatosensory cortex, organization is *somatotopic*, i.e., point-for-point mapping of the bodily surface onto the distribution of fibres within pathways, onto thalamic nuclei, and onto the somatosensory cortical surface.

Proprioception

This aspect of sensation covers body and limb movement and

awareness of position in space. The relevant receptors include various of the touch mechanoreceptors already mentioned, located in and around limb joints. Awareness of limb movement (kinaesthesia) also involves receptors located on muscle fibres sensitive to muscle stretch. Proprioceptive sensory input enters the central nervous system along the somatosensory tactile pathway, via the spinal dorsal column, medial lemniscus, thalamus, and finally the post-central somatosensory cortex.

A vital contribution to proprioception is made by the vestibular apparatus, located in the inner ear. This organ is crucial to the sense of balance. In outline terms it consists of three semicircular canals and the otolith organs. These structures are continuous with each other, but arranged in space so as to cover all possible orientations – the semicircular canals lie perpendicular to each other. The whole arrangement is fluid-filled, and displacement of the fluid, produced by movement of the head in any direction, is picked up by specialized hair cell receptors and converted into afferent sensory impulses along the eighth cranial nerve (p.28). After a synapse in the brainstem, information travels to parts of the cerebellum, which are in turn connected to eye muscles and descending motor pathways to the spinal cord. The system controls body balance and the coordination of head and body movements. (For a more detailed discussion of proprioception and other material covered in this chapter, see, e.g. Kandel and Schwartz, 1985.)

Taste

The sensation of taste depends upon a molecular combination between the substance and a taste receptor. The receptors themselves are modified skin cells, and occur in groups of around fifty on a *taste bud*. The taste buds are found clustered in small numbers in *papillae*, folds in the surface of the tongue. Taste buds turn over (are replaced) every ten days or so as a matter of course, while their normal functioning is dependent upon trace elements such as zinc (see Chapter 9).

Experiments on the subjective experience of taste suggest the existence of four primary taste qualities: bitter (e.g. quinine), sour (e.g. dilute acids), salt (e.g. sodium chloride), and sweet (e.g. glucose). However, although different taste buds may respond maximally to different primary tastes (e.g. bitter tastes are better sensed at the back of the tongue), it does not appear that there are four specific taste receptors corresponding to the four tastes. Rather, single receptors may respond preferentially to one of them, but will still respond in some way to all. Activity in an afferent fibre will then represent this graded response across the population of taste receptors innervated by the fibre, and the final taste 'experience' will represent the pattern of activity across all sensory fibres. This would account for the fact that some tastes do not appear to represent one of the four primary qualities, or even a combination of them, and may in fact be literally indescribable.

Taste afferent sensory fibres travel via the cranial nerves to the nucleus solitarius in the medulla, and thence to a relay in the thalamus and on to the cortex. The cortical representation of taste is in the post-central somatosensory cortex, just below and in front of the zone dealing with somatosensory (touch) information from the tongue. The taste, or gustatory, pathway branches extensively in the medulla, sending inputs to limbic and hypothalamic regions which would be concerned with memory and emotional and motivational aspects of food taste. Chapter 9 describes a dramatic example of the importance of an intact gustatory system in psychological functioning.

Olfaction

The olfactory receptors lie in the olfactory mucosa at the back of the nasal air passages. They are effectively the endings of bipolar neurons (i.e. neurons with two long processes or axons), with the other long process extending centrally and making up the olfactory nerve. Interestingly the 100 million olfactory receptors are renewed every sixty days or so, thus representing one of the few examples of regeneration of neural (nervous) tissue.

Molecules representing the olfactory stimulus dissolve in the mucosal lining, bind to the receptor molecule, and initiate action potentials in analogous fashion to the mechanism of taste sensation. The analogy is continued in the suggestion that seven primary olfactory qualities (smells!) exist: ethereal (like ether), camphoraceous, musky, pungent, putrid, pepperminty, floral. However, evidence for highly specific receptors attuned to one or other category of smell is weak, and it appears that, as with taste, receptors show a category preference but will respond in some way to all smells. The smell finally perceived would then represent the graded pattern of activity across all olfactory sensory fibres.

The centrally extending axons of the olfactory receptor cells form the olfactory nerve. This passes to and synapses in the olfactory bulb in the forebrain or prosencephalon. Olfaction is the only sensory system whose first synapse is in the forebrain, and the only one not to possess a relatively direct pathway relaying in the thalamus on its way to the neocortex. Instead, the olfactory tract runs from the olfactory bulb to various palaeocortical (palaeocortex = 'old' cortex – see p. 41) structures which make up the initial cortical representation of olfaction. These structures include the olfactory tubercle, the prepyriform cortex, parts of the amygdala, and the entorhinal area of the hippocampus. There is an eventual link to the neocortex via a pathway from the olfactory tubercle to the thalamus and thence to the ventral surface of the frontal lobe (orbitofrontal cortex), which is probably responsible for the conscious perception of smell.

These structures technically make up the rhinencephalon ('smell-brain'), but there is much overlap with the 'limbic system' (p. 35), and the term 'rhinencephalon' is rarely used. The direct involvement of structures such as the amygdala and hippocampus in affective (emotional), and cognitive and motivational behaviours means that little emphasis is placed on their olfactory functions; this can be pragmatically justified as only lesions of the main olfactory centres, the olfactory bulbs and tubercle, result in drastic impairment of the sense of smell.

It is also notable that smell sensitivity has declined through mammalian evolution, so that we and the other primates are less sensitive and have correspondingly smaller olfactory bulbs than primitive mammals such as the insectivores (shrews and hedgehogs). This is probably associated with a shift from nocturnal to daytime living (and more dependence on vision), and from finding and holding food in the mouth (and under the nose) to the use of hands (Passingham, 1982).

Pain (nociception)

Pain pathways were outlined in the section on touch, but as this is an area in which major discoveries have occurred over the last decade, outlined in the previous chapter, I shall present a little more detail of how pain pathways are thought to operate.

All pain receptors are free nerve endings, while painful stimuli can be mechanical, thermal, or chemical. Information representing 'pain' can travel via the spinal nerves to the spinal cord over one of two routes. The first use axons covered with a fatty myelin sheath, while the other uses unmyelinated axons. The significance of the myelin sheath is that its presence enables nerve impulses to be transmitted much more rapidly along the axon; so the myelinated and unmyelinated pathways can be seen as representing 'fast pain' and 'slow pain' respectively. The actual conduction velocities are of the order 25 metres/second as against 0.5 metre/second, i.e. a transmission time difference of two seconds or more for stimuli travelling from hand or foot to the spinal cord, so explaining the experience of an initial sharp pain often followed by a duller and longer-lasting pain from the same stimulus event, e.g. putting your big toe in a hot bath.

Pain fibres synapse in the spinal cord, probably releasing the relatively recently discovered transmitter Substance P. Information is then transmitted up to the brainstem and thalamus via the antero-lateral spinal pathways. Many fibres synapse in the brainstem, especially in the region known as the midbrain, mesencephalic, or periaqueductal grey matter. Other fibres pass directly to the ventrocaudal nucleus of the thalamus, from where they are projected on to the somatosensory cortex of the post-central gyrus.

The precise role of these various brain regions in pain

perception is as yet unclear. Lesions and electrical stimulation of thalamic and midbrain sites have been shown to be effective in either producing the experience of pain or reducing it; indeed, thalamic lesions are still sometimes used to reduce chronic pain in human patients. In addition, the potent analgesic ('pain-reducer') morphine is now known to act at specific receptors found particularly (though not exclusively) in midbrain regions. These *opiate* (named after the family of drugs from which morphine comes) receptors are stimulated, in the normally functioning brain, by the naturally occurring ('endogenous') opiate enkephalin. It is assumed that enkephalin is released from pre-synaptic nerve terminals and acts on post-synaptic opiate receptors to produce a powerful analgesic effect (see Chapter 3).

The conditions under which enkephalin is usually released are more debatable. Certainly individual differences in pain sensitivity can be attributed to variations in the responsiveness of the endogenous opiate system, while instances of analgesia and effective behaviour in the face of severe injury (e.g. the great Bert Trautmann winning an FA cup medal with a broken neck) can be seen as situations where reaction to pain must be postponed until the action has died down. There is also a growing lobby in favour of explaining hypnotic and acupuncture-induced analgesia in terms of a stimulation of the release of endogenous opiates. But, although this explanation is appealing and this is even likely to be the case, controlled and convincing experiments in this area are rare, and the picture is still fuzzy. Indeed, one side-effect of the swing to enkephalin as a mediator of pain and pain phenomena has been a neglect of the descending neural influences on pain perception.

Substantial descending pathways exist between midbrain and hindbrain structures and the spinal cord which are almost certainly involved in modulating pain input at the level of the first afferent synapse in the spinal cord. Thus cognitive and emotional effects on pain perception will involve central pain pathways, structures, and neurotransmitters, and descending ('efferent') pathways which filter pain-related input in line with the current situation and past experience. (See Melzack and Wall, 1965: the Gate control theory of pain.)

Hearing

The sensory receptors of the auditory system, buried deep in the inner air, are mechanoreceptors. The stimuli, the sounds around us, exist as vibrations of molecules in the air which travel from the source to the ear as sound pressure waves, at around 1,000 feet/second. When the wave of molecular vibration arrives at the ear, it exerts a pattern of fluctuating pressure which corresponds to the original sound. It is this pressure pattern which the auditory receptors have to transduce into neural impulses in the auditory nerve.

They are very good at it. Sound waves have two basic properties, frequency and amplitude. Frequency is the number of cycles (waves) per second, and is roughly proportional to the perceived pitch of a sound; we are sensitive across a range of 15 cycles/second (15 Herz) up to around 20,000 cycles/second (20,000 Herz or 20 kiloHerz – 20 kHz). Amplitude corresponds to loudness or intensity, and is measured in decibels (dB). The loudness scale is logarithmic, so that the loudest sound the auditory receptors can cope with is around 120 dB, and represents a millionfold increase over the softest sound we can normally perceive (under 10 dB). It has even been claimed that under controlled laboratory conditions some subjects can register the random collisions of molecules in the air around them!

As with all sensory systems, other species show different capabilities associated with their particular ecological adaptations. Cats and dogs are sensitive to frequencies up to 60–70 kHz, while bats and dolphins, admittedly using different means of reception and transduction, can cope with frequencies above 100 kHz.

The human ear is divided into outer, middle and inner sections (see Fig. 4.1). The auditory canal acts as a resonator, collecting and guiding sound pressure waves to the tympanic membrane, or eardrum. Vibrations of the tympanic membrane are transmitted across the air-filled middle ear via the middle ear ossicles, three small bones (malleus, incus, stapes) which act as levers to increase the effective intensity of the tympanic membrane vibrations. The vibrations, representing the sound stimulus, eventually reach the oval window in the membrane

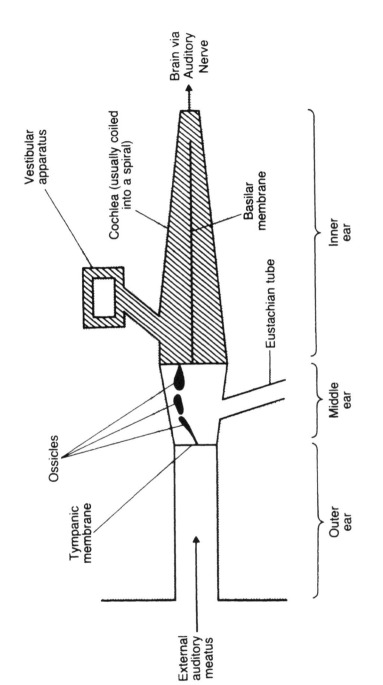

Figure 4.1 *Major components of the human ear (diagrammatic)*

separating middle ear from inner ear; movement of the oval window then produces correlated vibrations in the fluid-filled inner ear.

The inner ear includes the vestibular apparatus (see p.90), and the cochlea, a spiralled structure containing the auditory sensory transduction apparatus. In between two compartments of the cochlea lies the basilar membrane, on which are around 25,000 hair cell receptors. Vibrations in the fluid-filled inner ear produce oscillations of the basilar membrane and associated displacement of the hair cells. Movement of the hair cells leads to action potentials in the fibres of the auditory nerve to which they are directly connected, and so travelling sound waves in the auditory canal are finally transduced into neural signals.

As sound vibrations lead directly to oscillations of the basilar membrane and thence to afferent impulses in auditory nerve fibres, it would be extremely neat and parsimonious if sound frequency or pitch was coded by the frequency of afferent impulses. However, the limited number of hair cell receptors and the properties of the hair cell/auditory nerve fibre connection give a maximum response rate of only four to five thousand impulses per second in the auditory nerve, i.e. a frequency hypothesis can cope only with sounds up to 4 kHz.

The alternative 'place' hypothesis emphasizes the nature of the basilar membrane. This varies in width and thickness along its length, which means that different portions resonate maximally at different vibration frequencies, i.e. different frequencies may be coded by the *part* of the membrane vibrating most. A compromise and likely answer is that low-pitched sounds follow a frequency model while high-pitched sounds involve the place approach. What is clear is that further along the auditory pathway from cochlea to auditory cortex single fibres are found which are frequency specific, i.e. they transmit only sounds of a specific pitch.

Auditory nerve fibres travel from the cochlea in the inner ear to the cochlear nucleus on the same side of the medulla of the hindbrain, where they synapse. The auditory pathway then runs from the cochlear nucleus to the superior olivary body in the medulla, with each cochlear nucleus projecting to both olivary bodies, i.e. left inner ear cochlea → left cochlear nucleus → left and right olivary bodies. From the olivary bodies auditory fibres run in the lateral lemniscus to the inferior colliculus of the midbrain, thence to the medial geniculate nucleus of the thalamus from where they are projected to the primary auditory receiving areas in the temporal cortex.

There is evidence that the superior olivary bodies and the inferior colliculus are involved in sound localization, via a sophisticated comparison of the differences in time and intensity for the same sound arriving at the two ears (which are, of course, some distance apart). In addition, downward-travelling efferent fibres exist, such as those from the superior olivary body to the cochlea itself, which are concerned with modulation of auditory input at the periphery by central mechanisms.

The crossing-over of pathways at hindbrain levels means that there is an extensive *bilateral* representation of auditory input in the central nervous system, with each ear projecting to the auditory cortex of *both* hemispheres. As pointed out in Chapter 2, deafness after cortical damage requires substantial bilateral destruction of tissue.

Despite this bilateral arrangement, it is accepted that the contralateral pathway is functionally dominant, with left ear input being preferentially processed by the right hemisphere and right ear input by the left hemisphere. This is crucial for the rationale behind and the understanding of dichotic listening experiments, as discussed in Chapter 5.

Cortical mechanisms of hearing have not been so exhaustively investigated as those for vision. However, it has been found that the auditory cortex is tonotopically organized, with a systematic representation of different frequencies across the cortex. In addition the cortex has the columnar arrangement found particularly in the visual cortex (but likely to be a basic property of neocortex – see Chapter 2), and likely to be functionally significant; some neuronal columns have been identified as either binaural summation or binaural suppression columns, i.e. the neurons are responsive to input from *either* ear, but in the one case inputs from both ears summate and in the other they cancel each other out.

The frequency specificity of auditory fibres in the brainstem and of cortical neurons suggests a fundamental 'feature analysis' as the basis of auditory perception, i.e. complex environmental sounds are broken down into their basic frequency and amplitude components before being reconstructed at a cortical level. The results of the basic analysis of these frequency and amplitude components in primary auditory cortex are transmitted onto secondary and tertiary auditory cortical zones, where more complex processing and integration takes place. In these zones neurons have been identified which respond to complex 'whole' stimuli such as species-specific calls (Wollberg and Newman, 1972). So, what is known of auditory perception fits in with a view of perceptual processing as beginning with an analysis of complex stimuli into units, based on the fundamental properties of the stimulus. This is followed by a high-level resynthesis and reintegration of the results of the elementary processing into complex perceptual phenomena. As we see in the next section, this view of perception applies equally well to the visual system.

Vision

The visual system is the most complicated of our senses, as befits the sensory modality that we are most reliant on. A crude index of this complexity is the size of the optic nerves, each of which contains around one million nerve fibres, compared with the 30,000 or so in each of the auditory nerves.

Despite the daunting complexity, the visual pathways have been sufficiently studied, anatomically and functionally, to allow us to present a reasonably clear account of the early stages of visual form perception. The model of visual cortical organization that emerges, with function neatly associated with the modular arrangement of cortical neurons described in Chapter 2, may well serve as the basis of functional organization across the whole cortex.

Retina and optic pathways
The visual sensory receptors are contained in the multi-layered

retina covering the rear two-thirds of the eye (the retina, incidentally, is derived during development from the same embryological cells as the nervous system, and can be seen as a true outgrowth of the brain rather than a separate peripheral tissue). Light energy from the environment, in the form of electromagnetic waves composed of photons, passes through the cornea and pupil, and is focused by the lens onto the retina. The retina is also unusual in that the receptor layer, containing the photosensitive elements, lies beneath the other cell layers making up the retina (see Fig. 4.3); this means that the axons which eventually combine together to form the optic nerve travel across the retinal surface before passing through the back of the eye at the retinal blind spot (so called as it cannot contain

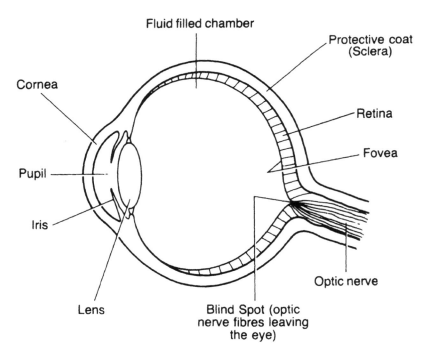

Figure 4.2   *The eye*

visual receptors and therefore cannot respond to light stimulation).

There are two types of visual receptor cells: rods and cones. Rods are specialized for vision in dim light, and cones for high acuity (resolution) and colour vision, which requires more intense light. Although there are 120–30 million rods and only 5–10 million cones in the primate eye, the cones are concentrated in the *fovea*, that part of the retina which represents the centre of the visual field. As we move across the retina, relatively fewer cones and more rods are encountered, with a consequent loss of acuity and colour vision. Thus, with eyes fixed straight ahead, we see most clearly the centre of the visual field in front of us, with a progressive loss of detail towards the edges as the cones become less frequent. As we shall see, rods are inoperative in daylight.

Both types of visual receptor cell transduce light energy into action potentials in the same way. Rods and cones contain molecules made up of retinal (a form of Vitamin A) in combination with an opsin. Absorption of photons of light energy produces a conformational change in the structure of retinal and a subsequent split in the retinal-opsin bond; the rupturing of this bond stimulates changes in the cell membrane of rods and cones, which eventually lead to the generation of action potentials (for more detail on this chain of events, see, e.g., Kandel and Schwartz, 1985).

Functional differences in the receptors are related to the different opsins found in them. The whole retinal-opsin molecule in rods is known as rhodopsin. To allow for vision in dim light, rhodopsin is highly sensitive to light, and in daylight it is permanently broken down into retinal and opsin, and therefore non-functional. When passing from bright into dim light, the period of adjustment we all experience represents the resynthesis of rhodopsin in the rods, upon which our night vision, such as it is, depends.

Each cone contains retinal in combination with one of three different cone opsins. The cone opsins make these receptors much less sensitive to light as such, but give them the ability to mediate high resolution of detail and colour in the visual world. In addition, the spectrum of colours we are able to perceive is based on the presence of the three different opsins, i.e. the range of colours we are aware of is produced by different patterns of light stimulation across the three types of cone receptor.

Action potentials generated in the rods and cones are eventually reflected in nerve impulses travelling along optic nerve fibres. However, the relationship is not simple, as around 130 million receptors must converge onto one million optic nerve fibres. This convergence is mediated by specialized neurons in the other retinal cell layers (see Fig. 4.3), and is not a simple channeling process. Rods and cones are directly connected to bipolar cells, which in turn connect with ganglion cells; the axons on ganglion cells constitute the optic nerve. Obviously many receptors contact the same bipolar cell, although a single

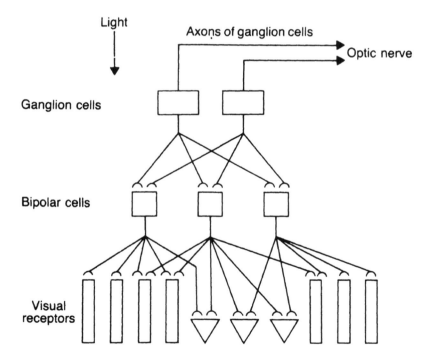

Figure 4.3   *Cell layers of mammalian retina (diagrammatic). Not shown are lateral interconnections via horizontal and amacrine cells*

receptor may interact with more than one bipolar cell. In addition, if the receptor → bipolar cell → ganglion cell is seen as a vertical pathway, there are important lateral interconnections as well. 'Horizontal' neurons mediate lateral connections in the receptor/bipolar region, while amacrine cells perform the same function in the bipolar/ganglion cell zone.

Thus substantial and sophisticated processing of visual input occurs within the retina itself. Although a detailed discussion is beyond the scope of this book, one key function served by the lateral interconnections is to increase the contrast between the activities of neighbouring receptors; i.e. if a single receptor is stimulated (in practice unlikely, given their size), one outcome mediated by horizontal cells would be the active inhibition of neighbouring receptors, to increase the relative output of the stimulated receptor. It is a general principle of neurons in the visual system that they respond best to sharply contrasted visual stimulation, and least well to diffuse stimulation of the whole retina. This is based in the organization of retinal receptive fields, which will be discussed in the next section.

Ganglion cell axons from all parts of the retina congregate and pass together as the optic nerve through the retina at the blind spot. The two optic nerves meet at the optic chiasma, where a systematic reorganization of fibres occurs. The axons from the inner halves of each retina (that half nearest the nose, the nasal hemiretina) cross over to the opposite side. The axons from the outer halves of each retina (the temporal hemiretina) stay on the same side (see Fig. 4.4). Each optic tract (not now a nerve, as we are within the brain) leaving the optic chiasma thus consists of 50 per cent axons from the left eye and 50 per cent from the right. The functional significance is that one tract represents the left side of the left eye and the left side of the right eye, and the other tract represents the right side of both eyes. A stimulus out to the right of the subject (i.e. in *the right visual field*) is received by the left side of both eyes and so stimulates activity in the left optic tract only. Analogously, activity in the right optic tract represents the *left visual field* (Fig. 4.4).

The visual system pathways are therefore partially crossed, in a highly systematic fashion. This allows us to predict, for instance, the effect of lateralized brain damage; loss of one optic

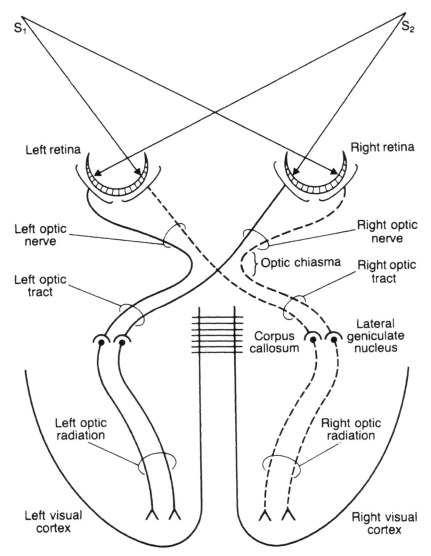

Figure 4.4   *Optic pathways. With eyes fixated to the front, a stimulus (S₁) to the left of the subject is received by the right half-retina (hemi-retina) of each eye and transmitted initially to the visual cortex of the right hemisphere. Stimulus S₂ to the right of the subject is received by the left half-retina of each eye and transmitted to the left hemisphere*

nerve (i.e. damage between retina and chiasma) leads to the loss of vision in one eye, while damage to one optic tract (i.e. between chiasma and thalamus) produces the loss of the half of the visual field opposite to the side of damage. In addition, visual system organization can be used to restrict reception of stimuli to one side of the brain only; a stimulus presented at the extreme edge of the visual field ('lateralized presentation') will elicit activity in only one optic tract, and is a vital technique in the study of functional differences between the hemispheres (see Chapter 5 for extensive discussion of this issue).

From the optic chiasma the optic tract passes to the lateral geniculate nucleus (LGN) of the thalamus. The LGN is arranged in six distinct layers, and although the optic tract contains fibres from both eyes, each LGN layer receives input from one eye only, i.e. at this level there is still complete separation of input from the two eyes.

From the LGN the visual projection continues as the *optic radiation* and eventually reaches the cortex of the occipital lobe – occipital, primary visual, or striate cortex, sometimes referred to as Brodmann's area 17. Visual cortex has the normal cortical arrangement of six layers of neurons. LGN input arrives and synapses in layer IV. There are extensive vertical interconnections between the six layers, and various output pathways. Layers II and III project to secondary visual cortex (Brodmann's area 18), and the cortex of the medial temporal lobe. Layer V is the origin of a pathway to the superior colliculus in the midbrain; the superior colliculus also receives a direct input from the retinal ganglion cells, and uses the combined information to control the orientation and movement of head and eyes in relation to visual stimuli.

The organization of the major visual pathways from the retina to the visual cortex results in the cortex of each hemisphere receiving directly a complete retinal mapping of the contralateral ('opposite-sided') half of the visual field. It should be remembered that the presence of the corpus callosum (see p.116) means that, although the visual pathways may be hemisphere-specific, the two visual cortical zones themselves are reciprocally interconnected.

Retinal receptive fields and the cortical basis of visual form perception

The technique used in analysing the neurophysiological basis of visual form perception revolves around the concept of 'receptive field'. This refers to an area of the retina stimulation of which (by carefully controlled patches of light) produces a response in a given fibre or cell. There is a systematic variation in the size, shape, and location of retinal receptive fields as we travel along the visual pathway from retinal ganglion cells to neurons in the various cortical processing zones; from this variation a picture has emerged of how elementary perception of form takes place.

In 1953, Kuffler identified what has since been established as the most basic type of receptive field in the mammalian visual system. He recorded from retinal ganglion cells (and would have obtained similar results from optic nerve fibres, as these are the axons of ganglion cells), and showed that their receptive fields consisted of concentric rings: a central circular area and a surround, each containing many receptors. A maximal 'on' response was obtained from the ganglion cell when a light stimulus exactly filled the centre area of its receptive field; response ceased if the stimulus moved to the surround area. The cell could, therefore, be classified as a centre-on, surround-off responder (Fig. 4.5). The opposite arrangement of these concentric receptive fields has also been found – centre-off, surround-on – and in both cases a light stimulus covering the

Figure 4.5 *Retinal receptive field of ganglion cell – centre-on, surround-off type*

whole field evokes no response; positive and negative stimulation cancels out.

Until recently, it was thought that mammalian retinal processing, shown by ganglion cell receptive fields, was elementary compared to some non-mammalian systems. A remarkable analysis by Lettvin *et al.* (1959) of retinal ganglion cells in the frog identified five classes of cells, each responding maximally to a different and complex light stimulus; examples include cells responding to a general dimming of illumination, cells responding to well-defined boundaries between objects, and cells responding to moving, curved, dark edges. These latter are best stimulated by a small spot, moving jerkily across the retina, and seem to be specific 'bug detectors'.

Such visual processing seems analogous to what the mammalian cortex does, rather than the mammalian retina, and in primates this certainly seems the case even now. However, Levick (1967) and Cleland and Levick (1974) claim to have discovered equally sophisticated processing in the retinal ganglion cells of rabbit and rat; and it may be that all visual systems incorporate a substantial amount of peripheral processing.

Optic nerve fibres respond best, therefore, to circular spots of light on the retina. Similarly, and although several ganglion cell axons (optic nerve fibres) connect with a single lateral geniculate nucleus neuron, LGN cell receptive fields match those of ganglion cells, i.e. the fields are concentric, and either centre-on surround-off or vice versa. Predictably, following the optic pathway to the cortex we find that the neurons of layer IV which receive direct input from LGN cells also possess concentric retinal receptive fields. However, visual cortical neurons beyond layer IV all respond best to *line* stimuli, e.g. a bright line on a dark background or vice versa, or an edge between light and dark regions. In addition they have *orientation selectivity*, in that the line stimulus has to be at a specific orientation (angle) on the retina; rotate the line a few degrees of arc and the firing rate of the neuron diminishes; at 90° to its characteristic orientation the neuron is virtually inactive.

Before considering the means by which the circular-spot-

responsive-receptive fields of LGN and layer IV neurons become the line-responsive receptive fields of other visual cortical
cells, it would be appropriate to acknowledge the history of
research in this area. It is unusual for any area of research to
become synonymous with the names of one or two particular
people, although it does occur, as with Roger Sperry and
split-brain research (see Chapter 5). Research into the
mechanisms of visual perception is similarly and indelibly
associated with the work of David Hubel and Torsten Wiesel.
Beginning in the late 1950s and continuing up to the present
day, they have established the structural and functional
architecture of the visual cortex, pioneering the most painstak-
ing and sophisticated experimental techniques; when only the
results are presented, it is easy to overlook the problems of
combining electrical recording from single cortical neurons
with a retinal stimulus of suitable size and shape to activate it.
In 1981 Hubel and Wiesel received, jointly with Roger Sperry,
the Nobel prize for medicine.

Hubel and Wiesel (for a review of their work, see Hubel and
Wiesel, 1979) identified several functional types of visual cortical neuron beyond layer IV. *Simple* cells respond to lines of a
specific orientation on a specific part of the retina. *Complex* cells
have receptive fields best stimulated by a line of specific
orientation anywhere on the retina. Although direct evidence is
lacking, the transition in receptive fields from concentric, to
linear in one part of the retina, to linear anywhere on the retina,
can be explained relatively simply. Suppose that a simple
cortical cell receives its input from a group of layer IV neurons
whose receptive fields are all of one kind (centre on – surround
off), and which lie in an overlapping straight line on the retina
(Fig. 4.6). The most effective stimulus for that simple cell will
then be linear, in a particular retinal location, and of a specific
orientation and thickness, such that it covers the overlapping
'on' zones of the receptive fields.

The next step in this converging flow of connections would be
that several simple cells project onto a single complex cell. The
simple cells would have in common a specific orientation
selectivity, and although each is location-specific, together
their receptive fields would cover the whole retina. Thus the

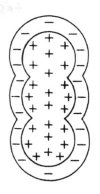 

Figure 4.6   *Overlapping retinal fields produce receptive field of visual cortical cell. Most effective light stimulus = line-shape*

optimal stimulus for the complex cell would be a line of appropriate orientation *anywhere* on the retina; in fact maximal activity is often produced by a line stimulus sweeping across the retina.

It seems that neurons in primary visual cortex perform a basic 'feature detection' on incoming visual stimuli. As in the case of the auditory system, complex visual input is initially broken down into fundamental units, before converging operations at increasingly higher levels of the visual system reintegrate the results of basic analysis at lower levels. One might suppose that the logical destination for converging operations in the visual system is a set of neurons specialized to respond only to whole complex visual stimuli, i.e. the notorious 'Grandmother' cell is waiting to be discovered. However, it is a general view, and one held by Hubel and Wiesel, that although convergence probably continues into secondary and tertiary visual areas (i.e. several complex cells connect to a single 'hypercomplex' cell, which will then respond to higher visual features such as angles, movement in a particular direction, etc.), primate visual perception does not depend upon a number of 'supercomplex' cortical neurons specialized to respond to 'whole' visual stimuli. This is not to say that such neurons do not have a part to play in perception, as we see later.

Besides line orientation, visual cortical neurons extract other features from visual input. Earlier in this section I mentioned how input from the two eyes, although travelling in the same optic tract, remained segregated at the lateral geniculate nucleus. This remains the case with the layer IV cortical neurons to which the LGN projects; these cells respond to stimulation of one or other eye, but not both, i.e. they are *monocular*. Simple cortical cells are also monocular, but roughly half the complex cells respond to stimulation of either eye, i.e. they are *binocular*.

As would be expected from the mechanics of line orientation selectivity, the convergence that produces binocular responsiveness in complex cells is highly systematic. If a complex cell responds to stimulation of either eye, then in each eye it has a retinal receptive field which can be plotted. It turns out that the two receptive fields are identical. Obviously, as for all complex cortical neurons, they are linear, but they also have precisely the same orientation, and subtler characteristics such as type of line (e.g. edge, slit) and width are also shared. There is variation between the eyes in one important respect: for rather more than half the binocular cells stimulation of one eye provokes a more intense response than stimulation of the other, i.e. these cells show an *ocular dominance* pattern. The degree of dominance varies from cell to cell, while for the remaining binocular neurons the eyes make equal contributions.

The functional significance of binocular cells showing a range of eye preference, from left eye dominant through equal contributions to right eye dominant, is as yet unclear; it is probable that they are vitally involved in stereoscopic depth perception. What is known, and has considerable implications for a general view of cortical organization, is the functional arrangement of primary visual neurons in relation to line orientation detection and ocular dominance.

A microelectrode making a perpendicular penetration of the visual cortex (i.e. at right angles to the surface) passes through the six layers of neurons. There is an orderly arrangement of cells, with those receiving the direct LGN input in layer IV, simple cells in layer III, and complex cells in layers II, III, and VI (the top layer, I, has few neurons, but mainly contains fibres travelling to and from the visual cortex). Simple and complex cells in layers II, III, V, and VI all have linear receptive fields of specific orientations, and Hubel and Wiesel were able to show that all the neurons encountered in a perpendicular penetration of the visual cortex (some hundred or so) had the *same* orientation, i.e. they could be considered an *orientation column*, in which optimum orientation of the retinal receptive field is constant for all the cells.

A similar penetration a millimetre away encounters a similar orientation column, but with the optimum orientation shifted round a few degrees, and it is clear that for the purposes of orientation selection, the visual cortex is architecturally subdivided into vertical neuronal columns. Hubel and Wiesel were then able to demonstrate the systematic organization of the orientation columns: a block of primary visual cortex one millimetre square and two millimetres deep (i.e. the cortical thickness) contains columns covering every possible stimulus orientation from vertical through 180° and back to the vertical.

As if this were not enough, it then turned out that columns of visual cortical neurons were also constant in regard to eye dominance – if the first cell recorded prefers the right eye, then so will all the rest. Repeating the exercise about half a millimetre away produces a switch in eye preference. Putting together the data for orientation columns and for ocular dominance columns, Hubel and Wiesel conclude that the one-millimetre-square block of cortex mentioned earlier will contain, besides columns covering all possible orientations, one set of ocular dominance columns for the left eye and one for the right. (Note that, although discussed separately, the same column of neurons will have an orientation specificity and a characteristic ocular dominance. There is, however, no evidence that the two response properties are systematically related across cortical columns.)

Such a block of tissue constitutes the elementary processing unit, or module, of the visual cortex, whose overall functional organization is assumed to consist of repeated versions of this unit module. Indeed, given the remarkable similarity in vertical organization of neurons across all cortical areas (described in Chapter 2), it is a reasonable guess that the functional organization of all neocortex is modular in nature. One major difficulty beyond the visual cortex, however, is to identify the 'features' which other sensory and associative areas are specialized to detect and operate upon. Feature detection in the visual cortex can be studied because simple visual stimuli are relatively easy to decompose into basic features such as orientation. Basic 'features' or units of somatosensory sensation, language, thought, or personality, are difficult or even impossible to imagine. It may be relatively easy to establish a *structural* modularity as basic to cortical function, but it is more difficult to identify the associated *functional* modularity.

Various efferent pathways leave the primary visual cortex. As mentioned earlier, connections from layer V neurons to the superior colliculus are involved in eye movement control, while layer VI cells send a projection back to the lateral geniculate nucleus; this is presumably involved in direct feedback modulation of visual input. The major pathways for the continued processing of visual information run from layers II and III to the secondary visual area (Brodmann's area 18), and, directly or indirectly via area 18, to regions within the temporal and posterior parietal cortex. The precise functions of these tertiary visual zones are unclear. Visual representation within them is exhaustive; complete retinal maps (i.e. stimulation of any part of the retina producing changes in neuronal activity) exist in temporal and parietal cortex, as well as in the primary visual cortex. There is a suggestion (Ungerleider and Mishkin, 1982) that separate pathways exist within the visual system for the processing of form and colour on the one hand and of movement on the other. This separation then persists into the tertiary areas, with parts of the temporal cortex concerned with the analysis of form and colour, and posterior parietal cortex given over to analysing movement.

Whatever the precise details of higher visual processes, an overall picture of the brain mechanisms of visual perception can be constructed. After elementary analysis into basic features, information is passed through a series of hierarchically ordered converging operations which reintegrate the results of elementary processing. In addition, the existence of several retinal maps in various cortical regions, perhaps dealing with independent aspects of vision such as colour and movement, supports the existence of *parallel* pathways for visual input. It also suggests that the end-point of visual processing is not a set of highly specialized super-complex cells, but perhaps a pattern of neuronal activity across several cortical areas. The analogy used in Kandel and Schwartz (1985) is of the way a photograph can be seen as represented by the individual grains making up the picture.

The existence of human clinical syndromes in which brain damage produces a loss of some aspects of vision, such as colour, while leaving others, such as form perception, intact, supports the view that high-level visual processing is distributed across the cortex. However, there may be at least one exception to this.

Chapter 2 discussed briefly the occurrence of prosopagnosia after damage to tertiary visual areas. This loss of the ability to recognize faces while leaving intact the ability to identify other objects has been associated with a possible specialized 'face-processer' in the right hemisphere (see Chapter 5). This in turn suggests a high-level tuning of a restricted region of cortex for complex 'whole' stimuli, which are, of course, of particular significance both for humans and for other animals. It has now been demonstrated that single neurons in the superior temporal cortex of rhesus monkeys are activated only by faces (monkey or human), or by the major features which go to make up faces (Perrett *et al.*, 1982). If such a face-coding system operates in humans, it would be an obvious candidate for the site of damage in prosopagnosia.

Plasticity in the visual cortex

Primate young are born with the basic architecture of the visual system essentially intact – retina, optic nerve, lateral geniculate nucleus, optic radiation, visual cortex, etc. However, there has been much interest in whether functional characteristics are inbuilt, or whether they can be modified in early experience. The short answer is that they can. Hubel and Wiesel again first demonstrated that cutting off visual input from one eye for as little as one week in the first weeks of life prevented the formation of ocular dominance columns in the cortex (see, e.g., LeVay, *et al.*, 1980); when tested with the eye open, optic nerve fibres and lateral geniculate neurons serving that eye functioned normally in terms of responsiveness and receptive fields, showing that it was a *selective* deprivation effect. In addition, binocular deprivation (cutting off visual input from both eyes) was much less effective in altering patterns of ocular dominance in the cortex. This finding and other work together suggest that for the development of ocular dominance columns and the functions they probably mediate, such as stereoscopic depth perception, the cortex needs balanced competition and activity from the two eyes, from birth.

A similar picture emerges for the line orientation selectivity of cortical neurons. Blakemore and Mitchell (1973) reared cats in the dark. Exposure to a vertically striped cylinder for as little as one hour at about four weeks of age modified cortical cells so that the majority were selectively responsive to vertical lines only. In 1973 Pettigrew and Freeman showed that early experience without lines prevented orientation selectivity, or even line-responsivity, developing.

So visual perception in mammals may be very much environmentally determined. This makes sense if we see an animal's early environment as usually being its later environment, in which case early modification produces perceptual processes maximally adapted to the environmental contingencies the animal will be confronted with throughout its life.

5 Functions and asymmetries of the cerebral hemispheres

Anatomical considerations

Anatomical asymmetries in the human brain

As with feet, the right side of the brain is not always anatomically identical to the left. As brain anatomy must correlate in some as yet unknown way with function, there is the possibility that anatomical asymmetries may act as a pointer to functional asymmetries.

The major stimulus to contemporary research in this area was the report by Geschwind and Levitsky (1968) of significant left–right differences in an area of the cerebral hemisphere known as the planum temporale (temporal plane). This is a cortical zone on the upper surface of the temporal lobe, and is thought to function as auditory association cortex, i.e. analysing auditory input after initial processing in the auditory receiving area. As such it overlaps with the region of temporo-parietal cortex known as Wernicke's area, where damage results in receptive language disorders.

Geschwind and Levitsky found that in a series of post-mortem brains, the temporal plane was longer in the left hemisphere in 65 per cent, longer in the right in 11 per cent, and equal in 24 per cent. This leftward asymmetry fits in with the left hemisphere specialization for language (Chapter 2), assuming that more means better when applied to brain tissue.

Subsequent research has validated their observations (e.g. Wada et al., 1975). Additionally, Witelson and Pallie (1973) found the same asymmetry in post-mortem brains of newborn infants, while Chi et al. (1977) reported a larger temporal plane in the left hemisphere of human foetuses as early as thirty-one weeks post-conception. If this anatomical asymmetry does relate to functional language asymmetry, these findings would imply an early if not genetically preprogrammed tendency for language to develop in the left hemisphere. It should be remembered, however, that functional asymmetries do not emerge until at least the age of four or five, and that the brain is extremely 'plastic' at birth.

Probably associated with this asymmetry in temporal regions is a similar significant tendency for the lateral Sylvian fissure of the left hemisphere to be longer than that of the right (LeMay and Culebras, 1972) in adults and foetuses (see Fig. 2.6). This difference, and a tendency for it to follow a slightly different route in the two hemispheres (Rubens *et al.*, 1976), suggests that Sylvian fissure geometry and the size of the temporal plane are closely related (Galaburda *et al.*, 1978).

There are other anatomical asymmetries in the human brain. Seen from above, the right frontal lobe is wider than the left, while the left occipital lobe, making up the posterior chunk of the brain, is wider than that on the right, i.e. the brain, generally speaking, is wider on the front right and the back left, giving an impression of being 'skewed' round to the right. Despite some suggestions that these particular differences may be less striking in left-handers (LeMay, 1976), we do not on the whole have any idea of the functional significance of these gross anatomical asymmetries. It is worth bearing in mind that we do not have any precise idea of how brain tissue functions, i.e. of how behaviour emerges from its underlying physical substrate. The temporal plane may be larger on the left in the majority of people, and the control of language is predominantly left-sided in the majority of people; it is a compelling correlation, but no more. How the temporal plane is involved in language, and why it should need to be larger to fulfil any specialized functions it has, are mysteries.

The corpus callosum
A final anatomical consideration before discussing functional asymmetries in the human brain concerns the corpus callosum. This structure is a 'commissure', a bundle of fibres (axons) running transversely across the brain connecting one side with

the other. It is not the only commissure. Transverse pathways are found at hindbrain and midbrain levels. In the mammalian forebrain there are, in addition to the corpus callosum, an anterior commissure (connecting areas of temporal cortex in the two hemispheres) and a hippocampal commissure (connecting the two hippocampi). However, the corpus callosum is usually the major inter-hemispheric fibre bundle, containing around 250 million axons in humans, criss-crossing from one side to the other (125 million axons in each direction); in contrast, the anterior commissure contains of the order of 3.2 million (Blinkov and Glezer, 1968). Variations to this pattern do exist in primitive mammals: wombats, kangaroos and other marsupials possess a developed anterior commissure and no corpus callosum.

In higher mammals the axons making up the corpus callosum connect areas of the neocortex with homologous areas on the other side, i.e. visual cortex to visual cortex, motor cortex to motor cortex, frontal association cortex to frontal association cortex. If all cortical areas had callosal inter-hemispheric connections, then a small lesion in one hemisphere should lead to a zone of degeneration in the identical area in the opposite hemisphere, carried along the degenerating callosal axon. If an axon is damaged, then degeneration travels back along the axon ('retrograde degeneration') until it involves the neuronal cell body and the dendrites; the gradual death of the neuron can be traced in the primate brain using histochemical staining with horseradish peroxidase. Using this technique it can be shown that some parts of the cerebral cortex are without callosal connections, while the concentration of callosal fibres and terminals is uneven across the cortex, so that some cortical zones have many terminals, i.e. receive many callosal afferents, but send out very few fibres in return.

Primary sensory areas tend to have fewer callosal connections. As an instance, sub-regions of visual cortex concerned with processing input from the vertical centre of the normal visual field show extensive inter-hemispheric callosal pathways. In contrast, sub-regions dealing with input from the periphery of the visual field are without callosal connections (Wolff and Zaborszky, 1979).

Association cortex has extensive callosal inter-connectivity, and overall the commissures of the forebrain provide a sophisticated facility for transferring information from one side of the brain to the other, with the corpus callosum being the major contributor. Transmission of information can take variable amounts of time. Between 50 and 60 per cent of corpus callosum axons have a fatty myelin sheath, and can conduct impulses at up to 13 metres/second; the remainder are unmyelinated and conduct at around 0.3–0.5 metres/second. Median conduction velocities are 2.8 metres/second (Swadlow and Waxman, 1979). Given a very approximate inter-hemispheric distance of 100 mm, these axonal properties mean that the inter-hemispheric transfer of information can take less than 8 milliseconds or more than 300 milliseconds. Presumably these different populations of callosal axons have different functions, but, given that we still lack a generally agreed model of what the whole corpus callosum does, the specific roles of its sub-components remain elusive; although it has been established that the most posterior portion (the 'splenium') is involved in the inter-hemisphere transfer of visual information.

Hemisphere asymmetries of function – split-brain studies

Introduction and overview
Epileptic attacks may range from the hardly noticeable to the disabling 'grand mal' seizures. In every case there is an abnormal discharge of electrical activity, which can rapidly spread across brain tissue via neuronal axons which are, of course, excellent conductors of electrical impulses. The origin of the abnormal discharge is often a site of physical brain damage – perhaps scar tissue from a previous brain operation or from a traumatic accident, but more often from brain injury at birth. If labour is prolonged, the baby may suffer a lack of oxygen; this provokes violent electrical discharges, which in turn may permanently damage brain tissue (often in the temporal lobe, where structures such as the hippocampus seem to be prone to such paroxysmal electrical activity). Later in life, this damage may provoke disabling epileptic attacks.

Where the epilepsy has an identifiable and localized site of origin ('focus'), it may be possible to remove the focus surgically, e.g. via a unilateral temporal lobectomy (see Chapter 6). Drugs can control some forms of epilepsy sufficiently for life to proceed normally. However, in a minority of cases the attacks are so severe and so frequent (e.g. several each day), uncontrollable by drug therapy and without a single localized focus, that more drastic means have been used to help the patient.

If the epileptic attack begins in one hemisphere, it rapidly spreads to the other hemisphere via the corpus callosum, so disabling the whole forebrain. Cutting the corpus callosum would at least restrict the attack to one hemisphere, and should reduce the severity of the epilepsy. So in the 1940s Akelaitis (1940) and Van Wagenen and Herren (1940) introduced this operation as a possible treatment for severe intractable epilepsy, and found, as predicted, significant therapeutic benefit. What was more surprising was the apparent lack of any severe behavioural side-effects from cutting the major pathway interconnecting the two hemispheres. Post-operatively patients appeared to possess a normal range of psychological processes.

The operation continued to be used for severe epilepsy, but in the early 1960s, stimulated by the work of Myers (1956) and Sperry (1961) on split-brain (the term still used for subjects whose cerebral commissures have been sectioned, in whole or in part) animals, Sperry and Gazzaniga (e.g. Gazzaniga *et al.*, 1962) began a more detailed psychological examination of patients given a commissurotomy (sectioning of the corpus callosum, anterior commissure, and hippocampal commissure) for the relief of chronic disabling epilepsy.

Their findings have been followed up over the last twenty years, and helped stimulate the enormous contemporary interest in the different functions of right and left cerebral hemispheres. Sperry was awarded the Nobel Prize in 1981 for this and other contributions to neuropsychology (sharing the prize, incidentally, with Hubel and Wiesel – see Chapter 4), reflecting the enormous contribution of the split-brain studies to brain research.

Using the anatomy of the visual pathways (see Fig. 4.4), Sperry's group developed a relatively simple technique to present stimulus material to either hemisphere. Figure 4.4 demonstrates how a stimulus (S_1) presented in the left visual field (i.e. to the left of the subject as they view the world), is picked up by the right half of each retina, and is then transmitted initially to the visual cortex in the occipital lobe of the right hemisphere. Similarly the stimulus (S_2) presented in the right visual field is registered by the left half of each retina and passed to the visual cortex in the left occipital lobe.

The optic tract from each eye partially crosses over ('decussates') at the optic chiasma, so that each eye projects to both hemispheres. As the visual fields for our two eyes have considerable overlap (close each eye in turn and see how little the view changes), and while there are substantial involuntary and voluntary eye movements while viewing, the visual cortex of the right hemisphere normally receives a significant binocular input (i.e. from both eyes). Only by using a central fixation point and presenting lateralized stimuli can either hemisphere be preferentially stimulated.

In intact subjects the hemispheres communicate via the corpus callosum. So a stimulus presented initially to the right hemisphere will rapidly be transmitted over to the left. In the commissurotomized split-brain patient this transfer cannot occur, and any stimulus presented to the right hemisphere stays there. Thus Sperry had a means of selectively presenting stimulus material to each hemisphere. How could he determine the response of each hemisphere?

With the left hemisphere there was little problem. Since the work of Dax, Broca and Wernicke in the nineteenth century it had been established that in virtually all right-handed people the control of language resides in the left hemisphere (see p.55). So the left hemisphere can read and hear, as assessed by its ability to write, talk and obey commands. Testing the right hemisphere is more difficult. Although the neural control of the vocal articulatory apparatus (larynx, tongue, etc.) is bilateral, actual control is dominated by the left hemisphere (see Bradshaw and Nettleton, 1981), while right-handed people quite naturally write with their right hand, which is, of course, controlled by the left hemisphere. However, the right hemisphere does have control over the left arm and hand, and it was this response system that Sperry used in his experiments.

The early split-brain studies, reviewed by Sperry (1967), were unambiguous. As expected, any task involving language functions showed a left hemisphere (i.e. right visual field) superiority. With right visual field presentation, words could be read aloud and copied using the right hand, pictures of objects could be named, and so could objects felt with the right hand. The right hemisphere was mute; with left visual field presentation, the patient could not read words, copy words using the left hand, name objects presented visually, or name objects felt by the left hand. The subject could not copy with the right hand words presented to the right hemisphere. A clear dissociation or 'disconnection' syndrome was demonstrated.

The right hemisphere did demonstrate some linguistic ability (and more of this later). When object names were flashed to both hemispheres simultaneously, the left hand could select from a range of objects hidden behind a screen that object whose name had been flashed to the right hemisphere. If asked to name it the subject would respond with the name of the object flashed to the left hemisphere. A consistent finding was a failure of the left hemisphere to describe what the right hemisphere was doing, to the extent of denying that the left arm and hand were in any way part of the same body.

These results confirmed the dominance of the left hemisphere for language functions, and suggested an intimate connection between language and self-awareness. However, other tasks demonstrated that the right hemisphere was not entirely a sleeping partner. When patterns, drawings, or faces were simultaneously presented to both hemispheres, that presented to the right hemisphere was consistently picked out at a subsequent recognition test involving pointing with *either* hand; when naming is the required response, a left hemisphere dominance prevails. The left hand/right hemisphere is better at copying drawings and learning finger mazes. Nebes (1971) demonstrated that the right hemisphere is better at estimating the size of circles from sample arcs of varying sizes presented either visually or tactually. Generally, the right hemisphere shows a superiority at what have been called visuo-spatial tasks, particularly where the task involves mapping spatial contexts on to the motor activities of the hands. Finally, and to reiterate, subjects consistently fail to describe or even acknowledge their performance on tasks where that performance is mediated through the right hemisphere. They are unconscious of what half of their cerebral cortex is doing.

Language in the split-brain subject, and some problems with split-brain research

The early work just summarized leads to the conclusion that the right hemisphere in the split-brain subject is effectively non-linguistic; at best, there is some reading and understanding of simple concrete nouns, and some verbal production, as the left hand can rearrange scrabble letters into simple words. There was no evidence for any semantic or syntactic understanding – no comprehension of meaning or ability to read sentences – no speech, and a failure to carry out even the simplest command (in experiments using visual presentation or dichotic listening techniques; see p. 133).

Since then, a closer study of the split-brain patient has led to a reassessment of right hemisphere linguistic ability, with associated disagreements and controversies. The debate is of some significance. If the isolated right hemisphere of the split-brain patient has significant linguistic ability, one might wonder why the patient aphasic after left hemisphere damage usually shows minimal recovery of language functions (Glass *et al.*, 1973); the right hemisphere is still intact, and might be expected to produce at least minimal language. Moscovitch (1976) links the reports of right hemisphere language in split-brain patients with the surprising sparing of some language functions in the few instances where the entire left hemisphere of adults has been removed in cases of severe epilepsy or tumour invasion (e.g. Smith and Burkland, 1966; see Walsh, 1978, for a review of infantile and adult hemispherectomy – note that 'hemispherectomy' is inaccurate, as it is cerebral cortex only, and not subcortical hemispheric structures, that is usually removed). Moscovitch orders right hemisphere language performance in various samples as:

Hemispherectomy > Split-brain > Aphasics > Normals

and suggests that the usually dominant left hemisphere inhibits the language centres of the right hemisphere; completely in normals, almost completely in aphasics, partially in the split-brain patient (via subcortical interconnections or through competition for output pathways), and least in the hemispherectomized patients. It should be noted that subsequent observations suggest that the published reports greatly over-estimated the language capacities of adult hemispherectomized patients (M. Coltheart, personal communication).

On the other hand, if the language ability of the right hemisphere in the split-brain patient is usually minimal or absent, then permanent aphasia after left hemisphere damage is entirely predictable, and any instances of recovery in left-hemispherectomized patients must represent unusual pre-operative brain organization, e.g. bilateral representation of language. Such an explanation could also explain the *occasional* split-brain patient with substantial right hemisphere language; it would need to be demonstrated across most of them to be convincing.

It is here that opinions diverge. There are undoubtedly split-brain patients with impressive right hemisphere language, to the extent of expressive speech. What weight do we attach to such patients? Zaidel attaches great weight. Using a contact lens system to control for eye movements and so allow prolonged presentation of complex stimulus material, he has shown that the right hemisphere can point to pictures refer-ring to words, but cannot point to spelled words that rhyme; it can match two pictures whose names rhyme (without reading the names), but cannot match a spelled word with a picture having a rhyming name (Zaidel and Peters, 1981). He con-cludes that the right hemisphere reads ideographically rather than phonetically, seeing words as visual gestalts without being able to convert visual input to sound (grapheme – phoneme conversion). This is supported by the results of Levy and Trevarthen (1977), who showed that the mute right hemis-phere was superior for the visual perception of written words when meaning was not involved, but could not read phoneti-cally, converting words to sound; this is a left hemisphere function.

Summarizing his position, Zaidel (1983) states that the right hemisphere generally has no speech, good auditory language comprehension, with a larger auditory word store than visual. This auditory input predominance may be due to its lack of grapheme–phoneme correspondence rules, necessary for handling the written word efficiently. The right hemisphere can interpret subject–object relations and active–passive tenses, and also has limited comprehension of spoken sentences and can follow simple commands.

A critique of Zaidel's general view of right hemisphere language comes from Gazzaniga (1983). He points out that of forty-four split-brain patients only five show clear evidence of right hemisphere language (a point acrimoniously disputed by Zaidel, 1983). Gazzaniga does not deny these cases, and describes in detail two recent patients (i.e. recently operated) who demonstrate normal language comprehension, including some semantics, in the right hemisphere, which can also generate written answers to questions and express itself through speech. However, everything we know of right hemisphere language in the split-brain subject is derived from less than ten patients, and the most detailed knowledge from two or three (e.g. Zaidel and Peters, 1981). Gazzaniga would argue that these cases are not representative, but reflect abnormal pre-operative brain organization, i.e. bilateral language areas, enabling either hemisphere to mediate linguistic functions.

It is important to remember that split-brain patients have the operation because they have a chronic disabling brain malfunction, usually as a result of injury at birth. The age at which the epilepsy manifests itself varies, the age at which the commissurotomy is performed varies, and the age at which psychological testing occurs varies.

The following patient profiles are taken from Levy and Trevarthen (1977):

Patient	Sex	Age at operation	Age at testing	Pre-operative neurological signs of hemisphere malfunction
N.G.	F	30	37	Bilateral
L.B.	M	13	17	Bilateral
A.A.	M	13	17	Bilateral, mostly left
C.C.	M	13	18	Left
R.Y.	M	43	47	Right

All except R.Y. were presumed to have suffered birth damage; R.Y. was in a car crash. N.G. and L.B. show substantial right hemisphere language (they were also the subjects in Zaidel and Peters, 1981). N.G. is female; epilepsy developed at age eighteen. L.B. is male, with epilepsy first developing at age three and a half. He illustrates a potential confounding in split-brain work specifically, and in clinical neuropsychology generally. At three and a half the brain is still immature and developing. Handedness has often not stabilized, and hemispheric functional asymmetries not fully developed (e.g. Witelson, 1976). The corpus callosum is not fully myelinated until around the age of ten (Yakovlev and Lecours, 1967); as the fatty myelin sheath is essential for normal functioning of myelinated neurons, one can conclude that the corpus callosum is not fully functional until around age ten.

Therefore damage to the brain in the early years can result in substantial functional reorganization. The most extreme case would be that of infantile hemiplegia, in which an infant born with a convulsive epilepsy disabling one hemisphere (producing a contralateral paralysis of one side of the body, or hemiplegia), has that hemisphere removed and still exhibits little or no cognitive impairment when adult (e.g. Smith and Sugar, 1975). Thus brain damage at birth and subsequent early epilepsy could easily result in a reorganization of cognitive functions across the hemispheres; findings from such split-brain patients may be dramatic, but should be generalized to the normal brain only with caution. If, as Gazzaniga (1983) states, only five out of a total of forty-four split-brain patients give clear evidence of right hemisphere language, with at least two of those having incomplete commissurotomies sparing the anterior commissure, then caution is even more clearly indicated.

The heterogeneity of the patient samples and inconsistency in results can be shown in areas other than language. Zaidel and Sperry (1974) concluded that split-brain patients have impaired verbal and non-verbal short-term memories. Unfortunately, although their sample was quite large (eighteen), they had no pre-operative baselines, and had to use test norms established from the general population. LeDoux, Risse, Springer, Wilson, and Gazzaniga (1977) examined one subject both pre- and post-operatively. He was fifteen at the time of commissurotomy (sparing the anterior commissure), performed to alleviate chronic epilepsy which developed after a severe encephalitic infection at the age of ten. On a range of verbal and non-verbal tests this subject showed an *improvement* in memory and IQ performance after the operation. LeDoux *et al.* conclude that Zaidel and Sperry's results were unreliable in the absence of pre-operative performance baselines, and that efficient cognitive processing is more dependent upon *intra*-hemispheric integrity than upon *inter*-hemispheric integrity.

However, unlike most of Zaidel and Sperry's patients, the subject in LeDoux *et al.*'s study had an intact anterior commissure. Experiments on monkeys show that the anterior commissure is capable of significant inter-hemispheric transfer in the absence of the corpus callosum; Butler (1979) used a series of visual discrimination tasks in monkeys, and found that colour discrimination transferred perfectly from hemisphere to hemisphere even when the corpus callosum had been cut, while there was still some transfer of shape, size, and orientation discrimination. All transfer was abolished when total commissurotomy was performed.

So the anterior commissure can be functional in cognitive tasks. Additionally, split-brain patients show massive individual differences, and LeDoux *et al.* did only have one subject. Huppert (1981) examined three patients, all with total commissurotomies and including L.B. and N.G. Her context was the memory deficits found in Korsakoff and temporal lobectomized subjects (see Chapter 6). By reasoning that a lesion of the hippocampal commissure might lead to hippocampal dysfunction, resulting in some memory loss, Huppert predicted that split-brain patients would show some anterograde amnesia in a picture recognition learning task. Two subjects did behave like Korsakoff patients, needing more time at acquisition but with normal retention once acquisition had been satisfactorily attained. The third subject, L.B., had no memory impairment at all, with normal acquisition and normal retention. Huppert relates this to his early onset epilepsy and the subsequent efficient reorganization of functions in a still-plastic brain. At the least it emphasizes the idiosyncratic nature of the split-brain patient, and a dislocation between the split-brain with impressive bilateral language abilities (L.B. and N.G.) and the split-brain with unimpaired pictorial memory (L.B., but not N.G.).

Models of hemisphere function derived from the split-brain work obviously intertwine with research using normal subjects, and so I will reserve overall conclusions until the end of that section. Before moving on to hemisphere asymmetries in the normal population, however, there are some fascinating aspects to the split-brain patient which should be mentioned.

Split brains and split consciousness?

It is difficult to adequately describe the extraordinary sight of a split-brain subject doing a standard test of hemisphere function. 'Scissors' has been flashed to the right hemisphere. The left hand is guided behind a screen to an array of objects. It selects a pair of 'scissors' and gives them to the experimenter. When asked why he has done it, the subject denies, confabulates, or just says that he doesn't know.

Perhaps more impressively, the patient in everyday life shows few signs of the 'split-brain' syndrome. Head movements during reading and scanning the world are exaggerated to ensure that both hemispheres receive all input. Actions appear controlled and integrated, although there are momentary confusions; the right hand (left hemisphere) lights the gas, and a moment later the left hand (right hemisphere) turns it off; the patient uses her right hand to choose a dress to wear, and simultaneously the left hand darts out and chooses another one.

On the whole, however, it is still impressive that only skilled testing reveals the psychological consequences of commissuro-tomy.

The left hemisphere is verbal, and such self-awareness as the patient can communicate always refers to the activities of the left hemisphere/right-hand system. If 'self-awareness' is synonymous with 'consciousness' then the right hemisphere is unconscious. But it is functionally quite advanced, probably up to the level of higher mammals such as primates, and we would not call non-verbal animals 'unconscious'. The right-hemisphere lacks language-dependent self-awareness, but possesses a consciousness of sorts. Does it have any sense of 'self'?

Sperry (1982; Sperry *et al.* 1979) believes it does. The right hemisphere can recognize photographs of itself (of the patient, that is, not an isolated right cerebrum), family, and friends, and acknowledge historical and political figures, generating apparently appropriate emotions. It has a sense of time, past, present, and future. LeDoux, Wilson and Gazzaniga (1977) tested one of the most recent commissurotomized patients (P.S.), who turned out to have bilateral language representa-tion to the extent of expressive speech being present in both hemispheres. (This was not a result of residual inter-hemispheric pathways; stimuli, for instance, could only be matched if presented to the same hemisphere, and not if one went to the left and one to the right, i.e. apart from language, the classical disconnection syndrome was present).

The right hemisphere of P.S. could be asked questions (flashed on cards), and reply by assembling words from Scrab-ble letters with the left hand. The first project was to rate various people, ideas, and objects (e.g. War, Mother, Sex, Truth) as 'good' or 'bad' on a scale of 1–7. The right hemis-phere had consistently more negative ratings than the left over the sixteen items, being more positive only for 'Sunday', equally attracted to 'Car' and 'Money', and equally disliking 'Vomit'. Some time later a similar test was given, with 'Like/ Dislike' ratings being given to various items (e.g. School, Mother, Nixon, Beer). This time the right/left ratings were impressively similar. LeDoux, Wilson, and Gazzaniga noted that P.S. was quite calm during this test session – both hemispheres in harmony? – but quite disturbed and difficult during the first session – hemispheres at odds with each other?

The right hemisphere was asked various questions via visual display. It knew who it was (giving 'Paul' as the response to 'who are you?'), who its girlfriend was, what its favourite hobby was. It did, however, want to be a racing driver ('What job would you choose?'), in contrast with the left hemisphere which wanted to be a draughtsman.

By generating answers to ambiguous subjective questions it appears that the right hemisphere in P.S. has 'its own independent response priority-determining mechanism'. Each hemisphere has a sense of self and its own set of values and attitudes, which can show massive overlap; as LeDoux, Wilson, and Gazzinga point out, the two hemispheres share the same life experiences over many years, so such overlaps can be expected. But the disparities are equally impressive – on the first test, and in terms of ambition. LeDoux, Wilson, and Gazzaniga conclude that each hemisphere has its own distinct consciousness, and that consciousness is linked to linguistic sophistication (although it should be noted that they use consciousness as synonymous with self-awareness; as I pointed out earlier, this would render most of the animal kingdom unconscious).

The key problem is how two surgically separated hemispheres are functionally integrated in the everyday life of the split-brain patient (or not, as the case may be: P.S. perhaps demonstrated functional conflict during the first test session; an assessment of his everyday behaviour would be of great interest). In an attempt to shed light on this, Sergent (1983) studied a recently commissurotomized patient, J.W. J.W. does not have significant right hemisphere language, with only limited comprehension and no production. He can read letters, and the task involved categorizing letters as vowels or non-vowels; preliminary testing showed that the two hemispheres were equally competent at the task. In the main task, each letter of a pair simultaneously presented went to different hemispheres. Using one hand to press keys, the subject had to decide if *either* of the letters was a vowel. Rather than one hemisphere (presumably the left) taking over the task, or even confusion and hesitation when conflicting stimuli went to the two hemispheres (e.g. vowel to the right, consonant to the left), J.W. displayed perfect accuracy under all conditions of stimulation and response (left or right hand). Sergent then flashed pairs of letters to the two hemispheres, and asked J.W. simply to match them, i.e. respond as 'same' or 'different'. Performance was random, as expected from classical split-brain research.

The interpretation of this experiment is not straightforward. Each hemisphere can identify letters, and categorize them as vowel or consonant. The letter identification is *not* transferred (J.W. fails on a simple matching task), while the results of the categorization within each hemisphere are integrated and the results of the integration (vowel present or vowel absent) made available to both hemispheres (so the response is equally accurate whichever hand is used). Sergent associates the high-level supervisory/evaluative integration with deep subcortical neural structures undivided by the commissurotomy, and linked with the two hemispheres. Sergent did not run a condition in which J.W. had to match two letters simultaneously presented to the two hemispheres as same/different in terms of whether they were vowels or consonants. This would have been of some interest. To do letter matching the subject does not actually have to 'read' the letter – it could be done as a simple pattern recognition/feature analysis task. To do categorization matching (vowel or consonant) the letter has to be 'read' and identified; one might predict that as this is the major part of the categorization task used in Sergent's experiment, such matching should be possible even by the split-brain patient. So one would have the surprising result that J.W. could not match the identity of single letters across hemispheres, but could match the *categories* of those letters.

It is clear that the split-brain patient has provided, and will continue to provide, much fascinating information on brain function. The problems discussed earlier imply that findings are not always directly applicable to brain function in the normal subject, but must rely for corroboration upon experimental work involving intact people and other brain-damaged populations. It is equally clear that in one or two areas – and I have in mind particularly the nature of human

self-awareness and its relation to language and consciousness –
the commissurotomized patient has a paramount and enduring
relevance.

Hemisphere asymmetries of function – studies of other brain-damaged patients and normals

Introduction
The previous section concentrated upon the split-brain studies
of hemisphere function. However, the vast majority of contemporary investigations use normal subjects, while a persistent
minority of papers over the years have reported the consequences of accidental brain damage on hemisphere function.
The causes of this brain damage may be divided into three
major types: epilepsy, cerebro-vascular disorders, and
traumatic brain injury. (There are many other categories of
brain damage, including tumours and bacterial or virus infec-
tions. These have not, on the whole, provided insights specifically into hemispheric functional asymmetries.)

Epilepsy was discussed on page 118. Cerebro-vascular disorders include any interference with the blood supply to the
brain, and include strokes (where the blood supply to a part of
the brain is suddenly cut off by a thrombosis – a blood clot or air
bubble plugging a narrow blood vessel) and haemorrhages
(massive bleeding from blood vessels within the brain, usually
caused by high blood pressure and/or congenital weaknesses in
the cerebral circulation). Cerebral haemorrhage is always
sudden and often fatal. Strokes may be equally sudden, but are
less likely to be fatal, depending upon the extent and location of
the cerebral tissue normally supplied by the obstructed blood
vessel. Brain neurons deprived of oxygen for more than ten
minutes die, and strokes therefore produce infarcts, areas of
dead and dying brain cells, and usually some behavioural
impairment. Strokes are usually unilateral, and the side of
damage may be obvious from a subsequent temporary or
permanent motor paralysis, i.e. left hemisphere stroke damage
would result in a right-sided paralysis (or 'hemiplegia') of the
body musculature. When there is no paralysis, interference

with language functions may suggest left hemisphere damage in a right-handed patient, while the electroencephalogram and more modern neurological procedures such as CAT scans (see Chapter 1) can localize brain damage in the living patient.

Similar procedures can be used to investigate the consequences of traumatic brain injury caused by car, industrial or domestic accidents, or by penetrating missile wounds. Patients with traumatic head injury usually form a more heterogenous group than those suffering from cerebro-vascular accidents, as particular cerebral arteries seem especially vulnerable to thrombosis and haemorrhage. However, there are fewer of the latter group, and most clinical work in the area involves epilepsy and head injury.

In all these clinical groups and in normal subjects the corpus callosum and other forebrain commissures are more or less intact. Thus the divided-field tachistoscopic technique developed in order to lateralize stimuli to one or other hemisphere in split-brain subjects cannot be used without modification – a single stimulus presented to one hemisphere will immediately be relayed to the opposite hemisphere. The simple modification is to present *two* stimuli simultaneously, one in each visual field, and therefore projected one to each hemisphere. The subject is asked to report any stimulus seen, and with short exposure durations (e.g. fifty milliseconds) will report only one of the two. It is assumed that the stimulus reported will be the one processed and identified fastest: e.g. of two words presented, that presented in the right visual field and projected to the left hemisphere will be the one reported; the other, projected to the right hemisphere, has to be relayed across the corpus callosum to be processed by left hemisphere language centres before it can be reported.

Shape recognition is regarded as a speciality of the right hemisphere. So, if two shapes are simultaneously presented, one in each visual hemifield, that projected to the right hemisphere of a right-handed subject should be reported. Note that verbal report has been shown to be a left hemisphere function. Thus even the reported stimulus has to pass from the right hemisphere, where it has been analysed, to the left hemisphere to be reported. However, the stimulus projected to the left hemisphere has, in theory, to make the trip twice – once over to the right hemisphere to be analysed, and then back to the left hemisphere to be reported. Thus identification should favour the left visual field–right hemisphere pathway where shapes are concerned.

A similar 'competitive' technique can be used with the auditory system. Stimuli are presented simultaneously through headphones, one to each ear ('dichotic listening', Kimura, 1961). Subjects are asked to report what word or sound they hear. As the auditory pathways are predominantly crossed (i.e. a weak ipsilateral ear–cortex pathway is dominated by a contralateral ear–cortex pathway), stimuli presented to the right ear are initially processed by the left hemisphere and stimuli presented to the left ear initially processed by the right hemisphere. Results are presented as 'ear advantages', i.e. a right ear advantage (REA) implies preferential processing by the *left* hemisphere.

The patterns of performance with these visual and auditory techniques should reflect the organization of the hemispheres for processing certain kinds of stimuli, and patients with uni-lateral brain damage would also be expected to show deficits on tasks considered to preferentially engage that hemisphere. The most obvious and important examples of this would be the language disturbances following left hemisphere damage, in-itially reported by Dax and formally described by Broca (1861) and Wernicke (1874). Tachistoscopic and dichotic listening techniques can be used with these patients, but more common in clinical neuropsychology is the use of test batteries for assessing a range of cognitive abilities. Deficits as compared with normals may be shown on the 'verbal' sub-tests of, e.g., the Wechsler Adult Intelligence Scale (WAIS), and indicate left hemisphere pathology. Deficits on the 'performance' sub-tests may reflect right hemisphere pathology.

The study of hemisphere function in normal and brain-damaged subjects is a massive enterprise. Of the order of ten journals publish such papers, and there may be twenty to forty papers each month, while two or three books emerge every year on aspects of hemisphere asymmetries of function. It is not possible to review such an accumulation of data in the space available here, and I shall concentrate upon major points and controversial issues. A good overview of the area is provided by Springer and Deutsch (1981), and by Bradshaw and Nettleton (1981, with following commentaries).

The two major problems in this area are circularity and replicability. If a given task gives a significant right visual field superiority, we assume it has a 'verbal' nature and is best processed by the left hemisphere. If it gives a significant left visual field superiority, we assume it has a 'visuo-spatial' nature and is best processed by the right hemisphere. We use the fundamental verbal/visuo-spatial dichotomy to validate our stimuli, and then use the stimuli to investigate hemisphere asymmetries of function; a fundamentally circular approach. Its usefulness depends upon the undoubted specialization of the left hemisphere for language functions, as revealed by clinical studies of brain-damaged patients and by use of the Wada test. This test involves injecting the anaesthetic sodium amytal into the carotid artery supplying one side of the brain. For the duration of the anaesthesia that hemisphere is non-functioning, and if it mediates language then language abilities are lost for that short period. Use of this test shows that 95–99 per cent of right-handers have language in the left hemisphere (Rasmussen and Milner, 1977). However, the Wada test usually involves speech production only, in line with the majority of clinical neurological studies, and does not imply that all stages of word perception and production are equally lateralized. Remember that with the split-brain studies the isolated right hemisphere often revealed some rudimentary language ability, but rarely produced speech.

Thus the finding that up to 30 per cent of right-handed subjects may show *left* visual field superiorities for verbal stimuli (Berlin and Cullen, 1977) may not be due to inappropriate stimuli (Levy and Reid, 1978), but may merely reflect individual differences in how we cope with the complexity of human word processing, where different stages may be differentially lateralized; e.g. visual feature analysis in the right hemisphere, and actual word naming in the left (Pirozzola and Rayner, 1977).

The problem of replicability is common to all research, but

seems particularly acute in the area of hemisphere function. One reason for this is the minuteness of the differences being sought. For instance, if a tachistoscopic reaction time procedure is used and subjects are asked to press a button if a *word* is presented in *either* visual field, then a *significant* right visual field advantage may be on average less than ten milliseconds. Such data may then be used to suggest major processing differences between hemispheres, between males and females, between familial and non-familial left-handers, etc. Follow-up studies may fail to find the same effects, or demonstrate differences in the opposite direction. Examples will be given in the next and subsequent sections, although I have tried to emphasize those findings which are more or less accepted; any single finding, however convincing it appears, should always be treated with caution.

Overview
Assessing hemisphere involvement via visual field superiorities (LVF = right hemisphere, RVF = left) and ear advantages (LEA = right hemisphere, REA = left hemisphere), various types of stimuli elicit consistent hemisphere laterality effects.

Brightness and colour discrimination, localization of dots within a matrix, line orientation, depth perception, pattern recognition, and faces, all produce an LVF advantage. Words, letters and digits all produce an RVF advantage, as does the localization of letters within a matrix.

In dichotic listening tasks, recognition of environmental sounds and various aspects of music such as duration, timbre and emotional tone may all produce an LEA. Spoken digits, words, nonsense syllables, backwards speech and normal speech produce an REA.

So far so good, with reasonable hemisphere separation in terms of 'effective' stimuli. In some cases this is most impressive; using the same matrix of cells, an LVF advantage is obtained if the subject is asked to report whether a given cell is filled or unfilled, and an RVF advantage if the question is to report whether the cell contains a particular letter or digit (Robertshaw and Sheldon, 1976). In general, the hemispheres may be characterized either by the stimuli that most effectively engage them, or by the mode of processing they employ. It is this latter approach that has been most popular, and it has led to a series of mutually overlapping and redundant dichotomous descriptions of the two hemispheres. The simplest of these uses the two types of stimulus material which best distinguish the hemispheres – language and faces. Language is verbal, segmented, sequential, temporally ordered, and needs analysis into its components before it can be interpreted. Faces are constellations of visuo-spatial features, usually recognized via parallel gestaltic processes rather than via verbal mediation. Thus the original description sees the left hemisphere as verbal and the right hemisphere as non-verbal and visuo-spatial.

Since then, dichotomies have proliferated. The following table presents some of them:

Processing

Left hemisphere	Right hemisphere
Verbal	Visuo-spatial
Sequential	Simultaneous
Analytic	Synthetic, gestalt
Temporal	Spatial
Rational	Intuitive
Digital	Analogue
Intellectual	Emotional

Most can be reduced to the straightforward verbal/non-verbal distinction, while for more romantic notions (Western thought/ Eastern thought; Masculine/Feminine – see Ornstein, 1977) there is little evidence and great reliance on (right hemisphere based?!) intuitive appeal.

What has been constructive has been the growing awareness that individuals may bring to the same problem of stimulus analysis different processing strategies, while different stages in the processing chain may be differently lateralized. I have already mentioned the discrepancy between Wada test based estimates of left hemisphere language production, and divided visual field estimates of left hemisphere language perception. Similarly with music, where an early study led to a simple account of how we process music. In 1974, Bever and Chiarello found that non-musicians show an LEA for the recognition of melodies (gestalt, holistic appreciation via the right hemisphere?), while trained musicians show an REA (analytic, chord-by-chord appreciation via the left hemisphere?).

Subsequent studies have either supported this view (e.g. Johnson, 1977), failed to replicate it (e.g. Zatorre, 1979), or extended it. Thus Shanon (1980) found a consistent REA for complex musical tasks regardless of training, as have other investigators (e.g. Carmon, 1978; Mills and Rollman, 1979), suggesting that when subjects are forced by the nature of the task to attend to musical *details*, a left hemisphere advantage emerges. It is important to note that music and language are physically similar, being temporally ordered sequences capable of segmentation into meaningful chunks, and that a left hemisphere involvement in musical analysis is therefore unsurprising.

Using this and a whole range of experimental and clinical evidence, Bradshaw and Nettleton (1981) propose that the left hemisphere is specialized for the analysis and production of temporally ordered sequences of stimuli and motor activities. Thus its dominance of language comprehension and production, its fine-grained bilateral control of the oral musculature and the sequencing of skilled manipulative movements of limbs, hands and fingers (Kimura, 1977), are all manifestations of the same fundamental property.

Whether the Bradshaw and Nettleton model is another example of dichotomania (Springer and Deutsch, 1981), or a catalytic and innovative approach (see commentaries following Bradshaw and Nettleton's paper, 1981) remains to be seen, but it does serve as a framework for analysing data, and appears no worse than alternative approaches. Its use may be seen when considering face recognition.

Faces seem to be the right hemisphere stimulus *par excellence* – so much so that it has been proposed that a specialist face-processor exists in the right parietal lobe (Carey and Diamond, 1977). Evidence that face recognition is not part of the right hemisphere's general facility with pattern stimuli is the disruption of the LVF advantage by inverting the faces (Leehey *et al.*, 1978), a manipulation that does not affect any ability of the left hemisphere to recognize faces. However, an RVF advantage can be obtained with famous or very familiar faces (Marzi *et al.*, 1974; Marzi and Berlucchi, 1977), although this may be interpreted as reflecting verbal mediation ('naming').

Bradshaw and Sherlock (1982) were concerned to alter visual field advantages in face recognition by forcing subjects to employ either an *analytic* or a *holistic* strategy. To minimize the emotional content of facial expression (which would artefactually lead to an LVF advantage if the right hemisphere is better at processing 'emotional' stimuli; see p.152), faces were drawn using squares, triangles, and shapes, for facial features such as eyes, nose, and mouth. In the analytic condition the distinctive feature of target versus non-target faces was an apex-upwards triangular nose compared with an apex-downwards nose. In the holistic condition the distinction between targets and non-targets was the general separation of feature elements (eyes, nose, and mouth, far apart or close together). After extensive practice, stimuli were presented using the divided field technique, and reaction times for identifying them as 'target' or 'non-target' recorded.

The predicted effects – an LVF advantage in the 'holistic' condition and an RVF advantage in the 'analytic' condition – were obtained for both target and non-target stimuli, although more strongly for the former.

Although calling the processing of feature-elements-separation 'holistic', while the identification of triangular noses as pointing upwards or downwards becomes 'analytic', may be debated, the experiment is a neat demonstration of how the same stimuli can give rise to different visual field (and hence hemisphere) advantages depending upon the precise strategies used by the subjects. As the two task conditions cannot easily be slotted into a verbal/visuo-spatial dichotomy, the authors' interpretation of their results as supporting an 'analytic' left hemisphere and a 'holistic' right hemisphere distinction seems defensible.

Sinistrality and sex

The reasonably clear picture of functional hemispheric asymmetries presented in the previous section can now be used as a stable background to some complicating issues. The picture works best when applied to male right-handed subjects with no family history of left-handedness. It becomes distorted when left-handedness ('sinistrality': note that the Latin root for 'left-handed' and 'sinister' is the same) and/or sex is introduced as an additional variable.

Before becoming immersed in detail, a couple of general statements may be made. Between 50 and 65 per cent of left-handed subjects have language in the left hemisphere, most of the remainder have language in the right hemisphere, while a proportion may have language bilaterally represented, i.e. in this latter case showing more of a functional hemispheric symmetry than an asymmetry. The right-handed female subject shows, in general, the same pattern of asymmetries as the right-handed male, but to a lesser degree, i.e. there is evidence (McGlone, 1980) that the female brain is less lateralized than the male brain.

Sinistrality and sex are considered here under the same heading, as recent work suggests that there may be complex and important interactions between them, to the extent of suggesting that, where hemisphere asymmetries are concerned, a family history of sinistrality is of more significance than your own sex and, indeed, handedness.

In line with the warning given at the beginning of this chapter, the debate on laterality, handedness, and sex is fuelled by apparently convincing experiments contradicted by other equally convincing experiments, leading to a further fragmentation of paradigms and variables, e.g. are divided field visual tests equivalent to dichotic auditory tests for assessing laterality effects? Are previous reports of sex differences in asymmetries confounded by the use only of right-handed subjects with no family history of sinistrality (familial sinistrality, FS), bearing in mind that in the population a positive history of FS is as common as a negative history?

Even the definition of left-handedness can be debated. The

three basic means of assessment are self-report ('Are you now, or have you ever been, left-handed?'), the handedness questionnaire ('What hand do you use for writing, holding a screwdriver, pushing a broom, etc?'), and performance measures (e.g. hand differences in speed of tapping, gripping a dynamometer, peg-sorting, etc). Performance measures have the advantage in assessing the level of skill or strength in a hand non-preferred simply because it is more efficient to use and become practised with the preferred hand, rather than through any dramatic and fundamental difference between the hands.

Whatever methods are used, estimates of left-handedness vary between 1 and 30 per cent, centring in the range 9–10 per cent of the population (see Hardyck and Petrinovich, 1977, for a review of left-handedness). A severe criterion of left-handedness (i.e. no reports of right-handed preference in the handedness questionnaire) reduces the frequency to around 4 per cent (Annett, 1978, 1980). Around 65 per cent of the population are classified as purely right-handed, while around 25–30 per cent are classified as mixed-handed, varying from the predominantly right-handed to the predominantly left-handed. Consistently, left-handedness is more frequent in males than in females, in twins, in some instances of mental retardation, in epilepsy, in mathematicians, and in dyslexics (Hardyck and Petrinovich, 1977; Annett, 1980). Of course, several of these instances involve a perfect confounding of sex and group, i.e. more males than females are dyslexic, more males than females are mathematicians. There is no evidence of any causal connections.

Despite early suggestions that left-handers have impaired spatial abilities (Levy, 1969), it now appears that there are no convincing reasons for assuming overall intellectual differences associated with handedness (Hardyck and Petrinovich, 1977). This is not to say that cerebral functional asymmetries may not distinguish right- and left-handers, and in fact there is a popular view that, particularly in regard to linguistic processes, left-handers are less lateralized, particularly those subjects with a positive family history of sinistrality (FS+) (Hardyck and Petrinovich, 1977; Springer and Deutsch, 1981). The clearest evidence for a less stable pattern of cerebral organization comes from the aphasic consequences of unilateral brain damage. Left-handers tend to have a slightly higher incidence of aphasia following right hemisphere lesions than do right-handers (13.7 per cent versus 6.7 per cent), and equivalent levels following left-sided damage (22 per cent versus 24 per cent: Hardyck and Petrinovich, 1977). Data on visuo-spatial disturbances are comparable for the two groups.

There is also some evidence that left-handers show smaller ear asymmetries in dichotic listening tasks, and smaller field differences in tachistoscopic tests (see, e.g., Levy and Reid, 1978). However, there are those who criticize these data. Annett (1980) points out that an experimental group of left-handers will produce a mean asymmetry score (i.e. ear difference or field difference) of around zero if *all* have significant cerebral asymmetry but with half showing a reversed pattern – language in the right hemisphere and visuo-spatial abilities in the left (see figures quoted earlier on language asymmetry in left-handers). She quotes this precise pattern in the work of Lishman and McMeekan (1977). Additionally, if left-handers have a higher incidence of reversed asymmetry, then they will automatically suffer more frequent aphasic consequences from right hemisphere brain damage.

However, a reflection of the tendencies in the literature would be that left-handers show a higher incidence of reversed asymmetry and of reduced asymmetries in comparison with right-handed subjects. This pattern seems more marked in FS+ than in FS− left-handers (Lishman and McMeekan, 1977), whose cerebral organization follows that of right-handers (Hardyck and Petrinovich, 1977).

The study of sex differences in cognitive processes and in cerebral laterality has a chequered history. Some authoritative reviews (e.g. Maccoby and Jacklin, 1975) conclude that males are superior on spatial tasks and that females excel on verbal tasks, differences that emerge in the years ten to twenty rather than before. These differences can then be related to hemisphere functional asymmetries, with the male brain being seen as more lateralized and the female brain as more symmetrical (e.g. Levy and Reid, 1978; McGlone, 1980; Inglis *et al.* 1982), usually in the direction of a bilateral representation of language. Other, equally authoritative reviews conclude that sex differences in cognitive abilities and/or lateralization are minimal and can effectively be ignored (Fairweather, 1982). Certainly, given the effort expended in the search for sex differences in cognition and brain organization, the results are not impressive either in amount or in consistency. Even the search for anatomical differences in brain structure has revealed little. The female brain is smaller in absolute terms, but not as a proportion of body weight. There are no gross differences. Lacoste-Utamsing and Holloway (1982) reported that the splenium of the corpus callosum (the posterior portion) was larger in females than in males, on a sample of five female and nine male brains. Witelson (1983) failed to replicate this, but concluded instead that a ratio of corpus callosal area to brain weight did differentiate the sexes, with females scoring higher than males. It is all rather unconvincing.

In a series of studies, McKeever has tried to combine the previously separate analyses of the effects of handedness and sex on hemisphere function, and so to resolve some of the contradictions in the literature. Using male ($\circlearrowleft$) and female ($\circleddash$) subjects, both left-handed (LH) and right-handed (RH) as assessed via inventory and performance measures, with either a positive (FS+) or negative (FS−) family history of sinistrality (remember that around half the population, including many right-handers, have a family history of left-handedness), he obtains patterns of laterality data from tachistoscopic visual and dichotic listening paradigms. In one of the first studies (McKeever and Van Deventer, 1977), using tachistoscopic letter recognition and dichotic digit recognition (both presumed to engage the left hemisphere preferentially), the following pattern of results emerged:

Group	Visual	Auditory
RH FS− $\circlearrowleft$	no asymmetry	REA
RH FS+ $\circlearrowleft$	no asymmetry	REA
RH FS− $\circleddash$	RVF	REA
RH FS+ $\circleddash$	RVF	REA

Group	Visual	Auditory
LH FS− ♂	no asymmetry	REA
LH FS+ ♂	RVF	no asymmetry
LH FS− ♀	no asymmetry	Tendency to REA
LH FS+ ♀	RVF	REA

RVF = Right visual field advantage
REA = Right ear advantage

Although complicated, some simple conclusions emerge from the data which have implications for all research on hemisphere differences.

1 The pattern of results differs for the two tests, suggesting that tachistoscopic and dichotic presentations are tapping different components of laterality (now becoming a popular view, e.g. Bryden, 1973; Tapley and Bryden, 1983).
2 On the visual task, a sex difference emerges for right-handed subjects, with females being *more* lateralized. A sinistrality effect emerges for left-handed subjects, with FS+ subjects being *more* lateralized.
3 The auditory task does not distinguish between subgroups of right-handed subjects. Amongst left-handers, only FS− males and FS+ females show an REA.
4 Over both tasks, the *most* lateralized groups are right-handed females (FS− or FS+) and left-handed FS+ females.
5 Performance on laterality tasks is a complex interaction between the specific task, sex of the subject, their handedness and their family history of left-handedness.
6 At least, where asymmetries did emerge in the right-handed groups, they were in the predicted direction of a left hemisphere advantage.

In a subsequent study (McKeever and Hoff, 1982), McKeever looked in more detail at sinistrality effects in right-handed subjects. There was a suggestion in the data just described that a positive history of left-handedness reduced the RVF effect in right-handed males (although neither RHFS+ or

RHFS— males showed a significant RVF, the latter were less insignificant!), and to extend this suggestion they introduced two different visual tachistoscopic tasks. The first involved the lateralized presentation of various pictures (e.g. apple, shoe, moose), and the recording of the latency in milliseconds to name the object (Object Naming Latency Task, ONLT). The second used lateralized presentation of words and non-words, and recorded the latency to press one of two buttons indicating the stimulus as a word or a non-word (Lexical Decision Latency Task, LDLT). Differences in latencies were expected depending upon which hemisphere the stimulus was presented to.

There were sixty-four right-handed subjects, spread equally across the four groups FS+ and FS— females and FS+ and FS— males. The results may be summarized as follows:

Group	ONLT (LVF–RVF difference in msecs)	LDLT (LVF–RVF difference in msecs)	
		Words	Non-words
Female FS+	+29.6	+20.5	−2.8
Female FS−	+18.1	+10.0	+26.0
Male FS+	+19.2	+18.7	+9.4
Male FS−	+30.0	+18.4	+18.3

Positive latencies indicate faster reactions in the right visual field (left hemisphere). All groups show a significant RVF on the object naming task, although a Sex × Sinistrality interaction emerges, with FS+ females and FS— males being most lateralized and FS— females and FS+ males least lateralized. (Note that a comparison of FS— females and males – the usual groups in studies of sex differences – would suggest that females are *less* lateralized than males. In fact, in this study, FS+ females were as lateralized as FS— males.)

The data from the lexical decision task are messier. There was no overall sex difference or Sex × Sinistrality interaction.

FS+ subjects had larger RVF advantages for words, while FS− subjects had larger RVF advantages for non-words; the different pattern of results over three of the four groups for words and non-words suggests that the psychological processes underpinning the recognition of words as words and of non-words as non-words are differentially organized in the two hemispheres.

Conclusions (5) and (6) to the previous study are reinforced by this experiment. Laterality data reflect complex interactions between task, sex, handedness, and familial sinistrality, but, generally speaking, verbal tasks engage the left hemisphere preferentially. It is noticeable that the letter recognition task of McKeever and Van Deventer (1977) produced a different and weaker pattern of RVF advantage in right-handed groups compared to the ONLT and LDLT of McKeever and Hoff (1982); this again emphasizes the task specificity of laterality experiments, but does follow a predictable course, as tasks requiring 'deeper' linguistic processing (ONLT, LDLT) should perhaps be more left hemisphere specific. McKeever and Hoff themselves emphasize one specific conclusion because of its relevance to previous work – apparent sex differences in their experiment were in fact a Sex × FS interaction, and, as FS+ is as common as FS− in the population, studies which report sex differences in cerebral lateralization without incorporating the variable of familial sinistrality are incomplete. Only where all possible combinations of FS and sex are used can valid sex differences emerge, as in McKeever and Van Deventer's (1977) data on tachistoscopic letter recognition in right-handed subjects.

I have quoted McKeever's work in some detail not because it is necessarily 'true', but because it embodies a degree of theoretical and practical sophistication lacking in much of the experimentation in this area. It points out the hazard of even thinking in straightforward dichotomies – male versus female, left-handed versus right-handed. Studying one homogeneous group is an alternative approach avoiding the pitfalls of simplistic theorizing, but the introduction of additional variables immediately renders questions such as 'is the female brain less lateralized than the male brain?' meaningless. There is of course a danger that variables beyond the intuitively relevant may affect performance on laterality tests. After reading several papers at one sitting, the feeling can steal up on one that dividing the subjects into Tall and Short would produce significant performance differences, so subtle are the influences on behaviour. However, I am sure, in the cold light of day, that this is not the case!

Evolution and the origins of handedness and cerebral laterality

Humans differ from other animals in having a pronounced rightward bias; the majority are right-handed, right-footed, and have a dominant right eye (which eye do you use for viewing through a telescope?). The majority of right-sided people have language in the left hemisphere. While some authors consider the link between 'sidedness' and language to be strong enough for handedness and footedness to predict the language hemisphere (e.g. Levy and Levy, 1978; Strauss and Wada, 1983), others emphasize the imperfect correlation between laterality indices – 30 per cent of right-handers are left-eyed, 30 per cent of left-handers are right-eyed (Annett, 1980).

As mentioned earlier, more than 90 per cent of right-sided people (hand and foot preference) have left hemisphere speech, and although the proportion may be lower for other language functions such as comprehension, most attempts to explain the lateralization of language in the human brain involve an intimate relationship between language and handedness.

There is no pronounced evolutionary trend towards lateralization. Handedness and pawedness in primates and rats are distributed normally – around 25 per cent will prefer one side for a task involving one hand or paw, around 25 per cent the other, and around 50 per cent will exhibit no consistent preference. Such a distribution is consistent with an entirely random environmental determination of 'sidedness', although *degree* of lateral bias may involve a genetic influence (Collins, 1975; Annett, 1978).

The brains of rats show no anatomical asymmetries, although a chemical asymmetry in the dopaminergic nigro-striatal tracts exists (Glick *et al.*, 1977). Injections of a dopamine-stimulant drug such as amphetamine can induce consistent rotation even in intact rats, presumably by uneven stimulation of the parallel nigro-striatal pathways in the forebrain, implying a lateralized imbalance in normal dopamine function (see Chapter 3 for a fuller discussion of the 'rotating rodent'). A similar imbalance in neurotransmitter concentrations in the human brain has been reported, with more noradrenaline being found in the left pulvinar region of the thalamus and in the right somatosensory cortex than in their contralateral equivalents (Oke *et al.*, 1978); and while Chapter 12 also considers the recent evidence of dopamine asymmetries in the schizophrenic brain, it must be emphasized that the functional correlates of these human neurochemical asymmetries are unknown.

Anatomical asymmetries have occasionally been reported in the brains of Great Apes, but the evidence so far is not impressive (see Harnad *et al.*, 1977, for reviews). However, there are some pronounced functional asymmetries in the brains of non-human animals. Most notable are the left hemisphere specialization in chaffinches and canaries for the production of species-specific song (Nottebohm, 1977), and the less well-established possibility that the left hemisphere of the macaque monkey is specialized for the production and reception (analysis) of species-specific calls (Petersen *et al.*, 1978).

In an exhaustive review of laterality in the vertebrate brain, Walker (1980) points out the tempting speculation that these functional asymmetries may represent precursors of language lateralization in humans. However, such speculations can only be tentative at this stage, although some believe that further functional asymmetries in the animal brain can be revealed by using species-specific tests (for a review, see Denenberg, 1981).

The problems of replicability in this area may be illustrated by two studies of face recognition in macaque monkeys. As reviewed earlier, humans may possess a specialized 'face-processor' in the right hemisphere, and facial recognition is disrupted if the stimuli are inverted. Monkeys are adept at discriminating faces of other monkeys, although there is no evidence that this ability is lateralized. Bruce (1982) reports that the performance of macaques on facial discrimination is unaffected by inversion, implying that faces are treated in the same way as neutral patterned stimuli, where orientation does not matter. However, Overman and Doty (1982) found that inversion *did* disrupt the recognition performance of macaques, relative to pictures of birds, butterflies, and landscapes, where recognition was not affected by inversion. They conclude that faces (of humans and other monkeys) are significant stimuli to the macaque and treated differently to other classes of stimuli. Bruce (1982) comments on some problems with their design and the interpretation of the data, but there is still a residual incompatibility between the two studies. To coin a cliché, more work needs to be done to decide if monkeys have a 'face-processor' independent of their other sophisticated perceptual abilities. Indirect support comes from the discovery of 'face-specific' neurons in monkey visual association cortex, described in Chapter 4.

Given the lack of any obvious evolutionary continuity in brain lateralization, it is hardly counter-intuitive to associate the degree of lateralization in the human brain with the major functional discontinuity between humans and other animals, i.e. language. The question of how and why language, particularly speech, evolved in the left hemisphere is less easy to answer. One of the most plausible conjectures, based on anthropological studies of living primates, is that pre-linguistic humans evolved a complex gestural communication system, using hand and arm movements to represent, i.e. symbolise, objects and the relationships between them, space and territory, ideas, and perhaps present, past and future (e.g. Hewes, 1973). Although this could involve either arm and hand, one can postulate a selective advantage in having one side and its cerebral control mechanisms with a predisposition to develop and handle (!) this communicative function (based, perhaps, on a general left hemisphere tendency to control intra-specific communication, as revealed in the chaffinch, finch, and macaque monkey studies mentioned earlier). It would then require the superimposition of a linguistic code to fulfil and extend the

functions of the gestural code, in a hemisphere already specialized for those functions. Lateralization would be initially a
hangover from the skilled right arm and hand, but might be
sustained by the need for efficient unilateral control of a speech
apparatus innervated by *both* hemispheres, and by the continuing need for a high level of skilled movement in the right
hand (following Kimura's (1979) ideas on the intrinsic relationship between the control of sequential articulators in
speech and the control of sequential arm and hand movements
in skilled motor tasks).

Similar but more detailed ideas have recently been put
forward by LeDoux (1982). He emphasizes the basic language/
spatial abilities dichotomy between the hemispheres, and then
concentrates upon an area of the hemisphere known as the
inferior parietal lobule (IPL). Lesions to the left IPL in humans
result in severe language disturbances, while lesions to the right
IPL impair the patient's ability to attend to and interact with
the spatial environment. In the primate brain the IPL in
both hemispheres handles the monkey's interactions with the
spatial environment. LeDoux then addresses the question of
why language functions should evolve in an area previously
devoted to spatial abilities.

The answer, he suggests, lies in the cross-modal nature of
spatial perception and the need to move around in a spatial
environment, i.e. perception of objects and movements towards
or away from them requires a complexity of processing and
integration that goes beyond a single modality (sensory system) to require *supramodal* mechanisms. The IPL is reciprocally
connected to several *polymodal* cortical regions, areas where
several different sensory pathways converge and presumably
are integrated. The IPL can then be seen as a supramodal
structure devoted to the elaborate processing of sensory information (Mesulam *et al.*, 1977).

Language, LeDoux states, is the ultimate supramodal function, moving beyond the final products of all sensory inputs and
their analysis and synthesis into the realm of symbols, syntax,
and semantics. It would therefore be logical for it to evolve in
that area of the brain already concerned with the supramodal
processing of spatial information. Lateralization to the left

hemisphere is explained along the lines discussed earlier, via a linkage with the arm and hand superior in skilled movement, with the added advantage that the right IPL can still be dedicated to spatial functions. Damage to the right IPL results in severe deficits in orienting and behaving in the spatial environment, e.g. when the patient is asked to draw a clock-face with his right hand, all the numbers are lined up vertically on the right-hand side. However, as LeDoux points out, if this drawing is then tachistoscopically presented to the left hemisphere the patient comments on what a funny-looking clock it is, i.e. the intact left hemisphere still possesses complex visuospatial abilities (as one would expect from the argument presented earlier on the bilateral representation of visuo-spatial functions in the monkey brain), but finds difficulties in regulating spatially directed motor responses.

This account, while perhaps doing less than justice to LeDoux's detailed and complicated argument, does show how his ideas both fit in with general views on the nature of the evolution of lateralization in a fundamentally symmetrical brain, and emphasize the continuity in the evolutionary progression (for an engrossing discussion of the possible selection pressures leading to the evolution of high-powered sensory systems and their cross-modal and supramodal intergration, see Jerison, 1973).

As a final comment in this section, I will briefly return to the left-handed subject. The hypotheses described above were designed to explain the 'standard' human brain – right-handed and left-brained for speech and other aspects of language. Is left-handedness, in combination with left-, right-, or rarely, mixed-brainedness, a genetic aberration? Annett (1978, 1980, 1984) takes the attitude that as 'sidedness' in animal populations is environmentally determined and symmetrically distributed between left and right, then what has to be explained is why humans are biased to the right side (and left half of the brain), rather than why some humans are not.

Her model proposes an inherited factor shifting laterality preferences to the right hand (the right shift factor, RS), possibly as an incidental side-effect of the genetic determination of left hemisphere language. Left-handers do not possess (by definition) the right shift factor. Their handedness and language laterality are independently determined by environmental factors. The children of two left-handed parents will again, by definition, lack the RS factor. If handedness is then determined environmentally, the distribution should follow that found in animals, with the proviso that fewer mixed-handers will be *obvious*, as human circumstances (e.g. writing) demand a high level of skill in one hand or the other and practice will lead to a preference for one side consistently.

Using inventories and performance tasks to isolate pure right-, pure left-, and mixed-handers, Annett has shown that handedness in the children of left-handers follows the frequencies predicted from the model, with, for instance, between 40 and 50 per cent writing with the left hand and 50–60 per cent with the right (a difference accountable via cultural bias); additionally there were no significant differences between the hands on various tests of skill. Thus, to reiterate, when the risk of sinistrality is greatest (two left-handed parents), the child's preferences appear to represent chance variation and there is no difference between the hands in skill, i.e. there is no inherited right shift factor.

Annett's is a parsimonious genetic model, with a single gene in two forms (or alleles), one inducing the right shift and the other neutral. Levy and Nagylaki (1972) produced a more complicated model, involving two genes each existing as two alleles. The first pair determines the hemisphere controlling speech and the preferred hand, and the second pair determines whether the preferred hand should be ipsilateral or contralateral to the controlling hemisphere. As Annett (1978) points out, a model requiring four independent genetic mutations and which treats handedness as a simple dichotomy has inherent disadvantages. The model also makes specific predictions about handwriting position and language lateralization. Specifically it predicts that 'inverted' writers (pen tip pointing towards the writer) have language in the ipsilateral hemisphere, whereas normal writers (non-inverted) have language in the contralateral hemisphere. As 40–50 per cent of left-handers are inverted writers, as are a few (< 1 per cent) right-handers, these predictions can be tested using tachistoscopic and dichotic techniques.

Levy and Reid (1978) produce evidence in support of these predictions. However, others have only partially replicated them (Tapley and Bryden, 1983), or failed to replicate them (McKeever and Van Deventer, 1980), with the former study suggesting a different basis for 'inversion' in right- and left-handers, and the latter producing evidence for significant sex differences in the consequences of inversion for cerebral organization. These suggestions would match perfectly conclusions as to the sophisticated interactions which determine performance on divided-field and dichotic investigations of functional hemispheric asymmetries. Annett's single-gene model certainly seems more attractive at this stage, although it must be emphasized that it is based mainly on handedness data, and may have to be extended to incorporate the occasionally uneasy relationships between handedness and lateralization of language.

Emotion and psychopathology

The study of hemisphere differences reaches into every corner of psychological research. Without attempting to be overinclusive, there are another couple of corners which I shall illuminate in this section, partly out of personal indulgence and partly to illustrate the broader significance of the field.

There has been a persistent following for the idea that 'emotion' is particularly associated with the right hemisphere (in right-handed males). Electro-convulsive shock therapy (ECT) for depression has occasionally been found to be as effective when applied only to the right hemisphere as when applied across the whole cerebrum (Kendell, 1981). Divided-field tachistoscopic studies have shown that the right hemisphere (left visual field) is superior at identifying emotional expression in photographs of human faces (Ley and Bryden, 1979; Safer, 1981; Natale et al., 1983) while there is a left-ear advantage in identifying the emotional quality of tonal sequences (Bryden et al., 1982). Emotional expression may also be judged as more intense on the left side of the subject's face (i.e., the side controlled by the right hemisphere) (Sackheim et al., 1978).

Two of the most frequently quoted studies in this area are those of Gainotti (1972) and Dimond *et al.* (1976). Gainotti rated the emotional consequences of unilateral brain damage in 160 patients, 80 with left-sided and 80 with right-sided lesions, His emotional categories, assessed during neuropsychological testing, were:

Catastrophic reactions   (Anxiety, Tears, Aggression, Refusal, Boasting, etc.)

Depressive mood   (Discouragement, Anticipated Incapacity, Rationalizations, etc.)

Indifferent reactions   (Indifference, Jokes, Minimization, Denial of illness)

Gainotti concluded that left-sided lesions (intact right hemisphere) were associated with a higher incidence of Catastrophic reactions, while right-sided lesions (intact left hemisphere) were associated with Indifference reactions. The association of Catastrophic reactions has been used to substantiate the right hemisphere/emotion connection, but it is worth pointing out several reservations with regard to this conclusion. Firstly, of the eight separate measures of Catastrophic reactions, only five differentiated left-sided and right-sided groups, and in no instance did more than 50 per cent of the left-sided group present the symptom (the highest incidence was twenty-eight out of eighty who swore during testing). Secondly, as expected, the incidence of aphasia was greater in the left-sided group, and was positively associated with a higher incidence of Catastrophic reactions; thus the increased 'emotionality' of the left-sided group was at least in part, and understandably, due to the loss of the main system for communicating with the outside world. Thirdly, the two groups were not differentiated by the incidence of depressive mood. Thus the interpretation of the study as demonstrating an emotion/right hemisphere link depends upon a very restricted definition of emotion (see also Chapter 8 for more discussion of the problems of defining emotion), and an uneven pattern of significant results.

However, recent work using CAT scans on right-handed

stroke patients and exhaustive neuropsychological assessment of mood has provided more convincing data. Robinson *et al.* (1984) demonstrated an association between left frontal damage and severe depressive symptoms, and between right frontal damage and an unduly cheerful but apathetic mood state. Left frontal depression was largely independent of any aphasic symptoms. The authors speculate that the depressive state may be induced by asymmetrical damage to the bilateral noradrenergic pathways ascending to the cerebral cortex, thus linking their depressed stroke patients with the brain chemistry models of naturally occurring depression outlined in Chapter 12.

Dimond *et al.* (1976) used an entirely different procedure. A divided-field technique involving contact lenses enabled stimuli to be presented to either hemisphere for prolonged periods. These stimuli were films, approximately three minutes long, of a Tom and Jerry cartoon, a surgical operation, and a travelogue of Lucerne. Normal subjects were asked to rate the films on humour, pleasantness and unpleasantness, and how horrific they were.

Films presented initially to the right hemisphere were rated as significantly more unpleasant (all films) and more horrific (Tom and Jerry and the medical film) than when presented initially to the left. Left hemisphere judgments were not significantly different from those of a control group viewing the films in free vision (i.e. both eyes). The authors conclude that the two hemispheres have 'essentially different visions of the world', with the right hemisphere producing emotional judgments more in line with the depressed patient than with normal controls.

Although unilateral presentation of single stimuli to intact subjects has been used fairly frequently to elicit hemisphere differences (e.g. Levy and Reid, 1978), it is still impressive that the degree of inter-hemispheric communication possible in a three-minute period does not eliminate any hemisphere differences in emotional judgments. Such prolonged presentation does, however, admit the possibility that the functional asymmetries that do emerge are not immediately comparable with either short duration exposure of lateralized single stimuli or with short duration simultaneous exposure of stimuli in both visual fields. The results certainly do not fit with a general dominance of the right hemisphere in processing emotional stimuli, as suggested by the work on facial expression and emotional tone stimuli mentioned earlier. They do correspond to the hypothesized role of the right hemisphere in depressive states, as suggested by the rather sketchy ECT data, perhaps by Gainotti's study, and more convincingly by Robinson *et al.*

In fact the left hemisphere presentation data in Dimond *et al.*'s experiment suggest that it is the *left* hemisphere which normally dominates emotional reactivity, a finding which is not necessarily at odds with the facial expression and dichotic studies as these were concerned with *perception and interpretation* rather than with *reactivity*. Given the problems in defining and analysing 'emotion', it seems unlikely that clear and replicable data will emerge to enable a positive association of emotion with one or other hemisphere. The problems do not, however, prevent the types of grand theorizing which characterize all areas of hemisphere research. In a particularly appealing article, Galin (1974) presents a model of a conscious left hemisphere dominating mental life, but in uneasy accord with an 'unconscious' right hemisphere mediating those 'darker' processes described by Freud as unconscious or preconscious but which are of immense significance to the psyche, e.g., repression.

Ideas on an association between 'emotion', normal and abnormal, and hemispheric functional asymmetries, lead naturally to considerations of other relationships between psychopathology and the sides of the brain. There has been much work, and many suggestions have been made (see, for instance, the two volumes on Laterality and Psychopathology, edited by Gruzeilier and Flor-Henry, 1979, and by Flor-Henry and Gruzelier, 1983). Perhaps the most coherent statement has been made by Flor-Henry *et al.* (1983). Bringing together evidence from neuropsychological testing, EEG and skin con-ductance recording, traditional tachistoscopic and dichotic studies, and from various other sources, he suggests that schizophrenia and manic-depressive (bipolar) psychosis represent the extremes of a continuum running from a predominantly left hemisphere dysfunction (schizophrenia) to a predominantly right hemisphere dysfunction (manic-depression and other affective emotional disorders).

Along similar lines, Gruzelier (1983) has for some years emphasized a left temporal lobe involvement in schizophrenia, mainly on the basis of deficits in the skin conductance orienting response and its habituation (see Chapter 12). Two groups of schizophrenics emerge – those with excessive orienting responses which show prolonged habituation (Responders), and those who show little or no orienting (Non-responders). As some animal work suggests a limbic involvement in orienting and its habituation (reviewed in Green, 1983), Gruzelier views schizophrenia as a temporal-limbic pathology, while lateralized hand differences in skin conductance orienting characteristics point to a left hemisphere location.

Both Flor-Henry and Gruzelier emphasize the dynamic equilibrium between left and right hemispheres, reflecting processes of mutual inhibition. Thus an *overactive* left hemisphere leads to larger *left*-hand skin conductance orienting responses (there is some evidence for ipsilateral control of hand sweat gland activity, although the idea is not undisputed), and the high verbal output and florid hallucinatory and delusional symptoms of the 'positive' schizophrenic (Gruzelier, 1983; see Chapter 12 below for a further discussion of schizophrenic symptomatology). An *underactive left* hemisphere produces, through diminished cross-callosal inhibition, a dominant *right* hemisphere, leading to larger *right* skin conductance orienting responses and the speech poverty and psychomotor retardation of the 'negative' schizophrenic. In both cases, therefore, the neurophysiological dysfunction is located in the left hemisphere.

It is indisputable that no one task or psychological function engages only one hemisphere, and that the corpus callosum and other commissures mediate complex dynamic interactions between the sides of the brain. Such a 'balance' view of hemisphere relationships is much more plausible than a static allocation of functions to side, and can encompass individual variation over time in laterality test performance and in psychiatric symptomatology, e.g., the periodic nature of the acute florid schizophrenic episode. It may even explain the therapeutic action of drug therapy in terms of a normalizing of inter-hemispheric relationships; Gruzelier presents data in support of this interpretation.

However realistic the 'dynamic balance' approach may be, it suffers from the disadvantage of inclusivity – virtually any finding on any type of laterality test can be slotted into the model by simply positing various combinations of unilateral hemispheric pathology and inter-hemispheric inhibition (the same problem arises, of course, in relation to a dynamic balance approach to hemispheric function in the normal brain). Unambiguous data are hard to find.

In addition, the view of schizophrenia as a left hemisphere pathology is not universally accepted. Taylor and Abrams (1983) present evidence from neuropsychological testing that schizophrenics suffer from a profound bilateral impairment, while Venables (1983) considers that there is evidence for schizophrenia being a predominantly right hemisphere dysfunction. Chapter 12 reviews some of the neurochemical and neuropathological work relevant to schizophrenia. Some findings – lateralized asymmetry in amygdaloid dopamine, the association between left temporal lobe damage and schizophrenic-like symptoms, etc. – support a left lateralized impairment, while others, such as the enlargement of the corpus callosum, the *bilateral* enlargement of the lateral ventricles, and unreplicated work on somatosensory evoked potentials, suggest, if anything, an *inter-hemispheric integration* impairment.

It may be that the general interest in hemispheric functional asymmetries has simply spawned another set of 'explanatory' principles for schizophrenia and other psychopathologies, in the same way that the explosion of interest in brain chemistry in the 1960s produced the dopamine model of schizophrenia and the catecholamine models of affective disorders. However, despite the essentially empirical nature of research within physiological psychopathology, I am optimistic that the various enthusiasms which capture the researcher's imagination – dopamine pathways or lateralized hemispheric pathology – do produce some significant and enduring findings which will eventually be seen as advances rather than distractions.

6 Brain mechanisms of memory and learning

Introduction

The term 'physiological substrates' covers a range of biological systems whose role in behaviour can, at least potentially, be studied. Each of the behaviours studied by psychologists may involve all or any of these biological systems, generating a variety of links, or areas of investigation, between behaviour and physiology. 'Motivation' involves brain structures, chemical pathways in the brain, and peripheral endocrine and autonomic nervous systems. 'Sleep' can be studied from the angle of brain mechanisms, general body metabolism, or behavioural function. 'Emotion', too, may be correlated with various brain structures, and with circulating levels of hormones.

These various physiological substrates represent biological systems at similar levels of analysis. In the context of reductionism, to analyse behaviour in terms of brain structures is no more or less reductionist than to analyse it in terms of blood levels of adrenaline. Occasionally the analysis may involve recording the electrical activity of single neurons, e.g. in studies of habituation (Chapter 7), and this does represent a shift in levels. We can use the term 'macrophysiological' to refer to that level incorporating brain structures, pathways, peripheral endocrine and autonomic systems, etc., and the term 'microphysiological' to refer to studies of single cells and to intracellular biochemical and molecular processes; the problem may then arise of how to coordinate findings from macrophysiological and microphysiological investigations of the same behaviour.

Although there is a burgeoning interest in the brain's microphysiology in general, physiological psychology has concerned itself in the main with macrophysiological systems – the role of amygdala and septum in emotion, of the hypothalamus in motivation, of the pituitary-adrenal cortex system in stress and arousal, etc. It is only in the area of memory and learning that the problem of microphysiological–macrophysiological coordination is absolutely central, and where attempts to resolve it have been, with a few exceptions, unsuccessful. The consequence is that the physiological psychology of memory and learning divides into a number of effectively independent research areas, defined by the level of physiological analysis attempted. Microphysiological substrates include single cell electrical activity and its correlation with the course of learning (as in the formation of CS-CR bonds in classical conditioning), changes in intracellular protein synthesis correlated with learning, and changes in synaptic structure (e.g. growth of new dendritic 'spines'), associated with learning. Macrophysiological analysis concerns itself with the effects of brain lesions and stimulation on learning and memory, correlates between evoked potentials or EEG patterns and learning, drug-induced modifications in learning and memory processes, or perhaps autonomic and endocrine factors in the acquisition and storage of new information.

If this were not confusion enough, there are several levels of conceptual analysis applied to the behaviour itself. A general definition of learning – 'the more or less permanent change in behaviour as a result of experience' – covers a multitude of behavioural responses and experience. At the highest level, studies of brain-damaged patients have illuminated psychological models of human information processing; at the lowest, there has been a less than constructive debate on whether flatworms can really learn anything at all.

A topic that embraces classical conditioning of the isolated cockroach leg, electro-convulsive-shock-(ECS)-induced retrograde amnesia for passive avoidance learning in the rat, and selective loss of the ability to transfer new information to long-term memory in brain-damaged human patients, is by its nature fragmented. I shall focus upon microphysiological investigations and the role of small molecules, the psychological nature of the deficit in ECS-induced retrograde amnesia in rats, and, using macrophysiological data, review the involvement of brain structures and pathways in learning and memory. This latter discussion will involve the problems of extrapolating both brain structure and behaviour across species, and will concentrate on the nature of hippocampal function in humans, monkeys, and rats.

The neuroanatomy of memory

Various forms of accidental brain damage, specific lesioning or stimulation of brain structures, or generalized trauma to the brain, may all disrupt memory. The deficit may involve an inability to recall previous experiences (retrograde amnesia), or a failure to learn material encountered after the brain damage (anterograde amnesia), or both of these syndromes.

Retrograde amnesia is the more frequently encountered in everyday life. Sudden brain trauma, e.g. blows to the head via car crashes, etc., often produces a retrograde amnesia, wherein the patient cannot recall the events immediately preceding the accident. Similarly, but under more controlled conditions, electro-convulsive shock therapy (ECT) used on depressive or schizophrenic patients can produce a retrograde amnesia.

Anterograde amnesia is less common but more dramatic, as an example will show. Patient H.M. suffered from disabling epileptic seizures for eleven years. It was known that structures buried deep in the temporal lobe were often the site, or focus, of epileptic attacks, and when anti-convulsant drugs ceased to be effective it was a regular procedure to surgically remove these medial temporal areas. In 1953 Scoville performed a bilateral temporal lobectomy on H.M., removing the overlying neocortical tissue, the anterior half of the hippocampus, the parahippocampal gyrus, and the amygdala, on both sides (see Fig. 6.1).

The operation did substantially reduce the epileptic attacks, but left H.M. with a patchy retrograde amnesia for the three years preceding the temporal lobectomy, and a devastating global anterograde amnesia. People and events encountered after the operation are, in general, not remembered. Thus a

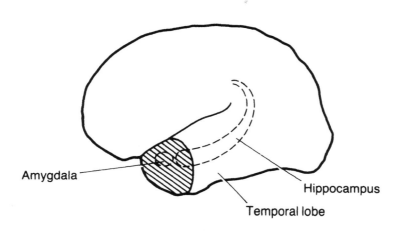

Figure 6.1   *Temporal lobectomy. The operation removes the tip of the temporal lobe, including the amygdala and a variable amount of the hippocampus. In the case of H.M., the operation was bilateral*

nurse meeting H.M. day after day for months will, each time, be greeted as a stranger. Early memories are intact – thus family and old friends are remembered. His general intelligence and range of perceptual-motor skills are unchanged, and his memory for new material does exist in a limited fashion. This has been shown by psychological testing carried out initially by Brenda Milner (Scoville and Milner, 1957), and continued up to the present by a variety of postgraduate students and research workers (e.g. Huppert and Piercey, 1979).

To summarize a range of experimental findings, it appears that H.M. has a functional short-term store, but cannot transfer material into a long-term consolidated form. Thus he can recall a short list of words as long as he can continually rehearse them in between initial presentation and recall; a distraction of any sort will mean the inevitable loss of the word list. The serial position effect in free recall of word lists has been used to support a distinction between short-term and long-term memory stores; the superior recall of words presented either early (primacy) or late (recency) in the list representing retrieval from a long-term and a short-term store respectively. H.M. shows a normal recency effect but no primacy effect; recently presented words are still held in a short-term store and are available for recall, while words presented early in the list have been displaced from short-term memory by subsequent items, and have not been transferred into long-term memory as occurs in normal subjects.

Vernon Gregg, in a companion volume (Gregg, 1986), deals in detail with the psychological relevance of studies of amnesic patients; my purpose is to reach some general conclusions concerning the nature of the deficit, and to relate them to the initial neuroanatomical damage. So in the case of H.M. we appear to have an intact long-term store, in that his retrograde amnesia is not severe and people and events encountered before surgery can be recognized and recalled (this also implies that his retrieval processes are intact, a point we consider in more detail later). He also possesses a normally functioning short-term memory store where new information can be temporarily held, but fails to transfer material from this into long-term permanent store.

Until an autopsy becomes possible and is performed, we do not know the precise extent of the surgical damage in H.M. However, particularly when compared with cases of accidental brain damage, we do have a good idea of the major structures involved (Scoville, 1954). Of these, damage to the hippocampus has been implicated in the amnesic syndrome of H.M., and as the defining feature of this syndrome is a failure to transfer material from STM to LTM, we may then tentatively conclude that the hippocampus in humans is involved in the STM–LTM channel, and that hippocampal lesions produce amnesia by blocking this transfer.

The importance of H.M. to neuropsychology cannot be overestimated; he provides support for the most enduring neuroanatomical model of memory, and for one of the more enduring psychological models of memory (i.e. separable short-term and long-term stores).

Once the drastic effects of a bilateral temporal lobectomy

were known, the operation was dropped from the anti-epilepsy therapeutic battery. However, unilateral operations have continued, as epileptic foci are often unilateral and the one-sided removal of medial temporal structures does not have the dramatic outcome of bilateral damage. Nevertheless, some behavioural effects have been reported. Corsi (referred to in Milner, 1971) has demonstrated significant memory loss after unilateral temporal lobectomies, with the nature of the loss depending upon the side of damage. Left temporal lesions disrupt verbal learning and memory, while right-sided operations impair the patient's ability on tests of spatial learning and memory (this would, of course, correlate with hemisphere functional asymmetries). The degree of impairment was roughly proportional to the amount of hippocampal tissue removed.

Penfield and Mathieson (1974) report two cases of severe memory loss following unilateral temporal lobectomies. In each case a standard operation, removing the amygdala and the anterior half of the hippocampus, was followed by a gross memory loss, consisting of a retrograde amnesia (stabilizing at a few months in one case and at around four years in the other) and a global anterograde amnesia. The significant feature of this report is that the first patient, operated on in 1946, has now died and an autopsy has been performed. This revealed that the hippocampus remaining on the intact side was in fact shrunken, with major loss of neurons; Penfield and Mathieson conclude that this chronic hippocampal damage was the result of physical trauma at the time of birth, and that their operation unfortunately removed the patient's only functioning hippocampus, i.e. an effective *bilateral* temporal lobectomy, and with the same outcome as in the case of H.M. (This also implies that the epileptic attacks were likely to have originated from the damaged hippocampal tissue on the unoperated side, and that, doubly unfortunately, Penfield removed the wrong hippocampus from a therapeutic point of view.)

Thus temporal lobe damage may produce both retrograde and anterograde amnesia. There are, then, two major questions to be resolved: is it certain that it is damage to the hippocampus which produces temporal lobe amnesia, and do other well-established amnesic syndromes also involve the hippocampus?

With regard to the second question, there are a number of reported single cases of amnesia following brain damage of various sorts. However, the only other relatively homogeneous category of patients exhibiting substantial memory loss are those with Korsakoff's syndrome (also referred to as Wernicke–Korsakoff's syndrome). This syndrome occurs as a consequence of thiamine deficiency, usually produced by chronic alcoholism; the high alcohol intake disrupts the liver's metabolic pathways, leading to a failure to absorb the vitamin in sufficient quantities. Thiamine deficiency causes degeneration of neural tissue in diencephalic areas of the brain, and this cerebral degeneration eventually leads to an amnesic syndrome. There are significant numbers of Korsakoff patients around, and most of the work on the human amnesic syndrome involves such subjects. They demonstrate an anterograde amnesia apparently similar to H.M.'s, although whether or not this is associated with a retrograde amnesia is still debated. Seltzer and Benson (1974) claim that Korsakoff subjects are worse on recalling recent events and better on the more remote, i.e. they do have a retrograde amnesia. Warrington and Sanders (1971), on the contrary, demonstrate that memory for recent events is quite good, and only falls off with the more remote, i.e. a pattern similar to normal controls, with no retrograde amnesia.

On a variety of short-term memory tasks Korsakoff patients have the same problems as H.M., exhibiting a global anterograde amnesia. Accepting for the present that a bilateral temporal lobectomy and the cerebral degeneration associated with Korsakoff's syndrome do produce the same amnesic syndrome, we would expect them to involve the same brain structures. The hippocampus has been held responsible for temporal lobe amnesia, and should therefore be involved in Korsakoff's. However, a problem with degenerative neural diseases is that the distribution of tissue breakdown varies from patient to patient. It can be so extensive as to produce a general 'dementia', and it can be difficult to identify the common elements.

Certainly Korsakoff degeneration need not directly involve

the hippocampus. It is mainly a diencephalic disorder, with damage associated with diencephalic structures such as the mammillary bodies and the thalamus, but usually sparing telencephalic structures such as the hippocampus. However, this need not be a problem for the hippocampus–memory hypothesis; because the mammillary bodies are directly linked to the hippocampus via the fornix pathway, mammillary degeneration would secondarily disrupt hippocampal function. Unfortunately, a major review by Victor *et al.* (1971) collated the results of a number of autopsies on patients dying of Korsakoff's syndrome, and found a higher correlation between memory disorder and thalamic damage than with damage to the mammillary bodies. In some cases the latter were virtually destroyed, with the patients exhibiting little sign of the amnesic syndrome.

Amnesia may also follow viral encephalitis or carbon monoxide poisoning (such patients have been extensively studied by Warrington's group at the National Hospital in London – see, e.g., Warrington and Weiskrantz, 1970), but in neither case is strict neuroanatomical localization possible. Brain damage sparing the hippocampus and its associated structures can produce an amnesic syndrome; McEntee *et al.* (1976) report an H.M.-like anterograde amnesia following a tumour invasion of the caudate nucleus and medial and dorso-medial thalamus, while patient N.A. shows a persistent anterograde amnesia following a fencing accident, in which the tip of the blade entered the base of the brain via the right nostril, and probably damaged the dorso-medial nucleus of the thalamus (Teuber *et al.*, 1968; Squire *et al.*, 1981).

It is therefore possible that the amnesia associated with Korsakoff's syndrome may not involve the hippocampus, and it is probable that amnesia can result from damage to structures other than the hippocampus and its immediate neighbours. Returning to the effects of temporal lobe damage on memory, we can now ask whether the hippocampus is, as assumed for many years, the site of the effective lesion.

The brief answer is that we do not know, although we are less certain than we used to be. The strongest evidence in favour is the precise nature of the surgical intervention, and the probability that simultaneous damage to other structures, e.g. the amygdala, is not responsible for the dramatic outcome. (Chapter 8 reviews attempts to reduce hyper-aggressive behaviour by lesioning the amygdala, attempts which may not be effective but which certainly do not affect memory and learning along the way.)

An alternative interpretation of the temporal lobectomy findings is put forward by Horel (1978), in the course of a substantial review of the neuroanatomical basis of human memory. Pointing out problems with the hippocampal hypothesis, some of which have been mentioned above, he suggests that the crucial lesion actually involves damage to the temporal stem, a fibre pathway connecting temporal lobe cortex to subcortical structures. It is almost impossible to avoid damaging the temporal stem in the course of a temporal lobectomy, as it runs alongside the hippocampus for part of its course.

The subcortical targets for temporal stem fibres are the basal ganglia and the dorso-medial regions of the thalamus. Given the substantial evidence linking damage to the dorso-medial thalamus with the amnesic syndrome associated either with Korsakoff degeneration or with tumour and accidental injury, Horel concludes that temporal stem damage incurred during a temporal lobectomy could produce amnesia via a secondary disruption of thalamic function, i.e. he is replacing a hippocampal hypothesis with a dorso-medial thalamic hypothesis.

Before considering experimental work with animals that sheds light on the hippocampal hypothesis of memory, some semantic problems have to be clarified. An elementary model of memory would involve acquisition, short- and long-term storage (consolidation), and retrieval. Memory malfunctions such as anterograde amnesia are observed when test performance is inadequate, i.e. material cannot be retrieved when asked for. Such a breakdown in a recall or recognition test could imply any one of several problems. The material may not have been 'acquired' in the first place, through defective perceptual or short-term processes. The material may be lodged in a short-term store, but fails to be consolidated into a long-term memory. Finally, the material may be consolidated and stored away, but cannot be retrieved on demand.

Brain damage to any structure involved in any of these processes might then result in amnesia; but we could not state whether that structure was a substrate for acquisition, storage, or retrieval processes in memory. We would also expect lesions to a wide range of structures to result in memory disruption – acquisition, storage, and retrieval of information may involve many different pathways and centres within the central nervous system. (For a discussion of these general issues, see Morton, 1985, and Squire, 1980.)

It is therefore unjustified to assume that any one structure is the site of 'memory', or that all cases of anterograde amnesia represent a homogeneous group with a single psychological and physiological malfunction. The controversy over the last decade as to whether the human anterograde amnesic syndrome represents deficient initial processing (Cermak *et al.*, 1974; Glosser *et al.*, 1976; Huppert and Piercey, 1978) or deficient retrieval (Warrington and Weiskrantz, 1970, 1974) may be undermined by such a false assumption. Warrington and Weiskrantz have been criticized (Butters and Cermak, 1974) for using as an experimental group a mixed bag of Korsakoff, post-encephalitis and unilateral temporal lobectomized amnesic patients. There is evidence that Korsakoff amnesics are psychologically distinct from post-encephalitic amnesics (Cermak, 1976; Mattis *et al.*, 1978) and from the bilateral temporal lobectomized patient H.M. (Huppert and Piercey, 1979).

These issues are discussed in more detail in Vernon Gregg's (1986) volume in this series. A broad conclusion is that Korsakoff amnesics show impaired semantic encoding of new information and a failure to 'time-tag' stored material, making retrieval difficult, but can show normal forgetting of information once the acquisition deficit is overcome. H.M. shows an inability to retain information in store, although initial acquisition can be normal. Of course, if Korsakoff amnesics have a different psychological impairment to H.M., then whether or not their hippocampus is involved becomes a superfluous question. H.M. gave rise to the hippocampal model of memory; however, as his precise deficit is a failure of STM → LTM

transfer, it should be called a hippocampal model of STM →
LTM transfer. Only if Korsakoffs shows a similar failure
should their particular pathology involve the hippocampus,
and the evidence suggests that they do not. In fact a division
that is becoming accepted is one that distinguishes 'diencephalic' amnesia (e.g. Korsakoff patients, and case N.A. with
thalamic damage) from 'temporal lobe' amnesia (H.M.), both
psychologically and neuroanatomically (Squire, 1982).

As mentioned previously, the relatively limited retrograde
amnesia found in cases of human amnesia implies that patients
can recall material stored prior to the brain trauma; i.e.
retrieval processes are operating, and a global retrieval-deficit
hypothesis of human amnesia is untenable (Squire, 1980).
What is even more confusing is that the anterograde amnesia,
while extensive, is not complete. H.M. can acquire simple
visual-motor skills such as mirror drawing and maze-learning;
repeated practice over days shows substantial learning,
although H.M. himself denies, each day, ever having seen the
task before! When tested on word lists, which he cannot recall,
he does appear to remember the task at hand, i.e. he *tries* to
remember, and so must have acquired the idea that a task is to
be attempted.

Observations such as these have led to the suggestion that
there are separable systems for different sorts of information,
e.g. perhaps along the lines of Tulving's episodic and semantic
memories (Warrington, 1975). Corsi's observation (quoted in
Milner, 1971) that the type of amnesia produced varied with
the side of a unilateral temporal lobectomy (see p.163) also
supports the view that to conceptualize in terms of a single
memory system is as unrealistic as to expect all human amnesic
patients to suffer from the same psychological deficit.

This point is particularly relevant when we consider the
comparative neuropsychology of memory, i.e. the effects of
systematic lesions upon learning and memory in animals. The
hippocampal hypothesis of human amnesia – securely, it was
thought, based upon H.M. and similar cases – has been widely
accepted. It appeared to be a rare example of damage to a
specific brain structure producing a specific psychological
deficit in man, and therefore a crucial test of the rationale for

extrapolating from animals to man within physiological psychology. If the hippocampus mediates human memory, it should, to justify the general approach of extrapolating from animal data to the human brain, mediate memory in animals.

Hippocampal function

In the mammalian brain the hippocampus is a prominent forebrain structure. It is classified as archicortex, or 'old' cortex, as distinct from the neocortex, or 'new' cortex. As you may have gathered from the description of the temporal lobectomy performed upon amnesic patients, the hippocampus is buried within the temporal lobe of the cerebral hemisphere, i.e. it is technically 'subcortical', although itself a primitive form of cortex (see Chapter 2).

The hippocampus has long attracted the attention of physiological psychologists. It is large, and easily accessible for purposes of lesioning or stimulating. It also possesses a characteristic organization, with layers of neurons being interconnected by identifiable axon pathways and inter-neurons. A diagrammatic representation of the hippocampus suggests, at first glance, the wiring of a small computer, and this inbuilt structural organization, along with its size and position, points to a specialized role in behaviour.

The anatomy and connections of the hippocampus do not appear to have altered drastically from the evolutionarily primitive primates such as the lemurs and tarsiers, to the advanced groups such as monkeys and humans. There are no dramatic changes which might suggest a radical shift in function during the course of evolution, and the various hypotheses of hippocampal function in animals are usually presented without regard for the species used as experimental subjects. Since the early 1960s, these hypotheses have ranged from the mediation of orienting and attentional processes to the control of behavioural inhibition and an involvement in voluntary motor activity. The work on animals is notable for the absence, until recently, of any great emphasis upon memory and learning, in direct contrast to the human memory–hippocampus link which has been prominent in clinical neuropsychology for the last twenty years.

The most influential model of hippocampal function in animals has related it to the control of processes of internal inhibition (Douglas, 1967, 1975; Kimble, 1968; Gray, 1982). This concept was derived initially from Pavlov's work on classical conditioning, and refers to the inhibition or suppression of a behavioural response on the basis of learning or experience. The salivation response to the bell in a classic Pavlovian conditioning experiment will gradually diminish if the food reinforcement no longer follows the bell, i.e. it will extinguish if the S-R connection is not adequately reinforced. Extinction is seen not as a gradual 'fading away', but as the active inhibition or suppression of a response that is no longer rewarded. The same process is seen in operant conditioning; a bar-press response is learnt via regular reinforcement, but will be inhibited and extinguished if the reinforcement is omitted.

This idea of inhibition as an active process comes over more clearly where behaviour has to be suppressed if punishment or non-reward is to be avoided. Some operant schedules, referred to as 'differential reinforcement of low rate' (DRL) schedules, involve periods of non-responding, where the animal has to withhold bar-pressing for a certain period to obtain a reward; if he keeps pressing, he is never rewarded. Another clear example of internal inhibition at work is the suppression of behaviour in order to avoid shock, as in passive avoidance. In the classic situation a rat is placed upon a small raised platform. When, in the course of exploration, he steps down on to the grid floor, he receives a mild foot shock. If replaced upon the platform either immediately, or an hour or a day later, he does not step down; he has learnt in one trial to avoid punishment by inhibiting the step-down response. This is an example of passive avoidance.

Habituation (Chapter 7) is the fading away of a behavioural or physiological response to novel stimuli; as with extinction, this fading away is not a passive fatigue process, but an active inhibition of the orienting or exploratory response as the stimuli become less novel. Habituation, therefore, joins extinction, responding on DRL and punishment schedules, and passive avoidance, as an example of internal inhibition at work.

There is now a vast amount of experimental evidence showing that rats with hippocampal lesions perform poorly on tests requiring behavioural inhibition. They keep responding during extinction procedures in operant conditioning, over-respond during DRL and punishment schedules (therefore receiving fewer rewards in the one case and more electric shocks in the other), and are very poor at learning passive avoidance – after training they do not, like control animals, remain on the platform, but step straight down. In habituation tests, hippocampal rats persist in orienting towards and exploring stimuli to which they have been repeatedly exposed, and to which control animals have habituated.

It appears, therefore, that the hippocampal lesion disrupts the processes of internal inhibition, and a key phenomenon in support of this hypothesis is that hippocampal rats are actually better than controls at learning tasks in which inhibitory processes impede performance. Such a task is shuttle-box active avoidance.

In its simplest form the shuttle-box consists of an enclosed runway with electrified grids at either end. The rat receives a mild footshock at one end, A, which it may escape by running to the other end, B; to avoid a footshock at this point, it must rapidly return to A, and so on. By efficient shuttling back and forth footshocks can be avoided, but each avoidance response involves running to an area where the rat has previously been shocked; i.e. an area to which the animal has learnt powerful passive-avoidance tendencies. These tendencies, to remain still and safe, act against the active avoidance response, and slow down the acquisition of shuttle avoidance. Hippocampal rats, with impaired internal inhibition, are less prone to the passive-avoidance tendency, and happily shuttle backwards and forwards without the conflict – to approach and to avoid – of control animals; they acquire shuttle-box avoidance faster than controls, which is a powerful argument in favour of the hippocampus as the site of behavioural inhibition.

So the dominant hypothesis of hippocampal function in animals has not obviously involved memory, in contrast with the human work. I say 'not obviously' as, although hippocampal rats can acquire complex behavioural skills such as active avoidance and clearly do not suffer from global anterograde amnesia, it is sometimes difficult to disentangle inhibitory and memorial processes.

Efficient extinction of a bar-pressing response requires that the animal remembers whether or not previous presses have been rewarded. Habituation, as pointed out in Chapter 7, is a function of stimulus novelty, which can only be assessed by remembering previous stimulus presentations – have I seen this before or not? So the inhibition of the orienting response depends in turn on the memory process involved in comparing a current stimulus with previously presented stimuli (Sokolov's match/mismatch comparator model of the hippocampus revolves around the hippocampus-memory link). Even the passive-avoidance deficit found with hippocampal rats can be seen as a simple failure to learn the stimulus-response link (platform – remain still), although in view of their ability to acquire active avoidance responses it does seem unlikely.

In recent years one area of research has emerged which supports a more specific link between the animal hippocampus and memory. The hypothesis is that this large and highly organized structure serves as the substrate for spatial memory in the rat; its primary function is to locate the animal in space and in relation to relevant features of the environment such as food, water, danger, etc. The experiment of Blanchard *et al.* described on page 316 is a good example of the importance of a spatial map to the rat.

The information upon which the spatial map is built up comes from exploration (i.e. this hypothesis is a return to the 'cognitive map' ideas of Tolman; see p. 314), and some of the more convincing experiments in favour of a hippocampus/ spatial memory hypothesis depend upon the rat's systematic approach to exploration.

Given a free choice of the two arms in a simple T-maze, a rat will, let us say, turn left. Returned to the choice point and allowed to choose again, it will, with a probability of 80–90 per cent, turn right. Repeated trials produce a systematic pattern of alternating choices of left and right, and give the behaviour the name 'spontaneous alternation'.

If allowed to explore freely a novel Y-maze, a rat will again choose arms systematically; over a prolonged trial it will consistently enter that arm least recently explored; i.e. if arms are arbitrarily labelled A B and C, a sequence of entries might be recorded as A, B, C, A, B, C, B, A, B, A, B, C, A, B, C, etc. Alternation, as in the T-maze, is not perfect, but consistently non-random.

Olton (1976) has extended the range of observations to include an eight-arm radial maze, with arms radiating from a central platform. Rats had few problems with even this complicated maze, taking only nine or ten choices to explore all eight arms. Only with a seventeen-arm maze did performance begin to break down, with choices becoming less systematic and more random.

What does this systematic approach to maze exploration depend upon? The two earliest hypotheses were either that the rat learnt a consistent *response* tendency (always turning left will produce efficient exploration in a Y-maze or in Olton's radial mazes), or that their responses were guided by intra-maze stimuli, i.e. they recognized arms as being familiar or novel. Douglas (1967) showed convincingly that their exploratory behaviour was guided by stimuli rather than being a response tendency; using a T-maze with a movable approach arm he demonstrated that the rat will alternate arms regardless of whether it has to repeat or alternate responses.

Olton has similarly demonstrated, by shifting arms around in the course of a single trial, that the decisive feature for the rat in his radial maze is whether an arm is novel or familiar, not whether it is always the one to the left of the previously explored one.

Douglas argued that spontaneous alternation in the T-maze reflected internal inhibition at work. At the choice point, the rat is confronted with two arms, one of which, after the first trial, is always more familiar. Inhibition, in the context of habituation and exploration, depends upon the degree of familiarity, with orienting and exploration being inhibited as stimuli become familiar and less novel. At the T-maze choice point, therefore, the rat will choose to explore the more novel arm; on the following trial this arm is now more familiar, internal inhibition will be greater, and the alternate arm will now tend to elicit the exploratory response. And so on, building up a pattern of spontaneous alternation.

Hippocampal lesions disrupt spontaneous alternation in the T-maze, and free-running alternation in the Y-maze or in Olton's large radial mazes. Choice of arms becomes essentially random. Douglas suggests that this reliable finding supports the hypothesis that the hippocampus mediates internal inhibition, as without inhibition exploratory responses cannot be made on the basis of relative familiarity. (An intriguing phenomenon described by Douglas is the development of spontaneous alternation in children; using a giant T-maze, he has shown that systematic alternation does not appear before the age of about three, which coincides with the maturing of the fully functional human hippocampus!)

An alternative and not contradictory hypothesis is that the lesion destroys the spatial map built up by the rat on the basis of exploration. If the animal cannot distinguish one arm as familiar (explored) and another as novel (unexplored), then inhibitory processes have nothing to work on and all arms, being equally novel, will have an equal chance of being entered. Thus responding becomes random. Powerful evidence in favour of the hippocampus as the site of a spatial map has been put forward over the last few years by O'Keefe and Nadel (1978) and by Olton (1976, 1979). We know, from Douglas's early work, that the rat recognizes maze arms on the basis of stimuli. These stimuli may be of many sorts – olfactory (scent marking), tactile (texture of floor), or visual (intra-maze cues such as colour or shape, extra-maze cues such as objects in the experimental room, chairs, lights, even the experimenter himself). The rat constructs a map of the maze during his exploratory behaviour by registering configurations of the available stimuli. He therefore 'knows' when he is in a certain part, and the physiological correlate of this 'knowledge' is the firing of certain neurons in the hippocampus. By recording directly from hippocampal cells, O'Keefe and Nadel have identified neurons which fire only when the rat enters a certain part of the maze; they call these neurons 'place units', and hypothesis that they represent a topographical map of the maze, i.e. a point-by-point correspondence of parts of the maze with parts of the hippocampus.

Hippocampal lesions then destroy the spatial map and lead to random exploratory behaviour. Intriguingly, the deficit in hippocampal rats can be overcome by giving them powerful stimuli to cue the correct responses; for instance, a hippocampal animal will spontaneously alternate if one arm of the T-maze is painted white and the other black. Olton has shown that hippocampus rats can negotiate his radial maze efficiently if a cue, such as a light, signals when an arm has been explored – the animal remembers that the cue means familarity. Thus even the rat has alternative strategies for exploration, usually employing place-learning on the basis of a spatial map, but able to use a cue-learning strategy if place-learning is prevented by a hippocampal lesion.

The spatial memory hypothesis of hippocampal function in the rat is not inclusive of *all* hippocampal functions. The deficits shown by lesioned animals on DRL and punishment schedules, or in orienting to specific novel stimuli such as tones, suggest that other mechanisms may be disrupted. Vinogradova (Chapter 7) has identified hippocampal neurons whose activity mirrors habituation of the behavioural orienting response, while Thompson *et al.* (1980) have found populations of neurons whose increases and decreases in activity follow precisely the formation of stimulus–response connections in a classical conditioning procedure (conditioning the eyeblink response to a puff of air with a bell).

To help account for this range of deficits following hippocampal damage, Olton has subsequently produced an alternative model of hippocampal function (Olton *et al.*, 1980). He conceptualizes his radial maze task as involving both 'working' and 'reference' memory components. If eight arms of a seventeen-arm maze are baited with food, a hungry rat freely exploring has to learn and remember, over a series of trials, which eight arms are consistently baited, and which of the eight it has already visited on a given trial. Aspects of the task which are unchanged from trial to trial, such as food locations, involve reference memory, while information of temporary relevance, such as which arms have been visited on a given trial, involve short-term working memory. Normal rats rapidly learn the task and perform efficiently. Olton demonstrated that lesions of the fornix bundle (a major input to the hippocampus), disrupting hippocampal function, produce a systematic pattern of errors in the radial maze. Over a series of trials, lesioned animals learn to avoid the non-baited arms, but in a given trial repeatedly re-enter baited arms they have already visited, i.e. their reference memory is intact ('which arms are consistently baited?'), but working memory is impaired ('have I visited this arm already on this trial?'). So Olton concludes that the hippocampus in the rat is involved in short-term working memory processes.

Given the range of behaviours affected by hippocampal damage, it may be that a unitary hypothesis of hippocampal function is unrealistic (see, e.g., Schmajuk, 1984). Attempts have been made to resolve apparent differences between behavioural inhibition and the various memory hypotheses (e.g. Gray, 1982), and there are substantial grounds for assuming anyway that the rat hippocampus is involved in several aspects of learning and memory. This would have the advantage of tying in with the hypothesized role of the hippocampus in cases of human amnesia.

This latter hypothesis was extensively discussed earlier in the chapter, and two critical points raised. Firstly, human amnesic patients show a heterogeneous array of psychological symptoms, which include retaining the ability to learn a range of perceptual-motor tasks, and secondly, particularly in Korsakoff's syndrome, the hippocampus may not be involved. The first point introduces a general problem with locating learning and memory within the brain. Human amnesic patients show severe semantic deficits, but have few problems with what one can call simple S-R associative learning – Korsakoff patients, as an example, acquire classically conditioned responses as easily as control subjects. H.M. is aware that a task has to be performed, but cannot learn lists of words, suggesting a distinction between Tulving's semantic and episodic memories. Hippocampally lesioned rats show a severe 'spatial' amnesia, but can learn active-avoidance responses quite easily. It has been assumed for many years that instrumental (operant) conditioning in rats requires an intact neocortex; Oakley (1979) has shown that this is not the case, as neodecorticate animals can acquire high fixed ratio schedules under appropriate conditions. However, it is indisputable that even a brain is unnecessary for classical conditioning, which has been demonstrated in such simple neuronal preparations as the isolated cockroach leg.

So different forms of learning seem to involve different mechanisms in both human and animal brains, with the corollary that any attempt to isolate, e.g., the hippocampus as the site of a global 'memory' is doomed to failure. The psychological differentiation of learning and memory processes is equally as important as the sophisticated anatomical and neurophysiological procedures used to investigate their neural substrates.

The second point – that the hippocampus may not be crucial in all cases of human amnesia – is supported by a vast range of animal work. As the early investigations of the rat hippocampus failed to show a dramatic and consistent effect upon learning and memory, other structures have been implicated. One outcome has been a series of papers by Thompson (e.g. Thompson, 1974, 1978; Thompson *et al.*, 1976) in which he attempts to localize various memory systems within the rat brain; thus, on the basis of lesions involving up to fifty different sites in the brain, he concludes (Thompson, 1978) that the passive-avoidance memory system incorporates a wide range of structures, in line with the wide range of behavioural processes needed. The basal ganglia look after sensorimotor integration, the posterior thalamus, amygdala, and frontal cortex are involved in all fear-initiated responses, the cerebellum, anterior thalamus, and parietal cortex are required for somatosensory functions, and finally the occipital cortex, hippocampus, and mammillary bodies have a cognitive mapping duty. These functional blocks may then be excited or inhibited by brainstem mechanisms (raphe nuclei and brainstem reticular formation).

Such an analysis may not be parsimonious, but it does have the merit of plausibility. Sensory, integrative, and motor aspects are accounted for and, as one might predict, consequently incorporate large regions of the brain. As pointed out previously, given that all behaviour is complicated, 'memory' will not be localizable to any one structure, and a cursory glance through any physiological psychology journal will find support for Thompson's contention that many parts of the brain must be involved. In fact we should also remember that the notion of 'a structure' is one that we apply to the brain as a descriptive, not a functional, term, and there is not a logical imperative that says that the brain's functional systems will coincide with our structural descriptions. I have discussed the effects of hippocampal lesions as though the hippocampus exists in isolation; it does not, and disrupting it will immediately affect those structures (neocortex, septum, mammillary bodies, etc.) with which it is directly interconnected.

Brain scientists are not unaware of these complications, and their discussions of 'hippocampal function' take as read the fact that life is not as simple as it sounds (see, for instance, the issue of *Physiological Psychology* devoted to the hippocampus, Vol. 8, No. 2, 1980). Their hypotheses are heuristic devices to temporarily integrate a vast amount of data, and in this light the hippocampus/memory hypothesis can be seen to be one of the more successful. The human clinical data may still be interpreted in its light, despite criticisms mentioned earlier, and there is now sufficient evidence for a role for the hippocampus in some aspects of rat learning and memory. Recent work also describes severe deficits in hippocampectomized monkeys (Mahut *et al.*, 1981) in their ability to distinguish novel from familiar objects and to learn relations between objects and rewards.

In an important development of this line of research, Mishkin (1978) and Zola-Morgan (e.g. Zola-Morgan and Squire, 1985) have shown that *combined* removal of the hippocampus and amygdala on both sides of the brain produces a profound anterograde amnesia in monkeys on a range of learning tasks. More importantly, several of the tasks are ones on which human amnesics also show learning deficits. An example is delayed non-matching to sample (Zola-Morgan and Squire, 1985). A sample object is presented, and after a variable delay the original object is re-presented along with a novel object; the subject to choose the *novel* item. Both lesioned monkeys and human amnesics have great difficulty with this task.

So it may be that the bilateral hippocampal-amygdala lesioned monkey will prove to be a viable model of human amnesia. One problem to be resolved is the psychological and neuroanatomical distinctions between, e.g., H.M. and Korsakoff amnesics, discussed previously. No one animal model is likely to accommodate both syndromes, and on neuroanatomical grounds one would expect the Mishkin/Zola-Morgan monkey model of amnesia to resemble H.M. rather than Korsakoff amnesics, as both have combined damage to hippocampus and amygdala. Incidentally, the bilateral amygdalectomy suffered by H.M. is almost ignored when his case is discussed, although he could potentially tell us as much about amygdaloid function as about the hippocampus. Recent work does implicate the damage to the amygdala in a relative failure of H.M. to be aware of, or at least comment upon, internal states such as hunger, thirst, and pain (Hebben *et al.*, 1985).

I have used the various approaches to hippocampal function in humans and animals to illustrate the rationale behind the use of animals in physiological psychology. If it were completely unjustified to extrapolate from rat to man – if the hippocampus in rat had no behavioural correlates remotely similar to those of the hippocampus in man – then much of the physiological approach to psychology would lose its point. This is why clinical patients such as H.M. are so important; we have a mountain of animal data, but a molehill of human data.

Before leaving the hippocampus and its role in learning and memory, we must remember that, as a component of the forebrain limbic system, it is also involved in other psychological and physiological functions. Chapter 8 mentions it in relation to some aspects of emotion, while the following chapter details the role it plays in feedback control of the pituitary-adrenal axis. Hippocampal neurons selectively take up corticosteroids from the bloodstream, thus monitoring the level of pituitary-adrenal activation during stress and arousal; via its connections to the hypothalamus, the hippocampus can then modulate adrenocorticotrophic hormone release from the pituitary gland. Whether those parts of the hippocampus involved in the behavioural and physiological aspects of emotion and stress are identical with the areas implicated in learning and memory is unclear. Functional differentiation within this large structure is accepted, with, e.g., neurons whose activity tracks the formation of conditioned stimulus – unconditioned response (CS–UCR) bonds in classical conditioning seen as distinct from O'Keefe and Nadel's 'place units'. There is no logical reason why behavioural and endocrine functions should be distinct. They interact in an area such as 'emotion', and there is intriguing evidence that the cognitive capacity of memory is also subject to endocrine modulation. Some of this evidence is described in Chapter 9; an alternative approach was that of Holloway and Wansley (1973). They trained rats on a passive-avoidance task, and simply tested groups at various intervals after training. Recall, measured by the latency to enter the footshock chamber, was found to vary significantly with time of testing; peaks and troughs of retention scores occurred at six-hourly intervals, producing over a three-day period a sinusoidal curve (〜〜〜〜〜). Such variations in memory recall, due simply to time of testing, have also been found with humans (Folkard, 1977) and probably represent an association between original learning and internal biological stimuli present at the time of learning. A popular candidate for this role of internal stimulus is the activity of the pituitary-adrenal axis, represented by blood levels of corticosteroids. These levels are subject to a circadian rhythm, varying systematically with time of day. One might then hypothesize that retention is best when blood corticosteroid levels match those present at original learning, and worst when levels are at the opposite point of the cycle. Retention will then vary with the time of day (or point in the circadian rhythm) at which testing takes place. As the hippocampus is implicated in both memory and in control of the pituitary-adrenal axis, such an interaction between passive-avoidance memory and the circadian rhythm of blood corticosteroids is quite conceivable. Additionally, it is also been shown that the phasic retention curve in rat passive-avoidance memory is eliminated by lesions of the supra-chiasmatic nucleus (Stephan and Kovacevic, 1978). This nucleus, further discussed in Chapter 10, is directly involved in the control of the body's endogenous (natural) circadian rhythms.

Retrograde amnesia in the rat – consolidation or retrieval?

The human amnesic syndrome has both anterograde (inability to learn new material) and retrograde (inability to retrieve previously acquired information) components, with the former being the more dramatic and more studied. In animals, and in particular the rat, the use of electro-convulsive shock (ECS) to induce retrograde amnesia (RA) has enabled the phenomenon to be systematically studied, producing data of great relevance to theories of learning and memory.

The basic findings were made by Chorover and Schiller in 1965. They used a straightforward step-down passive-avoidance task, which has the great advantage of producing substantial learning within a single trial. On the acquisition trial, animals step off the platform and immediately receive a mild footshock from the grid floor. When replaced on the platform, they do not step down; the degree of learning is proportional to the latency (delay) before the step-down response occurs on this retention test, with perfect acquisition producing extremely long latencies (thus necessitating a cut-off point at which the experimenter accepts that learning is 100 per cent), and retrograde amnesia reflected in extremely short latencies (comparable with naive rats placed on the platform for the first time).

Using alligator-clip electrodes attached to the rat's ears, Chorover and Schiller applied an ECS (the parameters for ECS in this sort of work are in the range of a fifty-milliampere current lasting for 0.3 second) at various intervals after the animal had stepped down and received the footshock on the acquisition trial. They found that if the footshock–ECS interval was no greater than around thirty seconds, then the animals would show significant amnesia on the retention test; animals not given ECS showed perfect retention of the passive-avoidance response. Footshock–ECS intervals of a minute and over did not result in retrograde amnesia, as though the association between response (step-down) and stimulus (foot-shock) was now immune to the amnesic effects of ECS.

Such data provide powerful support for a two-stage view of consolidation processes in memory (Hebb, 1958). The first stage consists of reverberating neuronal activity, with action potentials generated in those brain circuits mediating passive-avoidance learning. This stage, learning as electrical activity, would be vulnerable to disruption by the overwhelming electrical discharge induced by the ECS. After a minute or so the reverberating neuronal activity, if uninterrupted, will be translated into structural modifications to the neurons concerned, perhaps via synaptic growth or via permanent alterations in neurotransmitter release. At this point the memory becomes impervious to ECS as it is no longer dependent upon electrical activity.

So we would have qualitatively distinct neural substrates for short-term and long-term memory processes, which would also accord with the human experience. Retrograde amnesia as a consequence of brain trauma in humans tends to diminish with time, but there is always a residual memory loss for the period immediately preceding the trauma, as though the memories of that period were particularly vulnerable.

After an accident, human retrograde amnesia can be extensive, but reduces with time. This implies that the trauma has affected not only storage of information, but its retrieval; three-day-old memories are initially unavailable, but gradually become accessible, as though retrieval processes were slowly recovering. Only information not permanently stored is permanently lost, i.e. the memories, in the form of neuronal electrical patterns, for the minute or so preceding the trauma.

The distinction between a failure to recall because retrieval processes are inoperable and a failure to recall because information has not been stored has become a central debating point in the study of amnesia. The failure to perform adequately on tests of recall or recognition is an operational definition of amnesia. However, it does not distinguish between a failure to consolidate or store information in memory and a failure to retrieve that information from memory. An extreme position would be that we *always* store *everything* and all cases of amnesia – human, animal, retrograde or anterograde – reflect a basic inability to retrieve the appropriate information at the appropriate time.

Since Chorover and Schiller's original work, the passive-avoidance/ECS paradigm has become a favourite with the physiological psychologist interested in memory processes. It was soon shown that the degree of retrograde amnesia varied not only with the footshock–ECS interval, but with the intensity of the ECS. More elegant demonstrations included the application of ECS to specific structures; McGaugh and Dawson (1971) showed that amnesia appeared to depend upon the disruption of the characteristic EEG pattern of the hippocampus (the theta waves). Then, in 1973, Miller and Springer presented an alternative explanation for ECS-induced retrograde amnesia. Moving away from the traditional and widely accepted two-stage view of memory consolidation, they propose that the ECS disrupts a cataloguing system rather than a storage system. Their view is that information is consolidated in a permanent structural form within fractions of a second, and that it is therefore invulnerable to ECS. However, a set of retrieval cues has also to be stored, to facilitate retrieval processes; their analogy is with a library, where a given book is not only stored on the shelves, but an entry is made in a cataloguing system to facilitate retrieval of the book when necessary. If cataloguing takes of the order of a minute, it could be disrupted by ECS, and the book, or information, would be stored but retrieval would be an inefficient and slow process.

The evidence in favour of a retrieval hypothesis comes from experiments on the effectiveness of 'reminder treatments' in reducing ECS-induced amnesia. A standard passive-avoidance paradigm is used, with footshock followed a few seconds later by ECS. Then, in between the ECS and the retention test, a reminder treatment is presented. This can take several forms, but all have to have in common an association with the original learning task; it may be a mild footshock, delivered in the rat's home cage (and therefore referred to as a non-contingent footshock), or it may be a brief exposure to some aspect of the learning situation – a box of the same colour, for instance. On the subsequent retention trial in the passive-avoidance apparatus, animals given the reminder treatment tend to show less amnesia than controls, i.e. their step-down latencies are longer. The basic finding is summarized below:

	seconds		hours	Reminder treatment	hours	Retention
Acquisition trial for passive avoidance	$\longrightarrow$	ECS	$\longrightarrow$	e.g. non-contingent footshock	$\longrightarrow$	test shows reduced amnesia

Control subjects would not have the reminder treatment.

Miller and Springer (see also Spear, 1973) argue that the association learnt at acquisition is not simply between the step-down response and the electrified grid floor, but between the response and various internal and external stimuli, or cues, present at the time. These can include the level of stress or arousal, affective state, shape and size of the apparatus, level of lighting, etc. A complex of these cues, representing the 'state' of the animal at the time of learning, serve as the catalogue entry for the learnt avoidance response, i.e. reinstatement of some or all of these cues acts to retrieve the response. ECS prevents the laying down of these retrieval cues, but the reminder treatment which, by definition, has to be one of the relevant stimuli, helps to restore the link between the response and the test situation. The specificity of a reminder treatment can be shown by comparing passive avoidance with a spatial discrimination learning paradigm (Miller and Springer, 1973). Non-contingent footshock is an effective reminder in the former, where footshock is a feature of original learning, but not in the latter, where it is not; exposure to the original apparatus works in both instances, to reduce ECS-induced amnesia.

As an incidental point, the idea that responses are learnt in association with the 'state' of the animal at the time of learning is relevant to the time-dependent variations in memory mentioned in the last section. If learning is associated with, say, a given level of circulating corticosteroids, then the hypothesis predicts that recall will be best when the level during the retention test matches the level at original learning.

The proposition that ECS-induced retrograde amnesia is a failure of retrieval rather than of consolidation is not universally accepted. The efficacy of reminder treatments can be difficult to demonstrate clearly, and works best with a within-subject design:

Gold and King (1974) point out that the first retention test and the reminder treatment could function as additional learning experiences, as all experimental stimuli are present in some form. In support of their view they show that reminder treatments improve the test performance of animals not given ECS, but in whom only a weak 'memory' has been established by use of mild footshock on the acquisition trial. As ECS amnesia is often incomplete, there would usually be a residual memory present for the reminder treatment to work on; the reduction in amnesia observed on the retention test would then be due to additional learning rather than the reinstatement of retrieval cues.

This position would predict that the effectiveness of reminder treatments would be directly proportional to the residual memory after ECS, i.e. the weaker the ECS-induced amnesia, the more substantial the residual memory, and the more effective the additional learning. A retrieval-deficit hypothesis of ECS-induced amnesia, in which reminder treatments act by reinstating contextual retrieval cues, would predict the opposite; the more complete the amnesia, the more scope for the reinstatement of cues and the more effective the reminder treatment.

In a direct test of these two predictions, Riccio *et al.* (1979) modulated the strength of induced amnesia for passive avoidance by varying the interval between training and the amnestic agent (hypothermia, caused by immersion in cold water: experimental brain trauma can be produced by many means, including hypothermia, exposure to a lack of oxygen or increased carbon dioxide – all can result in amnesia). It has long been established that the shorter this interval, the greater the amnesia. The reminder treatment (partial re-cooling) significantly improved retention performance in the short-interval group (thirty seconds), slightly improved retention performance in the medium-interval group (five minutes), and had no effect in the long-interval group (ten minutes). Performance of control groups (no reminder treatments) indicated that the degree of amnesia did vary with the training–hypothermia interval, with the ten-minute group showing less amnesia than the others but still enough to allow for an effect of reminder treatment.

Riccio *et al.* conclude that the effectiveness of their reminder treatment was proportional to the severity of induced amnesia, i.e. was best seen when the training–hypothermia interval was short, and therefore inversely proportional to any residual memory. This would support the interpretation of the reminder effect as a reinstatement of retrieval cues rather than as a supplementation of residual memory.

Given the problems of assessing learning and memory in animals, it is unlikely that a straightforward resolution of the retrieval versus storage argument is possible (see Riccio and Richardson, 1984, for a comprehensive review). The parsimonious view that memory is in a vulnerable short-term form for a few seconds after learning has been criticized on grounds other than the reminder treatment phenomenon. Different experimenters using the same passive-avoidance paradigm with ECS produce different estimates of the duration of short-term memory, ranging from seconds to minutes (Schneider, 1976). Amnesia can apparently be produced by injecting protein synthesis inhibitor drugs some *hours* after the acquisition trial, while there is also evidence that memory is still available for a few seconds *after* an amnestic treatment; American footballers concussed in the course of a match can recall the incident for a minute or so afterwards – only later do they show complete amnesia for it, the events leading up to it, and the rest of the match (Yarnell and Lynch, 1979). This sort of observation suggests that STM cannot be obliterated by the trauma – otherwise it could not possibly be available for even a few seconds afterwards.

However, the most reliable and central finding in studies of retrograde amnesia in animals is that an ECS given immediately after learning is the best way of producing amnesia; the longer the learning–ECS interval, the less the amnesia. Whether the ECS disrupts an STM store or a cataloguing process (itself a form of consolidation), it is clear that some aspects of the memory process are vulnerable for a brief period after learning, and become less vulnerable with time. Thus the original model of a short-term process consisting of patterns of neuronal discharges merging into a long-term store consisting of structural change still holds, at least in outline.

Another facet of these animal studies bears on the relationships between different sorts of learning. The standard experiment examines amnesia for a learnt operant or instrumental response – usually passive avoidance. As the avoidance paradigm involves painful footshock, the animal also acquires various *classically conditioned* 'fear' responses. We can operationalize 'fear' in the rat by measuring defecation rates, heart-rate, or various other autonomic responses; when replaced in an area it has previously been shocked in (as on the retention test in passive-avoidance training) the animal defecates more and shows a short-lived heart-rate deceleration response (bradycardia). Defecation and bradycardia responses represent the autonomic correlates of fear or anxiety, and are classically conditioned to the stimuli present on the passive-avoidance acquisition trial. The rat learns not only to avoid (operant conditioning), but to show 'fear' (classical conditioning).

It has been shown (Springer, 1975; Miller and Kraus, 1977) that these two categories of learnt behaviour are differentially affected by ECS. At the ECS intensities adequate for producing amnesia for the operant response, the classically conditioned responses can still be present. So on the retention test the animal is placed on the platform, and immediately steps down (showing amnesia for the operant passive-avoidance response), but at the same time exhibits increased defecation and bradycardia, i.e. it has remembered that it should be 'scared', but not how to avoid the fear-inducing stimulus.

The autonomic fear responses are conditioned to the stimuli present on the acquisition trial – apparatus, footshock, etc. – and will be elicited when the animal is exposed to all or any of them. It has been suggested (Springer, 1975) that this is what happens when a reminder treatment is given, or when a first retention test is given in the within-subject design mentioned earlier. Their importance is that these consolidated classically conditioned responses, cued by the reminder treatment, may then in some way facilitate the relearning of the operant response, i.e.:

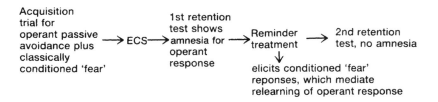

However, in a direct test of this hypothesis, Miller and Kraus (1977) used a sufficiently intense ECS to produce amnesia for both an operant response and for classically conditioned defecation and heart-rate bradycardia, i.e. on a retention test, control animals (given ECS but no reminder treatment) were completely amnesic, showing no 'fear' responses. Even then, reminder treatments were effective in restoring the operant response, and Miller and Kraus conclude that the 'reminder' phenomenon does not depend upon residual conditioned autonomic responses; the most parsimonious explanation is still that reminder treatments restore retrieval processes.

In their study, ECS-induced amnesia for conditioned defecation was also reduced by the reminder, but that for conditioned bradycardia was not. Springer (1975) had demonstrated that the ECS intensity necessary to produce amnesia for the bradycardia response was greater than that effective for defecation, which in turn was greater than that for the operant response. So overall we can differentiate between operant and classical conditioning, and between individual classically conditioned responses, on the basis of their vulnerability for ECS-induced amnesia.

This has some implications for modelling the physiological bases of memory. If, to be effective, ECS has to be more intense, it is presumably because convulsive activity has to spread to more of the brain than would normally be affected. We can therefore conclude that not only are operant and classically conditioned stimulus–response associations stored or represented in different parts of the brain, but the various classically conditioned associations are themselves stored independently of each other. This supports the evidence mentioned earlier that the neocortex, while not essential, facilitates operant learning, but is not necessary for efficient classical conditioning. There is no evidence as yet on the separable subcortical locations of bradycardia and defecation responses learnt in the course of passive avoidance training, though it may be suggestive that Thompson's work implicates the hippocampus in classical conditioning of the eyeblink reflex.

Finally, there are implications for definitions of amnesia. H.M. has a profound anterograde amnesia for some sorts of material but not others; he cannot be said to be completely amnesic. Similarly, the rat given an ECS after acquisition may be amnesic for the operant response, but still exhibit the conditioned fear response; it cannot be said to be completely amnesic. Different types of learning involve different psychological processes and involve different physiological substrates, and may be differentially affected by brain trauma.

Microphysiological approaches

We have considered some of the attempts to localize various aspects of learning and memory to particular areas and structures. Each structure is an agglomeration of many millions of neurons and their interconnecting synapses; the behavioural function of the structure will then correlate with the activity of its constituent neurons. A change in behaviour, such as learning, must involve a change in the functional state of a structure, which is to say, in the neurons making up that structure. If the hippocampus is involved in the transition from STM to LTM, then hippocampal neurons should show significant changes in activity when the transition occurs.

The search for the microphysiological correlates of learning and memory has been enduring and not particularly successful.

There are various reasons for this, which may roughly be divided into the technical and the tactical. Technically, the study of the neuron, its inter-neuronal synaptic processes and its intra-neuronal metabolic systems, is prohibitively complex. To identify and measure changes in RNA and protein formation, or growth of new synaptic connections, sophisticated biochemical and radiography techniques are employed which are inaccessible to those not trained in them; even to the biochemists who use them, results are often ambiguous or unreplicable. Because the technology is itself so complicated, and often employed by non-psychologists, the behavioural analysis is frequently rudimentary. If you are searching for changes in RNA base ratios as a correlate of learning, you choose the simplest form of 'learning', i.e. you train rats to climb a sloping wire (Hyden and Egyhazi, 1962). Only in the last decade or so have even the grosser subdivisions of learning and memory (short-term and long-term storage, consolidation versus retrieval) became generally accepted as subjects for the microphysiological approach.

Tactically, the level of physiological analysis – changes in and between individual neurons – is inappropriate for the level of behavioural analysis. The processes of learning and memory will not be confined to individual neurons, or even groups of neurons; when sensory input, short- and long-term storage, and retrieval are considered they will not even be confined to individual structures. Microphysiological analysis can only buttress models based on macrophysiological studies. The electrical activity of single hippocampal neurons may mirror the progress of classical conditioning (Thompson – see earlier in this chapter), or of behavioural habituation (Vinogradova – see Chapter 7), but our models of hippocampal function are based on relatively gross lesion and stimulation work.

That is not to say that microphysiological studies are unimportant. The deliberate use of primitive behaviour in primitive organisms (e.g. behavioural habituation in the sea-hare, Aplysia – see Chapter 7) has told us a great deal about the neuronal processes underlying elementary responses in simple nervous systems. The fact that decreased neurotransmitter release appears to mediate behavioural habituation in Aplysia may represent a fundamental feature of neuronal plasticity, and one which may operate in the mammalian brain; but variations in neurotransmitter release in one neuron will not constitute the physiological correlate of learning in mammals. It may be a part of it, but it is the combined learning-related changes in millions of neurons which will be the realistic correlate.

In an ideal world, data may accumulate at both macro- and micro-physiological levels to give a coherent account of structures and their function; we may establish that the hippocampus mediates the transition from STM to LTM, and that the physiological basis is a pattern of change in neurotransmitter release in hippocampal neurons. Both levels of analysis are necessary for a comprehensive explanation.

The single most convincing demonstration of the value of the single-cell approach within physiological psychology is the work of Hubel and Wiesel on neurons in the visual cortex (see Chapter 4). By identifying 'feature detectors', i.e. neurons responding to individual properties of stimuli such as orientation, they showed how visual perception is constructed step-by-step as information is processed through the brain's visual pathways. It may be that 'feature detectors' exist in systems other than sensory pathways, although the problem is then to define what would constitute a 'feature' in, say, a passive-avoidance learning paradigm. Optimistically, one could say that habituating neurons (Chapter 7) are coding the feature 'novel or familiar'.

Progress is being made in this area, in the face of daunting methodological problems. It is one thing to identify neurons coding for novelty, but quite another to control for the possibility that other groups of the brain's 15×10^9 cells can also code for novelty. It is in the accumulation of data from many laboratories using different levels of investigation that the neural bases of, e.g., novelty and familiarity will be established. One elementary question is whether there is just one such 'processor', handling the property of 'novel or familiar' for all stimuli regardless of modality, or whether each modality – visual, auditory, somatosensory, etc. – has its own. This bears on a possible fallacy in the approach to brain function which expects behavioural functions to be localized, whether at the level of speech comprehension in Wernicke's area, or 'novel versus familiar' in individual neurons. Such 'microphrenology' may turn out to be as misplaced as the bumps-on-the-head approach of the nineteenth-century phrenologists; but, as discussed in the last section, most brain scientists realize the danger but accept localization of function as a practical approach which has served them well up to the present time.

Microphysiological approaches to learning and memory have taken as a basic assumption the idea that more or less permanent changes in behaviour as a result of experience (learning) will be embodied in similar changes in neurons and inter-neuronal connections somewhere in the brain. The precise nature of these physiological correlates is unknown.

Initially, learning will probably be represented by altered electrical activity – a popular candidate for the neuronal bases of learning and memory has always been the formation of new bioelectric circuits in the brain (see, e.g., Hebb, 1958, and his concept of 'cell assemblies'; or Ungar, 1974). Such circuits could be formed in several ways. New synaptic connections could be made, linking formerly independent neurons (it was once thought that the brain and its constituent neurons, once mature, were inflexible; it is now known that if a pathway is severed, then the axons of a neighbouring intact pathway will branch to replace the lost synaptic connections, i.e. neurons can show anatomical plasticity). Neurotransmitter release at existing synapses may be increased or decreased, activating or deactivating neuronal circuits. On a more molecular level, there may be increases or decreases in the sensitivity of the pre- or post-synaptic membrane to the neurotransmitter that is released, thus affecting the flow of impulses across the synapse. Finally, unique molecules, synthesized as a direct result of the learning experience, may in some way 'label' synapses, directing impulses through circuits in a manner analogous to that of directional signposts at road junctions (Ungar, 1974).

All of these possible mechanisms for producing new bioelectric circuits correlated with learning involve protein synthesis within neurons. Intra-neuronal metabolism is controlled by the genetic material contained in the cell's chromosomes within the cell nucleus, i.e. DNA. The executive function is performed by molecules of RNA, which pick up commands from the physically fixed and stable DNA, move from nucleus into the cytoplasm, and there organize the synthesis of new proteins from the raw material, amino-acids. New patterns of neuronal activity require specific changes in protein synthesis, which in turn will require changes in RNA. An early and enduring hypothesis of the molecular basis of learning and memory therefore implicated an alteration in neuronal RNA consequent upon learning leading to altered patterns of protein synthesis within the neuron. (It should be noted that RNA structure is ultimately determined by the stable DNA in the nucleus, and changes in RNA should be reflected in some change in the functional state of nuclear DNA. This step, learning $\rightarrow$ DNA, has never been satisfactorily modelled.)

There have been various approaches attempting to identify the role, if any, of RNA and protein synthesis in memory. I wish to consider briefly two of the more enduring ones: firstly, the effects of protein synthesis inhibition upon memory, and secondly, the transfer of memory via brain extracts.

There are several drugs which, by interfering with RNA or amino-acids, prevent the synthesis of proteins in cells. These drugs – cycloheximide, acetocycloheximide, puromycin, etc. – can also produce amnesia in animals if injected before or shortly after a learning trial, suggesting that protein synthesis is indeed necessary for consolidation of learning. There are, however, severe problems with this apparently straightforward approach.

Many drugs induce amnesia, via the phenomenon of 'state-dependency' rather than via any effect on protein synthesis. This phenomenon occurs when material learnt under the drug state cannot be retrieved when the effect of the drug wears off. Only when the drug is reinjected does the animal show 'learning'. On the anecdotal level, behaviour while under the influence of alcohol is notoriously difficult to recall when sober. More systematically, rats can be trained to turn left in a T-maze after injection of amphetamine, and to the right after injection of the anticholinergic drug scopolamine. The responses are specific, or conditioned, to the drug state (Overton, 1966), and whether a trained rat turns left or right depends only on what drug it is given. Interestingly, the training can show limited transfer; if injected with another anticholinergic, e.g.

atropine, the rat turns right, while another amphetamine derivative produces a left turn.

State-dependency can be a powerful determinant in behaviour. Animals given passive avoidance training under the influence of scopolamine show amnesia if tested when undrugged, but evidence of learning if tested after another injection of scopolamine; the transfer of training is from drug state to drug state, and not from drug state to non-drug state. Any drug study involving a drug state → non-drug state transfer lends itself to a general state-dependency interpretation, rather than to more specific effects. Fortunately for the protein-synthesis hypothesis, amnesic effects of the inhibitor drugs have also been demonstrated when they are injected immediately *after* training, a procedure which reduces the possibility of state-dependency complications as the training and testing are both under non-drug conditions.

The central criticism of this area lies in the non-specificity of the drugs' actions. Protein synthesis is basic to the survival of the body, and every cell in the body is a protein factory, constantly metabolizing new and replacement proteins for tissue repair or to maintain their normal functions. In the brain, the turnover of chemicals is stupendous; it has been estimated that the whole of the brain's acetylcholine is resynthesized every few hours. A protein-synthesis inhibitor injected into the peripheral bloodstream can potentially affect all of these metabolic activities, and such a widespread interference could easily, as a side-effect, disrupt performance on a learning task.

Some of these problems can be eliminated by injecting the drug directly into the brain; even then, protein synthesis inhibition can be widespread and severe (Barondes and Cohen, 1957, reviewed in Barondes, 1970, show that around 80 per cent inhibition is necessary to affect memory in mice). Given that normal neuronal function is dependent upon constant synthetic activity, it is unsurprising that drastic interruption of protein synthesis in the brain interferes with learning and memory. However, with increasingly sophisticated techniques, the effects of these potent drugs are being localized – both anatomically and pharmacologically. Eichenbaum (1975) found that small amounts of cycloheximide injected into the hippocampus, amygdala or postero-lateral thalamus, immediately after training, disrupted memory; injections into the reticular formation, antero-lateral thalamus, or neocortex were ineffective. Following this up, Berman *et al.* (1978) investigated the effects of cycloheximide (one, ten or twenty micrograms) applied to the amygdala, frontal cortex, or internal capsule, on memory for passive avoidance in rats. The paradigm was standard, with water-deprived animals allowed to enter a goal box and drink from a water spout. At a given amount they received a footshock; when retested, control animals refuse to enter the goal box. However, animals injected with ten or twenty micrograms of cycloheximide into the amygdala immediately post-footshock showed amnesia for the passive avoidance response when tested twenty-four or forty-eight hours later. A group injected thirty minutes before training were also amnesic, but injections twelve hours after training were ineffective, as were all injections into other brain sites whether immediately post-footshock or not.

Simultaneous electrical recording and autoradiography established that the effective injections of cycloheximide did not induce abnormal electrical activity (i.e. they were not disrupting memory formation by inducing non-specific seizures), but did inhibit protein synthesis significantly in the amygdala, and less dramatically in some other brain regions. The authors conclude that protein inhibition in the amygdala was responsible for the amnesic effects of the drug.

There were other interesting observations. All groups, even those apparently amnesic at twenty-four hours, showed normal retention when tested thirty minutes after footshock and injection (i.e. when protein synthesis inhibition would have begun). On the other hand, the drug was not active twenty-four hours after footshock and injection, implying that the amygdala-injected animals were amnesic at this time in the presence of normal protein synthesis.

These results imply that the short-term process responsible for retention at thirty minutes is not dependent upon protein synthesis. However, protein synthesis at this time is necessary for the consolidation of learning into a form in which it can be recalled twenty-four hours later. The similarity to the models of memory based upon ECS-induced amnesia is obvious; it is even conceivable that both manipulations operate via the same mechanisms, as the effects of ECS on protein synthesis are unknown. Equally, the dispute on whether ECS-induced amnesia represents storage or retrieval problems applies to cycloheximide-induced amnesia, and is similarly unresolved.

While accepting that cycloheximide is not a 'clean' drug in that it blocks cholinergic synapses and inhibits some neuro-transmitter enzymes, it is hard not to agree with Berman *et al.* that protein synthesis within amygdala neurons is necessary for the storage and/or recall of new information. The work of Eichenbaum and others implicates hippocampal and thalamic sites, suggesting that Thompson's model of the brain systems underlying passive avoidance learning (see p. 177) is quite realistic. Unfortunately we are no clearer as to purpose of protein synthesis in learning. Berman *et al.* favour the setting up of new neuronal networks via synaptic growth, changes in the pattern of neurotransmitter release, or alterations in membrane sensitivity, ideas which have been around for some time.

A more specific hypothesis on the role of proteins in memory is that unique molecules are synthesized when learning occurs, which then serve to 'code' neural pathways – the 'signpost' approach mentioned earlier. This hypothesis is particularly associated with the work of Ungar in the field of memory transfer via brain extracts. Since its beginning in the work of McConnell and Jacobson in the 1950s this field of research has generated massive enthusiasm in its supporters and massive scepticism in everyone else. The early controversies centred on the problem of 'learning' in the flatworm, and whether the curling response could be genuinely classically conditioned. When rats were used as subjects, with the brains of trained animals being extracted, mashed, and injected into naive recipients, the entire feasibility of the enterprise came under fire. If learning resulted in alterations to RNA molecules in the brain, then it is theoretically possible to extract such molecules. However, when injected into the bloodstream of the naive recipient, such large molecules cannot pass the blood–brain barrier (a membrane lining the walls of cerebral blood vessels, designed to prevent the passage of large molecules into the brain cells). Even if they entered brain tissue, one then has to explain how these RNA molecules diffuse into the appropriate neurons in the appropriate brain structure, become incorporated into the cellular metabolism, and enable the naive brain to exhibit 'learning'. It all seems very unlikely.

The whole enterprise relies on the demonstration that 'memory' can be transferred in this way; the naive recipient must show 'learning' when compared with a completely naive control. Reviews by Chapouthier (1973; 1983) and Ungar (1974), while cautious, point out that positive results have been reported in over a hundred papers from around forty different laboratories, sufficient to establish the phenomenon of 'memory transfer'. The key problem is replicability; Ungar himself points out that a successful transfer experiment has never been replicated under identical conditions of training, preparing the brain extract, subjects, etc. The phenomenon, in that sense, is elusive, with the learned behaviour transferred to the recipient being less pronounced and more variable than that shown by the originally trained donor animal.

It was noticed early on that memory transfer decreased as the purity of the RNA extracted from the donor brain increased. This shifted attention from RNA as the memory molecule, and led Ungar to search for and to find a large molecule (macromolecule) in extracted brains that appeared to be responsible for the transfer of passive-avoidance learning to naive recipients. This macromolecule, a polypeptide (for the relations between amino-acids, peptides, and proteins, see p. 261), was called scotophobin (fear of the dark) as it coded for avoidance of the dark compartment in Ungar's standard passive-avoidance paradigm. To confirm the status of scotophobin as a specific memory molecule, Ungar and others have synthesized it and shown that it facilitates dark-avoidance learning in naive rats (Ungar *et al.* 1972; see Chapouthier, 1983, for a review). Subsequently Ungar and his group have isolated and identified polypeptides coding for habituation to a tone, and passive avoidance in goldfish to either blue or green compartments, although much of this work remains to be replicated and confirmed. He has also shown that 'memory molecules' are remarkably specific, with dark-avoidance memory not transferring to step-down passive avoidance.

Ungar uses the signpost analogy to explain how memory molecules work. During dark-avoidance training, scotophobin is synthesized in the brain and attaches itself to certain synapses. Its presence influences the flow of impulses through these synapses, and effectively creates new bioelectric circuits; these are the substrate of learning and memory.

Chemical labelling of synapses by molecular markers such as scotophobin is an attractive idea. There are potentially millions of polypeptides, sufficient to code each learning experience. Whether this actually happens, though, is still in the realms of speculation. There are many physiological psychologists who treat with scepticism all experimental work in this area, and the problems of replicability and reliability mean that no one piece of experimental evidence is decisive. In many ways we are left with our original hypotheses. Learning and memory must involve changes within and between neurons. Such changes will in their turn involve RNA, DNA, and protein synthesis, and work such as that of Berman *et al.* confirms the hypothesis. But quite what the nature of the microphysiological change is (synpatic growth, synthesis of a specific molecular marker, etc.) remains to be determined; and this leaves aside the analysis of learning and memory into their component psychological processes, each of which probably involves its own distinctive microphysiological correlate.

7 Habituation – attention and memory

Introduction

A cardboard cut-out hawk is flown over chaffinch territory; the chaffinches' 'mob' the supposed predator, but over repeated trials the mobbing response dies away as the chaffinches realize that a cardboard cut-out hawk is not too dangerous. A human subject sits in a soundproof room, strapped to a chair, with recording electrodes attached to his hands and headphones over his ears, under instructions to remain perfectly still and try to relax; after a few minutes, a single, unexpected tone is sounded in his ear, and a galvanic skin response (GSR; or the skin conductance response, SCR; see Chapter 9) is recorded from the electrodes. As the tones are repeated, the SCR dies away.

On the sea-bed sits Aplysia californica, the sea-hare. As a mollusc, Aplysia has gills, attached to a gill mantle. When a puff of water is directed at the mantle, it is withdrawn, protectively; as the puffs of water are repeated, so the gill-withdrawal response fades away.

A rat is placed in a novel maze. At first he explores enthusiastically; as time passes, he becomes less active and finally goes to sleep in what is now a familiar environment.

These are a few examples of response habituation. Defined as a waning of a response over repeated presentations of the same stimulus (Harris, 1943), habituation can be shown to occur at all levels of the animal kingdom, from protozoa upwards, and at all levels within an organism, i.e. behavioural responses right down to the activity of single neurons.

Responses which habituate are to stimuli which are initially significant to the organism, and which therefore demand to be 'attended to'; once they are assessed as being harmless and irrelevant, the response habituates. Novelty is often cited as a potent stimulus property for producing habituating responses – the rat in the maze explores, presumably because the maze is novel, and ceases exploring (habituates) when it has become familiar. More commonly, the stimulus is not in itself novel, but appears under novel circumstances; we have all heard tones at one time or another, and Aplysia has felt puffs of water before, but we and Aplysia still respond to the stimulus if, for instance, it appears out of nowhere. Subsequent presentations of tone and water-puffs are no longer surprising or deserving of 'attention'.

Some stimuli are intrinsically significant, and responses to these do not habituate. Biological relevance is often involved, for instance in the case of the chaffinches, where real predators must be responded to every time. Consummatory responses to food, water, mates, do not habituate. At a more cognitive level, overhearing your own name being mentioned at a party elicits an orienting response which does not habituate; your own name is highly familiar, but also highly significant.

I keep using words like 'attention', and 'orienting', even if they are in quotation marks. The reason for the quotation marks is the occurrence of habituating responses in lower animals like Aplysia, and in single cells in, for instance, the cat hippocampus. Does Aplysia 'attend'? Do individual neurons 'orient'?

Over the last twenty years there have been two major approaches to the study of habituation. The Eastern Europeans, led by Sokolov (building on the original observations of Pavlov on orienting responses in his classical conditioning paradigm), have developed the theoretical and empirical investigation of habituation of autonomic and behavioural orienting in humans and higher animals; Thompson, Groves and Spencer, in the United States, have evolved a more comprehensive theory to include all instances of habituation from amoeba up to humans.

Sokolov's approach has encouraged the use of autonomic

responses (e.g. SCR to tones) to study attentional processes in man, where the simple equation is that the presence of a stimulus-specific SCR implies attention, while absence of an SCR implies habituation or lack of attention. If pathologies of attention are suspected, as, for instance, in schizophrenia, then this technique can be of great value.

The approach of Thompson *et al.* has concentrated on the precise characteristics of response habituation, with less emphasis on the psychological considerations. Their aim has been to define a number of parameters (or characteristics) which, if present, serve to define habituation. These parameters can, in theory, be investigated in any instance of response decrement, and, if present, that response can be considered genuinely to habituate. So it is not enough to observe the gradual fading away of the gill-withdrawal response in Aplysia for it to be called habituation; ideally it should be shown to possess the parametric features of habituation as defined by Thompson *et al.*

Before considering each of these approaches in detail, an alternative view of habituation should be considered. The key feature of a habituating response is that it represents the result of stimulus processing; the orienting response to a simple tone habituates, but if the frequency of the tone is changed, the response returns. Unlike fatigue processes, habituation leaves the response system intact but inhibited. The basis of this inhibition is that a given stimulus is similar to the preceding stimulus, and for the similarity to be assessed some representation of preceding stimuli must be kept. The foundation of habituation is that incoming stimuli are compared with previous stimuli, and the closer the similarity the more the orienting response will be inhibited (i.e. habituate). A mismatch between stimuli results in disinhibition of the orienting response.

So, besides representing mechanisms of attention or orienting, habituation represents information storage, i.e. memory. As an example of a change in response level on the basis of experience, habituation may therefore be seen as a simple form of learning.

This analysis applies to all examples of habituation, so that even the lowly sea-hare is demonstrating a form of elementary learning. As some of these primitive organisms have very limited nervous systems, i.e. systems in which every cell can be identified and recorded from, they are ideal subjects for studying the electrophysiology and neurochemistry of learning. Whether the results of such a study can be extrapolated to complex learning in complex organisms, however, is arguable, and was briefly considered in the previous chapter.

Models of habituation – Sokolov

Sokolov (1963; 1975) described the orienting response (OR) to mild, novel (in the sense of unexpected) stimuli. It consisted of a pattern of behavioural and autonomic changes, such as physically turning towards the stimulus, pricking up your ears (rare in humans, but often seen in cats), EEG desynchronization, occurrence of skin conductance responses, heart-rate deceleration followed by acceleration, and constriction of blood-vessels in the extremities to ensure the supply to brain and heart. The overall pattern is one of phasic (i.e. momentary) central and peripheral arousal.

With repeated presentations of the stimulus, the OR habituates, but returns if the characteristics of the stimulus alter significantly, leading Sokolov to suggest that comparison of stimulus characteristics is the basis of habituation. His model of the OR and its habituation has three major components (see Fig. 7.1): the incoming stimulus is analysed at the cortex, the results of the analysis are passed to the hippocampus for comparison with the stored representations of previous stimuli, and if a mismatch or discrepancy occurs the OR is elicited via the reticular formation. If the incoming stimulus matches previous input, the hippocampus inhibits the reticular formation and the OR does not occur, i.e. the OR habituates.

Thus we have a relatively simple stimulus – comparator model of habituation, which is intuitively appealing and for which there is substantial evidence. Habituation can be observed to occur to the semantic properties of verbal stimuli. Siddle (1978) has shown that an SCR orienting response to town names habituates; if habituated subjects are then tested

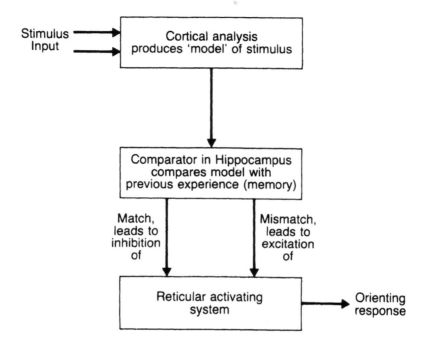

Figure 7.1   *Simplified version of Sokolov's model of the orienting response*

with the name of a car the OR recovers, but if tested with another, different, town name there is no recovery, i.e. the subjects have habituated to the semantic category, town names. The reverse procedure also works – subjects can be habituated to the semantic category, car names, and then show OR recovery if tested with a town name but not if tested with another car name. Such semantic habituation must involve cortical analysis of stimulus features.

Direct evidence for hippocampal involvement in habituation of the OR comes from the work of Vinogradova (1975), who records from single neurons in the cat's brain. These respond with bursts of activity to novel stimuli, and habituate if the stimulus is presented repeatedly, i.e. an analogy at the neuronal level of what can be observed at the behavioural level.

Other regions of the brain demonstrate some response plasticity (particularly the amygdala), but none to such a degree as the hippocampus. The hippocampus also receives multiple sensory inputs from the cortex, which would suit its role as a general stimulus-comparator.

The reticular formation is clearly important in elicitation of the OR. Stimulation of the reticular formation produces EEG activation via ascending pathways, and various peripheral components of the arousal response via the autonomic control centres which are embedded in it. Wester (1971) has produced behavioural orienting in the cat (orienting which appears identical with that seen naturally) by stimulating the thalamic component of the ascending reticular system. A slight complication is that the brainstem reticular formation also contains plastic neurons, which show response habituation to repeated stimuli (Groves and Lynch, 1972) in a similar fashion to hippocampal neurons. It may be that the distinction between the hippocampal comparator and the reticular OR generator is not as clear-cut as we might wish, but overall Sokolov's model does appear to have a sound basis in what we know of the brain.

The role of the hippocampus in OR habituation reflects a general view of this structure as being involved in attentional processes and the control of inhibition (see p. 213). Bagshaw and Benzies (1968), recording skin conductance responses to neutral tones in monkeys, showed that hippocampal lesions apparently prevented habituation of the OR, while amygdala lesions prevented any elicitation of the OR in the first place. An intriguing parallel has been drawn between the SCR characteristics of these two groups of monkeys – one group respond but do not habituate, while the other do not respond – and two groups of schizophrenics (Gruzelier and Venables, 1974). Recording SCR responses to neutral tones, these workers were able to differentiate a group of schizophrenics who responded but who did not habituate, and another group who did not respond. Using the animal data, the conclusion was drawn that responders reflect some sort of hippocampal malfunction, and non-responders some sort of amygdala deficit.

Although these findings are still subject to much critical debate (e.g. some normal control subjects are non-responders, while even schizophrenic non-responders may produce ORs if asked to *count* the tones, i.e. if the tones are given attentional significance; the problem of controlling for chronic drug treatment has still to be solved), they do represent one of the few attempts to integrate constructively human and animal data.

Models of habituation – Thompson and Spencer

Thompson and Spencer (1966) and Groves and Thompson (1970) take a phylogenetic perspective on habituation. The problem was to integrate such diverse examples of response habituation as gill-withdrawal in Aplysia, exploration and acoustic startle in the rat, and reflex leg extension in the cat. Their solution, based on empirical observations, was to list a set of parametric characteristics which would serve to identify an instance of habituation. These characteristics are presented below.

1 If a stimulus elicits a response, repeated presentation of the stimulus will lead to a decrement in the response.
2 If the stimulus is withheld, the response recovers over time ('spontaneous recovery').
3 If repeated series of habituation training and spontaneous recovery are given, habituation becomes faster.
4 The more rapid the frequency of stimulation, the more rapid the habituation.
5 The weaker the stimuli, the more rapid is habituation; strong stimuli may not habituate.
6 Effects of habituation training may go beyond asymptotic response level. This would be shown by a slower rate of spontaneous recovery.
7 Habituation to a stimulus will exhibit generalization to similar stimuli.
8 Presentation of another, strong, stimulus, will produce response recovery; this is referred to as dishabituation.
9 With repeated presentation of a dishabituating stimulus, the amount of dishabituation produced habituates, i.e. habituation of dishabituation.

Thus we have an operational definition of habituation – any response which fulfils the stated requirements qualifies as an instance of habituation, without regard to type of organism or level of response (behavioural or neuronal).

The major advantage of this approach relative to Sokolov's is the potential integration of all the varied instances of response habituation into a single theoretical framework. Sokolov's emphasis on OR habituation in complex organisms eliminates from consideration animals with no cortex, hippocampus, or reticular formation (e.g. Aplysia), and responses recorded at, for instance, the neuronal level (although he might incorporate single-unit data as evidence for his model). There is no particular reason why the model should be inclusive of all responses; indeed, it seems obvious that OR habituation to semantic stimuli in humans bears little resemblance to habituation of the gill-withdrawal response in Aplysia. We might see the Thompson and Spencer approach as fundamentally empirical; to establish the nine criteria for even one response involves a massive amount of empirical research, but at least the data collected from various responses would be systematic and comparable. And if the comparisons show substantial similarities between very different responses, then we can start theorizing about a ubiquitous phenomenon called 'habituation'. Sufficient empirical data has accumulated for several responses to be classified as habituating responses. These include hindlimb extension to electrical stimulation in the cat (Thompson and Spencer, 1966), the gill-withdrawal response in Aplysia (Castellucci and Kandel, 1976) and the startle response of the rat to a very loud noise (Davis, 1972). Several single-neuron studies have, surprisingly, also demonstrated the parametric characteristics of habituation; these include neurons in the brainstem reticular formation (Groves and Lynch, 1972) and in the frog spinal cord (Farel *et al.*, 1973).

It is obvious that the two approaches – Sokolov, and Thompson *et al.* – are very different in style and aim, but are not directly in conflict until we consider the proposed mechanisms proposed to underlie habituation. Sokolov's is essentially a single-process model, with observed habituation to a stimulus depending only upon the cortical-hippocampal-reticular hab-

ituation pathway; Groves and Thompson specifically suggest a
dual-process model, with observed habituation reflecting the
final outcome of two independent processes.

These processes are 'habituation' and 'sensitization'. Any
stimulus has a tendency, they suggest, to induce a decrease in
responding via an habituation pathway, and a tendency to
induce an increase in responding via a sensitization or arousal
system. If a loud tone is sounded, we jump. If it is repeatedly
presented, we may gradually habituate to it; however, if it is too
loud, we continue to jump. In this latter case, we are fully
familiar with the characteristics of the stimulus (i.e. we have
technically habituated to it), but the loudness of the stimulus
activates our non-specific sensitization system (i.e. the reticular
formation) so much that we continue responding (see Fig. 7.2).

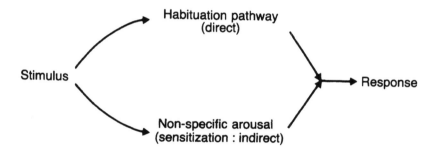

Figure 7.2   *Response habituation as a product of habituating and
sensitizing pathways*

Sensitization has masked any habituation that may have occurred; using this approach we have to distinguish between *observed*
response habituation, which represents internal processes of
sensitization and habituation, and the *inferred* internal process
of habituation.

There are various situations in which the dual-process
theory has proved useful. Individuals vary in their responsiveness to even mild stimuli, and the same person will vary from
day to day – clearly, response level can be determined by our

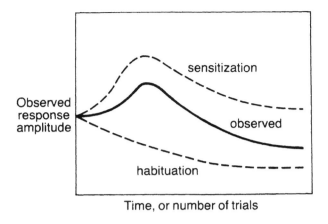

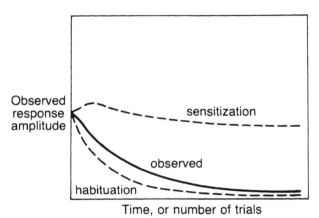

Figure 7.3 *Possible relations between observed habituation and the theoretical processes of habituation and sensitization (based on Groves and Thompson, 1970)*

non-specific arousal state. The range of observed response habituation curves is infinite, from the classic exponential decline to an initial increase followed by a decrease (see Fig. 7.3); these curves can be explained by postulating different mixes of sensitization and habituation.

The major stimulus variable influencing sensitization is intensity. The stronger the stimulus, the greater the non-specific arousal, and the less likely we are to see response habituation. Mild stimuli induce very little sensitization, and consequently elicit maximal habituation; it should be remembered that Sokolov's paradigm involves orienting responses to such mild stimuli, while some of the animal work involves very intense stimulation (e.g. the acoustic startle response in the rat).

An experimental finding suggested by Groves and Thompson to discriminate between the dual-process model and Sokolov's single-process model in favour of the former is the 'incremental stimulus intensity effect'. Reported by them using the hindlimb leg flexion in the cat and by Davis and Wagner (1969) using acoustic startle responding in the rat, the effect is diagrammatically portrayed in Figure 7.4. Habituation to a test stimulus is greatest when it comes at the end of a series of stimuli of gradually increasing intensity, compared with when it comes at the end of a series of constant intensity tones. The latter should be more amenable to the building of a stimulus model, as the stimuli are unchanging; however, the incremental series allows for the dissipation of low levels of sensitization induced by the early stimuli, and consequently habituation predominates at the end.

Davis (1972; 1974a,b) has studied acoustic startle in the rat intensively, and, quite apart from the incremental stimulus intensity effect, has shown the value of the dual-process model in explaining his results. The amplitude of responding systematically depends upon the level of masking white noise in the chamber before startle tones are presented – high levels of noise arouse the animal, making him 'jumpier'. Whether habituation is observed or not depends upon both absolute tone intensity and tone intensity relative to the background white noise (i.e. signal-to-noise ratio).

Systematic variations in startle amplitude are, at the moment, best explained in terms of habituation and sensitization processes, and not in terms of a Sokolov-style model. But given the very different approaches, it may not be reasonable to compare the two models.

I would suggest that the approach chosen depends upon the problem you are investigating. No one would deny that arousal level affects response amplitude, but if the central problem is to analyse the psychological function of habituation, then arousal can be controlled and then ignored. The habituation of a brainstem-mediated reflex such as acoustic startle involves the use of stimuli which are very loud and arousing, but not very interesting. Habituation to semantic categories utilizes stimuli which are not arousing, but very interesting; one can quickly see how refinements could be introduced to investigate other aspects of complex information processing in humans. On the other hand, to study the neuroanatomical and neurochemical substrates of habituation necessitates the use of animal models (see next section).

In an integration of human and animal approaches, Wagner (e.g. Wagner and Pfautz, 1978) introduced a paradigm for recording autonomic orienting responses in rabbits. The value of autonomic measures is that they are much more sensitive than skeletal responses such as startle, so mild stimuli can be used to elicit reflexive orienting, and direct parallels can be drawn with data on the human SCR, also an autonomic orienting response.

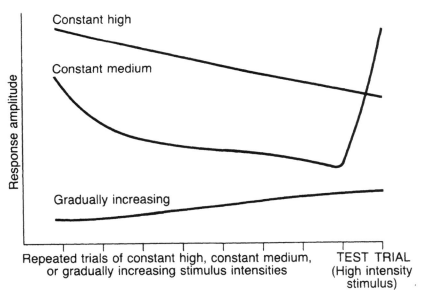

Figure 7.4   *Incremental stimulus intensity effect. Habituation shown in a test trial using a high-intensity stimulus is greatest when it comes at the end of a gradually increasing series than at the end of a series of constant high or constant medium stimuli*

Wagner uses a vasomotor constriction response, recorded from blood-vessels in the rabbit's ear (the technique is suited to rabbits, who have big ears; skin conductance activity can be recorded from animals, e.g. rats and monkeys, but the recordings are usually contaminated by movement artefacts). Whitlow (1975) has shown that the vasoconstrictive response to presentation of neutral tones habituates over repeated presentations, and recovers if tone frequency is altered, i.e. it is stimulus specific. If the inter-stimulus interval is extended to 150 seconds, habituation does not occur; as Wagner and Whitlow believe that observed habituation is dependent upon the comparison of successive stimuli in the rabbit's short-term memory, then the maximum inter-stimulus interval at which habituation is observed may represent the duration of STM (i.e. as habituation is produced by comparing one stimulus (S_1) with the next (S_2), then the representation of S_1 must be held in STM until S_2 comes along; if the S_1–S_2 interval is longer than about 100 seconds, then the representation of S_1 in STM decays before S_2 is presented, and habituation cannot occur).

Human STM has a limited capacity, with incoming stimuli displacing previous input when STM is 'full'. If habituation relies upon the simultaneous representations of S_1 and S_2 in STM, then irrelevant stimuli introduced between them might satiate STM and displace S_1 before S_2 is presented, even though the absolute S_1–S_2 interval is less than the duration of STM. Whitlow has demonstrated this effect; irrelevant stimuli such as a flashing light, a mild electro-tactile stimulus, etc., if presented between two identical tones S_1 and S_2, will reduce the amount of habituation shown to S_2, relative to a control condition in which the S_1–S_2 interval is unfilled.

Although needing replication by other laboratories, these findings do suggest ways in which orienting and habituation in animals and humans may be accommodated within the 'information-processing' approach of contemporary cognitive psychology. The questions being asked concern the psychological function of the orienting response and its habituation.

Physiological substrates

Alternative questions can be aimed at the physiological substrates of habituation. We have seen how Sokolov's model details the various structures involved in the OR and its habituation, and the difficulty it would have coping with habituation in lower organisms who do not possess a hippocampus. They do have primitive nervous systems, though, and the physiological bases of habituation in something like Aplysia may be analysed down to the individual neuron. Some reflexive behaviours in vertebrates also involve simple neuronal networks (e.g. Farel's work on spinal reflexes in the frog), and again the bases of the habituation process may be observed in a single neuron. For both Aplysia (Castellucci and Kandel, 1976) and the frog spinal reflex (Farel *et al.*, 1973), the physiological change correlated with observed response habituation is a decrease in the amount of a neurotransmitter released into the synapse. This is not just a case of the pre-synaptic neuron running out of neurotransmitter, as the response returns in full if the stimulus is altered.

Habituation in these simple neuronal systems is an example of response plasticity, or learning. The basis of this learning appears to be the synaptic release of neurotransmitters; and we saw in Chapter 6 how similar ideas may be applied to the complex learning of more complex animals.

Habituation in organisms with highly evolved central nervous systems is much harder to pin down, although some immediate general statements can be made. To emphasize the distinction between habituation of the OR in humans and of acoustic startle in the rat, the latter has been shown to be primarily a brainstem reflex. The pathways involved run from the ear via the auditory nerve to the inferior colliculus in the midbrain, and then descend down through the brainstem reticular formation to the spinal cord and out to the skeletal muscles. The OR to mild stimlui appears to be a forebrain-mediated reflex, although the final organization of the motor response probably occurs in the brainstem reticular formation.

As mentioned previously, Vinogradova has shown that the firing rate of hippocampal cells correlates with habituation of the OR in cats, and so supports Sokolov's suggestion that the hippocampus is the site of the stimulus comparator essential for habituation to occur. This is in accord with the large body of work involving the hippocampus in the general regulation of behavioural inhibition.

I have pointed out the view of habituation as an example of response plasticity, or learning. It also represents the active inhibition of responding as the stimulus loses its initial significance; i.e. the response is elicited by the first stimulus presentation, but then diminishes (or is inhibited) with repeated presentations, only to recover (or to be disinhibited) if the stimulus changes.

This view of habituation as inhibition is not incompatible with the view of habituation as a simple learning process; the subject is learning to inhibit responding on the basis of experience. However, it does allow habituation to be classified with other examples of behavioural inhibition, e.g. passive avoidance, where the animal learns not to respond in order to avoid punishment, or extinction, where the animal gradually ceases to respond as he is no longer being reinforced.

As described in Chapter 6, Douglas (1967; 1975) has been in the forefront of attempts to associate the hippocampus with the control of behavioural inhibition. He characterizes the behavioural effects of hippocampal lesions in terms of a loss of the normal inhibitory control of responding; so lesioned animals are slower to habituate (e.g. when exploring a novel environment), they over-respond during the extinction of operant behaviours, and are poor at learning passive-avoidance tasks as they cannot inhibit the punished response. Particularly convincing is the demonstration that hippocampal rats are actually better than controls in performing tasks in which inhibitory tendencies interfere with efficient behaviour, such as active avoidance (p. 171).

Several authors (Carlton, 1969; Douglas, 1975) have pointed out the similarities between the effects of hippocampal lesions and the effects of anticholinergic drugs. These latter block cholinergic receptors, so reducing activity in cholinergic pathways. One major cholinergic pathway in the brain (see Chapter 3) runs from the septal nucleus to the hippocampus, and has a major role in controlling hippocampal electrical activity. A blockade of cholinergic receptors in the hippocampus might therefore be equivalent to a functional lesion, and this would explain the similar behavioural effects of anticholinergic drugs like scopolamine and of hippocampal lesions. However, other pathways (e.g. the dorsal noradrenergic bundle, and also the central serotonin system – see Chapter 3) have also been implicated in the control of behavioural inhibition.

Despite the evidence for a role for the hippocampus in behavioural inhibition, other ideas have been put forward; we have met some of them already (Chapter 6), and will meet others in subsequent chapters. However, as part of its involvement in the control of inhibition, the hippocampus appears to mediate the habituation of orienting responses in humans, and of exploratory and orienting responses in complex animals. The brainstem reticular formation is concerned in the organization and production of the orienting response, which, as Sokolov points out, involves phasic peripheral arousal. If intense stimuli are used, arousal becomes a significant factor in response amplitude (along the lines of the dual-process model), and may represent a greater invovlement of the reticular formation. Groves and Lynch (1972) have suggested that the brainstem reticular formation is the site of both sensitization and habituation, as it contains neurons which increase firing with stimulus presentation ('sensitizing neurons'), and neurons which decrease firing with stimulus presentation ('habituating neurons'). These latter type of neurons resemble those identified by Vinogradova in the hippocampus.

At this stage it does seem clear that if the habituation of single-neuron activity reflects the involvement of a structure in behavioural habituation, then several structures immediately suggest themselves. The reticular formation, the hippocampus, and the amygdala all contain such neurons. The hippocampus we have already considered in some detail, and the importance of the amygdala (Bagshaw and Benzies, 1968) and the thalamus (Wester, 1971) for elicitation of the orienting reflex has been mentioned.

Wester's findings are particularly interesting. By using high-frequency electrical stimulation of various sites within the thalamus, he has obtained behavioural orienting in the un-anaesthetized cat. The thalamus is a complex structure (see Chapter 2), with many identifiable nuclei. Some of these (the sensory relay nuclei) receive inputs from the classical sensory pathways, and convey this sensory information on to the cerebral cortex; others (the intralaminar nuclei) appear to be an extension of the brainstem reticular activating system. Orienting responses elicited from the sensory relay nuclei habituate with repeated electrical stimulation, while the OR from the intralaminar nuclei does not habituate. However, this non-habituating response can be converted into a habituating response if the link between the intralaminar nuclei and the brainstem reticular formation is broken by a lesion at midbrain level. Wester concludes that the lesion interrupts a non-habituating pathway from thalamus to the brainstem (where the final orienting response is organized), although admitting that ascending fibres may also be involved.

Whatever the precise details, the experiment does support the distinction between elicitation of an orienting response and its habituation. Some structures will be involved in immediate stimulus registration and analysis (in which the orienting response presumably plays a part – 'what is it?'), while others will be involved in assessing the longer-term relevance of the stimulus ('is it important?'). In Sokolov's model, these functions are carried out by the cerebral cortex and the hippocampus respectively, with the integrated response being organized and produced in the reticular formation. Some of the evidence reviewed in this chapter supports the involvement of these structures, while other findings implicate other areas, such as the amygdala and thalamus.

I have suggested that the Thompson and Spencer dual-process model of habituation is less applicable to reflexive orienting to mild stimuli, where the arousing aspects of stimulus presentation are minimized. Attempts have been made to show that autonomic orienting responses, typically the dependent variable in human studies, follow the parameters of the dual-process conceptualization of habituation. However, findings are contradictory, and it has also been found that different components of the classical orienting responses (e.g. skin conduction responses; heart-rate deceleration) behave differently in a habituation paradigm.

Rather than becoming entangled in a parametric analysis of these various measures of response habituation to see if they do, after all, represent a common process, research should, I suggest, aim at the physiological functions of the responses and the physiological substrates underlying them, i.e. habituation as stimulus processing. A psychological emphasis implies the use of responses in relatively complex intact animals, and the search for the physiological substrates would then involve those same animals. The use of simple organisms with relatively simple nervous systems (e.g. Aplysia), or of limited neuronal networks (e.g. frog spinal cord reflexes), relates more to habituation as response plasticity and the molecular study of memory.

8 Emotion – physiological psychology and central mechanisms

Introduction

'Emotion' has been an elusive subject for psychology. It epitomizes those behavioural categories which anecdotally and intuitively are known to figure prominently in human life and experience, but which slip through the psychologist's fingers like so many soap ducks. What work the physiological psychologist does tends to be constrained by the need for observable emotional responses – this allows him to study emotions in animals with a minimum of anthropomorphizing, but ignores the subjective experience ('feeling') crucial to human emotional states. Many emotions have no dramatic behavioural correlate; we can, with some ease, identify euphoria, anger, rage, and fear in others, but happiness, envy, distrust, disappointment, may have no outward sign.

So, in this chapter and the next, the quoted experimental work will involve the more dramatic emotions, which have traditionally been the subject matter for the physiological psychologist. Other areas of psychology have attempted to grapple with the whole range of emotional behaviour and experience, and the review volume by Plutchik (1980) is an excellent survey of the terminological, methodological, and intellectual confusions which have to be faced. It also reviews the various experimental traditions in the study of emotion, and so serves as an ideal introduction for anyone wishing to delve further into this field.

Our concern is with the physiological bases of emotion, and immediately two experimental traditions may be distinguished. The first is in the mainstream tradition of physiological

217

psychology, and looks at emotions in animals with a view to identifying the brain mechanisms involved using the standard battery of central manipulative techniques – lesions and stimulation. The second studies emotions in human subjects, and is particularly interested in the role of peripheral arousal in the genesis of emotional states. It lies in the general area known as psychophysiology.

The two approaches overlap. Both are concerned with extreme emotions such as euphoria, fear, and anger, and work on animals has been used to justify brain surgery in the modulation of human abnormal emotional states ('psychosurgery': see later). However, the differences are more striking, and the next chapter discusses the evolution of these two entirely separate disciplines, and reviews the psychophysiology of emotion. This chapter is concerned with physiological psychology, and considers what animal research has revealed about emotion and the brain. Later sections will deal with the application of brain surgery in the control of human abnormal emotions (psychosurgery) and the role of the brain's transmitter pathways in mediating emotional behaviour. We begin with a brief review of the lesion and stimulation work on brain mechanisms of rage and aggression in animals.

Animal research

This approach first became popular in the 1920s and 1930s (e.g. Bard, 1928; Hess, 1954), and has remained a fertile area of investigation, characterized by continual refinements at both behavioural and physiological levels. Early work was aimed at determining the localization of aggression within the brain, albeit at a fairly gross level. This was supplanted by a finer-grained analysis, as improving techniques made this possible. Latterly there has been increasing interest in the topography of aggressive behaviour, i.e. an awareness that aggression does not always follow the same pattern and is not always for the same purpose. Different forms of aggressive behaviour may then have different physiological substrates in the brain.

Aggression in the cat is seen as a pattern of responses –

running, growling, unsheathing of the claws, piloerection (hackles rising), biting, striking with the claws, etc. Electrical stimulation of sites in the pons or medulla of the hindbrain elicits components of the pattern, but they are generally uncoordinated and undirected. Stimulation of the midbrain produces integrated threat and attack behaviour in the cat (for a detailed review, see Flynn, 1976), which is also dependent on the presence of a prey object such as a rat, i.e. it is directed and not automatic. Hess (see Hess, 1954) was the first to demonstrate the effectiveness of hypothalamic stimulation in producing aggressive behaviour in the cat, although Masserman (1941) felt that, as in his experiments the behaviour was undirected and independent of the sensory environment, it was a 'sham' rage rather than authentic emotional expression (but see Flynn, 1976). Stimulation of the other major diencephalic structure, the thalamus, may also elicit aggression in the cat, but sites in telencephalic structures such as the limbic system and neocortex are less responsive. Amygdala stimulation can lead to defensive threat, but generally speaking the role of these telencephalic structures in aggression is modulatory. Siegel *et al.* (1977) found that stimulation of the prefrontal cortex could suppress aggressive behaviour in the cat, and lesion studies also support this view of the telencephalon.

Removal of the cerebral cortex, i.e. neocortex, striatum, and limbic system (see Chapter 2), in the cat produces 'decorticate rage'; the cat becomes hyper-responsive and aggressive, but its responses are misdirected, as the ablation also disrupts sensory systems. If the neocortex only is removed, the animal appears placid (Bard and Mountcastle, 1947), while if neocortex and limbic system are ablated the animal seems normally responsive. The pattern (Flynn, 1976) is shown diagrammatically below:

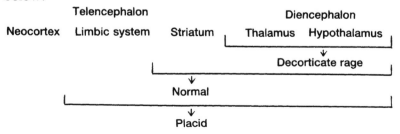

More specific telencephalic lesions have variable effects. Septal damage produces a syndrome of hyper-irritability ('septal hyper-emotionality') in rats and mice, but not in cats or primates. Amygdala lesions reduce fear and aggression in monkeys (Kluver and Bucy, 1939; see section on psychosurgery below), and, possibly, in humans, while effects in rats are unpredictable; King and Meyer (1958) found that septal hyper-emotionality in rats could be reversed by a subsequent amygdala lesion, suggesting perhaps a reciprocity in their actions.

As well as electrical stimulation, lesions of diencephalic, midbrain and hindbrain areas can induce aggressive behaviour. Damage to the ventro-medial hypothalamus produces a rage response in cats (Hess, 1954; Wheatley, 1944), while lateral hypothalamic lesions can antagonize aggressive behaviour (see review by Goldstein, 1974). The potency of stimulation and lesions of hypothalamic nuclei in affecting aggression might imply a major role of this structure in mediating emotional behaviour. However, if the hypothalamus is surgically isolated from the rest of the brain, aggressive responding is still exhibited by the cat, and can still be elicited by thalamic stimulation and from the midbrain. Conversely, midbrain lesions completely antagonize aggression induced by hypothalamic stimulation (Hunsperger, 1956).

This suggests that the individual components of aggressive behaviour are organized in the midbrain and hindbrain, and integrated into a pattern of responding by the midbrain. Higher structures of the diencephalon and telencephalon are involved in aggression by virtue of descending pathways connecting them with the midbrain; through these connections they modulate responding, enabling it to occur under appropriate environmental conditions.

As a response category, aggressive behaviour can be described in terms of the stimuli which elicit it (as we shall see later), and the sensory analysis necessary to link stimulus with response occurs in the forebrain (diencephalon and telencephalon). So an animal with the forebrain removed but with an intact midbrain and hindbrain will show integrated aggressive behaviour, but only to intense stimuli such as electric footshock. However, if part of the thalamus and the posterior hypothalamus are also left intact, the response is elicited by mild stimuli such as light, or may even become spontaneous (Bard, 1928; Carli *et al.*, 1963; reviewed in Flynn, 1976). The midbrain organizes the response, but higher brain structures control its manifestation.

We can see at a general level how this might work. In cats the neocortex contains visual and auditory centres, and is therefore important in selecting a target and directing the attack. An established rat colony will attack an intruder rat; recognition is via olfactory cues (Adams, 1979), and the analysis of olfactory input is a major function of the amygdala. Thus the amygdala has a crucial role in this particular example of aggression in animals, allowing the response to occur only to the specific stimulus of an intruder.

There are various forms of aggressive behaviour observable in animals. Moyer (1968) identified seven distinct categories:

1 Predatory attack.
2 Inter-male aggression, particularly to strangers.
3 Fear-induced aggression.
4 Irritable aggression, to frustration or pain.
5 Territorial defence (usually inter-male).
6 Maternal aggression, in defence of young.
7 Instrumental aggression (conditioned, via training).

Such a phenomenological classification is based on the observation of aggression in various situations, and need not imply that in each case the actual pattern of responding is dramatically different and likely to involve different brain substrates. Blanchard and Blanchard (1977) analyse aggressive behaviour in the laboratory rat. Their main conclusion is that the topography, or style, of attack behaviour against an intruder is exactly as that seen in wild rats, and therefore a valid experimental model of aggression. However, they differentiate this form of attack ('conspecific', as it is directed against a member of the same species) from reflexive fighting induced by footshock, and from predation. Both these latter are also popular in the laboratory. Pairs of rats in an enclosed space will fight if given footshock; Blanchard and Blanchard refer to this as pain-induced or reflexive aggression. Rats will attack, kill, and eat frogs; less frequently they will prey on mice (over 90 per cent will spontaneously attack frogs, while less than 20 per cent attack mice). The three forms of attack behaviour – conspecific, reflexive and predation – differ both in terms of the situations which elicit them and in the precise patterning of the aggressive behaviour, e.g. conspecific fighting involves piloerection, while predation does not. Thus Blanchard and Blanchard have shown that, of Moyer's categories, three at least (numbers 1, 2, 4) are situationally, behaviourally, and, therefore, likely to be physiologically distinct.

Convincing evidence of different physiological substrates for different forms of aggression comes from the work of Flynn, who has also analysed the patterning of sensory-motor reflexes in aggressive behaviour. Working with the cat, Flynn (1976; Flynn *et al.*, 1971) has identified two forms of predatory attack elicited by electrical stimulation. Both types appear identical to behaviours observable in the normal animal; however, many cats do not spontaneously attack mice or rats, and elicited attack provides a reliable and controllable model of aggression. One type of predation is an *affective attack* involving the components of rage mentioned earlier in the chapter: a claws-out, piloerection, hissing attack. The other is a stealthy, non-affective (non-emotional) attack, not preceded by any display of threat or rage; this is described by Flynn as *'quiet, biting'* attack Both forms have the same result, killing and eating of the prey.

Affective attack and quiet, biting attack can be elicited by stimulation of sites in the midbrain, and from hypothalamic stimulation. Within the hypothalamus, electrodes dorsal and rostral (i.e. anterior to) to the ventro-medial nuclei produce the affective type, electrodes lateral to these placements elicit quiet, biting attack. Thalamic stimulation is ineffective for affective assault, but can result in quiet, biting predation, while the opposite applies to the amygdala. There are also complex interactions between the various sites. Thalamic lesions eliminate affective attack produced by hypothalamic stimulation, while amygdala stimulation can modulate hypothalamically elicited quiet biting predation.

Predation in the cat relies upon appropriate sensory input. Thalamic stimulation does not result in quiet attack if the cat is blindfolded, in analogous fashion to the dependence of midbrain-elicited attack upon the actual presence of a prey object (Berntson *et al.*, 1976). Thus electrical stimulation does not activate pre-programmed motor systems; the response observed depends upon appropriate sensory feedback. Particularly impressive in this regard are Flynn's results on the effects of eliminating sensory feedback from the mouth and jaw regions of the cat. This can be achieved by severing the trigeminal nerve, and has unnerving results for the mouse. The cat, upon appropriate hypothalamic stimulation, quietly stalks and corners the prey using visual and olfactory cues. He places his mouth over the neck and back, but does not bite as he would normally, but rubs his mouth over the mouse's fur. The consummatory response of biting does not appear at the end of an unstoppable response sequence, but, as with other components of the aggressive pattern of behaviour, depends upon appropriate sensory feedback. The trigeminal nerve normally carries back to the brain sensory impulses generated by the presence of the mouse body in the cat's mouth; this feedback is necessary to complete a stimulus-response link which results in biting. With no feedback, there is no biting.

Flynn concludes that, although quiet attack in the cat can be conceptualized in stimulus-response terms, the S–R reflexes are in a complex pattern, and the behaviour as a whole is not 'all-or-none'. Given the range of sensory information necessary for this one example of aggressive behaviour to occur (visual, auditory, and olfactory distance receptors; tactile and gustatory proximal receptors), and the various categories of aggressive behaviour, it is not surprising that aggression can be influenced by lesioning or stimulating such a variety of structures in the brain.

It is unrealistic to associate aggression with any one structure. The results of lesion and stimulation studies point to a midbrain site organizing the response output that is recognized as aggressive behaviour; the appropriate manifestation of aggression is dependent upon the sensory-motor coordinating functions of diencephalic and telencephalic structures. In a gross sense, these could be said to alter the thresholds for aggressive responding, ranging from the extreme placidity of the amygdalectomized monkey to the hypersensitive rage of the decorticate cat.

Before proceeding to other aspects of aggression and emotionality, it is logical at this point to discuss the relation of brain mechanisms of aggression in animals to psychosurgical intervention in humans.

Psychosurgery

In 1935, the International Neurology Congress in London heard a paper given by Fulton and Jacobsen on the behavioural effects of destroying the frontal lobes in monkeys and chimpanzees. Among the audience was Egas Moniz, a Portuguese neurologist. He was particularly impressed by the post-operative docility and calm observed in one of the chimpanzees, and immediately saw the potential of such an operation in violent and difficult human psychiatric patients. A few months later, the first prefrontal lobotomy was performed in Lisbon under Moniz's supervision. In 1936 he reported on the first series of twenty such operations, carried out on chronic institutionalized patients with schizophrenia and other severe psychiatric disorders. According to Moniz, fifteen showed significant improvement, ranging from increased docility to complete cure.

Thus began the golden age of psychosurgery. Moniz himself was not destined to play the leading role, being shot and paralysed by a lobotomized patient in 1944 (an example of divine retribution, if one believes in such things). The Americans Freeman and Watts (Freeman, 1971) became the major proponents, being, alone, responsible for over a thousand frontal lobotomies between 1936 and 1950. Altogether, somewhere in the order of 50,000 operations were carried out in the same period.

The original operations of Moniz involved injections of alcohol into the frontal lobes, and later surgical removal of large amounts of tissue (a 'lobotomy'). Freeman and Watts realized that isolating frontal cortical regions from the rest of the brain would have the same effect, and devised techniques for severing the relevant fibre pathways (a 'leucotomy'). The procedures were not oversophisticated, but do demonstrate the robustness of the brain; hooked scalpels were inserted through holes drilled through forehead or temple regions of the head, and, literally, waggled up and down. The degree of waggling determined the grade of lobotomy: minimal, standard, or radical (Freeman, 1971).

Any form of physical intervention to modify behaviour involves social, ethical, philosophical and scientific issues. I am dealing primarily with the last, but even then it is impossible to ignore wider aspects. Statements in scientific papers – 'it [lobotomy] proved to be the ideal operation for use in crowded state mental hospitals with a shortage of everything except patients' (Freeman, 1971) – and proposals to use psycho-surgery to eliminate 'undesirable' social behaviour such as street riots in deprived urban areas (Mark and Ervin, 1970), prevent a purely objective assessment of the procedure. A critical analysis of these various issues is contained in Chorover (1976), Valenstein (1973), and Carroll and O'Callaghan (1983).

In 1937 Papez, building on the observation that rabies is associated with spontaneous rage and aggression, and also with the presence of negri bodies in the hippocampus (black deposits, seen on autopsy of patients dying of rabies), proposed that the hippocampus and other limbic structures constitute a circuit for the expression of emotional behaviour. MacLean (1949) revised and extended Papez's hypothesis, and the Papez–MacLean limbic model of emotion has been a major influence on research and theory. The original proposal supplied a rationale for the frontal lobotomy or leucotomy, as the operation severed links between frontal cortical functions relating to cognition and personality, and limbic-midbrain expression of aggression. However, as one might have predicted, the frontal lobotomy affected personality, blunting affect and intellect and reducing creativity, producing an apathetic, but, of course, more manageable patient. (For a discussion of the 'frontal syndrome', see p. 54.)

In the early 1950s, the use of the phenothiazine tranquillizers replaced the frontal lobotomy as the treatment of choice in schizophrenia, and psychosurgery faded away. More recently there has been a revival, associated with refinements in surgical procedures, and still based on the original limbic model of emotion. In 1939, Kluver and Bucy had reported that removal of the temporal lobes of the hemispheres produced in monkeys a syndrome of hypersexuality, hyperorality (placing of objects in the mouth), and extreme docility. It was soon established that the crucial structure was the amygdala, as a lesion restricted to this area produced all the components of the Kluver–Bucy syndrome. Therefore, ignoring the wider effects of amygdalectomy in monkeys (such as the inability to communicate effectively with other monkeys in the troop, leading to isolation from the troop and eventual death, Kling *et al.*, 1970), various psychosurgeons have lesioned the amygdala in an attempt to modify aggressive behaviour in humans.

One can sympathize with the problem. Violent aggression can be associated with various psychiatric conditions, such as mental subnormality, schizophrenia, autism, and psychopathy. However, the very nature of the condition means that the surgery is usually inflicted, as there is no possibility of informed consent (e.g. Kiloh *et al.*, 1974; Balasubramaniam and Ramamurthi, 1970: these latter specialize in amygdalectomizing younger patients, some less than eleven years old). So there are severe ethical problems; and as there is usually no psychological assessment by independent observers, with ratings of 'improvement' based upon improved manageability, the whole moral basis and purpose of the operation is dubious. Manageability is important, but whether it should involve destroying part of the brain is questionable. Scientifically, the previous section presented evidence that aggressive behaviour comes in various forms, that different forms have separable brain substrates, that many centres within the brain are involved in aspects of aggressive behaviour, and that there are significant species differences in the effects of brain lesions and stimulation on aggression. There is no scientific rationale for amygdalectomy in the treatment of human aggression; those who subscribe to it are retreating to a nineteenth-century view of the brain similar to Gall's phrenology, where individual and complete functions are localized in separate structures. The brain does not work like that.

A more sophisticated approach is adopted by a group at St George's Hospital, London (Kelly, 1973; Kelly *et al.*, 1973a, b). They return to the idea that an interruption of the fibres connecting the frontal lobe, which modulates emotional expression, and the limbic system, which organizes emotional expression, might modify pathological emotional states. Using a cryogenic technique of cooling the area around a probe to −70°C and rewarming, they can produce lesions 7–8 mm in diameter. Several of these lesions are performed, both in the region containing fronto-limbic fibres and in the cingulate gyrus, part of the main limbic circuit. The precise location of each lesion coincides with a 'physiologically active' centre, i.e. a site which, when electrically stimulated, produces signs of peripheral autonomic arousal such as increased respiration, forearm blood-flow, and skin conductance activity. Kelly and his colleagues reason that the various pathological conditions they were to treat had in common high levels of arousal – the conditions ranged from chronic anxiety states and obsessional neuroses to depression, schizophrenia, and depersonalization syndromes. Removal of physiologically active centres in the brain via a limbic leucotomy might reduce chronic peripheral arousal.

The forty patients had been ill for an average of eleven years, and been subject to a variety of therapies including psychotherapy, electro-convulsive shock, and drugs. Nine had already been given a prefrontal lobotomy. Before the operation they were assessed clinically and on scales of depression, anxiety, and various personality and IQ tests.

After the operation 67 per cent of all patients were clinically improved, ranging from 80 per cent of the depressives to 55 per cent of the chronically anxious. Overall the subjects were significantly less neurotic, less anxious, less depressed, and less phobic. IQ, if anything, increased pre- to post-operatively. Peripheral arousal levels were significantly lower after the operation. Long-term follow-up established that the effects of limbic leucotomy in these patients were not transitory.

This study exemplifies the problems and the benefits of psychosurgery. The site of lesioning has no particular justification from laboratory work, except that, on a general level, the limbic system is involved in some aspects of emotional expression. Precision is obtained by linking lesion sites with peripheral physiological arousal, a rationale involving a different line of reasoning from the 'limbic model of emotion' approach. However, although not built on a thorough understanding of the central and peripheral mechanisms of emotion, the technique appears to work, beyond merely making the patients more manageable. The long-term improvement in clinical and psychological ratings compares favourably with, for instance, the efficacy of phenothiazine drugs in schizophrenia; certainly one would expect most of the patients to have welcomed the operation (their attitude, before or after, is not reported). So, if the principle of intervention in mental illness is accepted, then the limbic leucotomy of the St George's group appears to be a useful therapeutic tool. It is light years ahead of the frontal lobotomy in technical sophistication, and the relatively small lesions render gross personality changes less likely. It is, though, subject to the same social and ethical constraints. Most psychosurgery for aggressive disorders is performed on patients unable to comprehend or to consent to the procedure, and the definition of pathological aggression is usually left to the psychosurgeon. Leaders of urban riots manifest a pathology of aggression; army commanders ordering the devastation of villages do not. These definitions are value-judgements, and value-judgements are not susceptible to scientific analysis.

A different approach to the modulation of emotional behaviour through brain manipulation is taken by Heath (1976; 1977). He theorizes that psychotic episodes are associated with abnormal electrical activity in the septum, and aggression with abnormalities in the hippocampus. By tracing out pathways using electrophysiological techniques, he has established that the cerebellum plays an important part in an 'emotion' circuit, connecting with limbic structures such as the septum and hippocampus. The cerebellum lies close to the skull, and is easily accessible once the cranial bone is opened. Heath fixes stimulating electrodes to the surface of the cerebellum in his human patients. Wires from the electrodes pass under the skin to the chest, where they emerge and are attached to a battery-operated stimulator carried by the patient in a pocket. When activated, the stimulator provides a 0.25 millisecond pulse at a frequency of one hunded pulses per second.

Patients used to test out this procedure include some with uncontrollable aggression, some chronically ill schizophrenics, and two with severe neurotic disorders (Heath, 1977). Duration, severity and overall chronicity of the disorder were key factors in selecting subjects.

The results, as reported, were dramatic. To give one example: a nineteen-year-old male, slightly retarded and first hospitalized when thirteen years old, showed such pathological self-mutilation behaviour and violent aggression towards others that he was physically restrained much of the time, despite massive doses of a variety of drugs; the day the stimulator was first activated, the outbursts of violence ceased. Along with this specific improvement, a general improvement has been noted in social adjustment and on a variety of psychological tests, and the patient is now rated as clinically symptom-free; he is no longer hospitalized and requires no medication.

A similar pattern of results was found for ten out of the eleven subjects. The only failure proved to have an organic lesion in the cerebellum, close to the stimulation site.

Such therapeutic effects are dramatic, particularly as the patients were characterized by severity and chronicity of symptoms. Heath hypothesizes that the rhythmic stimulation of the cerebellum is conducted via neuronal pathways to the sites in the septum and hippocampus where dysrhythmia (spiking activity) is producing the clinical symptoms. Applied stimulation recruits the electrical activity of these structures into a synchronized, rhythmic pattern, and alleviates the aberrant behaviour.

Only a few cases have been reported, and they have not yet been studied in the long term. The initial results are empirically encouraging, particularly as the technique is non-invasive, i.e. does not involve the direct manipulation or damage of deep brain structures. If it does not work with a given subject, the brain is still intact, in contrast to the psychosurgical approach. The arguments against using the procedure are ethical and social. Most patients suited, in Heath's terms, for this operation would be in no condition to give consent to it; society (via the medical profession) would inflict it on them.

I have dealt at some length with psychosurgery. It is one of the few areas where the behavioural analysis of brain mechanisms in animals is of direct relevance to current clinical practice with humans. Unfortunately the work with animals suggests that there is no sound scientific rationale for the specific surgical interventions used to 'treat' behaviour disorders in man. Such interventions proceed on a more pragmatic basis, i.e. do they work? However, 'improved' is often a synonym for 'easier to manage', while actual clinical improvement is much less impressive. A recent review of the effects of amygdalotomy concluded that only a third of patients benefit, and that the relationship of behavioural outcome to the surgery performed was indeterminate (Small *et al.*, 1977).

Brain chemistry and emotion

It should have become obvious that work on the brain structures involved in emotion in animals has been severely restricted; we could justifiably substitute 'aggression' for 'emotion'. The relationship of central neurotransmitter pathways to emotion has been studied on a broader scale, or at least along two distinct lines. The first is directly analogous to the 'structural' approach, and investigates the neurochemical bases of aggressive behaviour in animals. The second is a relatively recent development, stimulated by the therapeutic potency of anti-depressant drugs in humans. Emotional, or 'affective', disorders in humans have become, for various social and cultural reasons, a major area of psychiatric concern. Depression and manic-depression involve changes in mood state which may eventually require some sort of therapeutic intervention. Chapter 12 discusses in detail the use of drugs in alleviating depression, and uses what we know of drug pharmacology to relate mood state to neurotransmitters in the brain. Anticipating that discussion, the conclusion is that affective disorders in humans involve changes in the relative balances between the monoamine neurotransmitters, noradrenaline, dopamine, and serotonin, particularly noradrenaline and serotonin. No structural basis in the brain for depression and other affective disorders has yet been identified.

The neurochemistry of aggression in animals has followed the tradition of the structural analysis. Distinct categories of aggressive behaviour are identified, and drugs used to isolate any involvement of the central neurotransmitters. The results are generally ambiguous (Avis, 1973). Eichelman and Thoa (1973) conclude that predation is mediated via serotonin systems, being increased by the serotonin-depleting agent PCPA; spontaneous aggression could be elicited by the dopamine agonist apomorphine, and may therefore depend upon brain dopamine pathways, while irritable aggression probably involves the noradrenergic system. Avis (1973) used slightly different categories of behaviour in rats, and in a realistic review demonstrates that unambiguous conclusions are usually unjustified. Isolation-induced fighting and pain-induced aggression could be modified by various noradrenergic, dopaminergic, and serotonergic drugs. The most consistent finding was that drugs blocking central cholinergic pathways (anticholinergics) were effective at reducing isolation-induced, pain-induced, and predatory aggression, and that this inhibitory action was not species-specific. A prediction based on these findings would be that cholinergic-stimulating agents should elicit aggressive behaviour, and this has, in fact, been the most replicable result in the area of aggression and neurochemistry. Application of the cholinergic drug carbachol to the lateral hypothalamus elicits mouse-killing in rats (Smith *et al.*, 1970), a result replicated by Bandler (1970). Bandler (1971) has also elicited predatory behaviour by injecting carbachol into thalamic sites chosen on the basis of Flynn's electrical stimulation work; the behaviour is indistinguishable from natural predation. Berntson and Leibowitz (1973) induced affective threat and attack in the cat with cholinergic drugs, and showed that it could be blocked by subsequent injection of anticholinergic agents.

It therefore appears that predatory aggression in the rat and the cat is under the control of central cholinergic pathways. The apparent identity of the hypothalamic and thalamic sites from which either electrical or chemical stimulation can elicit predatory attack suggests that Flynn's electrodes were stimulating cholinergic neurons.

Not all forms of aggressive behaviour are amenable to cholinergic manipulation. Earlier in the chapter I pointed out that aggressive behaviour is not homogeneous; subtypes may be distinguished in terms of their topology (i.e. the precise form the behaviour takes) and their physiological substrates. A single example of aggression depends upon an intricate series of stimulus-response linkages, and therefore upon sensory and motor processes coordinated by a central mechanism. Obviously no one brain structure and no one neurotransmitter pathway will have exclusive control over such a complex behaviour as animal aggression.

Before leaving aggression, two areas of research, lying outside the scope of this book, should be mentioned. Endocrine studies show that hormones can play a significant role in aggression and other emotions. The presence of testosterone in the urine is a key trigger for aggressive behaviour in rats (Adams, 1979). Mouse-killing is seen only in male rats, and is abolished by castration (Avis, 1973), showing its dependence upon male hormones (androgens) such as testosterone. There are few sound studies of testosterone and aggression or criminality in humans, and no particular correlation emerges (Goldstein, 1974). A more general role for hormone levels in emotion is suggested by the mood changes seen in females during the menstrual cycle and occasionally observed after taking high-oestrogen contraceptive pills. These effects are likely to be mediated centrally as the brain contains a network of sites selectively responsive to hormone levels in the bloodstream.

Aggressive behaviour in animals can be systematically manipulated by breeding programmes. If mice either high or low in aggression are inbred, significant differences in aggressive behaviour between the groups emerge by the third generation. Similar results have been reported in dogs (Scott, 1958). Scott also demonstrated an interaction with the environment; 'aggressive' pups raised with an 'aggressive' mother showed more aggressive behaviour than 'aggressive' pups raised with a 'docile' mother.

The suggestion of a significant genetic component in aggression stimulated a search amongst the inmates of penal and psychiatric institutions for genetic abnormalities. The only finding of interest was the higher frequency of the XYY syndrome (i.e. a genetic complement with an extra Y, or female, chromosome) in institutionalized subjects; around ten in a thousand as opposed to one in a thousand in the normal population. However, not all XYY people are either aggressive or criminal, and not all pathologically aggressive criminals have the XYY syndrome (Goldstein, 1974). Social, cultural and developmental factors play a much greater part in human aggression, and it would be wrong, or at least naive, to extrapolate from experiments on mouse-killing rats and rat-killing cats, to the human condition.

9 Emotion – psychophysiology and peripheral arousal systems

Introduction

As mentioned in the previous chapter, the psychophysiological approach involves human subjects and is particularly concerned with the role of peripheral arousal systems in behaviour. To point the contrast with physiological psychology, I shall first review the general methods of the psychophysiologist, and then consider work specifically on emotion.

The psychophysiologist works with intact humans, and measures various aspects of their physiology and neurophysiology (see, e.g., Martin and Venables, 1980). They record, as direct correlates of central nervous system activity, electroencephalograms (EEGs; also used by the physiological psychologist), and evoked potentials to discrete stimuli such as tones and flashes. As correlates of peripheral nervous system activity they can record heart-rate, the skin conductance orienting response (SCR; formerly the GSR, or galvanic skin response), blood-pressure and blood-flow, skin temperature, and other responses controlled by the autonomic nervous system. Blood or urine samples can be analysed for the presence of hormones such as adrenaline, prolactin, or corticosteroids.

A key concept for the psychophysiologist is 'arousal', by which is usually meant peripheral arousal, i.e. the dominance of the autonomic nervous system by the sympathetic branch, leading to increases in palmar sweating, heart-rate, blood-pressure, and higher blood levels of adrenaline and noradrenaline. Associated with this autonomic arousal is the activation of the pituitary-adrenal axis (see next section), whereby secretion

234

of corticosteroids from the adrenal cortex is massively increased.

Whatever physiological responses are recorded may then be correlated with some change in behaviour. A comparison of schizophrenics with non-schizophrenics may show that the former have tonically high peripheral arousal levels and abnormal skin conductance orienting responses to simple tones. The emotion of 'anger' may correlate with high levels of blood noradrenaline. The latency of evoked potentials to flashes of light may correlate with IQ (all these are more or less realistic findings; for further examples, see the journal *Psychophysiology*). The pattern that emerges is of a physiological response being the dependent variable (what is measured), and some aspect of behaviour or personality the independent variable (what is allowed to vary). This contrasts with physiological psychology, where the dependent variable is usually some aspect of observed behaviour, and the independent variable some controlled interference with a physiological system (usually the brain).

All of the physiological responses recorded by the psychophysiologist are ultimately controlled from the central nervous system, and in some cases act in turn upon the central nervous system (i.e. 'feedback': see next section). The nuclei controlling the autonomic nervous system lie in the brainstem (medulla, pons, midbrain), and electrical stimulation of these regions can produce changes in heart-rate, blood-pressure, sweat-gland activity, etc. These centres are in turn modulated by higher brain structures such as the hypothalamus and limbic system. The EEG, although its precise nature is still uncertain (i.e. exactly how the activity of millions of individual neurons summates to produce identifiable brain waves), is a direct reflection of the brain's activity, as, on a more localized level, is the evoked potential. However, theorizing within psychophysiology has tended to concentrate on the correlations between peripheral measures and behaviour, and not on the brain mechanisms underlying both. Thus Sokolov's influential model of the orienting response (Chapter 7) was based on peripheral measures of orienting to simple tones – skin conductance responses, heart-rate deceleration, etc. – with central mechanisms of orienting and habituation tagged on without direct evidence. Ideas on abnormalities of arousal level in schizophrenia have been based purely on the peripheral measures referred to – increased skin conductance levels reflecting increased sweat-gland activity – with no convincing model as yet of a central malfunction to underly the observations.

Over the last decade there has been something of a coming together of psychophysiology and physiological psychology. Recording from single neurons in the brain has been used to identify the mechanisms underlying Sokolov's model of the orienting response (Chapter 7), while skin conductance recording in humans has been combined with data from the effects of limbic lesions in monkeys to form a limbic model of schizophrenia (Gruzelier and Venables, 1974). But there is still a way to go before the necessary and logical coalescing of the two disciplines is complete, and their more or less absolute separation can still be seen in the study of emotion.

The previous chapter described the physiological psychology of emotion, and we now turn to the psychophysiology. To help describe this the basic outlines of the peripheral arousal systems are presented in the next section.

Peripheral arousal systems

The two components referred to are complex physiological systems, and I am not dealing with them in detail. The volume by Van Toller (1979) is a particularly good review, by a psychophysiologist, of the role of the autonomic nervous system (ANS) in behaviour, with some additional comment on the pituitary-adrenal system (PAS).

Autonomic nervous system
The association of the ANS and PAS comes about through the nature of responses recorded by the psychophysiologist and used to define an 'arousal' state. I have mentioned them already. A state of arousal or alertness is characterized by increases in heart-rate, blood-flow, blood-pressure, increased sweat-gland activity and skin temperature, and elevated blood

levels of adrenaline, noradrenaline and corticosteroids. Apart from the last, all are produced by activation of the sympathetic branch of the ANS.

The ANS is a purely efferent (or motor) system, conducting impulses from nuclei within the central nervous system out to the effector organs in the body. Target organs include the striated muscle of the heart, the smooth muscle of the gastro-intestinal tract and the walls of blood vessels, and various glands such as the pancreas, sweat glands, salivary glands, and the adrenal medulla. Each target receives an innervation (i.e. a nervous supply) from both branches of the ANS, the sympathetic and the parasympathetic. The effects of the two branches tend to be antagonistic – where one increases muscle activity or glandular secretion, the other decreases it (this view is a little simplistic, but adequate for our purposes; for detail, see Van Toller, 1979). The antagonism is best seen in the overall pattern of effects. Domination of ANS activity by the sympathetic branch produces a picture of arousal, or preparation for activity, with increases in heart-rate and blood-pressure, constriction of peripheral blood-vessels (i.e. those not immediately necessary for supplying oxygen to the heart, skeletal muscle, and brain), release of adrenaline and noradrenaline from the adrenal medulla, and inhibition of the gastro-intestinal tract. Dominance by the parasympathetic branch produces a picture of quiescence, characterized by dilation of peripheral blood-vessels and mobilization of the gastro-intestinal tract for digestion and absorption of food; heart-rate and blood-pressure fall.

The balance between the two branches is regulated by centres in the brain and is usually unconscious and automatic. When we take vigorous exercise, we do not tell ourselves to sweat and go red, and after a meal we do not instruct our small intestine to start digesting and absorbing food. We are homeostatic organisms, maintaining as far as possible a constant internal environment. This constancy involves a range of the body's characteristics, from temperature and the brain's oxygen supply to heart-rate and blood glucose levels. Such homeostatic regulation is the essential function of the autonomic nervous system.

Homeostasis has to be maintained in the face of various challenges. Environmental temperatures go up and down, and regulation of our internal temperature may involve behavioural as well as purely autonomic measures such as sweating – we sit in the shade or put on thermal underwear. The provision of energy to meet the demands of the body must also fluctuate with need; skeletal movement requires substantial energy input from the body's reserves, which must then be replenished to maintain their homeostatically comfortable level. It is possible to see the sympathetic/parasympathetic division in terms of this latter example: sympathetic dominance or arousal involves energy expenditure (i.e. the sympathetic pattern is 'catabolic'), while parasympathetic dominance is aimed at energy replenishment or conservation (i.e. the pattern is 'anabolic').

What all this implies, and what must form the background to any discussion of the *psychological* significance of physiological responses mediated by the ANS, is that the system has evolved as a means of harnessing the body's metabolism to its physical needs. From this angle, the ANS has no prima facie involvement in psychological phenomena; which is not to say that correlations between, for instance, various emotions and hormone levels do not exist, but that the *physiological* demands of the emotional state must be considered before valid conclusions can be drawn. As a straightforward example, the orienting response to mild novel stimuli involves a short-lived heart-rate deceleration; however, a simple way to produce the same effect is to hold your breath momentarily, which reflexively stimulates the ANS to produce a compensatory heart-rate deceleration. So, to conclude that the heart-rate-orienting response is directly cognitive, one should eliminate the possibility that it is secondary to respiratory inhibition.

The psychophysiology of emotion lays great emphasis on the autonomically innervated adrenal medulla. The adrenal gland lies just above the kidney, and is divided into two functionally independent components: a cortex, which secretes corticosteroids as part of the activation of the pituitary-adrenal system, and a medulla, which secretes adrenaline and noradrenaline in response to sympathetic ANS activation.

These two hormones are, as their names imply, closely

related chemicals. Both are catecholamines, and by their physiological actions classified as 'sympathomimetics', mimicking the effects of general sympathetic arousal; that is, increases in heart-rate and blood-pressure, peripheral skin vasoconstriction, mobilization of glycogen and fat reserves in preparation for energy expenditure, and increases in blood glucose level. The relationship of adrenal noradrenaline to the sympathetic branch of the ANS is completely incestuous, as noradrenaline is also the synaptic transmitter released from the terminals of sympathetic axons where they synapse on target organs. Thus noradrenaline secreted into the bloodstream from the adrenal medulla has as a major action the potentiation of sympathetic arousal by a direct stimulation of these sympathetic synapses.

Despite their similarities, the physiological effects of adrenaline and noradrenaline (or epinephrine and norepinephrine, to give them their American names) are distinguishable. Noradrenaline causes vasoconstriction in skeletal muscle, and adrenaline vasodilation. Both increase blood-pressure, but noradrenaline does this more by increasing peripheral resitance (via vasoconstriction), and adrenaline more by a direct action on heart muscle. The hyperglycaemic response (increase in blood sugar) to noradrenaline is smaller than that to adrenaline release. These, and other differences, allow the pattern of peripheral arousal produced by noradrenaline to be distinguished from that produced by adrenaline by physiological recording techniques (see, e.g., Ax, 1953; Funkenstein, 1956: both referred to later).

The adrenal medulla contains unequal amounts of the two hormones, and the ratio varies from species to species. In humans it is around 5:1 in favour of adrenaline, in the rabbit around 50:1 in the same direction, in the lion around 1:1, and in the whale 3:1 in favour of noradrenaline (Von Euler, 1967). Of more interest to us are the relative amounts released in response to various arousing stimuli, and their correlation with behavioural and cognitive variables. This is discussed in detail later on.

Pituitary-adrenal system

The pituitary gland is suspended immediately below the

Table 9.1   Hormones released by the pituitary gland

Anterior lobe (Adenohypophysis)	
Growth hormone	(direct effects on metabolism to promote growth)
Thyroid-stimulating hormone	(stimulates thyroid gland to release thyroxin)
Adrenocorticotrophic hormone	(ACTH: stimulates adrenal cortex to release glucocorticoids and mineralocorticoids)
Follicle-stimulating hormone Luteinizing hormone	(act together to promote testosterone release and sperm cell growth in males, and oestrogen release and egg cell production and growth in females)
Prolactin	(promotes lactation, or milk production, by direct action on female mammary gland)
Posterior lobe (Neurohypophysis)	
Vasopressin	(anti-diuretic hormone: regulation of water loss via kidneys)
Oxytocin	(promotes milk release from breast, and uterine contractions during labour)

hypothalamus by a short stalk, the hypophysis; it is not part of the brain, but intimately associated with it. The gland comprises two lobes, the anterior (or adenohypophysis) and posterior (or neurohypophysis).

The two lobes are differentiated by the hormones they release into the bloodstream, and in the precise mechanisms whereby the release is effected. The posterior lobe releases oxytocin and vasopressin in response to neural impulses travelling down the axons of neurons whose cell bodies lie in the hypothalamus. The anterior lobe secretes a variety of hormones (see Table 9.1), in response to stimulation by chemicals manufactured in the hypothalamus, and travelling down to the adenohypophysis in the blood supply to the pituitary (the hypophysial portal system).

The pituitary gland has been referred to as the master gland of the body. Its hormones regulate, either directly or via an action on other glands, many aspects of the body's growth, metabolism, and reproductive behaviour (see Table 9.1). These aspects do not, in the main, concern us here, but we do meet some of the pituitary hormones again (p. 260). A detailed review of pituitary neuroendocrinology is contained in Donovan (1970).

The adrenal cortex is controlled by the adrenocorticotrophic hormone (ACTH) released from the pituitary gland. The secretion of ACTH is in turn regulated by a chemical releasing factor (ACTH–RF) manufactured in the hypothalamus. ACTH passes into the bloodstream, travels to the adrenal cortex, and there stimulates the release of corticosteroids.

There are many corticosteroids, broadly divided into two classes of mineralocorticoids and glucocorticoids. The former are involved in the balance of mineral salts and trace elements in the body, essential for normal functioning of, e.g., the nervous system. The latter are concerned with the conversion of fat stores to glucose and the suppressing of the body's immune response to infection or tissue damage; both these functions are part of the organism's preparation for energy expenditure and responsiveness to sudden stress – tissue repair can wait until danger has passed – and the release of glucocorticoids is the major component of the physiological stress response. Studies of the stress response usually involve measuring blood or urine levels of specific glucocorticoids such as cortisone and corticosterone (both from the group of 17-hydroxycorticosteroids, or 17–OHCS); alternatively one can measure blood levels of ACTH, as the release of corticosteroids is controlled by and therefore correlated with the amount of ACTH released from the pituitary.

The pituitary-adrenal system is extremely sensitive, with even mild but unexpected stimuli evoking an immediate release of ACTH and corticosteroids. If the stimulus is harmless, the system is damped down in an elegantly simple way; the release of ACTH from the pituitary is inhibited by circulating levels of ACTH and corticosteroids, so that as soon as the pituitary-adrenal axis is activated it is tending to return to normal. It is a perfect negative feedback system (see Fig. 9.1).

The initial activation can be triggered by stimulus perception and evaluation by higher brain centres, which then excite

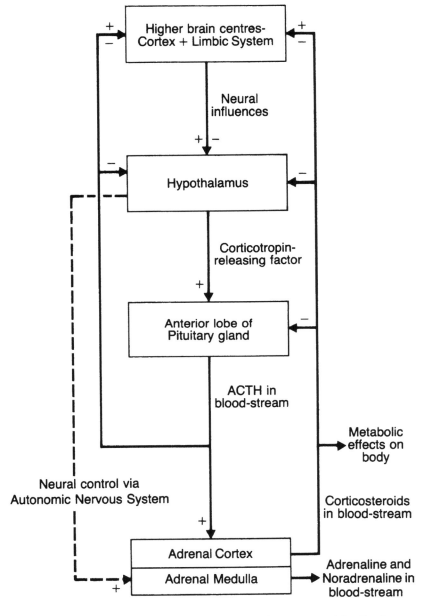

Figure 9.1   *Hypothalamic-pituitary-adrenal system, and feedback control of ACTH secretion*

the hypothalamus. If the stimulus is extremely threatening and/or arousing, these higher centres will override the negative feedback and sustain pituitary-adrenal activation at a high level; if the stimulus proves to be harmless, circulating levels of ACTH and corticosteroids are allowed to inhibit the pituitary and return the system to normal.

The autonomic nervous system and the pituitary-adrenal system

The peripheral arousal state correlated with extreme emotions such as fear and rage involves ANS sympathetic activation and excitation of the pituitary-adrenal system. One reason for their close association is the presence in the hypothalamus of centres controlling both systems. It should be clear from the last section that appropriate hypothalamic stimulation can activate the PAS, and it has been known for many years (Hess, 1954; Gellhorn and Loufbourrow, 1963) that hypothalamic mechanisms regulate the ANS. Stimulation in anterior areas produces peripheral parasympathetic dominance ('trophotropic zones'), and posterior hypothalamic stimulation leads to sympathetic arousal ('ergotropic zones'). Once stimulus evaluation has occurred in limbic and cortical structures, instructions to the hypothalamus will therefore produce an integrated peripheral arousal state. We discussed in the last chapter how hypothalamic stimulation can also elicit behavioural rage and aggression in the cat, and, more importantly, how animals with all the brain above the hypothalamus removed can still show integrated peripheral arousal and a behaviourally integrated, though misdirected, rage response. This implies that the peripheral arousal response can be a purely reflexive component of homeostatic regulation, with no need of intervening higher brain functions. However, as psychologists we are concerned with the more complex relations and contingencies between the organism and its environment, and it is clear that, e.g., the animal's perception of 'uncertainty', and the human's perception of taking an examination, involve the limbic system and cortex.

I have discussed the mechanisms of peripheral arousal as encountered within psychophysiology. We can now review attempts to correlate them with emotion and stress.

The psychophysiology of emotion

In 1884 William James invented this area. He proposed that, rather than an emotional feeling producing action, the action produces the emotional feeling. An object is perceived, and elicits a response, e.g. behavioural approach or avoidance, together with a range of peripheral changes in autonomic and endocrine systems. The brain receives feedback from these physiological responses, and interprets the pattern in terms of an emotional feeling. Thus the pattern of extreme peripheral arousal associated with the sight of an aggressive predator is interpreted by the brain as 'fear'. This conflicted with the more obvious view that the sight of the predator produces 'fear' which then leads to peripheral arousal and running away.

Around the same time the Danish physiologist Lange presented a similar hypothesis, although putting greater emphasis upon cardiovascular changes rather than general peripheral arousal. The model of emotional feeling as depending upon feedback from bodily changes is therefore known as the James–Lange theory.

The physiologist Walter Cannon (1929) was the next to pick up the argument, with a series of criticisms of the James–Lange model. He pointed out that animals still exhibit fear and rage responses after spinal transection (which eliminates sensory feedback from the viscera); that many non-emotional stressors such as high fever and anoxia (lack of oxygen) produce a peripheral arousal state apparently identical with the pattern supposed to produce 'rage'; that the sensory feedback system from the viscera (the 'visceral afferent system' – in some ways the sensory equivalent of the autonomic nervous system) is too primitive and too slow to code for a variety of rapidly occurring emotions; and finally that injections of adrenaline produce peripheral arousal, but do not lead to the experience of emotion.

Cannon proposed his alternative 'central' model of emotion, in which the thalamus was responsible for emotional experience, and the hypothalamus for emotional expression or behaviour, and which we considered in the last chapter.

Despite Cannon's criticisms, it seems intuitively likely that peripheral arousal is correlated with some extreme emotional states such as fear and anger, and may interact with stimulus perception and evaluation in the production of the subjective emotional experience. (It should be noted that James did restrict his ideas to the more 'primitive' emotions, such as rage, love and fear.) This hypothesis was given some encouragement by the work of Ax (1953). He used the known difference between the precise arousal patterns elicited by the release of adrenaline and noradrenaline from the adrenal medulla (see last section) to investigate possible correlations between emotions and peripheral arousal. Artificial laboratory conditions were set up to produce states of fear and anger in naive subjects. In both cases electrodes were attached to the body with leads to various electronic machines – the 'fear' condition involved dense smoke arising from the machines, while 'anger' was induced via an incompetent technician taking hours to fix the electrodes. Using a range of psychophysiological measures, Ax concluded that the state of fear (assessed via subjective self-report) was associated with adrenaline release from the adrenal medulla, and anger with noradrenaline release.

Funkenstein (1956) followed this up by correlating aspects of personality with adrenal medullary secretions. Subjects whose characteristic response to frustration was 'anger-out' showed the peripheral arousal pattern typical of noradrenaline, while those who demonstrated an 'anger-in' response had the arousal pattern typical of adrenaline.

This finding suggests a broadening of the theoretical base to include stable personality characteristics. We have already seen that peripheral arousal systems have as their main function the preparation of the body for energy expenditure whenever it is necessary. Adrenaline and noradrenaline have slightly different physiological actions, and their differential release in states of fear (or 'anger-in') and anger (or 'anger-out') may reflect the different anticipated demands of each situation on the body's energy stores. The anticipation will involve stimulus perception and evaluation, plus any inherited or acquired response tendencies, and so there can be substantial individual variations in behavioural and physiological reactions to emotional situations.

However, many non-emotional states, such as riding a bicycle, involve peripheral arousal, purely by virtue of their energy requirements. So if one is interested in correlations between adrenaline and noradrenaline release and behaviour, it might be more logical and useful to characterize the whole range of stimuli which elicit their release; then we might be able to define the precise situational requirements associated with, in the one case, adrenaline release and, in the other, noradrenaline release. Before discussing this enterprise, undertaken by Frankenhaeuser's group at the University of Stockholm but which necessarily takes us beyond 'emotion' as such, I will first outline the more recent history of the peripheral arousal/emotion story.

Schachter and Singer (1962)

There are few definitive studies in psychology, few experiments whose methodological and theoretical framework has stood the test of critical analysis and replication. Those that have, do so for a variety of reasons. They may actually be excellent studies, well designed, carried out, analysed, which produce significant and important results. Others, less impressive methodologically or in the pattern of results, survive to enter the folklore of psychology through their imaginative design and interpretation, and because their conclusions seem to make a lot of sense. Such a study is that of Schacter and Singer (1962).

Their starting-point was the conflict between James's view that peripheral arousal produces emotion, and Cannon's criticism that the same peripheral arousal pattern was common to different emotions. Ax had presented evidence that measurements of peripheral arousal could differentiate between fear and anger, with one being dominated by adrenaline release and the other by noradrenaline release. However Maranon (1924) had failed to produce a true emotional state by injecting subjects with adrenaline – one could have hypothesized that such induced peripheral arousal should elicit some emotional experience if James's ideas were valid.

Schachter and Singer point out that Maranon's subjects had a perfectly adequate explanation for their aroused state: they had been injected with adrenaline. They therefore hypothesized that subjects will always seek an appropriate explanation, or cognitive label, for subjectively perceived arousal, and if the explanation involves emotional stimuli, then an emotion will be experienced. A corollary of this is that if peripheral arousal is induced in subjects without their being given a suitable explanation, they will actively seek to interpret their state in terms of the immediate cognitive environment; if this environment is systematically varied, then different subjective emotional states might result.

Using the pretence of investigating the effects of a vitamin supplement ('Suproxin') on vision, Schachter and Singer injected male subjects with either adrenaline or a non-active placebo. Adrenaline-injected subjects were either informed of the expected physiological consequences (increased heart-rate, tremor, palpitations, etc.), misinformed, or left ignorant. Their cognitive environment was varied in two ways. In the Euphoria condition, a stooge acted in what might be classified as a manically happy way, playing with balls of paper and hula hoops, and flying paper aeroplanes. In the Anger condition, a stooge became progressively more angry and violent as he and the subject worked through an increasingly personal questionnaire (e.g. 'father's annual income?', 'do members of your family need psychiatric care?').

Schacter and Singer predicted that subjects experiencing a state of physiological arousal for which they had no explanation would interpret it in terms of their immediate cognitive environment; if the stooge was euphoric they would feel euphoric, and if the stooge was angry they would feel angry. Those subjects informed accurately as to the effects of the injection do have an appropriate explanation, and should therefore be unaffected by the stooge's behaviour. Subjects given the placebo should experience no peripheral arousal, and hence should feel no need to interpret their state in terms of their cognitive environment (the arousing consequences of injections were checked via pulse-rate recordings).

Induced emotional state was assessed via behavioural observations and subjective self-report. The quantitative predictions, in terms of degree of induced emotion, were:

Adrenaline Misinformed $\geqslant$ Adrenaline Ignorant $>$ Adrenaline Informed $=$ Placebo

Schacter and Singer conclude that their results conformed to expectations. Subjects given no explanation for the arousing effects of adrenaline injection felt and acted more euphoric or more angry than informed subjects or placebo-injected subjects in the same experimental conditions. Thus 'emotional state' is determined not just by a state of peripheral arousal, but by an interaction between the state of arousal and the cognitive environment, and is therefore a combination of peripheral and central factors.

This is the conclusion constantly referred to in subsequent reviews and descriptions of the psychophysiology of emotion. Recently, however, substantial criticisms have been levelled at the Schachter and Singer study. Two attempts at partial replication failed to reproduce their findings (Marshall and Zimbardo, 1979; Maslach, 1979), and although neither of these experiments is, in their turn, free from criticism (Schacter and Singer, 1979), they do emphasize the need to read the original 1962 paper closely. Initial data analysis showed that of the four dependent variables (behavioural observation of expressed emotion, and subjective self-reports, for the two conditions of euphoria and anger) only the behaviour ratings in the Anger condition produced a significant difference between the crucial groups, Adrenaline Ignorant and Placebo. Subsequent elimination of 'self-informed' subjects (those in the Ignorant and Misinformed groups who still attributed their physiological responses to the injection) from a post-hoc analysis produced significant Adrenaline Ignorant versus Placebo differences for both Euphoria and Anger conditions, but again, only for the behavioural ratings and not for the self-report scores.

This differentiation of subjective self-report from observed behaviour (i.e. emotional experience from emotional expression) is also seen in another study quoted by Schacter and Singer in support of their theoretical position. Schachter and Wheeler

(1962) observed that subjects injected with adrenaline laughed more at a slapstick film than placebo-injected controls; however, there were no significant differences between the groups in the subjective self-reports of emotional feeling. The two experiments are consistent in failing to show a correlation between peripheral arousal, cognitive environment, and subjective emotional experience.

So at the very least, the Schacter and Singer experiment does not confirm that emotional states necessarily involve an interaction between non-specific peripheral arousal and appropriate cognitive evaluation. It seems intuitively likely that perception of peripheral arousal does play some part in the genesis or maintenance of emotional states (Marshall and Zimbardo (1979) suggest that injection of adrenaline consistently induces an unpleasant feeling because its physiological effects are actually unpleasant), particularly more intense ones of euphoria, anger, and fear. An arousal/cognition interaction would help resolve the James–Lange/Cannon dispute; peripheral arousal would be necessary (*à la* James–Lange), but would not vary between emotional states (*à la* Cannon). Differentiation between states would be ultimately cognitive. Such a picture is appealing, which may account for the rather uncritical acceptance of the whole of Schachter and Singer's theoretical position during the last two decades. But it does seem that the relations between arousal and emotion are not straightforward, as is also demonstrated in approaches using other strategies.

Valins (1966) asked his male subjects to rate pictures of nude females for attractiveness. He gave them false feedback of their heart-rates via headphones, and found that increases in their supposed heart-rate were correlated with ratings of increased attractiveness. Valins concluded that feedback on peripheral arousal does not have to be real (or 'veridical') for it to play a determining role in emotional states, but just perceived as such.

There are obvious problems with this sort of study. Emotion is defined simply as an attractiveness rating. Heart-rate has an uneasy relation with other indices of peripheral arousal, with decreases occurring in some arousal states. Finally, Valins did not record his subjects' *actual* heart-rates, which may have co-varied along with the false heart-rates and so induced the changes in attractiveness ratings. Goldstein *et al.* (1972) performed a similar study, using male subjects and male nudes, and found that subjective emotional arousal varied with *actual* heart-rate changes and not with the false feedback.

The problems of using heart-rate measures of peripheral arousal were demonstrated by Hirschman (1975), who recorded heart-rate and skin conductance responses. Using slides of mutilated bodies, he found that increases in false heart-rate tended to be associated with increases in skin conductance activity (and, hence, increases in peripheral arousal), and with increasing subjective discomfort. However, if the subject was told that the false feedback was 'noise' rather than his heartbeat, the association with skin conductance responses was less obvious, suggesting that 'attention' was a crucial feature of the false heart-rate feedback experiments. Hirschman also reported that the correlation between increasing arousal, measured by skin conductance responses, and increasing subjective discomfort was not strong.

Reviewing the somewhat confused area of false heart-rate feedback and emotion, Harris and Katkin (1975) conclude that the various dependent variables did not usually represent 'emotion'. Valins, for instance, deals with the attribution of emotion ('attractiveness') to external stimuli, and not with any subjective experience. As they consider the latter as the definitive characteristic of emotion, Harris and Katkin suggest that only studies where subjects' self-reports are used, as in Hirschman (1975), deal with emotion proper.

As a step to clarifying this area of research, they propose a division into primary and secondary emotions. Primary emotions include peripheral arousal and the subjective perception of that arousal, while secondary emotions need not necessarily involve peripheral arousal, but may involve a subject's non-veridical perception of it, e.g. via false heart-rate feedback. Secondary emotions can therefore occur as emotional behaviour without peripheral arousal, as in the attribution of attractiveness reported by Valins.

Secondary emotions are dependent upon prior acquisition of primary emotions. Once acquired in the presence of peripheral arousal, release of some components of the emotion can occur in the absence of that arousal, and it is these that constitute a secondary emotional response.

As Harris and Katkin ably point out the methodological and theoretical confusions in the study of false feedback and emotion, they would seem to have little need to reconceptualize 'emotion' in such a complex fashion; the unjustified use of emotional expression and emotional experience interchangeably has been a permanent feature of research into emotion, and adequately accounts for the confusions to which Harris and Katkin draw attention. The lack of correlation between the two, as in Schachter and Singer's study, is the fundamental problem, and one which does not seem particularly illuminated by a further subclassification of emotions. It would also appear that the dependence of primary emotions on peripheral arousal leaves out in the cold all those emotions not involving arousal of any sort, e.g. guilt, remorse, etc.

We can see at this stage the complexity of the emotion/ peripheral arousal issue. Emotions themselves are multi-faceted, with subjective and objective characteristics which may, with certain levels of certain emotions, correlate with the presence or absence of peripheral arousal. Peripheral arousal itself is not a unitary concept; heart-rate need not correlate with skin conductance activity, and adrenaline excitation is not equivalent to noradrenaline excitation. Other problems of definition in this area are still unresolved. A recent debate on the role of cognition in emotion between Zajonc, who suggests that emotion or affect can be generated without prior cognitions, and Lazarus, who feels that emotional experience must depend upon a cognitive awareness of events and their significance, hinges in large part on how one chooses to define 'emotion' (Zajonc, 1984; Lazarus, 1984). Zajonc, for instance, puts forward the early development of emotions (fear, disgust, etc.) in babies as evidence that cognitions need not precede emotions, as babies have only limited cognitive capabilities. Lazarus disputes the latter point, and anyway *defines* emotions as requiring prior cognitive assessment. He is quite entitled to do this, and in fact a strict definition at least allows a theoretical position to be defended and criticized.

Some contemporary experimental work bearing on the links between cognition, emotion, and arousal has used a novel approach. Ekman (Ekman *et al.*, 1983) has for many years studied various aspects of non-verbal communication, including the use we make of facial expression in conveying emotion. Using video techniques to analyse expression, he can specify the precise pattern of contractions of the facial musculature which define any given emotion. The next step was to direct subjects in putting on a range of facial expressions to convey various emotions, i.e. precisely guiding the contraction of muscle groups into the appropriate pattern. Professional actors and scientists were used to minimize experimenter effects.

The emotional expression was held for ten seconds, during which physiological measures were taken, including heart-rate, finger skin temperature, skin resistance, and forearm muscle tension. When compared with pre-emotion baselines, changes in physiological measures significantly differentiated emotional expressions. 'Anger' was characterized by high heart-rate and skin temperature, and 'fear' and 'sadness' by high heart-rate and low skin temperature. 'Happiness', 'disgust', and 'surprise' were all associated with low heart-rate. Differences were less marked when subjects were asked to *relive* appropriate emotional experiences, an observation which will need to be analysed further. However, Ekman does seem justified in claiming that what he calls 'universal emotional signals' do elicit an emotion-specific autonomic activity. The precise mechanism is unclear, but extremely important. Facial expression is controlled from the motor cortex. The correlated autonomic pattern may then be a result of peripheral feedback from the facial musculature, or directly induced by the motor cortex (via the hypothalamus). If the latter, then specific autonomic arousal becomes an inevitable correlate of facial expression, and assuming that facial expression and subjective emotional experience are usually linked, an inevitable correlate of emotional experience. Whether it has a *causal* role in emotional experience would still be unresolved.

However, if autonomic arousal is an *indirect* result of contracting facial muscles, and not directly produced by the central nervous system, then it may be of lesser importance in emotional experience. So the original James–Lange/Cannon debate would still be unresolved, although Ekman's demonstration that different emotional expressions are associated with different patterns of autonomic activity would appear, if anything, to support the original suggestions of James and Lange. It would contradict the Schachter and Singer hypothesis of undifferentiated peripheral arousal being cognitively labelled into different emotional states.

Ekman reverses the usual approach, and uses peripheral arousal as a dependent variable (what is measured), and subjective state or objective behaviour as an independent variable (what is systematically varied). This takes us back to Ax's work, where induced fear and anger correlated with the physiological arousal patterns of adrenaline and nonadrenaline respectively.

More recently, Frankenhaeuser and her group (Frankenhaeuser, 1975, 1983; Frankenhaeuser *et al.*, 1976, 1978) have analysed the behavioural correlates of adrenaline and noradrenaline secretion in great detail, and their findings perhaps provide a more realistic and productive approach to the psychophysiology of emotional states.

The adrenal medulla, behaviour and personality

Adrenaline and noradrenaline are released from the adrenal medulla in response to activation of the sympathetic branch of the autonomic nervous system. Frankenhaeuser gauges their release by measuring urinary excretion rates, rather than measuring levels in the bloodstream, which, although more direct, involves the additional stress of taking the blood sample.

The human adrenal medulla contains more adrenaline than noradrenaline (about 5:1; Donovan, 1970), but urinary excretion rates are higher for the latter. However, a consistent and important finding has been that adrenaline release is much more responsive, or labile, to psychologically relevant stimuli; so much so that Frankenhaeuser's group work almost exclusively with adrenaline (noradrenaline release is increased significantly by physical stressors such as pain, cold, burns, and muscular work).

Like many chemicals in the body, including corticosteroids and synaptic transmitters in the brain, adrenaline levels show a pronounced diurnal variation. They are lowest early in the morning and peak between noon and mid-afternoon; any stimulus-induced response is then superimposed on a varying baseline level, which may well affect the efficiency of the response. If, as seems likely, adrenaline release correlates with a variety of performance and personality variables, its underlying rhythm may account for diurnal variations in performance and mood.

The extensive work of Frankenhaeuser's group on the nature of the psychological stimuli most effective at eliciting an adrenaline response produces some general conclusions. Overstimulation or understimulation both increase adenaline levels, with the rise correlating with perceived discomfort. Emotion-arousing films of any sort will elicit an adrenaline response, with no differentiation between amusing, violent, or horrific films. Similarly effective are tasks which are either pleasant (playing bingo), unpleasant (unsolvable puzzles), or just tedious (simple but prolonged mental arithmetic). Although in many cases the adrenaline response appears to involve an element of emotional arousal, or at least emotionally toned arousal, novel but emotionally neutral stimuli are effective, as are conditions of uncertainty. The response to these latter may represent a physiological preparation for any eventuality, and in some of the situations a complex interaction between psychological stimuli and physical responses is clearly occurring. Doing IQ tests is an example, where subjective involvement, emotional arousal (fear?), and intense physical activity (writing), combine to produce a massive release of adrenaline.

One of the more extraordinary findings reported by Frankenhaeuser is a sex difference in adreno-medullary reactivity. Females show little or no adrenaline response to a variety of stressors which are effective for males. These include cognitive tasks, and the taking of blood samples using a hypodermic syringe (Frankenhaeuser *et al.*, 1976); females showed no rise in adrenaline levels from control, relaxed, conditions. (It should be noted that adrenaline responses to achievement demands did not differentiate male and female engineers, bus drivers, or lawyers, i.e. what Frankenhaeuser refers to as 'non-traditional' roles for women (Frankenhaeuser, 1983).)

Particularly intriguing is the finding that the adrenaline response in males to the stress of taking an IQ test is correlated with test performance, i.e. urinary excretion of adrenaline is proportional to IQ. Good performance is also associated with a rapid and dramatic increase to the initial stress of the test, combined with a fast return to baseline when the test is over. In females, the adrenaline response to taking an IQ test is usually insignificant and is not correlated with either performance, which is on average better than males, or with subjective discomfort, which matches that in males.

Frankenhaeuser explains sex differences in adrenaline responsivity in terms of male/female differences in coping with achievement demands, and uses the apparent stability of their adreno-medullary system to explain why females on average live longer than males (Frankenhaeuser *et al.*, 1978). A key element in the damaging effects of stressful stimuli is the mobilization by adrenaline of the body's fat reserves, which results in high blood-levels of free fatty acids. These would be dissipated by physical effort, if such was the appropriate response to the stressor. However, many psychological stressors activate the adreno-medullary system but have no correlated physical response – we sit in the car, tense and occasionally angry, but perfectly immobile. Fatty acids accumulate in the bloodstream, and contribute significantly to the furring up of the cardiovascular system. Females, responding less dramatically to stressful situations, would accordingly suffer less physiological damage (Frankenhaeuser does emphasize that the subjective experiences do not differentiate males and females; in females, therefore, there is a dissociation between subjective stress and discomfort and peripheral physiological arousal).

Such a dramatic finding from one laboratory needs replication and extension before it can be fully accepted. If it were reliable, and assuming that the emotional repertoires of males and females are roughly equivalent, it would lessen the likelihood that adreno-medullary activity determines subjective emotion. The relative unresponsiveness of noradrenaline to psychological stimuli supports this conclusion, and casts doubt on the results of Ax and Funkenstein. Fear and anger, along with happiness, elicit a significant adrenaline response, and cannot be differentiated by patterns of adreno-medullary activation.

Besides a sex difference, urinary adrenaline excretion also correlates with aspects of personality (Frankenhaeuser, *et al.*, 1980b). Frankenhaeuser *et al.* (1980a) used an Activity Survey to divide a group of male subjects into Type A and Type B personalities. The survey assesses attitudes to work and leisure, and identifies a Type A personality which is significantly more susceptible to coronary heart disease. The groups were tested under conditions of work (mental arithmetic with noise distraction) and rest. Type B subjects showed higher levels of adrenaline excretion and heart-rate under work conditions than when resting, while Type A individuals were highly aroused under both conditions. They also reported feeling uncomfortable when resting, in comparison to the Type B's, which may account for their increased peripheral arousal in this condition; when working they may be happier, but the physical involvement ensures continuing high levels of adrenaline release. This example neatly points out the two major determinants of adreno-medullary activity. Physical exertion, with its direct dependence upon energy expenditure, is the most reliable activator, while subjective emotional involvement, especially if negatively biased, can also activate the system in anticipation of action which may or may not be necessary.

The pituitary-adrenal system, stress and arousal

Activity in the pituitary–adrenal system is highly correlated with activity in the sympathetic branch of the autonomic nervous system. Given that both are controlled from the hypothalamus, stimuli eliciting release of adrenaline from the adrenal medulla are likely also to stimulate the pituitary-adrenal axis, with a consequent secretion of corticosteroids from the adenal cortex into the bloodstream.

Research into the possible psychological relevance of the pituitary-adrenal system has not emphasized a role in different emotional states, but has looked at its relationship with stressful stimuli. Selye (1950) introduced the concept of the General Adaptation Syndrome, whereby different stressors would elicit a common stress response from the organism. The syndrome consists of a stage of 'alarm', when the stressor is first encountered, a state of 'resistance', in which the physiological systems of the body maintain normal functioning in the face of the stressor, and a stage of 'exhaustion', when the intensity and duration of the stressor overcome the body's resistance. Prolonged stressors may then produce various pathogenic symptoms, such as gastric ulceration and chronically raised blood-pressure.

Selye suggested that pituitary-adrenal activation was a central component of the stress response, and although he was primarily concerned with physical stressors such as pain, corticosteroid release is also an important response to psychological stressors. The definition of a stressor, or stressful stimulus, as something which elicits the stress response is circular; what is required is some idea of the characteristics of psychologial stimuli which prove to be stressors.

Prolonged stress causes gastric ulceration, possibly mediated by chronically elevated levels of corticosteroids in the bloodstream. Ulceration can therefore be used as a dependent variable to assess the stressfulness of various stimuli, particularly in animals. In 1958, Brady *et al.* reported a phenomenon that has become known as the 'Executive Monkey' syndrome. Monkeys were run on a Sidman unsignalled avoidance schedule. On this schedule, an avoidance response postpones a footshock for twenty seconds, but the imminence of shocks and successful avoidance are not signalled to the animal by lights or tones, etc. Monkeys were run in pairs, with one performing the avoidance responses and a yoked control passively receiving the same footshocks but unable to perform any avoidance responses. After many days, the executive monkeys died of severe gastric ulceration while the passive yoked controls remained healthy.

These results imply that footshock *per se* is not a severe stressor, but that a combination of active but unsuccessful responding (in that not all shocks are avoided) plus footshocks is. However, despite its prominence in accounts of the psychology of stress, this study has proved difficult to replicate, and Weiss (1972) has demonstrated that the experimental paradigm itself is more complicated than previously thought. He set up an analogous situation, with rats rather than monkeys, using a yoked control to isolate the effects of the physical stressor alone. A single trial consisted of a ten-second tone followed by a single footshock; if the 'executive' rat touched a panel with his nose during the tone, the footshock was avoided. There was one trial per minute, and the experiment was twenty-one hours long.

Weiss found that the executive rats developed slightly more ulceration than unshocked controls, showing that shock *per se* is a slight stressor. More dramatically, the yoked controls developed much more ulceration than the executives, in contradiction to Brady *et al.*, where the executive monkeys fared worse than the passive yoked partners.

The significant difference between the experiments was the presentation of a warning tone in Weiss's study. When an avoidance response was made, the tone was terminated, giving the animal immediate feedback that his coping response had been successful. If the coping response does not alter the animal's stimulus environment, as in unsignalled Sidman avoidance, relevant feedback is zero. Running this condition with rats, i.e. repeating the study but this time with no warning signal, Weiss obtained similar levels of ulceration in both executive and yoked control groups, showing that the warning tone did effectively reduce the stress of the situation.

This latter experiment was apparently analogous to the Brady *et al.* executive monkey study, but the results were still somewhat different, in that Brady *et al.* found the 'executive' condition to be much more stressful than the yoked condition. Weiss then pointed out that Brady's group selected for their executive monkeys those who naturally responded most, i.e. were most active. In all his work, Weiss has found a significant and positive correlation between activity level measured as response frequency, and tendency to ulcerate. He therefore suggests that Brady's executive monkeys were actually more prone to ulcers anyway, and conclusively validated his explanation by selecting as executives his most naturally active rats, and precisely replicating Brady's results. Active rats performing on a Sidman avoidance schedule with no relevant feedback, i.e. no warning signal, ulcerate more than any other of Weiss's experimental groups.

Two general conclusions emerge from this work. Firstly, coping responses can reduce levels of stress, but only if feedback is given; animals need not only to cope, but to know that they are coping. Secondly, susceptibility to the pathogenic effects of stress varies from subject to subject, much as adrenaline responsiveness varies from Type A to Type B personalities. This is particularly apparent with humans, where the perception of stressors is mediated through complex cognitive and emotional buffering systems, and where the adrenocortical response to stressors is consequently much more variable and unpredictable.

Mason has worked for many years on the adrenocortical and sympathetic adrenomedullary responses to psychological stimuli (for a comprehensive account, see Mason, 1968). By demonstrating that a rapid rise in external temperature is accompanied by corticosteroid secretion, while a slow rise to the same level is not, he has shown that the stress response is specific and sensitive to quite subtle stimuli. This goes against Selye's idea of a non-specific stress response, but Selye was much more concerned with gross physical stressors as encountered in medicine.

Mason has also shown that 'uncertainty' is a powerful activator of the pituitary-adrenal system. Mild novel stimuli are effective, as are unexpected changes in operant schedules. Sidman *et al.* (1962) trained monkeys until they were performing efficiently on an unsignalled Sidman avoidance schedule. When unexpected and gratuitous footshocks were given at random, a massive release of corticosteroids occurred. More recently, Hennessey *et al.* (1977) have shown that maximal pituitary-adrenal activation occurs in conditions of very high and very low uncertainty, perhaps analogous to the ability of both over-arousing and under-arousing conditions to elicit an adrenaline response from the adrenal medulla (see previous section).

Circulating hormones and cognition

In some areas of physiological psychology, explanations, particularly the more traditional ones, have involved a dichotomy between peripheral and central mechanisms. Hunger and the control of satiety, emotion and the role of autonomic arousal, can both be debated from either a centralist or a peripheralist position, although I hope the material presented in this chapter helps show the artificiality of such a division.

There is now evidence for a more direct interplay between hormones and chemicals circulating in the periphery and brain mechanisms mediating sensation, cognition, and overt behaviour. For some time we have been aware that the brain and body interact in a complex system involving cognition and peripheral physiological mechanisms; the field of psychosomatics is devoted to unravelling physiological problems apparently of psychological origin. The previous sections considered how the centrally mediated perception of an external emotional or stressful event could influence peripheral arousal systems, and we now, in turn, look at the possible feedback influence of peripheral chemicals on perception and other central processes.

The release of ACTH from the pituitary gland is controlled in part by the levels of ACTH and corticosteroids in the bloodstream. This feedback regulation involves receptive sites for ACTH and corticosteroids in the pituitary gland itself, in the hypothalamus, and in the higher levels of the brain (Fig. 9.1). Similar systems operate in the control of other pituitary hormones such as prolactin and growth hormone. Sexual identity and reproductive behaviour depend upon areas of the brain selectively responding to oestrogen, progesterone and testosterone, carried from the gonads to the brain in the bloodstream.

So we have been aware for some time that hormones can and

do reach the brain to influence either their own release or specific aspects of behaviour, but it is only recently that unexpectedly broad effects on perception and cognition have been shown. Along with discoveries on the precise nature of pituitary regulation, this has led to a specialized research area evolving – anatomical and psychological neuroendocrinology (for reviews see, e.g., Stumpf, 1975; De Wied, 1976).

To illustrate the psychological effects of chemicals of peripheral origin, I shall consider the involvement of ACTH in learning and memory, the influence of circulating corticosteroids on sensory thresholds and perception, and the role of trace elements such as zinc and magnesium on perception and cognition. The principles involved have a general relevance.

De Wied and his group at the University of Utrecht have for some years been studying the behavioural effects of ACTH in animals (De Wied, 1976, 1977; Wimersma Greidanus, 1977). They have demonstrated that the hormone facilitates the acquisition of active and passive avoidance, and also delays the extinction of learnt behaviours. It can reverse the amnesic effects of electro-convulsive shock (see Chapter 6) and other amnesic agents (Rigter and Van Riezen, 1975).

By using injections directly into the brain, they have shown that these actions are central, and not secondary to any peripheral changes. Important structures appear to be the hippocampus and the thalamus; this would certainly correspond with the established role of the hippocampus in feedback regulation of the pituitary-adrenal axis, through its selective uptake of ACTH and corticosteroids from the bloodstream (McEwen and Weiss, 1970). Intriguingly, corticosteroids appear to have behavioural effects opposite to those of ACTH – acquisition of avoidance learning is delayed, and extinction is speeded up.

De Wied has also studied the features of the ACTH molecule essential for its behavioural activity. Like most other pituitary hormones, ACTH is a polypeptide, i.e. a chain of peptides. Each peptide consists in turn of a chain of amino-acids, such as histamine, glycine, arginine, etc. Thus ACTH is known to contain thirty-nine amino-acid groupings (not of thirty-nine different amino-acids – human metabolism utilizes only around twenty-six different amino-acids, so long chains involve repetitions). De Wied split the ACTH chain into fragments, or peptides, and, using a straightforward numbering system (ACTH 1–10, ACTH 24–39, etc.) isolated their behavioural potency. He found that the peptide fragment ACTH 4–10 (i.e. consisting of a chain of seven amino-acids) was as active as the intact ACTH molecule on behaviour. However, it was ineffective at releasing corticosteroids from the adrenal cortex (the primary hormonal function of ACTH).

The detailed significance of De Wied's work is unclear. The function of neurohypophysial hormones in normal human behaviour is as yet unknown. ACTH circulates in the bloodstream, reaching the brain, and is taken up by brain structures. It presumably influences neuronal activity in those structures, and therefore could affect any behaviours these structures are normally concerned with; De Wied suspects that ACTH thus modulates motivation, memory, and learning in the intact organism, besides its established hormonal function in the periphery.

As other pituitary hormones, such as prolactin, thyroid-stimulating hormone, and vasopressin, have also been shown to have substantial and general effects on behaviour (De Wied, 1977), our division of physiological mechanisms into central and peripheral is becoming increasingly artificial. More alarming for those who wish to describe the brain in relatively simple terms is the discovery that short amino-acid sequences, or peptides, have significant behavioural activity. ACTH 4–10 is an example, but a better one is β-endorphin (see Chapter 3), This naturally occurring opiate, found in the brain, is a peptide whose amino-acid sequence also occurs as part of the pituitary hormone β-lipotropin (β-lipotropin 61–91). Besides making the pituitary gland a prime source for the extraction and purification of β-endorphin, the probability that the pituitary is a major source of synthesis for the body's natural complement of β-endorphin raises again the question of the general role of pituitary peptides in behaviour.

ACTH released from the pituitary stimulates the adrenal cortex to secrete corticosteroids into the bloodstream. There are two clinical syndromes in which corticosteroid secretion is abnormal: adrenal cortical insufficiency (Addison's disease), and adrenal cortical hyperfunction (Cushing's syndrome). Robert Henkin at the National Institute of Health in Maryland has made an extensive study of such patients and demonstrated some intriguing correlations between corticosteroid levels and sensory processes. Using mostly Addison's patients, Henkin has measured sensory thresholds in the untreated condition, and after replacement therapy with steroids such as prednisolone or cortisone. Taste acuity for the basic tastes of salt, sour, bitter and sweet was assessed using solutions of appropriate chemicals (sodium chloride, hydrochloric acid, urea, and sucrose) applied to the tongue. Olfaction was gauged by asking the subject to decide which of three solutions was different to the others using smell only; two were water and the other was one of the solutions used in the taste experiments. By varying the concentrations, taste and olfactory ability could be accurately measured. Detection thresholds for auditory signals were obtained using tones of standard intensity but of varying frequency.

The results (Henkin, 1975) were consistent across sensory modalities. Patients with untreated adrenocortical insufficiency, i.e. chronically lowered levels of circulating corticosteroids, had lowered sensory thresholds for taste, smell, and hearing. These subjects could detect lower concentrations of solutions either tasted or smelt, and could hear sounds of higher frequency than normal controls. After two or three days on steroid replacement therapy, sensory thresholds returned to normal. Results from patients with Cushing's syndrome were, as expected, in the opposite direction: chronically elevated levels of corticosteroids were associated with raised sensory thresholds, i.e. lowered sensory acuity.

That the increased acuity of untreated Addison's patients was not indicative of a general improvement in sensory functioning was shown by their problems with *recognizing* stimuli as opposed to simply detecting them. They could hear higher-frequency sounds than normals, but were worse at correctly recognizing words and in localizing sounds in the environment. Henkin concludes that low levels of circulating corticosteroids correlate with increased sensory acuity *per se*, but also with a decreased ability to recognize or integrate sensory stimuli. (Incidentally, it has been suggested that a similar combination – increased stimulus responsivity with a decreased ability to integrate or cope with it – is characteristic of schizophrenia. Henkin quotes anecdotal evidence that some patients so diagnosed have later been shown to have adrenocortical insufficiency.)

As these sensory abnormalities are consistently reversed by steroid therapy, it seems likely that circulating corticosteroid levels do have a direct influence on sensory and perceptual processes. The precise mechanism is unknown. Like ACTH, corticosteroids are selectively taken up by the hippocampus as part of the brain-pituitary-adrenal feedback system; perhaps this structure also mediates their perceptual effects. Addison's patients also have faster conduction velocities of neural impulses along peripheral sensory neurons, coupled with slower synaptic transmission. Henkin concludes that corticosteroids can have effects on the sensory receptor, on the peripheral neuron, and in the central nervous system.

Whether the effects of these stress hormones on sensory and perceptual processes play a significant role under normal conditions is debatable. Addison's disease and Cushing's syndrome are rare and severe physiological disabilities, and it may be that such extremes of adrenocortical functioning are necessary before significant sensory changes occur. On the other hand, the adaptive mechanisms of the body are constantly surprising us; it is possible to construct a scenario where increased corticosteroid levels lead to decreased stimulus sensitivity but an increased ability to perceive and recognize those stimuli that do register. This may be an aid to narrowing of attention and elimination, or filtering out, of irrelevant stimuli in an aroused, stressful situation, and a key to efficient responding.

The final example in this section again involves Henkin, and disorders of taste and smell. Many everyday (or at least, every other day) conditions involve abnormalities of taste and/or smell – pregnancy, influenza, hepatitis, alcoholic cirrhosis – and their precise aetiology (cause) is unclear. Occasionally a disorder of taste (dysgeusia) or loss of taste (hypogeusia) occurs without an obvious predisposing factor. These cases of *idiopathic hypogeusia*, as Henkin refers to them, are rare but dramatic. The clinical syndrome is evocatively described in Roueché (1977), who relates the tale of a pizza restaurant owner who spontaneously developed hypogeusia. The major symptom was that virtually all food eventually tasted rotten, like eating garbage. The subject lived on white grapes and vanilla ice-cream, which is not a good advertisement for a pizza house owner. Medical doctors were no help, and neither were the psychiatrists to whom they sent him. Eventually, and fortunately for this patient, his case was referred to Henkin, who had developed an interest in the syndrome. Along with the interest had come an hypothesis – that disorders of taste were related to a deficiency of zinc in the body.

Treatment with zinc sulphate tablets restored the pizza house owner to normal, confirming Henkin's prediction. He then, unbeknown to the patient, substituted placebo tablets for the zinc sulphate, to control for any non-specific effects of the medication. As expected, when the patient eventually reported back the hypogeusia had returned; unfortunately he was no longer a pizza house owner as he had sold up in despair when his 'treatment' had apparently failed (this implies no criticism of Henkin, who had emphasized that the patient should report back immediately any symptoms reappeared; this the subject had not done, as he did not wish to let Henkin down).

It is known that many conditions associated with abnormalities of smell and taste also involve lowered levels of zinc in serum, hair, or saliva. Of course, they may also correlate with other metabolic indices. However, Henkin *et al.* (1975) have shown that controlled drug-induced zinc loss produces a syndrome whose major feature is hypogeusia. Using the amino-acid histidine (which strips zinc from its binding sites in the body and allows it to be excreted), to reduce serum zinc levels, Henkin described a range of symptoms attributable to zinc loss in humans. Hypogeusia and hyposmia led to an immediate anorexia (reduced food intake). There were signs of cerebellar motor dysfunction, such as tremor and unsteadiness. More dramatically, there were also emotional, cognitive, and perceptual changes: lethargy, depression, forgetfulness, and, in one patient, auditory and visual hallucinations. All symptoms disappeared with zinc sulphate treatment.

The mechanisms mediating the effects of reduced zinc levels are unknown. The taste abnormalities are associated with an actual degeneration of the taste buds in the tongue, reversible with zinc sulphate therapy. Zinc is also found in many areas of the brain, with highest levels in the hippocampus, and significant levels in cortex, striatum, and cerebellum. Thus there is ample scope for explaining the motor, emotional, cognitive, and perceptual consequences of zinc loss. However, the role of zinc – and other trace elements such as copper and magnesium – at the cellular level is unknown, so precisely how neuronal function is affected we cannot say.

ACTH and corticosteroids are circulating hormones, with a massive increase in output in response to arousing and stressful tissues, but levels may fall in certain conditions. Besides their physiological actions, all these substances appear to have significant effects on various aspects of behaviour – effects which involve an action within the brain. Thus, in the case of ACTH and corticosteroids, cognition, motivation, and perception are directly modulated by chemicals more usually associated with peripheral arousal systems. Zinc is an example of how wide our search for the factors influencing the brain and behaviour has to be. Besides synaptic neurotransmitters, hormones, peptides, and trace elements play important parts in the chemical symphony of the brain.

As a final point, it is possible to see how this recent work relates to the original controversy regarding emotional experience and peripheral arousal. This chapter has reviewed that area in all its confusion, beginning with James's original view that peripheral arousal generated emotional experience. We can now see from the effects of ACTH on learning in animals and of corticosteroids on sensory processes in humans, that the physiological response to emotional and stressful stimuli – activation of the pituitary-adrenal axis – could in turn modulate the behavioural responses to those stimuli. The importance of increased levels of ACTH and corticosteroids in helping the organism adapt to stressful situations would not then be confined to the metabolic aspects, but would incorporate behaviour. Any direct influence they might have on emotion has not yet been investigated. If one were demonstrated, James's model of emotion could be revived, with the pituitary-adrenal axis given the role originally played by the autonomic nervous system.

10 Central mechanisms of arousal, sleep, and waking

Introduction

The previous chapter dealt with peripheral physiological arousal mechanisms. Although indices of peripheral arousal are not perfectly correlated (e.g. the phasic arousal associated with an orienting response produces an increase in skin conductance but a decrease in heart-rate), a combination of pituitary-adrenal cortex activation with general sympathetic arousal does serve to define our peripheral arousal pattern. The physiological state may correspond with behaviour, particularly during physical exercise and during the expression of intense emotion, or it may be behaviourally undetectable, as in some psychologically stressful or arousing situations in which responding is impossible or inappropriate. So our concept of 'arousal' has, even at this stage, to distinguish between 'behavioural' and 'peripheral physiological' components.

Psychologists also use 'arousal' as a theoretical construct, to help explain relationships between dependent and independent variables. This usage is epitomized in the inverted-U-shaped curve relating performance on a given task to the subject's level of arousal (Fig. 10.1); performance is poor at relatively low and high levels, and optimal at a moderate arousal level.

It should be emphasized that the inverted-U-shaped function is hypothetical, not a law of nature. It has to be empirically demonstrated for any given task, an endeavour fraught with many problems of which the most pressing is to systematically vary 'arousal' level. To do this we need to operationalize our theoretical construct, to choose a manipulation which directly

PERFORMANCE

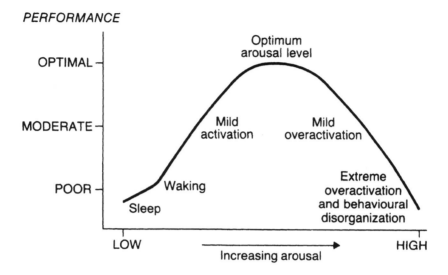

Figure 10.1 *Inverted-U-shaped curve of arousal and performance*

influences our subject's 'arousal' level.

At the extremes of a *behavioural* arousal dimension lie sleep and hysterical overactivity. It seems likely, even in the absence of experimental data, that task performance will be poorer in either of these states than during normal, alert waking, i.e. an inverted U could describe the function relating performance to these arousal states. So it is the range between these extremes that the experimental psychologist concentrates upon in the attempt to discover if, for instance, performance on a vigilance task can be improved with mildly arousing stimuli and impaired with very arousing ones.

The stimuli used tend to be stressors, such as white noise played through headphones, sleep deprivation, or incentives (i.e. where reward is proportional to performance). It is usually assumed that the intensity of the stressor is linearly related to the degree of the subject's arousal. The obtained relationship between stressor intensity and performance then represents the function relating arousal level and performance, and can be compared with the predicted inverted U-shaped curve.

It is perfectly legitimate for the psychologist concerned to deal only with his particular stressor, and to make no inferences beyond his own experimental paradigm. However, this narrow approach would not help to link the many studies of stressors and performance; it also makes sense to treat together experiments on, for instance, white noise and incentives when the interpretation of results refers in both cases to something called 'arousal'.

Even when widely used as an explanatory device, 'arousal' need not involve the experimental psychologist in an appeal to possible physiological mechanisms; it can remain a valuable theoretical construct for integrating a range of experimental data, rather like 'attention' or 'motivation'. In fact, the introduction of the probable physiological substrates of arousal can lead to great confusion. It is clear that different stressors have differential effects on performance, and their combined effects may be additive, independent, or even antagonistic (e.g. sleep deprivation and white noise). If they acted upon a common substrate of 'arousal', then their actions on behaviour should be similar and additive.

Cognitive performance depends, as we shall see, on central physiological arousal mechanisms. These are complex and interactive, not simple and independent. The notion of a single central 'arousal' system is now outmoded, and along with it any ideas that experimental psychologists may have about a common 'arousal' substrate mediating the effects of stressors on performance. This latter hypothesis was a fruit of the early work on the behavioural functions of the brainstem reticular formation, which demonstrated conclusively its major role in the control of sleep and waking behaviour. Before analysing this work in more detail, I shall first discuss in more general terms the phenomena of sleep and waking.

We spend around 30 per cent of our lives asleep, far more time than we give to eating, drinking, or, in most cases, learning. For centuries, the question of the function or functions of sleep has been discussed, and we still have no answer; or, more precisely, we have many suggestions, but no consensus. The basic phenomena are undisputed. Mammals, birds, reptiles, and fish sleep. Even molluscs and insects show behaviour indistinguishable from sleep. Some rare subjects manage on an hour or less per night; otherwise humans need, or think they need, between five and ten hours sleep in every twenty-four. If we are deprived of sleep, we feel tired, and tend to make up some of the deficit on subsequent nights.

These simple observations raise complex questions. The ubiquity of sleep across the phylogenetic scale implies that it has a necessary function, but does not distinguish between physiological hypotheses (e.g. tissue restoration), psychological hypotheses (e.g. processing of the previous day's experiences), or ecological hypotheses (e.g. safety from predation). The regularity of sleep patterns within the circadian cycle needs explanation. Is sleep actively triggered by the brain in response to darkness or to some intrinsic biological rhythm such as temperature; or perhaps by the daily build-up of some 'need for sleep' represented by, for instance, a drop in synaptic transmitter levels? Alternatively, sleep might be a passive process; the natural state, as it were, into which the brain falls unless incoming environmental stimulation is sufficient to arouse it.

No single chapter can deal with all the questions. I shall present some hypotheses relating to many of them, and then review the current status of the reticular formation as the physiological substrate of central arousal.

The states of sleep

Our definition of the various states of sleep relies heavily upon the electroencephalograph (see Chapter 1). Using EEG recordings, many levels of sleep may be identified; although for my purposes the subdivision of Meddis (1979) is the most appropriate. This distinguishes 'waking' from 'quiet' sleep (QS), and 'active' sleep (AS). The 'waking' EEG is characterized by desynchronized fast activity. 'Quiet' sleep consists of a synchronized EEG (i.e. there is a regular wave-form which may be identified by its amplitude and frequency); as one passes from light quiet sleep (LQS) to deep quiet sleep (DQS), the amplitude and frequency of the waves in the EEG increase and decrease respectively, i.e. the waves become bigger and slower. In 'active' sleep the EEG is desynchronized and fast, yet behaviourally the subject is sleeping most deeply, as very intense stimuli are needed to awaken him. Thus it is often referred to as 'paradoxical' sleep, or, as it is also associated with rapid eye movements, as REM sleep. A further alternative, following the work of Dement, Kleitman, and Aserinsky in the 1950s, is 'dreaming' sleep, as subjects aroused during this phase report dreams more frequently than if aroused during quiet sleep. However, a phylogenetic view of sleep incorporates animals who have no cortex (and hence no cortical EEG arousal), and no possibility of reporting dreams; so 'active' sleep is a more appropriate and inclusive term.

Birds and mammals exhibit all three states of sleep and arousal, oscillating between waking, QS, and AS. The pattern is highly consistent; animals fall from waking into LQS, and then to DQS. After some time in DQS, sleep lightens and they move back into LQS. At this point a phase of AS is triggered, from which they move again into LQS, and the cycle repeats itself: LQS → DQS → LQS → AS

In humans the cycle duration (from the triggering of successive phases of AS) averages around sixty minutes, so a normal night's sleep may contain six or seven AS interludes. As our sleep lightens towards morning we spend more time in LQS, and consequently the AS phases (apparently dependent upon prior LQS) become more frequent. Thus the dreaming associated with AS becomes more common and memorable as we approach awakening.

The patterning of awake → quiet sleep → active sleep represents a fundamental and intrinsic biological rhythm. Behavioural measures of the developing foetus *in utero* reveal rhythmic cycles of quiescence and activity. EEG measures of waking state, quiet sleep, and active sleep, in premature and full-term neonates, show that the periodicity (or cycle duration) at thirty-six weeks post-conception is similar to that in the eight-month-old infant (Stern *et al.*, 1973). So, although the ratio of active sleep to quiet sleep alters during the first post-natal year, with the proportion of active sleep gradually declining from 70–90 per cent to around 20–25 per cent of total sleep time, the complex cyclical pattern of waking and sleeping seems to be endogenous and therefore present from birth.

Quiet sleep and active sleep are qualitatively distinct states. Both have physiological and endocrinological correlates alongside their characteristic EEG patterns, and these have fuelled various hypotheses as to the functions of sleep. Active sleep is, in humans, also associated with the subjective self-report of dreams, and a range of psychoanalytically based interpretations have emerged to explain the content of dream imagery and by implication the function of dreaming and hence of active sleep (see, e.g., Freud, 1955). The effects of depriving humans and other animals of active sleep has been a popular device in the analysis of its functions, but it should be emphasized that active-sleep deprivation (or REM-deprivation, as it is often called) is not equivalent to 'dream deprivation'. Dreaming in humans may occur in the various phases of quiet sleep, while we do not know if the presence of active-sleep states in cats and rats implies the presence of dream imagery in these animals.

The functions of sleep

If sleep is necessary, total sleep deprivation should produce some physiological or psychological effects, analogous to the consequences of food deprivation. However, rather like prolonged hunger, the impetus to sleep increases without any dramatic breakdown in body or behaviour. We can endure hunger for many days without permanent ill-effects, and we can endure sleeplessness for many days without permanent damage; more impressively, performance on various cognitive tasks can be sustained at a high level even after several days of sleep deprivation.

This phenomenon has been used by some authors to demonstrate the absence of any psychological or physiological drive to sleep (Meddis, 1979), and has led to explanations on a more ecological level. Before considering these, it should be noted that, while we can survive and function effectively after days of food deprivation, eventually we die; similarly, prolonged sleep deprivation has been shown to produce psychotic breakdown in humans, and death in animals. When subjects eat after food deprivation, they do not consume the equivalent of all the meals they have missed; similarly, sleep rebound after sleep deprivation does not make up for all the sleep lost. It would appear that, in these respects, sleep does resemble the primary homeostatic drive of hunger.

An obvious feature of sleep is that the animal concerned is doing nothing to draw attention to itself, which could be seen as adaptive in a hostile environment. If there are periods in the day when foraging is either impossible (e.g. nighttime for animals specialized to operate in the day) or dangerous (daytime for small nocturnal mammals), then immobility during these periods would be an advantage (Meddis, 1979). An ecological explanation is also suggested by the predator/prey link, whereby total sleep time is directly related to predator status. Animals preyed upon, such as herbivores, tend to sleep much less (Oswald, 1980; Allison and Cicchetti, 1976). This contradicts any notion of 'sleep' being a particularly safe adaptation; if it were the dominant motivation, herbivores should sleep more. However, metabolic differences may account for the discrepancy; predators are carnivores geared to occasional but large meals, while herbivores have to graze most of the available time simply to fulfil their dietary needs. Predators therefore have more time to sleep, while it still makes ecological sense for herbivores to sleep and remain inconspicuous when grazing is impossible.

Although total sleep time has some relation to predator status, size is also important. Cows, sheep, and goats sleep for around four hours a day, while squirrels and tree shrews sleep for around fourteen hours. Size is inversely related to metabolic rate, so it is not surprising that total sleep time is directly related to metabolic rate (Zepelin and Rechtschaffen, 1974). High metabolic rates involve rapid energy expenditure when active, but substantial energy conservation and recovery when inactive or asleep. Horne (1979; 1978) proposes that energy conservation is therefore a major function of sleep in smaller mammals such as rodents. It is a period of anabolism, or tissue restoration, for the body.

In higher and larger mammals such as humans, periods of 'relaxed wakefulness' are interspersed with the normal sleep/ waking cycle. As energy expenditure during these periods is only about 10 per cent greater than in sleep, Horne suggests that anabolism can be carried out during relaxed wakefulness, leaving sleep available for alternative functions. As total sleep deprivation may produce some effects on cognitive perform- ance and on the cortical EEG (Horne, 1979), these alternative functions may include cerebral restitution; i.e. as the phy- logenetic scale is ascended, sleep becomes less important for the body and more important for the brain.

This view goes against a popular hypothesis of the separable roles of quiet sleep and active sleep, put forward by Oswald (1976; 1980). During the phases of quiet sleep the brain is unaroused in terms of the EEG, but there is much peripheral activity. Particularly impressive is the massive increase in the secretion of growth hormone from the pituitary gland; the effects of the hormone are to stimulate protein synthesis throughout the body, which suggests that quiet sleep is associ- ated with general tissue restoration (Adam and Oswald, 1977). As active sleep, or REM, involves high levels of cerebral activity (e.g. EEG arousal and an increase in cortical blood- flow of around 50 per cent over quiet sleep levels), Oswald (1976) suggests that this phase of sleep is associated specifically with recovery processes in the brain (see the related hypothesis of Stern and Morgane, discussed later in this chapter). The predominance of active sleep in the neonate is associated with rapid cerebral development, and supports this view of its functional significance.

Horne criticizes the hypothesis, pointing out that the effects of human growth hormone are widespread and in some cases unclear. Further, some mammals, such as cats and rats, do not show an elevated release during quiet sleep. He concludes that both active and quiet sleep are involved with general tissue restoration in smaller mammals, but that this role is taken over by relaxed wakefulness in higher mammals, leaving both types of sleep available specifically for cerebral restitution.

A phylogenetic perspective reveals some interesting data. Only birds and mammals demonstrate a cycle of two distinct sleep states. Reptiles, amphibia, and fish show only a single type of sleep, which, in the absence of EEG arousal and rapid eye movements, is assumed to be quiet sleep. Thus active sleep evolved only in the warm-blooded (homiothermic) birds and mammals. Meddis (1977) disagrees with this idea. He points out that metabolic rates in cold-blooded (poikilothermic) animals are significantly slower than in homiotherms, and so the signs of active sleep, such as an EEG arousal pattern and rapid eye movements, would be correspondingly less obvious, i.e. active sleep in reptiles would not resemble active sleep in mammals. As active sleep precedes quiet sleep in ontogeny (development of the individual), with neonates showing much more active sleep than adults, it would be parsimonious to suggest that it precedes quiet sleep in phylogeny (evolution). This is not a particularly sound argument, but Meddis does suggest why this pattern should evolve. Temperature regulation in active sleep is inefficient, with the blood-flow to the brain increased but the blood-flow to the periphery much reduced. Central temperature regulation is absent and therefore irrelevant to poikilotherms, but is essential to activity in homiotherms. Warm-blooded animals cannot allow their body temperature to fall too far or they will not recover. Periods of quiet sleep, in which temperature regulation is quite good, therefore have to be interspersed with phases of active sleep to prevent body temperature falling to dangerous levels. If one then postulates that sleep in poikilotherms is of the active sort, homiotherms would have to evolve quiet sleep in parallel with their warm-bloodedness. Thus, in evolution and in development of the individual, active sleep precedes quiet sleep (Meddis, 1979).

The study of sleep in poikilotherms has not advanced sufficiently to confirm the speculation; one obvious problem is that active sleep in mature mammals appears to be 'triggered' by a preceding phase of light quiet sleep (Stern and Morgane, 1974), a dependence opposite to the one predicted on an evolutionary view. However, a direct link between body temperature and sleep has been reported (Czeisler *et al.*, 1980). Volunteers spent months in isolation, without an indication of the time of day. Under these conditions sleep patterns became irregular, but the duration of sleep showed a high correlation with body temperature. Body temperature has a circadian rhythm with one peak and one trough every twenty-four hours, the trough often occurring an hour or so after midnight and the peak about twelve hours later. Isolated subjects retained this rhythm, although on average the cycle extended slightly to twenty-five hours. The length of time they slept could then be predicted from the point on their temperature curve at which they went to sleep. Usually they fell asleep when body temperature was low, and slept for seven or eight hours; occasionally sleep began when the temperature was high, and would then last for fifteen or more hours. There was no correlation between sleep duration and the length of time since they last slept.

Body temperature seems therefore to play a part in determining sleep duration. Sleep onset may also relate to this circadian rhythm, as most of the volunteer subjects eventually showed regular patterns of sleep onset and duration in phase with the rhythm of body temperature. However, many systems in the body show similar rhythms: levels of corticosteroids in the bloodstream, pain sensitivity, concentrations of brain neurotransmitters, etc. If a phenomenon such as sleep is in phase with one circadian rhythm, it must logically be in phase with any circadian rhythm (low body temperature may consistently coincide with a peak in blood corticosteroids; sleep onset and duration would be correlated equally significantly with both). Thus there is no simple cause-and-effect relationship to be inferred. What is more likely is that areas in the brain thought to be responsible for 'setting' all of these circadian rhythms are also involved in triggering sleep onset (see p. 291). As rhythms of rest and activity are observable in the foetus, and in subjects exposed to monotonous light conditions, these brain centres (such as the supra-chiasmatic nucleus) represent an endogenous (natural) oscillator which may be sensitive to day/night periodicity, but which is not influenced solely by such environmental contingencies. Any explanation of the function of sleep must therefore incorporate this biological predisposition to rhythms of sleep and waking, although it is quite possible that such a mechanism originally evolved in response to environmental pressures, e.g. the need to be inconspicuous while replenishing energy reserves and restoring tissues.

Deprivation of active sleep (REM-deprivation)

Sleep deprivation, in the short term, has few significant physiological or psychological effects in the normal subject. However, in the realms of psychopathology, there has been some interest in the possible therapeutic value of selective sleep deprivation. This interest has centred upon active sleep, or REM, and the various techniques of inducing REM-deprivation. During REM sleep, the muscles of the extremities twitch spasmodically, but the muscles controlling body posture relax. This is particularly obvious for the neck and head – when a cat falls asleep, the head is held erect until a phase of REM sleep begins, when the neck muscles relax and the head slumps forward. If the cat is on an island surrounded by water, its head will fall into the water and it wakes up; this happens whenever a phase of REM begins, and it is consequently deprived of this particular phase of sleep. Such a procedure (the 'flower-pot' technique) is uncomfortable and stressful for the animal, and is not used with human subjects. These latter will be awoken whenever EEG or behavioural signs of REM are observed. When this is done, a 'need-for-REM' develops and results in 'REM-rebound' when the subject is eventually allowed to sleep.

It has been reported that schizophrenics do not show REM-rebound after a period of REM-deprivation (Gillin *et al.*, 1974), but several studies (reviewed in Vogel, 1975) show no such link between schizophrenia and abnormalities of REM-sleep. A stronger case can be made for depression and REM. Depressions may be classified as reactive or endogenous, depending upon the presence or absence of an identifiable predisposing event. Vogel (1975) demonstrated that REM-deprivation significantly alleviated symptoms in a group of endogenously depressed patients; reactive depressions were unaffected. He suggests that the dramatic reduction in REM sleep produced by anti-depressant drugs reflects this same process; it is not a secondary and irrelevant phenomenon, but the basis of their therapeutic action.

A problem with this idea is that some drugs can reduce the amount of REM but have no anti-depressant activity. However, as Vogel points out, such drugs also result in significant REM-rebound when they are discontinued and the patient is allowed to sleep normally; anti-depressants do not produce an immediate REM-rebound, even though the reduction in REM is usually more severe (from 25 per cent to around 10 per cent of total sleep time).

This distinction between presence or absence of REM-rebound is crucial to biochemical hypotheses of the function of REM sleep. Many drugs suppress REM. If the suppression is followed by REM-rebound it can be inferred that a 'need for REM' has developed during the period for which it was suppressed. If the suppression is not followed by a subsequent rebound, it can be inferred that no 'need for REM' developed, presumably because the drug concerned actually fulfilled the normal function of REM sleep. In the first case, where rebound occurs, the drug inhibits the occurrence of REM without mimicking the function of REM.

There are hypotheses, considered in due course, vhich suggest that REM sleep is concerned with the resynthesis and replacement of brain neurotransmitter stores which become depleted in the course of waking activity. If a drug effectively replaces these neurotransmitters, albeit artificially, the need for REM is reduced or eliminated, and no rebound is necessary as stores of neurotransmitters are maintained.

This approach leads to a general consideration of the relationships between brain chemistry and sleep, an area dominated by the work of Jouvet.

Brain chemistry, sleep, and the reticular formation

Approaches to the brain mechanisms of sleep represent an interesting developmental picture of physiological psychology. Up to the 1960s, the area was dominated by neuroanatomical and electrophysiological investigations focusing upon the reticular formation. Then Jouvet (1969; 1972) suggested that the various phases of sleep (slow-wave and REM, using his terminology, rather than quiet and active) could be best understood in terms of neurotransmitters and chemical pathways, an approach consistent with contemporaneous studies of the brain chemistry of reward and punishment, hunger and thirst, etc. Since then, however, the neurotransmitter model of sleep has become extremely complicated, while the neuroanatomical model, whilst being constantly refined, has remained parsimonious and relatively straightforward.

Bremer, in the 1930s, provided two classical animal preparations in an attempt to resolve the active/passive dispute over sleep; this dispute was over whether sleep was actively generated by centres within the brain, or whether it occurred passively when sensory input fell below a threshold level, i.e. sleep, in a sense, as the natural state of the brain whenever incoming stimuli were insufficient to arouse it.

Working with cats, Bremer (1937) found that animals sectioned through the midbrain (*'cerveau isolé'*) showed persistent EEG sleep patterns; animals sectioned through the medulla/ spinal cord boundary (*'encéphale isolé'*: see Fig. 10.2) showed EEG sleep/arousal cycles. In both cases, Bremer assumed that sensory input to the forebrain (all sensory input from the periphery passes to the forebrain via the spinal cord, hindbrain, and midbrain) was minimal, in which case, following the passive theory of sleep, both preparations should sleep permanently. As the *encéphale isolé* cat shows periodic EEG arousal, sensory input is not, therefore, necessary for arousal to occur. The significant difference between *cerveau* and *encéphale isolé* preparations is that the latter has the midbrain and hindbrain still functionally and anatomically connected to the forebrain, and so, on Bremer's argument, there must be a built-in (or endogenous) arousal generator somewhere in these areas which can operate independently of sensory input.

When, in 1949, Moruzzi and Magoun first demonstrated the behavioural and EEG-arousing effects of electrically stimulating the reticular formation, it seemed that the locus of Bremer's endogenous arousal generator had been established. The reticular formation (or the *brainstem* reticular formation, to distinguish it from diencephalic systems which represent forebrain extensions of the reticular formation, and which are discussed later) is a core of tissue running through the brainstem, and therefore divisible into medullary, pontine and midbrain sections (see Fig. 10.2). It was originally thought to consist of a relatively homogeneous network (or 'reticulum') of

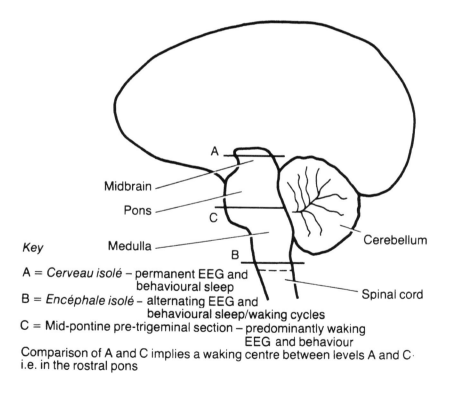

Key

A = *Cerveau isolé* – permanent EEG and behavioural sleep
B = *Encéphale isolé* – alternating EEG and behavioural sleep/waking cycles
C = Mid-pontine pre-trigeminal section – predominantly waking EEG and behaviour
Comparison of A and C implies a waking centre between levels A and C i.e. in the rostral pons

Figure 10.2   *Bremer's brainstem sections*

short-axoned neurons, whose single but essential function was to control, or modulate, the arousal state of the neocortex. This was achieved via ascending connections between the brainstem reticular formation and the neocortex, and hence the common term 'ascending reticular activating system'. This term can be slightly misleading in that reticular-cortical pathways are mirrored by cortico-reticular connections equally important in 'arousal', while the brainstem reticular formation itself sends descending pathways down through the spinal cord to influence autonomic and somatic motor functions. These are obviously important in any general analysis of the reticular system. (See also p. 31.)

In an attempt to confirm the role of the reticular formation as an endogenous arousal-generator, Lindsley *et al.* (1949; 1950) compared the effects of massive reticular lesions with the effects of lesions restricted to ascending sensory pathways in the brainstem. In the former case, the cats, with sensory input but no reticular formation, remained comatose after the operation and eventually died; in the latter instance, with no sensory input but an intact reticular system, the subjects exhibited normal sleep–waking cycles.

These results suggested that the reticular formation was, as predicted, essential for generating and controlling the brain's arousal states, and, moreover, could fulfil this function in the absence of sensory input. However, sensory input would not go away, literally or metaphorically. Bremer's *encéphale isolé* preparation eliminates input ascending via the spinal cord, but leaves intact the various cranial nerves which enter and leave the central nervous system at brainstem level. Particularly significant is the fifth, or trigeminal, cranial nerve, carrying touch and pain stimuli from the head and face. Roger *et al.* (1956) found that the arousal EEG of the *encéphale isolé* cat could be converted to a permanent sleeping EEG simply by severing the trigeminal nerve; this would imply that reticular formation-mediated EEG arousal was dependent upon the sensory input carried by the trigeminal nerve, and that 'sleep' occurred in the absence of such input and was therefore a passive phenomenon.

The next, and logical, step, was carried out by Batini *et al.* (1959). The trigeminal nerve connects with the brainstem at the level of the pons (Fig. 10.2), so that a brainstem section just anterior to this point would eliminate ascending sensory impulses travelling either via the spinal cord or via the trigeminal. Batini *et al.* showed that the cat with a mid-pontine pre-trigeminal section exhibited the 'normal' sleep-waking EEG pattern of the *encéphale isolé* preparation. In the absence of sensory input, this cortical EEG arousal must presumably be due to an endogenous arousal generator, situated in the brainstem reticular formation anterior to the mid-pontine area but posterior to the midbrain level (remembering that Bremer's midbrain-sectioned *cerveau isolé* preparation showed a sleep EEG). Moruzzi (1964) identifies the crucial arousal centre as the nucleus reticularis pontis oralis in the pons.

Such a finding veers away from the view that the brainstem reticular formation is a homogeneous structure with homogeneous functions. Long-axon neurons have been identified with cell bodies in the midbrain RF and many-branched axons extending into the forebrain, while around one hundred separable groups of cell bodies ('nuclei') have been identified in the brainstem reticular system, and, as we shall see, different groupings appear to have different functions in relation to sleep and arousal. Even the 'essential' role of the reticular formation in arousal has been questioned, with Adametz (1959) replicating the earlier studies of Lindsley *et al.* and showing that cats can recover from massive reticular damage if it is inflicted in two stages separated by about three weeks; single-stage damage led to the coma and death seen by Lindsley *et al.* Adametz concludes that the earlier findings represented the non-specific trauma of massive neural damage, which is reduced if the lesion is done in two stages. As such damage does not then prevent normal sleep–waking cycles, Adametz questions the primacy of the brainstem reticular formation in controlling arousal. (For an excellent and detailed review of this early period of research into the reticular formation and its function, see Thompson (1967).)

Jouvet
In the 1960s attention shifted from neuroanatomy to the neurochemistry of sleep and arousal. Sleep could be produced

by application of acetylcholine and other cholinergic drugs to a variety of sites in the diencephalon and telencephalon, leading Hernandez-Peon (Hernandez-Peon and Chavez-Ibarra, 1963) to suggest the existence of a limbic cholinergic sleep circuit. It was, however, the work of Jouvet which stimulated most interest into the neurochemical bases of sleep. Jouvet (1969; 1972) performed a series of lesion, drug, and combined lesion/ drug studies to investigate the mechanisms underlying active and quiet (REM and slow-wave, SWS, in his terminology) sleep in the cat. His manipulations focused upon two major systems within the brainstem reticular formation, the locus coeruleus and the raphé nuclei. The former lies in the pons, while the eight or so nuclear formations comprising the raphé system spread from the medulla through the pons to the anterior midbrain.

As we saw in Chapter 3 both of these systems are intimately associated with long-axon neurotransmitter pathways. The dorsal noradrenergic pathway originates from the locus coeruleus and innervates limbic, cortical, and cerebellar structures. The raphé nuclei give rise to most of the brain's serotonergic system, with the axons of neurons whose cell bodies constitute the raphé system innervating hypothalamic, limbic, and cortical areas. Thus, besides any other effects, locus coeruleus lesions will deplete brain noradrenaline, while raphé lesions will lead to a massive loss of brain serotonin.

Given these neuroanatomical and neurochemical correlations, one might expect a reciprocity in the effects of drugs and lesions. Drugs reducing the activity of noradrenaline in the brain should mimic the behavioural consequences of a locus coeruleus lesion, while raphé lesions should be paralleled by drugs blocking serotonergic activity. Alternatively, the effects of either locus coeruleus or raphé damage should be reduced or antagonized by drugs which functionally replace noradrenaline and serotonin respectively.

It is these sorts of predictions that Jouvet set about testing, after first establishing the crucial role of these reticular areas in the control of sleep and arousal. Using cats, he found initially that raphé lesions could produce a selective loss of SWS, while damage to the locus coeruleus produced a selective loss of

REM. Total destruction of the extensive raphé system led to an almost complete insomnia; anterior lesions were most effective at selectively reducing SWS, while posterior lesions appeared to affect mainly the REM component. The locus coeruleus and raphé nuclei are next-door neighbours in the brainstem, and there are reciprocal neuroanatomical connections between them (Morgane and Stern, 1974; Ramm, 1979). Jouvet suggests that a posterior raphé → locus coeruleus pathway is instrumental in triggering the onset of REM sleep, and it is this pathway that is damaged by the posterior raphé lesion. Such a triggering idea is appealing in view of the hypothesis mentioned earlier in the chapter, that phases of REM not only follow phases of SWS but are induced by them.

The role of a raphé serotonergic system in sleep is supported by neuropharmacological evidence. Injections of the drug para-chloro-phenylalanine (PCPA) deplete the brain of serotonin and produce an insomina akin to that seen after raphé damage; injections of the drug 5-hydroxytryptophan (5-HTP) increase levels of serotonin in the brain and reduce the insomnia observed after raphé lesions. However, injections of 5-HTP do not induce behavioural sleep in the intact cat, and neither does electrical stimulation of raphé nuclei, although it may produce synchronization of the cortical EEG pattern (Kostowski, 1971). These observations led Bremer (1977) to suggest that the raphé nuclei are *hypnotonic* rather than *hypnogenic*, i.e. they do not themselves induce sleep, but have a regulatory role in sleep states. In contrast, other workers maintain the 'induction of SWS' hypothesis for the raphé serotonergic system (e.g. Morgane and Stern, 1974; Dement *et al.*, 1976), and it is clear from the evidence that 'regulatory' is an insufficient description of the central role of this brainstem network in SWS. However, as we shall see, sleep can be induced by direct chemical or electrical stimulation of forebrain sites, and the precise functional characterization of the raphé system will probably emerge from a study of its interactions with these hypnogenic centres.

Compared to the relatively simple and popular raphé nuclei-serotonin-SWS hypothesis, Jouvet's ideas on the role of the locus coeruleus noradrenergic system in REM sleep are more controversial. Early experiments (Jouvet, 1972) suggested that lesions of the locus coeruleus led to a selective loss of REM, and that this area therefore represented a 'REM-executive', responsible for the induction and maintenance of the various phenomena which constitute REM sleep. Ramm (1979) has reviewed the large body of research on the functions of the locus coeruleus, and concludes, after a detailed survey, that damage to this nucleus or its projection pathways in fact has little or no effect upon REM or SWS.

The pharmacological evidence also is contradictory. If the locus coeruleus noradrenergic system is a REM-inducer, then depletion of brain noradrenaline should reduce and increases in brain noradrenaline should increase the occurrence of REM sleep. However, injections of the depleting agent α-methyl-para-tyrosine (α-mpt) *increase* the amount of REM sleep in cats (effects in rats are inconsistent; this reflects a general problem of species differences which has not yet been resolved); while decreases in REM are found with drugs such as tricyclic anti-depressants and amphetamine which, amongst other pharmacological actions, *increase* brain noradrenaline levels.

These observations led Stern and Morgane (1974) to propose an alternative hypothesis to Jouvet's. They suggest that the physiological function of REM sleep is to maintain the brain's catecholamine systems, i.e. noradrenergic and dopaminergic pathways. During normal waking behaviour (or after injections of α-mpt) these systems become 'neurally fatigued', and REM sleep is then essential for their replenishment.

Central to their argument is the logical point mentioned earlier in relation to Vogel's work on the anti-depressant efficacy of REM-deprivation. REM-deprivation leads, usually, to REM-rebound, as though a 'need for REM' (or, in Vogel's terminology, REM-pressure) had developed. Stern and Morgane argue that if a drug reduces the quantity of REM sleep with *no* subsequent REM-rebound, it must be preventing a 'need for REM' developing, presumably by being functionally equivalent to REM sleep. Of such drugs, the two major groups are the tricyclic anti-depressants and drugs which inhibit the enzyme monoamine oxidase (monoamine oxidase inhibitors, MAOIs); this enzyme is involved in the metabolic removal of monoamines (noradrenaline, dopamine, and serotonin) after their synaptic action, and its inhibition by MAOIs effectively raises the functional concentration of monoamines in the brain.

Tricyclics and MAOIs have in common the elevation of catecholamine levels, and, assuming that their ability to reduce REM without subsequent REM-rebound implies that they are functionally equivalent to REM sleep, then the function of REM is to increase and replenish catecholamine stores depleted in the course of normal waking activity.

This model predicts that the amount of REM sleep will be increased by drugs depleting the brain's catecholamine stores, in an attempt to restore working levels. In confirmation, Stern and Morgane point to the increases in REM seen in cats, monkeys and humans, following injections of the catecholamine-depleting drugs α-mpt and reserpine.

Stern and Morgane then turn to the problem of Jouvet's original observation that locus coeruleus lesions reduce REM, even though a major noradrenergic pathway has presumably been partially or completely destroyed – this loss of a catecholamine neurotransmitter should, if Stern and Morgane are correct, lead to an increase in REM rather than to a decrease. They cope with this apparent difficulty by postulating a distinction between the *function* of REM and the *mechanism* of REM. The function would be to replenish catecholamine stores, but the mechanism triggering REM need not necessarily involve catecholamines. By drawing attention to the presence in the locus coeruleus of cholinergic neuronal elements, they can tentatively explain Jouvet's observations by postulating the destruction of a cholinergic 'REM-trigger' by locus coeruleus lesions. There would then be two direct means of suppressing REM sleep: firstly using drugs which increase catecholamine levels effectively to replace the *function* of REM sleep, and secondly by destroying the REM-triggering mechanism.

Problems raised by Jouvet's original observations on the effects of locus coeruleus lesions tend to evaporate in the light of Ramm's (1979) critical work, mentioned earlier. As Ramm simultaneously emphasizes the unpredictable outcome of pharmacological manipulations on REM, and con ludes that the catecholamine hypothesis is not an adequate account of REM function, he brings little comfort to either Jouvet or Stern and Morgane. The position he arrives at is that neither the locus coeruleus nor its catecholamine systems are directly involved in the induction or maintenance of REM; however, bearing in mind the evidence just reviewed and the diffuse distribution of the locus coeruleus noradrenergic pathway, it does seem likely that catecholamine systems may play an indirect, modulatory role in REM sleep.

One point upon which both Ramm and Stern and Morgane agree is that the heterogeneous collection of phenomena collectively comprising REM sleep will involve many neuroanatomical structures and several neurotransmitter systems. Tonic (i.e. long-lasting) components such as cortical desynchronization can be induced by cholinergic and noradrenergic drugs (see Chapter 3). Phasic elements such as PGO spikes (electrical spikes in the pons, geniculate nucleus, and occipital lobe) can be induced by cholinergic drugs such as physostigmine, and suppressed by drugs increasing serotonergic activity such as 5-HTP. The precise pathways underlying rapid eye movements and postural muscle relaxation have yet to be traced, but are certain to involve equally complex interactions.

The paradox of REM, or active, sleep is that while we talk comfortably and at length about its phenomenology, phylogeny, function, etc., we are still hard put to it to give it an inclusive definition. The presence of any two or three out of the four or five signs which have become associated with REM sleep is usually sufficient to define that 'state' of the organism as REM, i.e. no one sign is necessary and sufficient. If no one component is 'essential', in the sense of always and only occurring in phases of REM sleep, then it becomes extremely difficult to isolate the function of REM and the way that function is exercised (Stern and Morgane, 1974).

The reticular formation and forebrain hypnogenic centres

So far we have concentrated upon the brainstem reticular

formation, involving arousal mechanisms in the midbrain (mesencephalon) and hindbrain (pons and medulla). As the effects of brainstem reticular stimulation are recorded at cortical level, via the EEG, it is obvious that structures and pathways in the forebrain (diencephalon and telencephalon) relay messages from brainstem to cortex, and so represent forebrain extensions of the reticular formation. It has also been known for several decades that electrical stimulation and lesions of forebrain structures can induce arousal or somnolence in their own right; such structures may therefore represent not just extensions to the more fundamental brainstem arousal system, but areas equally important in the control of sleep and waking.

Lesions of the posterior hypothalamus produce a sleep-like state (Nauta, 1946), more profound than the coma induced by lesions of the brainstem reticular formation (Feldman and Waller, 1962). The fine structure and arrangement of neurons and neuronal processes in the lateral and posterior hypothalamus are very similar to the classical 'reticulum' of the brainstem reticular formation, so leading to the suggestion that these forebrain diencephalic centres be considered as direct extensions to the reticular 'core' (Morgane and Stern, 1974). The other major diencephalic structure is the thalamus, and for some decades this too has been known to play a key role in mediating reticular influences on cortical EEG. Stimulation of thalamic nuclei can produce cortical synchronization or desynchronization, as well as behavioural correlates of waking or sleeping (Hess, 1954); Hunter and Jasper (1949) therefore considered the thalamic component of the ascending reticular system as equally important to the brainstem reticular 'core'.

The thalamus has many nuclear subdivisions (see Chapter 2), functionally divided into specific nuclei (such as the lateral geniculate, concerned with relaying visual signals from retina to occipital cortex – see Chapter 4), and non-specific nuclei, such as the mid-line and intra-laminar, which are involved in general functions such as 'arousal'. Reticular-thalamic-cortical interconnections are not straightforward. Stimulation of thalamic intra-laminar neurons can induce cortical EEG synchronization or desynchronization. However, the former effect can be blocked by lesions of the thalamo-cortical pathway, while the latter cannot be blocked by lesions of this direct pathway, but by a section *posterior* to the thalamus severing a thalamo-midbrain reticular formation pathway; i.e. the brainstem reticular formation cortex connection is not one-way and straight-through, but has several branches and many feedback loops.

The pathway essential for the synchronizing (i.e. EEG 'sleep' pattern) effect of thalamic stimulation leads to the orbito-frontal cortex, and stimulation of this area also produces electrophysiological and behavioural sleep (Bremer, 1977). The induction of sleep by electrical stimulation suggests, with reference to the question of whether sleep is an active or passive phenomenon, that sleep is actively imposed on the brain; there are centres whose normal function is to inhibit the waking patterns of brain and behaviour and to instigate the various sleep patterns. There is still the problem of what controls these 'hypnogenic' centres, to which we turn in a moment.

Besides the orbito-frontal cortex hynogenic centre there is a zone in the basal forebrain, just rostral (anterior) to the optic chiasma and usually referred to as the preoptic area, where electrical stimulation also produces sleep and lesions produce severe insomnia (Sterman and Clemente, 1962; Lucas and Sterman, 1975). The basal preoptic and orbito-frontal hypnogenic centres (Bremer, 1977) are functionally closely related, and also overlap with forebrain sites where stimulation by cholinergic drugs has been shown to induce sleep (Hernandez-Peon and Chavez-Ibarra, 1963). Hernandez-Peon suggested, after mapping the many sleep-inducing sites, that a limbic cholinergic sleep circuit existed, whose function was exercised by descending inhibition of the brainstem reticular formation. Putting all of these hypnogenic phenomena together, Morgane *et al.* (1977) suggested the existence of a fronto-limbic cortical sleep system, incorporating orbito-frontal, basal preoptic, and limbic mechanisms. Bremer (1977) is essentially in agreement, although adding a brainstem medullary hypnogenic centre on the basis of the mid-pontine pre-trigeminal preparation described earlier. This preparation shows persistent waking activity and Bremer argues that the MPPT section must free higher brain centres from an *ascending* hypnogenic influence probably emanating from the medullary region of the brain-stem.

It is now clear that there exist in the brain centres or mechanisms responsible either for the production of arousal or for the production of sleep, and the next obvious question is how they interact. Bremer (1977) has presented a model of how brainstem reticular arousal influences and forebrain hypnogenic centres coordinate their activities, and rather neatly incorporates some of the earlier 'is sensory input necessary for waking' debate.

His idea is that ascending reticular activity both arouses the cortex and inhibits forebrain hypnogenic mechanisms; these mechanisms are *tonically* inhibited, in the sense that they are continually activated but the manifestation of this activity, i.e. sleep, is suppressed so long as reticular arousal is sustained. Once reticular arousal falls below a certain threshold, the forebrain hypnogenic centres (e.g. orbito-frontal cortex and basal preoptic forebrain) are released from the tonic inhibition, exert their synchronizing influence on the brain, and produce sleep. As reticular arousal is a function of, among other things, general sensory input, sleep is both active, in the sense of being generated by specific sleep mechanisms in the brain, and passive, in the sense of being expressed only when general sensory input and consequent reticular arousal fade away (see Fig. 10.3).

Hypnogenic centres are undoubtedly exposed to other controlling influences. The endogenous nature of the sleep–waking cycle mentioned earlier in this chapter suggests that some form of rhythmic input occurs; it may be significant that the preoptic zone is anatomically close to the supra-chiasmatic nucleus, an area known to be involved in the genesis of endogenous physiological rhythms. The reticular-basal forebrain link would explain how the endogenous rhythm can be overridden if sensory stimulation, i.e. the environment, is demanding enough.

I discussed at length neurochemical hypotheses of brainstem reticular mechanisms. A similar analysis has not been attempted of forebrain synchronizing – sleep mechanisms, with only the early work of Hernandez-Peon guiding us towards a

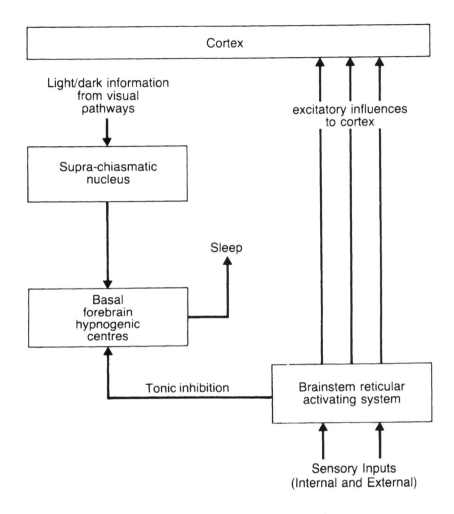

Figure 10.3   *Reticular formation and forebrain hypnogenic centres.*
Reticular arousal is modulated by sensory inputs. When it falls below a
threshold level, cortical excitability fades and tonic inhibition of hypno-
genic centres is removed; they may then impose their natural function —
sleep — on the brain. although they are still subject to control by endogenous
oscillators in the supra-chiasmatic nucleus. (Other important centres, such
as the thalamus and the midbrain waking centre shown in Fig. 10.2, are
omitted for the sake of simplicity)

substantial cholinergic component. As the cholinergic system mediates a major part of reticular influences on the cortical EEG (see Chapter 3), a general role in sleep and arousal would be expected.

An overall neurochemical perspective on sleep would therefore emphasize brainstem serotonergic and forebrain cholinergic systems on a general level, but with the cautionary note that the multifarious phenomena of slow-wave and REM sleep will probably be explained only by complex interactions between many neurotransmitters.

Finally, and in line with the current interest in small molecules and beha iour, it has been reported that a peptide isolated from the cerebro-spinal fluid of sleep-deprived animals can induce sleep in recipient animals (Pappenheimer *et al.*, 1975; Monnier *et al.*, 1977). The origin and role of this chemical are unknown.

11 Motivation

Introduction

The psychologist is aiming to explain behaviour. The most fundamental question that can be asked is, 'why behave at all?' Accepting that behaviour is not inherently pointless implies accepting that it has some purpose, or, in other words, is motivated.

The argument may be pursued at a philosophical level, debating the Nature of Man and the Meaning of Life. At a more mundane level, the motivational basis of eating in hungry rats, of object manipulation in monkeys, and of studying psychology in humans, may be compared and contrasted; can they all be incorporated into a single model of animal motivation?

Since experimental psychology became involved in the study of motivation, a popular and recurring approach has been to observe behaviour and list its various categories: fighting, playing, nest-building, eating, exploration, etc. Then each category is assumed to represent a unique motivational system, centring on a 'drive', or 'instinct' (McDougall, 1932), and so a spurious explanation is given for the behaviour. Animals explore because they have an exploratory drive; we know they have an exploratory drive because they explore.

This type of circularity has bedevilled the study of motivation, with many 'explanations' turning out to be merely alternative descriptions of observed behaviour. The problem is to break out of the circularity and find real explanations which go beyond the immediate observations upon which they are based. I deal with exploration in some detail later, but as an example of the problem consider the rat placed in a novel maze.

He runs around, exhibiting 'exploratory behaviour' energized by an 'exploratory drive'. However, if given the opportunity, the rat will escape from the maze and return to its home cage. The implication is that he does not find 'novelty' *per se* attractive or in itself worthy of exploration; he finds it aversive, and the observed exploratory activity is energized by 'fear' and the need to escape. We have then located the analysis of 'exploration' within the wider framework of the animal's general behaviour; it gives the animal information about its environment, which may then be used in the planning of behavioural strategies. The drive, or drives, underlying exploration can only be inferred by considering the subject in his adaptations to his surroundings.

There have been several attempts to conceptualize motivation in a realistic way. Some are more concerned with complex human behaviour: Maslow's (1970) hierarchy of drives considers the satisfaction of lower, 'primitive' drives as essential before one can ascend the hierarchy towards the final goal of 'self-actualization', while McClelland's (1961) 'needs', such as Need for Achievement and Need for Affiliation, while harking back to the sterile 'list' approach to motivation, are backed up by substantial and inventive experimental data. Other approaches are founded in animal work, and are directly relevant to the analysis of the physiological bases of motivation.

The simplest example of the concept of motivation and its explanatory value is the hungry rat. We assume that depriving a rat of food for twenty-four hours induces a state we may call 'hunger', reflecting a need for food to satisfy a physiological tissue deficiency. To fulfil this need, the rat will learn to press a bar in a Skinner box to obtain pellets of food; the pellets reduce the need, or drive, for food, and so eliminate 'hunger'. This sequence consists of energized and directed behaviour, i.e. a motivational sequence running from tissue deficiency to consummatory response and satisfaction.

Animals will learn in order to reduce such fundamental physiological drives, and 'drive-reduction' via 'reinforcers' provided the basis for Hull's (1943) global theory of animal learning. In this theory, all learning, from rats in Skinner boxes to complex human problem solving, was based originally in the satisfaction of primary physiological drives such as hunger, thirst, and sex.

The primary reinforcers for primary drives are obvious: food, water, the opposite sex. Stimuli consistently associated with primary reinforcing stimuli may themselves become reinforcers, i.e. capable of inducing and supporting secondary drives and learning based on secondary drive reduction. Thus maternal approval, consistently associated with primary nurturant reinforcers such as food and warmth, becomes a secondary reinforcer in its own right, and the infant's behaviour may then reflect the secondary drive of seeking maternal approval. So, although originating in the reduction of primary drives, infant behaviour can become detached from its physiological sources, and by introducing tertiary reinforcers (i.e. stimuli which have been consistently associated with secondary reinforcers), the explanatory power of the drive-reduction approach becomes impressive. Although the proposition that painting the Sistine Chapel, climbing Everest, or founding the Mongol Empire all reflect a need for maternal approval originating in the satisfying of the infant's hunger drive by the mother seems at first sight unlikely, an explanation could be constructed if necessary.

However, subsequent research has broadened our awareness of what makes animals behave, and relegated drive-reduction to a back seat, or at least to a very crowded front seat. Rats will learn to press bars for various non-nutritive and non-drive-reducing reinforcers such as saccharine or flashing lights, and, to anticipate some of the later discussion, their behaviour is now seen to be driven or guided by more than the reduction of simple physiological drives.

But hungry rats do learn complex responses for food reward, and cold rats will learn responses aimed at raising the ambient temperature; restoring tissue deficiencies is a prime concern of behaviour, and, by taking hunger as an example, I will show in detail how physiological and psychological research, starting with an apparently straightforward example of motivation, has given us a more realistic view of the regulation of food intake in animals and humans.

Hunger

The primary physiological drives are those behaviours aimed at maintaining homeostasis, i.e. sustaining a relatively constant internal environment. There are many indices of homeostasis, of which body weight, cellular and extracellular water content, and core temperature are commonly encountered within physiological psychology. Emphasis on these should not allow us to forget the others. Even within the field of hunger and the regulation of food-intake, we deal only with those foods which determine body weight, i.e. overall caloric intake in terms of fats and carbohydrates. Other dietary necessities, such as protein, vitamins, mineral salts, and trace elements, are equally as important for bodily functioning, but details of their regulation are comparatively unknown (however, see Chapter 9, where the effects of trace element deficiencies on behaviour are briefly considered).

Apart from abnormal overeating, dieting, or the dynamic phases of growth, body weight is regulated within impressively narrow limits in all animal species; even the obese ventromedial hypothalamic rat (see later) exhibits precise regulation, when he eventually settles down at his post-lesion weight.

One of the key aspects of the regulation of eating and drinking is that the ingestive behaviour is usually *anticipatory* of future need, rather than a direct response to a central tissue deficiency (Fitzsimons, 1972; Mogenson and Phillips, 1976). Animals normally take meals regularly, with water intake correlated with food intake, and neither is in response to extreme 'deficit' signals; intake is controlled by external stimuli, cognitive processes such as habit, and by internally controlled circadian rhythms. However, given the stability of body weight, actual intake in the short term (i.e. meal size) and in the long term (over weeks, months, etc.) must be regulated, regardless of whether feeding is in response to emergency deficit signals or is anticipatory of such signals. It is the nature of this regulation that concerns us.

There are several ways to classify the multitude of findings on the regulation of body weight. The original controversy over the relative importance of central versus peripheral factors was replaced, indeed swamped, by interest in the hypothalamus when the effects of ventro-medial and lateral lesions were demonstrated in the late 1940s. Latterly interest in peripheral mechanisms has revived, while the focus within the brain has shifted slightly from the hypothalamus to chemical pathways.

My approach will be to review the classical work briefly, retaining the artificial division between central (i.e. central nervous system) and peripheral (i.e. mouth, gastro-intestinal tract, circulatory, and endocrine systems) factors, and then describe recent findings relevant to this division. Then the ventro-medial hypothalamic obesity syndrome will be considered in detail, and an integrating hypothesis (Powley, 1977) presented which I feel represents the obvious direction research within this area must move in.

When rats or people eat, they do not eat for very long. Meal duration is reasonably consistent, and meal frequency also has a systematic pattern (Le Magnen, 1972). As we stop eating a given meal long before the food can have been digested and fully assimilated, factors other than body weight must be operating; we may therefore postulate another dichotomy between the control of 'short-term' satiety (meal duration) and of 'long-term' satiety (caloric intake over extended periods, regulating body weight).

Cannon and Washburn (1912) presented the first detailed hypothesis on the control of food intake. Theirs was a peripheral hypothesis, relating the sensation of hunger – and consequent eating – directly to the frequency of contractions of the stomach wall. These 'hunger pangs' correlated directly with the emptiness of the stomach, and subjectively seem a likely candidate for the regulation of feeding behaviour.

Although it was soon pointed out that animals with stomachs either removed or denervated (i.e. the sensory pathways from stomach to the central nervous system are severed), and humans with diseased stomachs surgically removed, could regulate their food intake and body weight reasonably well, it is now clear that the either/or approach to food regulation is unrealistic. A series of studies using an oesophageal fistula (for a review, see Morgan, 1965) were aimed at establishing precisely the contribution of peripheral factors to the regulation of meal size and overall weight; the fistula technique, whereby the oesophagus is cut between mouth and stomach and the cut ends brought to the surface, enables food to be passed through the mouth without reaching the stomach, or to be passed directly into the stomach via the lower cut end of the oesophagus. Thus we have an experimental separation of oro-pharyngeal (mouth + pharynx) and of gastric (stomach) factors.

The general conclusions to these studies were that animals could satisfactorily regulate meal size using either oro-pharyngeal or gastric factors alone; allowed to eat freely but with food passing straight out of the oesophagus, or to control the injection of liquid food directly into the stomach, animals would cease eating after a roughly appropriate time. Of course, in the long term, mouth-only feeders would suffer severe malnutrition, so it was feasible only to assess the contribution to short-term satiety.

As we shall see later, other mechanisms are now considered to operate alongside the presence of food in mouth and stomach, which would explain the failure to disrupt meal size regulation by experimentally removing one or the other. Just as clearly, oro-pharyngeal and gastric involvement are well established with, for instance, food-induced gastric distension inhibiting sensory (or afferent) impulses from stomach to brain (Le Magnen, 1972).

Hetherington and Ranson (1942) galvanized the study of feeding and hunger with their demonstration that lesions of the ventro-medial hypothalamus (VMH) produced a post-lesion hyperphagia (overeating), leading to a massive obesity in the long term. The hyperphagia was shown by a dramatic increase in meal duration, and led to the suggestion that the lesion removed a 'feeding cessation' or 'satiety' centre. When, in 1951, Anand and Brobeck reported that lesions of the lateral hypothalamus produced a post-lesion aphagia (prolonged failure to eat), it appeared that this lesion destroyed a 'feeding-initiation', or 'feeding' centre.

As the two major problems in this area were seen to be how

feeding was begun and how it was ended, the discovery of feeding and satiety centres apparently solved the dilemma. Ultimate control was central rather than peripheral.

An immediate question concerns the nature of the behaviour studied. Feeding involves tissue deficits, central and peripheral receptors receptive to these deficits, visual and olfactory sensory input, presence of food in mouth and gastro-intestinal tract, absorption and assimilation of foodstuffs via physiological and metabolic conversion, and the short and long-term regulation of input. It is on the one hand unlikely that one centre will have absolute control over these various aspects, and on the other hand unlikely that any brain structure involved in the control of feeding would exercise that control in the absence of sensory input or motor output. Put more simply, the ventro-medial hypothalamus may represent a satiety centre, but it still has to receive information from various mechanisms of 'satiety' telling it to inhibit feeding, and it has to have access to efferent, motor pathways to put that inhibition into operation. (One suggestion is that the VMH satiety centre acts by inhibiting the lateral hypothalamus feeding centre; this, of course, just begs the question, as one still has to identify the efferent pathways by which the LH exercises its effects. Direct VMH inhibition of the feeding centre has anyway been questioned (Aravich and Beltt, 1982).)

The identification of central satiety and feeding centres does not therefore eliminate peripheral mechanisms, and the last decade has seen a resurgence of interest in the central/peripheral interaction. Before turning to this, however, recent refinements of the 'satiety' and 'feeding' concepts should be considered.

In the early 1960s, Grossman (1960), in a series of elegant studies, showed that microinjections of chemicals into the hypothalamus could elicit feeding and drinking in the satiated rat. Feeding was under the control of noradrenaline (NA), in that it was produced by injections of that neurotransmitter, while drinking could be produced by injections of the neurotransmitter acetycholine (or of a similar drug, carbachol). Subsequently, while Fisher and Coury (1962) have traced out a limbic cholinergic circuit involved in drinking behaviour the involvement of noradrenergic pathways in feeding has been a subject of dispute.

Grossman found that NA increased feeding. Against this a potent anorexigenic (i.e. a suppressor of feeding) is the drug amphetamine, which potentiates NA activity in the brain. Leibowitz (1970) suggested that two sorts of NA receptor exist in the hypothalamus, with excitation or inhibition of feeding depending on which receptor is stimulated; noradrenaline and amphetamine preferentially stimulate different receptors, and so produce their opposite effects. More dramatically, Gold (1973) showed that knife-cuts within the ventro-medial hypothalamus did not produce obesity; only knife-cuts just posterior to the VMH led to post-lesion obesity. Further studies (Kapatos and Gold, 1973; Ahlskog and Hoebel, 1973) supported Gold's suggestion that the VMH obesity syndrome is due to the severing of the ascending ventral noradrenergic pathway. This pathway (see Chapter 3) supplies the hypothalamus with noradrenergic terminals as it passes through on its way from hindbrain to forebrain, and Ahlskog and Hoebel (1973) demonstrated a correlation between post-lesion obesity and the loss of hypothalamic noradrenaline. (It should also be noted that, as described in Chapter 3, the anorexigenic drug fenfluramine is thought to act by releasing serotonin from terminals in the hypothalamus, suggesting a sophisticated chemical balancing act in the control of eating).

A VMH lesion, if it destroys the NA terminals, produces obesity (the VMH syndrome, notwithstanding the unequivocal way it is usually presented in textbooks, is notoriously difficult to elicit); a more effective way to remove hypothalamic NA is to sever the ascending pathway supplying it, and this is then equivalent to a VMH lesion.

These data suggest that hypothalamic NA functions to suppress feeding – its loss leads to overeating and obesity – and explains the anorexigenic action of amphetamine; they still leave Grossman's original findings of an NA-stimulation of feeding to be incorporated into the model, and Leibowitz's ideas on this probably deserve more attention.

The syndrome of aphagia and adipsia produced by lateral hypothalamic lesions may also be mimicked by damage to other areas. Ungerstedt (1971a) first demonstrated that a lesion of the ascending nigro-striatal dopamine pathway (see Chapter 3: the lesions are usually produced by localized injections of 6-hydroxydopamine, 6-OHDA, a neurotoxin that selectively destroys DA and NA axonal terminals) leads to aphagia and adipsia. Unfortunately his animals were severely disabled in virtually every respect, and given the obvious point that it is easier to eliminate behaviour than to stimulate it, a loss of feeding and drinking need not be a specific deficit. However, subsequent work (Marshall *et al.*, 1974; Marshall and Teitelbaum, 1974; Baez *et al.*, 1977) has shown an impressive correspondence between the precise natures of the regulatory deficits following lateral hypothalamic or nigro-striatal lesions; this correspondence is particularly striking with regard to the stages of recovery from the aphagia and adipsia seen in rats given close post-operative attention.

To consider the physiological bases of obesity and aphagia in terms of pathways rather than neuroanatomical centres need not help explain the nature of the syndromes; we have simply switched terms; obesity may reflect a loss of hypothalamic noradrenaline, and aphagia a loss of hypothalamic dopamine. What has been added is an emphasis on sensory processes. A feature of the nigro-striatal lesioned animal is a severe sensory neglect. If the damage is unilateral, then the sensory neglect is to the contralateral side of the body – a failure to orient to stimuli presented on that side, and an apparent unawareness that that half of the body exists. Sensory neglect is also observed as part of the lateral hypothalamic (LH) syndrome in rats.

Zeigler (Zeigler and Karten, 1974; Zeigler, 1975) has pursued the basis of the LH syndrome in pigeons. Peripheral severing of the trigeminal nerve (which carries sensory information from the oral regions, e.g., the location of food and movements of the mouth), impaired eating, i.e. produced aphagia (note how this sensory impairment also disrupts aggressive behaviour in the cat: Chapter 8). Lesioning the central trigeminal nucleus in the diencephalon (i.e. the immediate destination of the sensory information carried by the nerve) produced aphagia and adipsia indistinguishable from the LH syndrome in rats. In addition to these motivational deficits there were sensorimotor problems, in parallel with the motivational and sensory aspects of the LH syndrome.

Sensory neglect in the LH rat recovers faster than the ingestive problems (Marshall and Teitelbaum, 1974), suggesting that they have separable physiological bases, and this is also the case for the rat with a unilateral nigro-striatal lesion (Baez *et al.*, 1977). So sensory impairment cannot be the whole explanation for the syndrome, although Zeigler's work implies a greater involvement than had been suspected. More recently, Schallert and Whishaw (1978) differentiated two forms of the LH syndrome; posterior lateral hypothalamic lesions produced a *passive* aphagia and adipsia, while anterior lesions led to an *active* aphagia, involving positive sensory rejection of food (i.e. finickiness).

We now return to recent work on peripheral mechanisms involved in the regulation of feeding. We have already considered the presence of food in the mouth and in the stomach (gastric distension). The precise effect of food in the mouth is unclear, although taste sensation is clearly important – rats will overeat pleasant foods (they are particularly fond of chocolate biscuits), and dietary obesity can be produced fairly easily (Sclafani and Springer, 1976). In humans, too, increases in food intake can be produced by simply varying sensory aspects such as colour and shape (Rolls *et al.*, 1982). Gastric distention is signalled directly to the hypothalamus. After the stomach, food passes into the duodenum and small intestine, and it is here that another short-term satiety signal comes into play. In 1972, Gibbs *et al.* identified a hormone that they suggested had as a major action the suppression of feeding. This hormone, called cholecystokinin, or CCK for short, has now been shown to suppress feeding in rats deprived of food for up to ninety-two hours (Mueller and Hsiao, 1979), and also reduces food intake in obese humans (Pi-Sunyer *et al.*, 1982). It is released from the upper intestine (i.e. duodenum and early portions of the small intestine) into the bloodstream, in response to the presence of fatty acids in the intestine. CCK can be effective in animals overeating after ventro-medial hypothalamic lesions (Kulkosky *et al.*, 1976), eliminating the VMH as a possible mediating mechanism for CCK, and its detailed mode and site of action are unknown. There is some evidence that it acts directly on the vagal nerve, which carries afferent sensory information from stomach and intestine to brain (Lorenz and Goldman, 1982).

Things become much more complicated after the food has been absorbed through the intestinal wall into the hepatic portal circulation of the liver. Carbohydrate input is reflected in blood glucose levels, and fat input in levels of blood free-fatty acids and lipids. Since the 1950s there has been a substantial debate on which of these indices is of more importance in the regulation of food input (see Grossman, 1967, for a full historical review). There are few decisive findings, but what has been established is the presence of receptors for blood glucose ('glucoreceptors') in both the peripheral hepatic circulation and in the ventro-medial hypothalamus. Activity in these receptors is proportional to the circulatory level of blood glucose, and in turn they affect activity in the neurons they are associated with. Peripheral glucoreceptors are served by branches of the vagus nerve, with glucoreceptor stimulation producing sensory impulses travelling via afferent vagal fibres to the central nervous system. Hypothalamic glucoreceptors are probably sited directly on hypothalamic neurones.

Levels of blood glucose respond rapidly enough to the ingestion and absorption of food for peripheral and central glucoreceptors to be given a role in the control of short-term satiety (Razek *et al.*, 1977), and make the list of such factors look something like this:

Control of eating and short-term satiety
Visual and olfactory stimuli associated with food
Presence of food in mouth
Presence of food in stomach (gastric distension)
Cholecystokinin (CCK) released from upper intestine
Central and peripheral glucoreceptors
Pancreatic hormones?

Pancreatic hormones include insulin and glucagon. The relevance of insulin to the hunger and feeding debate is established, and discussed fully in the next section. Glucagon has not been studied to the same extent (De Castro *et al.*, 1978; Martin and Novin, 1977), and its precise role is as yet unclear. It is released from the pancreas into the hepatic circulation of the liver, where it acts to increase blood glucose levels by breaking down, or catabolizing, fat stored as glycogen. Raising blood glucose levels alters peripheral glucoreceptor activity, and ultimately decreases food intake. The action of insulin on blood glucose is in the opposite direction; by stimulating the conversion of carbohydrates such as glucose into lipids which can be stored as glycogen, insulin reduces blood glucose. The precise control of blood glucose levels then probably involves a balance between the two hormones. Given the role of blood glucose in the regulation of food input, this hormonal balance must also contribute to the short-term and long-term control of feeding behaviour (De Castro *et al.*, 1978).

The ventro-medial hypothalamic syndrome

I have already mentioned the current dispute on the precise site of the obesity-producing lesion in the rat; whether it is purely intra-hypothalamic, or must involve the severing of extra-hypothalamic fibres. Whichever, the psychological and metabolic consequences are documented and agreed, although agreement does not extend as far as the fundamental malfunction leading to these circumstances. Psychologically, the VMH obese rat eats more of a palatable food, predominantly by increasing the duration of each meal. He (a mere convenience: VMH obesity is actually easier to produce in female than in male rats) is overinfluenced by the sensory aspects of food, eating abundantly of chocolate biscuits but refusing food adulterated with quinine, food which the unlesioned hungry rat would eat (see, e.g. Weingarten, 1982). The VMH rat will not work so hard to obtain food, being easily dissuaded by moderate operant schedules, or by mild footshock; he is apparently less motivated than deprived controls. He is also less active, more emotional (i.e. irritable) and less sexual.

Metabolically, the obvious characteristic of the VMH rat is that he is fat. This is descriptively and literally true, in that the post-lesion increase in weight is due almost entirely to increased deposition of fatty acids in the fat storage cells (adipocytes). If the behavioural hyperphagia (overeating) is eliminated by strict control of meal size, the VMH rat still becomes obese; if post-lesion weight gain is controlled to prevent obesity, the fat/non-fat ratio in the body still increases. These two observations suggest that the VMH rat suffers a profound metabolic malfunction, which shows itself in hyperphagia under appropriate circumstances. Apart from increased fat storage, other indicators of this malfunction are increased blood levels of insulin, increased glucose turnover (i.e. blood levels are roughly normal, although both synthesis and breakdown are increased), and high blood plasma levels of lipids and cholesterol.

The central role of fat metabolism in explaining the metabolic malfunction underlying VMH obesity was used by Nisbett (1972) in his model of the obesity syndrome. He suggests that the body-weight set-point, around which our weight normally fluctuates within precise limits, is regulated by the level of fatty acids in the adipocytes (fat storage cells). If the level falls or rises, hypothalamic centres are triggered to produce feeding or to inhibit feeding. Damage to the hypothalamus can permanently shift the body-weight set-point; ventro-medial lesions shift it upwards, and the animal eats more in order to pack more fatty acids into the adipocytes, while lateral hypothalamic lesions lower the set-point, and the animal eats less to reduce fatty acid levels in the adipocytes. Thus the hypothalamus is the effective controlling centre for body weight, and elicits or inhibits feeding behaviour in response to feedback (!) signals from the adipocytes. The number of these fat storage cells is determined by a combination of genetic factors and early nutritional experience; in later life the number is constant, and only their fat content can change. In Nisbett's view, the adipocytes – or 'ponderostat' – represent the ultimate target of feeding behaviour. VMH rats and obese humans, on this model, are working to maintain an abnormally high level of fatty acids in their 'ponderostat'; they are, literally, always hungry, where hunger is defined as a lowering of fatty acid levels below the target level. In VMH rats the target level is artificially high through damage to hypothalamic centres regulating body-weight set-point and target fatty acid content, while in the obese human target levels are artificially high through genetic and/or nutritional factors increasing adipocyte numbers. Nisbett points out some behavioural similarities between the VMH rat and the obese human – increased sensitivity to taste and smell of food, decreased activity, increased emotionality and irritability – to support his interpretation of both syndromes.

Keesey and Powley (1975), in a clear and concise account, also emphasize the alteration of a body-weight set-point after hypothalamic damage, with post-lesion feeding behaviour being aimed at meeting a new set-point. Lateral hypothalamic damage therefore produces aphagia as the animal decreases its body weight to meet the lesion-lowered set-point; they elegantly demonstrate that depriving the rats prior to the operation can reduce the body weight *below* the expected post-lesion level, and leads to post-lesion *hyperphagia* in lateral hypothalamic animals. Thus eating after hypothalamic damage is secondary to a basic alteration of body-weight point, and not a primary effect (as suggested by, e.g., Sclafani, 1976).

However, there are some problems with the Nisbett ponderostat. VMH rats become obese even if hyperphagia is prevented and eating is normal, suggesting a profound shift in metabolism rather than a simple shift in body-weight set-point. Human obese subjects probably represent a heterogeneous collection of causative factors – genetic, nutritional, developmental, psychological – and there is still much debate on their classification. Rodin (1975) has suggested a real distinction between normals, obese, and 'super-obese', with the latter being behaviourally more like normals than the straightforward obese, and it is clear that unitary explanations, whether psychological or physiological, of the human syndrome are simplistic. Leon and Roth (1977), reviewing work on human obesity, came to the same conclusions.

A further complication arose when Powley and Opsahl (1974) showed that VMH obesity could be reversed by cutting the vagus nerve just below the diaphragm (a sheet of tissue dividing the thorax from the abdomen) – a sub-diaphragmatic vagotomy. The vagus is one of the cranial nerves, arising from nuclei within the brainstem and travelling out to the periphery. As a nerve, it contains millions of fibres (axons and dendrites), some sensory and some motor, some autonomic(i.e. supplying internal organs) and some somatic (i.e. concerned with striped skeletal musculature and sense receptors dealing with the external environment). The vagus therefore is involved in a variety of functions – control of the musculature of intestines and the heart, taste sensation, sensory impulses from pharynx, larynx, thoracic and abdominal viscera, reflexive movements of pharyngeal and laryngeal muscles, and control of pancreatic secretions.

The nerve is severed below the diaphragm to minimize the disruptive effects. The major target sites below the diaphragm are the stomach, intestines, and the pancreas gland. When performed in VMH obese rats, the operation reverses the hyperphagia, reduces the elevated levels of gastric acid secretion in the stomach, and reduces the level of insulin secretion from the pancreas. Weight returns to its pre-VMH lesion level.

Injection of insulin in normals can increase eating, and elevated levels of insulin are found in VMH rats; given the establish control by the vagus nerve of pancreatic insulin secretion, Powley and Opsahl concluded that the VMH lesion releases the vagus from hypothalamic inhibition and produces chronically high blood insulin levels. The sub-diaphragmatic vagotomy reversed obesity in VMH rats by removing the pancreas from this unbalanced vagal control, and thereby reducing the chronically high blood insulin levels which were the direct cause of hyperphagia and obesity. Interestingly the behavioural correlates of the VMH syndrome – finickiness, irritability, etc. – are not reversed, suggesting a real physiological/psychological dichotomy in the syndrome.

One immediate problem with their data is the point made previously in connection with lesions producing aphagia and adipsia – it is much easier to eliminate behaviour than to produce it. The subdiaphragmatic vagotomy reverses obesity by reducing eating. King *et al.* (1978) have suggested that this effect is a general pathogenic action – the lesion, besides removing the vagal innervation to the pancreas, also denervates the stomach and gastro-intestinal tract, and this loss of intestinal motility would make swallowing and digestion difficult. Given the lack of apparent motivation to eat in VMH rats, they would react to such intestinal distress by not eating at all, and so reversing their obesity. Evidence in favour of their hypothesis, and against the major role for insulin levels as detailed by Powley and Opsahl, is that adapting animals to the pathogenic effects of a vagotomy *before* a VMH lesion does not prevent obesity developing, even though insulin levels are presumably normal.

Additionally, Opsahl and Powley (1974) themselves point out that the vagotomy operation does not reverse obesity in the genetically obese Zucker rat; King *et al.* (1978) explain this by the normal motivational state of Zucker obese animals, as compared with VMH obese animals, driving them to overcome the general debilitating effects of the lesion.

In a series of studies, Wampler and Snowden (1979) compared the effects of vagotomy before, simultaneously with, and after VMH lesions. Their conclusions agree with King *et al*. Besides a high mortality rate, vagotomized animals have substantial visceral discomfort which produces aphagia for normal food, but which may be overcome by a highly palatable diet.

The precise description and explanation of the VMH syndrome is still some way off. Carbohydrate and fat metabolism is physiologically so complex and so productive of chemical candidates for indexing energy consumption and body weight that the eventual realistic model will represent the ultimate fusion of physiology and psychology. Besides their complex interactions, even the number of major components is increasing; recent work, although in the very early stages, suggests a possible role for brown adipose tissue in some forms of obesity (Rothwell and Stock, 1979). This tissue is a centre for thermogenesis, producing heat by metabolizing fat stores in response to the sympathetic branch of the autonomic nervous system. Its major role is obviously to help maintain body temperature under external cold conditions; Rothwell and Stock suggest that thermogenesis can also be diet-induced, literally burning up caloric input and preventing weight increases, perhaps with heat production serving as a genuine satiety signal to the hypothalamus (Glick, 1982). A deficiency in amount or efficiency of brown adipose tissue would then predispose to obesity; an intriguing notion, but, as with all the other candidates, unlikely to be the sole explanation for the obesity syndrome in rats or humans.

In all areas of psychology, the inexorable accumulation of empirical data forces models and the hypotheses derived from models to become more complicated. The study of hunger and feeding behaviour has reached the stage where the simple peripheral versus central argument can be seen to be inadequate and increasingly unproductive. We know enough to realize that a minimally adequate model must incorporate the whole range of relevant findings on short-term and longer-term regulation of caloric input, and will consequently not be simple.

A representative attempt to explain in such realistic complexity the ventro-medial hypothalamic obesity syndrome is that of Powley (1977). He introduces in a major role the cephalic reflexes of digestion. By these he means those autonomic and endocrine responses set off by contact with the sensory aspects of food, i.e. sight, smell and taste. It is obvious that these sensory qualities are important in regulating food intake; dietary obesity can be induced by presenting rats with novel and highly palatable foods (Sclafani and Springer, 1976), and hungry rats will prefer non-nutritious but sweet saccharine to nutritious but non-sweet standard diets. Powley points out that the sight, smell and taste of food set off preparatory reflexes in the autonomic and endocrine systems relating to digestion; saliva and gastric secretions increase, pancreatic insulin secretion rises, gastric and intestinal motility increases. The reflexes are geared to preparing the gastro-intestinal tract for the digestion and absorption of food, and stimulating the viscera in preparation for the metabolism and storage of food.

As with classical reflex circuits, the cephalic phase reflex has an afferent (sensory) and an efferent (motor or response) limb. The afferent limb involves sensory input relating to food from eyes, nose and mouth; given the organization of sensation at the anterior (cephalic) end of the body, this information must pass initially to reception centres in the brain. After sensory analysis, the efferent limb of the reflex is activated, involving autonomic and endocrine pathways and producing the preparatory responses described above in gastro-intestinal tract and viscera.

By hypothesizing that the key relay centre in the brain mediating between afferent and efferent limbs of the reflex is the ventro-medial hypothalamus (or, at least, the site of the functional lesion in cases of VMH obesity), Powley can then relate the characteristics of the VMH rat to the disruption of the normal cephalic phase reflex to the presence of food.

The finickiness to the taste and smell of food and the hyperphagia of a palatable diet can be explained by a lowering of the threshold and an increase in the amplitude of the reflex, which might also shift the metabolic responses of the body towards energy conservation and storage, i.e. an increase in overall metabolic rate and in the proportion of fat stored in the adipocytes.

Such an inclusive hypothesis is difficult to evaluate in a single empirical study. Powley points to some direct anecdotal evidence, where human patients fed, for a variety of reasons, via a direct intra-gastric fistula (i.e. food goes straight into the stomach) prefer to chew the food first, even though swallowing is impossible. This, in Powley's view, triggers off the cephalic phase reflex and prepares the gastro-intestinal tract and the relevant viscera for the digestion, absorption, and metabolism of food. The importance of these preparatory reflexes is demonstrated by the beneficial effects of chewing the food on the patient's health and weight maintenance.

Throughout this section I have referred to various findings and approaches in the physiological psychology of hunger and feeding behaviour. The importance of the cephalic phase hypothesis is the emphasis given to an integrated framework for these various findings and approaches. Precise roles for cholecystokinin, peripheral glucoreceptors, adipocytes, etc., have still to be described, but at least an overall pattern, or system, may emerge; as the body has evolved along the lines of systems rather than of individual and isolated components, this approach must be more realistic and productive.

I have talked at length about the control of caloric intake (fats and carbohydrates) and body weight. As mentioned at the beginning, we do eat, and need, other things, and work is slowly extending to these other areas. Musten *et al.* (1974) showed that rats will self-select the protein component of their diet as precisely as the carbohydrate component. This was followed up by Anderson *et al.* (1979), who, by demonstrating similarly precise regulation of protein intake in obese VMH and Zucker rats, demonstrated that animals have at least two independent dietary regulatory systems, one for protein and one for carbohydrates; even when one is malfunctioning, the other can be normal. Central and peripheral factors in the control of protein intake have not yet been identified.

Thirst

Thirst and drinking behaviour will not be described in detail. Drinking, as a behaviour, is the province of the psychologist, but has proved a highly specialized research topic, beyond the scope of this text.

Detailed analyses of the physiological bases of thirst have been made, and comprehensive review papers exist (Fitzsimons, 1972; Blass and Hall, 1976; Andersson, 1978). Hypothalamic osmoreceptors (neurons responsive to the ion concentration of the blood) and the renin–angiotensin system of the kidney play key roles. As with hunger, genuine thirst is almost never experienced, as drinking is regulatory and anticipatory of such a deficit. It is also highly correlated with feeding.

The last section mentioned how the hypothalamic involvement in the control of hunger and eating had been recently extended to include various neurotransmitter pathways. Similarly, thirst has been known for some years to be under the control of a circuit of structures, ranging beyond the lateral hypothalamus. Grossman, in a classic paper in 1960, made a profound contribution to the concept of 'chemical coding of behaviour' when he reported that injections of a noradrenergic agonist into the hypothalamus stimulated eating in a satiated rat, while hypothalamic injections of a cholinergic agonist stimulated drinking. Immediately building on this, Fisher and Coury (1962) identified a network of sites where cholinergic stimulation elicited drinking, and proposed a limbic cholinergic circuit underlying thirst and drinking behaviour.

Non-homeostatic drives

Animal behaviour occurs in situations where no obvious physiological, homeostatically based need exists. A complete acceptance of the 'drive' approach to explaining behaviour implies that all responses involve drives and reinforcers, and must therefore hypothesize non-homeostatic drives in order to cover these situations. Hebb (1958) has shown that monkeys prefer to watch a roomful of other monkeys rather than an empty room. They will do manipulative puzzles endlessly, with no reward other than some form of intrinsic satisfaction. Rats will learn to press bars in order to switch on the Skinner box light (Tapp, 1969). A satiated rat will run around a novel environment, apparently 'exploring'.

All these examples represent behaviour not based on satisfying a primary homeostatic drive such as hunger or thirst. To introduce non-homeostatic drives such as curiosity, manipulative and exploratory drives has, as mentioned at the beginning of the chapter, the problem of circularity; too often, the so-called explanation is simply an alternative description of the behaviour. This section discusses exploratory behaviour, as a representative of these non-homeostatic responses, and attempts to show how contemporary approaches to its understanding result from a fusion of behavioural and neuropsychological research.

Exploration

Besides eating and drinking when hungry and thirsty, animals 'explore' a novel environment. We say they 'explore' by analogy with our own behaviour in similar circumstances – an example of anthropomorphizing.

Since the rat became a favoured laboratory subject in the early 1900s, its exploratory behaviour has, with varying degrees of intensity, been continually studied. One of the earliest and major controversies was the dispute in the 1930s between Tolman and Hull. The latter, developing his inclusive drive-reduction model of animal behaivour, explained exploratory behaviour in terms of its previous assocation with food-seeking behaviour. Tolman put forward a cognitive view; when rats explore, it is to develop an internal 'spatial map' of their environment. Their different approaches can be exemplified by considering a hungry rat at the entrance to a complex maze. He has previously learnt the correct path through the maze to a food reward, so, when positioned at the start, he can rapidly and accurately run to the food.

In Hull's view, the entrance to the maze has become associated, in a relatively straightforward stimulus-response way, with the food reward. The rat is guided through the maze by a chain of these S-R connections ('fractional antedating goal responses'), until the food box is reached. Tolman, in complete contrast, sees the rat at the beginning of the maze as actually possessing, in his brain, a map of the maze built up by previous experience; he 'knows' the complete route before he starts, and does not rely on a chain of mechanistic connections between the stimuli of the maze and the response of running.

Tolman's cognitive view became rather lost in the subsequent behaviouristic controversy over the validity or otherwise of Hull's drive-reduction model, but lately it has been revived in the light of recent neuropsychological research. We turn to this later.

In the 1950s and 1960s attention switched to possible drive-reduction explanations of exploration in the satiated rat. If an exploratory drive exists analogous to hunger, it should possess certain characteristics. It should be elicited by deprivation of the primary reinforcer, and satisfied by contact with the reinforcer. Immediately we have the problem of identifying the primary reinforcer. Is it a novel environment, or would a novel object suffice? Does a 'need for exploration' exist before the animal is presented with a novel environment, i.e. in his home cage, does the 'need' develop the longer he is deprived of the opportunity to explore? If not, then exploration is elicited by a novel object and reinforced by a novel object, which is rather like saying that hunger is only elicited in the presence of food and is also reinforced by food.

Attempts to see exploration in drive-reduction terms have consistently had recourse to the Yerkes–Dodson curve, the theoretical inverted-U-shaped curve relating performance efficiency to arousal level (see Fowler (1965) for a historical review of this and other attempts to explain exploratory behaviour). The argument supposes that animals are continually seeking an optimal arousal level. Departures from this level then lead to behaviour geared to readjusting arousal, with an overaroused animal avoiding stimulus contact and an underaroused animal seeking stimulation, e.g. by indulging in exploration, manipulative or curiosity behaviour. Such an explanation, while fixing exploration firmly in the homeostatic family of behaviours ignores the specific information-processing aspects of behaviour. This is not to ignore the underpinning of all behaviour by 'arousal'; if there were no arousal, there would be no behaviour, and extremes of under- or overarousal have obvious consequences for stimulus seeking and stimulus avoidance (this is the whole basis of the Eysenck introvert–extravert dichotomy in studies of human personality). So monkeys may play with wire puzzles rather than do nothing, and rats find lights flashing a sufficient reward for lever pressing; these sorts of behaviour seem clear examples of 'boredom' avoidance (but see the closing discussion to this chapter).

However, exploration is not related to arousal level in any simple way. If this were the case, then highly aroused animals should consistently explore less than underaroused animals, and this is not the case. Usually taking defecation rate as an index of arousal level or 'emotionality', several hundred papers have, over the years, attempted to define the relations between emotionality and exploration. Conclusions, even today, cover all possibilities. Emotionality may increase exploratory responding (Halliday, 1966), decrease it (Aitken, 1970), or, apparently, be independent of it (Whimbey and Denenberg, 1967). There are several good reviews of the conceptual and experimental confusion in this area (e.g. Russell, 1973; Archer, 1973).

It has been known for many years that the motivational basis of exploration is not straightforward. Welker (1959) demonstrated that a rat, given the opportunity to escape from a simple novel maze, will take it, i.e. the maze running we call exploration involves a significant escape component. Besides escape, or avoidance, exploratory behaviour should, intuitively, be giving the animal information about his immediate whereabouts, and Blanchard *et al.* (1974) showed how this information could be used. Two groups of rats were confronted with a cat in the middle of a maze. Group A has been allowed to explore the maze prior to the confrontation, Group B had not. The maze was escape-proof. When faced with the cat, Group A froze into immobility, while Group B ran further into the maze. One explanation for the difference is that, given the two possible responses to a large predator of either freezing and hoping to remain unnoticed or running to safety, the latter, if feasible, is safest. Group B, not knowing there was no way out of the maze, took a chance on running and finding one; Group A did know, via their prior exploration, and, knowing that running would only attract attention, froze.

On this model, exploration of a new environment is simply the acquisition by the animal of relevant information; it always makes biological sense to have a sound grasp of one's immediate environs. This does not mean that animals will always explore if given the chance; the home cage is familiar and safe, and voluntary exploration of a new environment is usually tentative, with frequent retreats to the safe haven. But it does occur, suggesting that novelty *per se* does have some attraction for the animal.

The neuropsychology of exploratory behaviour

We measure exploratory behaviour by observing and measuring responses in a novel environment or to a specific novel object. One obvious problem, ignored to a surprising extent in this area of physiological psychology, is that of distinguishing between non-specific locomotor activity and specific exploratory responding. Many brain lesions and many drugs have been found to increase locomotor activity in a novel environment, but the crucial comparison, and one often omitted, is with the effect on activity in a familiar environment. One thing we are convinced of concerning exploration, is that it involves novelty, and only responses involving novelty should be affected if conclusions on the neuropsychological bases of exploration are to be drawn. So drugs which decrease acetylcholine activity in the brain increase activity, but do so in both novel and familiar environments (Mulas *et al.*, 1970).

The mass of experimental work in this area does not suggest that any one brain neurotransmitter pathway is specifically involved in the control of exploratory behaviour. However, there is evidence that, of the various brain structures, the hippocampus is of central importance in some aspects of exploration. We need here to return to Tolman's cognitive approach to the rat in a novel maze: the idea that exploration enables the animal to build up a spatial map of its environment. The work of O'Keefe and Nadel (summarized in O'Keefe and Nadel, 1978) through the late 1960s and 1970s has reviewed and substantiated this hypothesis, and also located the 'map' within the hippocampus.

Their approach involved recording the electrical activity from single neurons in the hippocampus, while allowing the rat to explore an elevated maze (i.e. no sides, so the animal can see distance stimuli in the room). They found that a given neuron would fire only for a given position on the maze. By using complex combinations of maze orientation and animal location they demonstrated that the firing pattern of hippocampal neurons faithfully recorded the animal's position in its environment, i.e. that the environment was topographically represented, with a point-to-point correspondence, in the hippocampus, and that Tolman's spatial map had a physiological substrate.

They use this view of the hippocampus as a cognitive mapping system, wherein significant objects such as food and water are located within the enviroment, to explain the various behavioural deficits which appear after hippocampal lesions (this hypothesis was contrasted with alternative approaches to hippocampal function in Chapter 6).

If exploration represents an information-gathering behaviour essential for the animal's adaptive adjustment to its spatial environment, it is independent of drive-reduction and reinforcement; i.e. as a representative non-homeostatic drive, it can be seen to lie completely outside the traditional approach to the motivation of behaviour. Its physiological substrate appears to centre upon limbic system structures rather than the hypothalamus, and as a behaviour essential for the efficient organization of many other behaviours (e.g. eating is simplified if you know where food is to be found), exploration is probably best considered outside the framework of the purely homeostatic behaviours of feeding and drinking. This eliminates the apparently fruitless quest for a specific 'exploratory' drive, and places this aspect of animal behaviour firmly in the information-processing approach of contemporary cognitive psychology.

Other non-homeostatic behaviours such as manipulation and curiosity have been less studied, but one would predict that a similar functional approach – how does it aid the animal in its adaptations to its environment? – would be fruitful.

Electrical self-stimulation of the brain (ESB)

The discovery by Olds and Milner in 1954 of rewarding ESB opened up a Pandora's box for physiological psychology. Stimulation of certain sites in the brain represented the most powerful reinforcement one could give an animal, preferable to food for the hungry or water for the thirsty. Bar-pressing for ESB could be sustained for many hours at rates of 200–300 presses per hour, until fatigue intervened. The classic mapping work of Olds (Olds and Olds, 1965) and Stein (referred to in Chapter 3) showed that rewarding ESB could be elicited from a range of sites within the brain, particularly from placements along the median forebrain bundle (MFB), a large tract containing neuronal fibres ascending and descending from hindbrain to forebrain. The phenomenon seems ubiquitous, demonstrable in rats, cats, monkeys, dolphins and humans.

At first glance, ESB appears very different from natural rewards. It is extremely persistent, but extinguishes almost immediately when the bar-press is not rewarded with stimulation. After an inter-session interval, an animal may not spontaneously bar-press on reintroduction to the test chamber;

only after a few free 'priming' stimuli does he begin pressing. Performance deteriorates rapidly at long inter-stimulus intervals, and, similarly, acquisition of partial reinforcement schedules is poor. Finally, despite its effectiveness as a primary reinforcer, ESB will not support secondary conditioning, i.e. stimuli (e.g. a tone) consistently associated with ESB do not themselves become capable of supporting learning or the bar-pressing behaviour.

These chararcteristics are not, generally, seen with natural reinforcers such as food and water. However, apart from the last, they each emphasize the importance in ESB of the time since the last stimulus, i.e. inter-stimulus interval or ISI. The longer the ISI, the poorer the ESB performance. Natural reinforcers are tested with long Response–Reinforcement intervals and hence long ISIs – the delay between pressing the bar and locating, eating and digesting the food pellet can be quite substantial – and this introduces the possibility that distinctions between ESB and natural reinforcers might be procedural rather than fundamental.

There is some evidence that shortening the response–reinforcement interval (and hence ISI) in natural reinforcement paradigms reduces the distinction from ESB. A rat rewarded for bar-pressing with immediate intravenous glucose injections shows remarkable persistence, rapid extinction, and poor acquisition of partial reinforcement schedules, suggesting to some (e.g. Mogenson and Phillips, 1976) that there are no fundamental differences between the natural and artificial reinforcers.

Even those who consider them distinct (e.g. Gallistel, 1979) admit that complex interactions between them exist. Gallistel points out that hungry rats take longer to extinguish rewarding ESB and can acquire relatively high partial reinforcement schedules. His explanation is that each stimulus induces a drive-like after-effect which decays very rapidly, thus making the ISI crucial in ESB experiments. Hunger, making its own contribution to the animal's overall drive-state, adds to and prolongs this drive-like after-effect, enabling longer ISIs to be tolerated.

A further complication is introduced by the finding that the lateral hypothalamus, besides being involved in the regulation of hunger and thirst, is also a powerful supporter of ESB. In fact, in some instances, ESB, eating, and drinking can be elicited by appropriate stimulation of the same hypothalamic site. This does not necessarily imply that in each case the same physiological substrate is being activated; earlier in the chapter I referred to Grossman's neurochemical differentiation of noradrenergic eating and cholinergic drinking in the hypothalamus, and it is clear that many actually independent circuits may be physically intermeshed in the same hypothalamic area.

Despite procedural problems and the interactions between ESB and natural reinforcers, there is still a fundamental difference between the two. ESB does not satiate, and is therefore not based on any present or anticipated tissue deficiency. It appears to activate a higher-order reinforcement network, which is presumably also activated by the various natural reinforcers when they are encountered.

More recent attempts to explain the phenomenon have in some degree followed the tendency for the wider study of motivation to consider enviromental stimuli as increasingly important. Even the traditional 'tissue deficiency → drive → behaviour leading to drive reduction' had to give external stimuli at least a guiding role in motivated behaviour. Nowadays it is accepted that such stimuli can have a more dramatic influence. Normal rats can be made obese by suitable dietary control, while sensory stimuli such as a tone or light can support bar-pressing behaviour (Tapp, 1969). As pointed out earlier, eating and drinking are normally regulatory, guided by external cues, habit, and circadian rhythms, and are independent of any acute tissue deficiency. Valenstein *et al.* (1970), from the same hypothalamic electrode, elicited either eating, drinking, or gnawing, depending on whether food, water, or blocks of wood were made available to the rat. They refer to such behaviour as 'stimulus-bound'.

The realization that motivated behaviour could be initiated by external stimuli as well as by primary deficits can be combined with the 'cognitive' approach to exploratory behaviour to suggest that, yet again, physiological psychology is becoming more complex and more realistic. Simple drive-reduction has been to some extent replaced by the concept that behaviour can be initiated by external stimuli, a concept referred to as 'incentive motivation'. Bolles (1967) in a complex book, presented a detailed theory on the role of stimuli in motivated behaviour, and suggested that it is the initial association of neutral stimuli with biologically significant stimuli that enables them to independently elicit a response. Thus taste and smell, associated with food, themselves acquire the ability not just to reinforce behaviour (in the straightforward way of a secondary reinforcer), but to elicit or arouse it in the first place. This 'incentive' arousal would be independent of the actual reinforcement property of the stimulus, so allowing, e.g., non-nutritive saccharine to be a potent incentive for the rat.

One may then speculate that rewarding ESB is activating the physiological substrate of incentive motivation, arousing the animal but not satiating it. The idea of a separate system for incentive or arousal has been put forward several times (Gallistel, 1973; Crow, 1973), always centring on the ability of a stimulus both to arouse and to reinforce behaviour; pure incentives such as lights and tones emphasize the arousing properties of stimuli, while biological reinforcers, such as food in the presence of tissue deficits, emphasize the reinforcing properties. There would be separable physiological substrates for incentive, and for drive-reduction reward.

There are still major problems of interpretation in this area. If ESB operates via pathways controlling incentive motivation, pathways which are normally activated by incentives such as sight, taste and smell, there still appears no reason why it should not extinguish. If incentives acquire their motivational properties by association with primary reinforcers, then their arousal potential would decline if, e.g., the smell was repeatedly presented in the absence of food. This does not happen with ESB.

However, Valenstein (1967) has shown that responding for a saccharine-sucrose mixture is extremely persistent, and it is possible that the combination of high incentive value (e.g. sweet taste) with little or no primary drive-reducing ability is crucial for any stimulus to elicit prolonged responding. This also implies that some incentive stimuli are unconditioned, i.e. they have biological significance (in that responses to them do not habituate) in the absence of primary drive-reduction. We can then associate, e.g., sweet taste (or, more properly, stimulation of the 'sweetness' taste receptors) with ESB in their effects on behaviour, and point to a common locus in the brain's incentive motivation pathways.

I have referred to pathways consistently, as current hypotheses relate the behavioural arousing effects of incentive stimuli to the central nigro-striatal dopamine pathway (Crow, 1973; Mogenson and Phillips, 1976). Crow also suggests that drive-reduction reward is mediated by the dorsal noradrenergic pathway, in line with Stein's views on the reinforcement role of the brain's noradrenergic system (see Chapter 3). So, in Crow's view, both nigro-striatal dopaminergic and dorsal noradrenergic pathways can support ESB, as in the former case the electrode plugs into an incentive arousal system, and in the latter into a straightforward reward system.

The neurochemical basis of ESB has been discussed in Chapter 3. Briefly, it seems likely that the catecholamines dopamine and noradrenaline are involved, while a more recent paper suggests that enkephalins might have a part to play (Belluzzi and Stein, 1977).

This chapter has reviewed the physiological bases of motivation. In the sense that all behaviour is normally motivated, i.e. aroused and directed, we have covered only a fraction of the possible subject matter. However, the broad division into homeostatic and non-homeostatic drives allows us to evaluate the traditional approach, and to see immediately that the classic drive-reduction approach to behaviour is inadequate. Hunger represents an amalgam of cognitive processing, external stimuli, and complex preparatory metabolic adjustments, even before food is ingested and digested; short- and long-term regulatory factors also play their part. Exploration shifts emphasis to external stimuli and cognitive processes, with 'drive' concepts perhaps unnecessary. Rewarding electrical self-stimulation of the brain certainly avoids the classic drive-reduction approach, but is now seen to be more similar to natural rewards then had been thought; the key to this has been the shift in emphasis from a tissue-deficiency 'driving' behaviour to incentive stimuli 'pulling' behaviour. Both naturally occurring stimuli and ESB can, therefore, initiate and sustain behaviour in the absence of primary drive-reduction.

12 Brain chemistry and psychopathology

The topics covered in this book have emphasized the physiological bases of normal behaviour. Given that all behaviour has a physiological basis, we can also investigate abnormalities, or psychopathologies.

There are many entries in a classification of psychiatric disorders (see *Clinical Psychopathology* by E.M. Coles, in this series), and this chapter does not attempt to be comprehensive. On the basis of their currently high profile within the general field of brain research therefore, the discussion is limited to schizophrenia, the various depressive syndromes, and anxiety. Although each has possible neuroanatomical correlates, it is in the field of brain chemistry that the most dramatic and useful findings have emerged, and simultaneously fresh attention has been given to the whole problem of using animals to study brain function; this will, I hope, emerge as we proceed.

Schizophrenia

Chapter 3 discussed the evolution of the 'chemical pathway' approach to brain structure and function, and along the way mentioned how the analysis of drug therapy in schizophrenia catalysed the process. Schizophrenia, the 'Sacred Symbol of Psychiatry' (Szasz, 1976), has fascinated people for many years. Any psychotic condition, with psychosis defined as a complete or partial breakdown in the normal links between the behaviour of an individual and the world around, has a roman-

324

tic and fantastic aspect. In a prosaic world, any hint of contact with what many people hope is a more fundamental mode of experience has tremendous appeal; a short-cut to meaning and truth.

A debate on the moral and ethical aspects of psychiatric diagnosis is beyond the scope of this book. It is indisputable that schizophrenics, depressives, and anxiety-disabled patients have been helped by drug therapy, in the sense that some or all of the symptoms they presented on initial diagnosis are alleviated by the treatment. It is equally indisputable that physical treatments such as drugs or electro-convulsive shock have sometimes been used indiscriminately and with no theoretical or even empirical justification. Indeed, one of the by-products of the current intense interest in brain function may be a more rational basis for physical intervention in human psychopathology. Also, to demonstrate the neutrality of research, the analysis of the physiological bases of, e.g., schizophrenia may indicate how non-physical therapy can be effective: there are undoubtedly links between brain chemistry and environmental variables such as stress and diet.

One of the enduring frustrations of research into schizophrenia is the practical irrelevance of many of the major discoveries. Given that the aim is to diagnose a disorder reliably, and for that diagnosis to have implications for aetiology (i.e. cause and development) and prognosis (i.e. eventual outcome, with or without treatment), we have not come far since the 1950s. The major discoveries since the introduction of drug therapy have been the identification of a genetic component in the transmission of schizophrenia, and the realization, already referred to, that the effective neuroleptic (anti-schizophrenic) drugs had in common an anti-dopaminergic action.

A genetic component has led to the suggestion that certain children are 'high-risk' for schizophrenia, being progeny of parents at least one of whom is schizophrenic; such children appear to have characteristically abnormal skin conductance orienting responses, and longitudinal studies are at present under way in Denmark and Mauritius to validate these suggestions (e.g. Venables, 1983).

A degree of genetic loading also encourages the search for an inherited neurophysiological malfunction, although it should be remembered that social and cultural factors are also involved in schizophrenia, e.g. the correlation between prevalence of the disorder and social class.

The identification of the dopamine synapse as the site of action of neuroleptic drugs has galvanized research into brain dopamine pathways and behavioural functions (see Chapter 3). However, it has, as yet, made little difference to the schizophrenic patient. There is still no more effective treatment than the phenothiazines (e.g. cholorpromazine) or butyrophenones (e.g. haloperidol), although other recently developed drugs may be equally effective at lower doses. For the diagnosed schizophrenic in 1980, as in 1960, the standard treatment is to be given chlorpromazine (trade name, Largactyl); in cases where emotional 'poverty' is suspected, ECT may be used as well. There is still very little correlation between severity or subtype of schizophrenia, drug therapy, and outcome; in a major review, Davis and Garver (1978) analysed some eighty controlled studies and found a significant improvement reported for 75 per cent of patients on phenothiazines and for 25 per cent of patients on placebo. There are, therefore, many schizophrenics who are unresponsive to drug treatment, and many who do well without drug treatment.

Why are researchers fascinated by this disorder? It is the single most common psychopathology among patients in psychiatric hospitals, having an impressively consistent cross-cultural incidence of around 1 per cent of the population; it has been estimated that there are world-wide around ten million schizophrenics, a substantial number of whom will need, or are at present receiving, long-term institutionalization with constant maintenance drug therapy. A solution to the aetiology of the disorder, leading to increased prevention and more effective treatment, would be as beneficial a contribution to the plight of mankind as the elimination of slavery.

The dopamine hypothesis of schizophrenia may well be seen in the future as a decisive breakthrough; at present, its almost incidental contribution to our understanding of basal ganglia movement disorders (see Chapter 3) has had more immediate impact. I suspect that the reason for the failure to influence dramatically the treatment of schizophrenia lies in the nature of the psychotic breakdown, and the failure to conceptualize adequately the behavioural breakdown in terms that might be experimentally investigated in animals. To illustrate the point, let us return to some of the material first discussed in Chapter 3.

The original and elegant work of Olds, Stein, and others on the neurochemistry of rewarding electrical self-stimulation of the brain (ESB) led them to propose neurochemically coded reward and punishment pathways. By then defining schizophrenia in part as failure to respond appropriately to rewarding stimuli, Stein could postulate a fundamental malfunction in the noradrenergic reward system of schizophrenics. As, in common with all the long-axon neurotransmitter systems, noradrenergic fibres innervate cortical, limbic, and diencephalic structures (see Chapter 3), he could account for the cognitive and affective (emotional) symptoms of schizophrenia. Although largely swamped by the dopamine tidal wave of the 1970s, Stein's presentation of his hypothesis (Stein and Wise, 1971) does illustrate some of the problems involved in brain models of psychopathology. He knew a large number of findings had to be incorporated – the genetic loading, the peak of onset at puberty, the broad range of symptoms, the deteriorating course if untreated, and the efficacy of drug treatment.

To explain the basic malfunction in the noradrenergic system, Stein postulated a genetically controlled enzymatic deficiency which, given the intimate, indeed contingent, relationship between dopamine and noradrenaline in terms of synthesis, would produce an overproduction of dopamine and an underproduction of noradrenaline. The synthetic sequence in a noradrenaline neuron is given below:

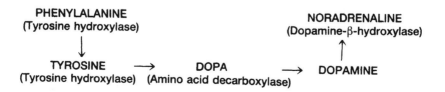

PHENYLALANINE   NORADRENALINE
(Tyrosine hydroxylase)   (Dopamine-β-hydroxylase)

TYROSINE   →   DOPA   →   DOPAMINE
(Tyrosine hydroxylase)   (Amino acid decarboxylase)

Dopamine is converted to noradrenaline by the action of the enzyme dopamine-β-hydroxylase (DBH); the only practical difference between the noradrenergic and the dopaminergic neuron is the presence of this enzyme. The genetically based absence of DBH would prevent the conversion of DA to NA, and lead to an overproduction of dopamine in the nor-adrenergic neuron. The excess DA would be broken down by a variety of routes, and one conceivable breakdown product could be 6-hydroxydopamine (6-OHDA). 6-OHDA is a well-known neurotoxin, i.e. it destroys neurons, and in this instance would eliminate the noradrenergic neuron it was being pro-duced in and around. The gradual build-up of 6-OHDA would explain the gradual onset of schizophrenia, while the failure of drug therapy in chronic schizophrenia would be explained by the irreversible destruction of the noradrenergic neurons; the relative efficacy of drugs in early-onset schizophrenia would be explained by the neuroleptics blocking the uptake of 6-OHDA into noradrenergic terminals and so protecting them.

Stein's 6-OHDA-mediated destruction of NA reward path-ways in schizophrenia was the first comprehensive and plaus-ible model of the disorder in terms of brain chemistry and based on systematic animal experimentation. Direct evidence from human subjects has been inconsistent, giving little support to any of the neurochemical hypotheses. Stein himself reported the predicted reduction of DBH levels after post-mortem analy-ses of the brains of schizophrenics (Wise *et al.*, 1974), while Wyatt *et al.* (1975) concluded that schizophrenics and normals did not differ; a reinterpretation of their data by Stein (Wise and Stein, 1975) suggested that paranoid patients did show a trend in the expected direction. It should be borne in mind that all post-mortem studies of schizophrenics suffer from the fun-damental and almost insoluble problem of controlling for the weeks, months, or years of drug therapy. The ideal control group would be normal patients who have experienced identi-cal drug treatment, which in practice never occurs; alterna-tively, drug-free schizophrenics could be used, but nowadays these are few and far between.

There is little direct evidence for Stein's hypothesis, but it does stand as a yardstick against which to assess alternative neurochemical hypotheses. They all have to account for aetiology, diagnosis, prognosis, and treatment, and usually attempt to do so in terms of a single biochemical model. What can vary is the starting-point; Stein began with an animal model of reward pathways, while the dopamine hypothesis began with the mode of action of neuroleptic drugs.

Chlorpromizine was originally developed as an antihistamine sedating agent, and was then serendipitously found to be effective in schizophrenic states. It was only in the 1960s that the anti-dopamine action of the commonly used neuroleptics was discovered (see Carlsson, 1978, for a review), and stimulated research into the behavioural functions of central dopamine pathways, especially as they relate to schizophrenia.

Before considering the DA-hypothesis in detail, and to throw attempts to 'model' schizophrenia in animals into perspective, let us consider the diagnostic problem. Table 12.1 presents two of the many approaches.

The classical system of Bleuler splits the various symptoms

Table 12.1   Symptoms of schizophrenia

(a) Bleuler	Fundamental	Accessory
	Disturbances of affect Disturbances of associations Autism Ambivalence	Delusions Hallucinations Catatonia
(b) Schneider	First rank symptoms	
	Audible thoughts Voices arguing Voices commenting	Auditory hallucinations
	Influences playing on body Thought withdrawal Thought insertion Thought broadcasting	
	'Made' feelings 'Made' impulses 'Made' volitional acts	Delusions of control by outside agencies
	Delusional perception	

into those he considered inevitable corollaries of the disease process (i.e. it was a medical model, in that while rejecting cases with clear evidence of organic brain damage, the fundamental pathology is seen as a physiological process with predictable consequences), and those that may or may not be present in a given case.

Schneider had a more pragmatic approach. His experience as a clinician was used to classify symptoms in terms of their usefulness in diagnosing schizophrenia, and defined a 'nuclear' syndrome featuring some or all of his first-rank symptoms. As can be seen from the list (see Mellor, 1970, 1982, for a fuller account), Schneider emphasized auditory hallucinations and experiences of 'passivity', and outside influences controlling emotions and actions.

Schenider's system is in relatively common use, and illustrates the range and complexity of schizophrenic symptomatology. It does, however, have many competitors; a study by Bland and Orn (1979; 1980) found that the system of Feighner *et al.* (1972), which incorporates duration of illness and measures of pre-morbid (i.e. before diagnosis) social and economic functioning, was a more accurate predictor of eventual outcome than the severity of illness gauged on the Schneiderian system.

The diagnosis of schizophrenia is essentially phenomenological – certain symptoms, generally agreed upon, are present in the absence of obvious organic brain damage or of a prior history of drug-taking. The symptoms, such as those of the first-rank, are not individually exclusive to or diagnostic of schizophrenia. They can occur in association with various organic and 'hard' neurological disorders, such as pituitary tumours, encephalitis, and temporal lobe epilepsy (see Davison and Bagley, 1969, for a comprehensive review), as well as in other psychopathological conditions such as manic-depressive psychosis. There is, therefore, substantial ambiguity over the behavioural aspects of schizophrenia, although it would be accepted to be a mixture of perceptual, cognitive, affective, and conative (motivational) variables. Does this provide an adequate basis for generating an animal model?

The dopamine hypothesis begins with the mode of action of

neuroleptic drugs. There is an impressively high correlation between the clinical effectiveness of neuroleptics and their ability to block dopamine receptors; chlorpromazine, used in relatively high doses in schizophrenia, is a less effective dopamine-antagonist than pimozide, which in turn is clinically effective at lower doses than chlorpromazine (see Carlsson, 1978; Van Pragg, 1977b, for reviews of the neuroleptic/ dopamine connection).

If neuroleptics act by reducing dopamine activity in the brain, then schizophrenia should represent an overactivity in dopamine pathways. Logically, then, an animal model of schizophrenia would be *pharmacologically* produced by injection of drugs which increase brain dopamine activity; the behavioural correlates of the dopamine hyperactivity in animals might then be said to be homologous with schizophrenic symptomatology, in that they are mediated by the same substrate in the brain.

As a concept, homology may also be applied to behavioural function: complex visual processing occurs in frogs, who have no visual cortex, and humans, who do. There is no possibility of structural homology, but there is an obvious functional one (the various conceptualizations of homology and analogy in relation to the evolution of anatomy and behaviour are somewhat subtle and arbitrary; for a discussion of these issues, see Hodos and Campbell, 1969).

The function of schizophrenic symptomatology cannot be defined; all that can be said is that it represents malfunctions in one or more behavioural systems – perceptual, cognitive, emotional, etc. Similar systems operate in other animals, in that perceptual, cognitive, and emotional behaviour may be assessed in rats. However, controlled manipulations of these systems in an attempt to mimic human psychopathologies cannot reproduce exactly the consequences of the same manipulations in human subjects – as previously described, the diagnosis of schizophrenia depends heavily upon the presence of thought disorder, hallucinations, and feelings of passivity and external control. These are assessed via the diagnostic interview, and are impossible to identify in animals.

We are, therefore, working with primarily a pharmacological

parallel, using drugs to stimulate the same neurochemical pathways in animals as in people, and looking for behavioural parallels which cannot exist in exactly the same form.

Chapter 3 presented some of the animal data on the behavioural correlates of brain dopamine activity. The analysis of the nigro-striatal pathway and its role in the control of motor output does reveal a fairly close parallel between animals and humans, and as we shall see, the motor effects of dopamine stimulants in animals play a large part in any discussion of models of schizophrenia. However, manipulations of the motor output system can be seen directly, with few, if any, possibilities of adaptive mechanisms intervening. In contrast, an attenuation of perceptual input, assessed via behaviour, i.e. response output, involves the much greater 'processing distance' between perception and response; this would allow the intervention of compensatory mechanisms and, consequently, much greater inter-individual variability in response output. Add in the vast qualitative differences in compensatory mechanisms and response processes between animals and people, and it can be concluded that the observed consequences of perceptual malfunction in animals will not parallel those in humans.

With tightly controlled experimental conditions, eliciting only a narrow range of behavioural processes, drug effects on specific systems may be identified – the work of Warburton on the cholinergic control of stimulus sensitivity is a good example (Chapter 3). But when drugs are injected and free-range behaviour observed, narrow conclusions may be unjustified as the behaviour could represent a direct action on motor output, or attempts by the animal to compensate for a primary interference with perceptual, cognitive, or other processes.

This short but general discussion does have a specific relevance to models of schizophrenia. Hemsley (1977) has proposed that the wide range of schizophrenic symptomatology represents individual variations in the patient's attempts to compensate for a primary malfunction in an attentional filter mechanism (Broadbent, 1971). This is an attractive attempt to provide a unifying concept in this difficult and somewhat disorganized field; however, no attempts have yet been made to isolate any dopaminergic involvement in the attentional processes of either animals or humans, and any that are made will be subject to the problems just discussed.

Bearing in mind these necessary constraints on animal models of complex human psychopathology, we can now consider the effects of overstimulating dopamine pathways in animals in the attempt to mimic schizophrenia. Substantial dopamine overactivity results in behaviour beyond the normal limits; the syndrome is referred to as 'stereotypy', and may be induced by a range of dopamine-agonist drugs such as amphetamine, methylphenidate, and apomorphine.

The syndrome varies slightly from species to species and from strain to strain. Table 12.2 is a representative description and rating system for stereotyped behaviour in the rat; in general, the commonest features are the repetitive licking, gnawing, and pawing. This central aspect of repetition characterizes stereotypy, and has been related to the stereotypies of behaviour seen in some chronic schizophrenics. These may include repetitions of thought patterns and of motor movements; the latter are seen in a wide range of chronic psychiatric patients, and probably represent non-specific aspects of institutionalization (Mayer-Gross *et al.*, 1977), while stereotypy in general does not play a significant part in the diagnosis of schizophrenia.

The stereotypy syndrome induced by dopamine stimulants is antagonized by neuroleptic drugs such as chlorpromazine. As we know that they are dopamine blockers it is perhaps not surprising that a behaviour induced by increasing dopamine activity should be reduced by decreasing it. What is of interest is that some clinically used drugs do not antagonize

Table 12.2   Stereotypy following injection of dopamine stimulant drugs in rats

Low doses:	Increased general locomotion
Medium doses:	Increased circling in restricted areas, sniffing at certain points
High doses:	Stereotypy. Repetitive licking and gnawing, rearing, little gross movement, rapid sideways head shakes

amphetamine-induced stereotypy in line with their clinical potency, calling into question the validity of the syndrome as either a model of schizophrenia or as a test-bed for potential neuroleptic agents.

In Chapter 3 the failure of thioridazine to antagonize amphetamine-induced turning in the unilateral nigro-striatal lesioned rat was attributed to its potent anticholinergic properties; the simultaneous blockade of both striatal dopamine and acetylcholine receptors maintained the dynamic imbalance between them produced by amphetamine. A drug like chlorpromazine, blocking only the dopamine receptors, reduces the dopamine overactivity induced by amphetamine and so restores the striatal DA/ACh to normal. As Iversen (1977) has localized amphetamine-induced stereotypy to the nigro-striatal dopamine pathway as well, the same argument can be applied to the failure of thioridazine to antagonize stereotypy.

Chapter 3 also pointed out that the extra-pyramidal side-effects of neuroleptic drugs were probably due to their dopamine-blocking action in the striatum, and could be prevented, using suitable drugs, leaving their anti-schizophrenic potency untouched. This latter effect cannot therefore be localized in the nigro-striatal dopamine pathway, which, by exclusion, implies that the meso-limbic cortical dopamine system is the one involved in schizophrenia. The striatally based amphetamine-induced stereotypy, while an interesting and important example of a dopamine-mediated behaviour, cannot therefore serve as a model of schizophrenia.

It has recently been suggested that a stereotypy syndrome seen after injection of the drug phenylethylamine represents a better model of the disorder (Borison and Diamond, 1978). The syndrome is similar to that induced by amphetamine, but is blocked by all the standard neuroleptic drugs, including thioridazine. Phenylethylamine is a naturally occurring biogenic amine, found in high concentrations in the limbic system. This fits in with the argument just outlined implicating the meso-limbic-cortical dopamine tract in schizophrenia, and also with a popular view that this particular psychopathology must involve limbic structures (Stevens, 1973; Torrey and Petersen, 1974).

Besides their effects in animals, dopamine agonists also have dramatic effects in people. Amphetamine can produce a toxic psychosis phenomenologically indistinguishable from acute paranoid schizophrenia, while methylphenidate can precipitate psychotic episodes in schizophrenic patients. These human data are more convincing as regards the dopamine model of schizophrenia than the animal models of dopamine hyperactivity; particularly the amphetamine-induced psychosis, as, in the whole range of drug-induced psychoses and hallucinogenic episodes, it is the only one which precisely mimics the human psychopathology. However, the data are still equivocal as amphetamine is pharmacologically a 'messy' drug, increasing activity in both dopaminergic and noradrenergic pathways, while the behavioural effects of the 'cleaner' methylphenidate can be antagonized by cholinergic agonists such as physostigmine (Janowsky *et al.*, 1972); the latter agents are ineffective in schizophrenia itself.

Other sources of data relevant to the dopamine hypothesis are post-mortem studies on the brains of schizophrenics, and the analysis of neurotransmitter metabolites from living patients. There is some evidence from post-mortem studies of an elevation of dopamine metabolites in the limbic system and cortex of schizophrenics (Bird *et al.*, 1979; Bacopoulos *et al.*, 1979); this was attributed by the authors to the selective therapeutic action of neuroleptic drugs, which alleviate the psychotic symptoms by increasing dopamine metabolism in the limbic system and cortex. (An increase in DA metabolism via a neuroleptic-blockade of DA receptors is quite feasible, although a full description is beyond the scope of this text. The important feature of this work is the regional localization of neuroleptic action in the brain.) Post-mortem studies in general cannot avoid being confounded by years of drug therapy. It is a fundamental aspect of brain function that the brain will attempt to compensate for any chronic (long-term) interference with its normal metabolism. So it is likely to respond to a chronic blockade of dopamine post-synaptic receptors by neuroleptic drugs with an increased production of dopamine (with a resulting increase in dopamine metabolites), and by increasing the number and sensitivity of post-synaptic dopamine receptors. All of these changes have, variably, been identified in post-mortem studies, but along with the identification goes an unresolved debate on whether they are drug-induced or whether they are in some 'true' sense related to the pathology of the schizophrenic process. In a recent review, MacKay (MacKay *et al.*, 1982) concludes, cautiously, that an increase in the amount of brain dopamine may represent a real and significant difference in the schizophrenic brain relative to controls.

The analysis of metabolites *in vivo* (i.e. in the living patient) is difficult. After synaptic release and action at the receptor, neurotransmitters are, in part, broken down into various metabolites. One excretion route for these chemicals is via the cerebral ventricles within the brain. These spaces are continuous with the canal which passes down the middle of the spinal cord, and the whole is filled with cerebro-spinal fluid (CSF). Samples of CSF, extracted from the spinal canal via a lumber puncture will therefore contain neurotransmitter metabolites, which may in their turn reflect neurotransmitter activity in the brain – dopamine overactivity should result in increased breakdown and higher levels of CSF metabolites.

Unfortunately, there is little or no evidence that such is the case in schizophrenia. Measurements of CSF levels of the dopamine metabolite homovanillic acid (HVA) show no systematic relation with the diagnosis of schizophrenia,

Table 12.3   Crow's type I and type II syndromes

	Type I (Acute schizophrenia)	Type II (Chronic schizophrenia)
Symptoms	*Positive* – thought disorder delusions, hallucinations	*Negative* – speech poverty, emotional flattening, psychomotor retardation
Response to drug treatment	Good	Poor
Outcome	Favourable	Unfavourable
Pathology	Overactivity in dopamine pathways	Loss of brain cells via possible viral infection

although higher levels are associated with aroused, anxious, or agitated schizophrenics (Van Praag, 1977b). This has led to the suggestion that CSF HVA reflects central activation per se rather than schizophrenia (Bowers, 1974).

So, overall, there is no decisive evidence from patients for the dopamine hypothesis (for an extended review, see Hornykiewicz, 1978), and there is still significant support for alternative models involving other neurotransmitters e.g. noradrenaline (Hornykiewicz, 1982). We are effectively driven back to the original association of anti-psychotic action with dopamine-blocking potency. It is impressive that, given the world-wide interest in schizophrenia and the range of substances empirically tested for anti-psychotic action, the drugs of first choice are still dopamine-blocking agents. There are intriguing exceptions; clozapine is ineffective against amphetamine-stereotypy, and appears to act via noradrenergic receptors (Burki *et al.*, 1975), while clinical trials suggest significant anti-psychotic activity for the noradrenergic blocking drug propranolol (Gruzellier, 1978).

One factor specifically reinforcing the dopamine–schizophrenia link is the testing of potential neuroleptics on animal models of dopamine overactivity – rotation (see Chapter 3) and stereotypy. By definition, the effective agents selected for subsequent clinical trials will be dopamine antagonists. This has not completely inhibited the search for original drug therapies; even the recently discovered enkephalin and its antagonist naloxone have been tested in schizophrenia with inconsistent results.

We have spent some time considering links between brain chemistry and schizophrenia, links which have been a driving force behind brain research through the last decade, and one outcome of this intense interest in the pharmacology of schizophrenia has been an alternative approach to classifying patients. I mentioned earlier that, although drug therapy revolutionized the treatment of schizophrenia, a substantial number of patients do not improve with neuroleptics, i.e. a dopamine hypothesis of the disorder, *based on the effectiveness of drug treatment*, is automatically restricted to those patients who respond well. Immediately you can divide schizophrenics into drug-responsive and drug-unresponsive categories.

The dopamine hypothesis concerns only the former group. In addition, drug-responsive schizophrenics, by definition, improve, i.e. their prognosis (long-term outcome) is better than for the drug-unresponsive group. This has the interesting side-effect of implying that chronic patients institutionalized in long-stay hospitals are primarily drug-unresponsive. Because of their availability, most post-mortem studies will involve such patients. So the evidence from post-mortem data supposedly in favour of the dopamine hypothesis actually comes from a drug-unresponsive group to which the dopamine hypothesis does not apply anyway.

Although, looking back, such a drug-based division into two groups seems obvious, it was only in the middle and late 1970s that Crow formally proposed such a division, and also described other distinguishing characteristics between the groups. A major catalyst for his ideas was the discovery in his unit that a significant proportion of schizophrenic patients have enlarged ventricles (Johnstone *et al.*, 1976). The ventricular system is a fluid-filled set of linked chambers in the brain, continuous with the spinal canal running down the middle of the spinal cord. A horizontal X-ray through the brain, taken with a CAT scanner (see Chapter 1), allows the size of the ventricles to be measured as a ratio with total brain size. There is reliable evidence that increases in the ratio, corresponding to a relative increase in ventricle size, are associated with a loss of brain substance. Most of this evidence comes from studies on chronic alcoholics suffering from Wernicke–Korsakoff syndrome (the main symptom of which is partial or complete amnesia; see Chapter 6), and Crow's group were the first to extend the observations to schizophrenia.

Following the discovery that a sub-group of schizophrenics have enlarged ventricles, presumably associated with a loss of brain tissue, Crow (1980) went on to define two types of schizophrenia (Table 12.3). Type I is characterized by positive, florid symptoms of hallucinations and delusions. Intellect is unimpaired, response to drugs is good, and long-term outcome optimistic. The basic brain malfunction is an overactivity of dopamine pathways. Type II is characterized by negative symptoms of speech poverty, slowness of thought and action, and a general inertia. Intellect may be impaired, drugs are ineffective, and the course of the illness is a progressive and irreversible deterioration. The underlying malfunction is a pathological process which destroys brain tissue.

Type I is therefore an acute form of schizophrenia, while Type II represents schizophrenia as originally conceptualized by Kraepelin and Bleuler, with a chronic deteriorating and irreversible course, i.e. it is 'true' schizophrenia. Although the separation of the two syndromes is incomplete – chronic long-term patients can exhibit periods of florid symptoms – and the association of ventricular enlargement with negative symptoms and poor outcome is not yet established (see, e.g., Jernigan *et al.*, 1982), there is general agreement that pathological loss of brain tissue occurs in some schizophrenics. It is still not clear whether it precedes the onset of schizophrenic symptoms, is produced by them or perhaps by drug treatment, or is entirely unrelated to schizophrenia (enlarged ventricles are found in alcoholics, in some manic-depressives, and as a component of normal ageing).

Crow assumes that the loss of tissue is fundamental to the disease process of Type II schizophrenia, and his most controversial suggestion is that it represents a viral infection of some sort (e.g. Crow, 1984). He takes as his model a psycho-pathology called Creutzfeldt-Jakob syndrome. This is a rare form of senile dementia, involving confusion, amnesia, delusions, etc. In New Guinea, Creutzfeldt-Jakob syndrome exists in the native tribes as 'kuru', and many years ago it was established that kuru was transmitted via the cannibalistic habits of the natives; specifically, by eating the brains of sufferers. This would point to a transmissable agent such as a virus.

Subsequently cases of transmission of Creutzfeldt-Jakob syndrome have been identified in this country, involving the inadequate sterilization of recording electrodes used first in the brain of a Creutzfeldt-Jakob patient and then for recording from an uninfected patient (Corsellis, 1979). Presumably an infective agent has been passed between them, and a psycho-pathological condition produced, i.e. Creutzfeldt-Jakob dementia represents a virus-like infection of brain tissue.

Schizophrenic symptoms such as delusions and hallucinations can occur in association with the inflammations of the brain produced by viral meningitis and encephalitis, so it is not by any means unreasonable to suggest, in principle, that Type II true schizophrenia is caused by a virus-like agent in the brain. Unfortunately, confirming evidence has not emerged. Analyses of the cerebro-spinal fluid of schizophrenics have proved negative, while attempts to transmit either neurological or behavioural abnormalities via injections of supposedly infected tissue into monkeys have been largely unsuccessful (Baker *et al.*, 1983). However, the reliable division of patients into drug-responsive and drug-unresponsive sub-groups does imply some, perhaps fundamental, physiological difference between them, and research is proceeding at a lively pace.

In Chapter 5 mention was made of the work on asymmetries of hemisphere function in psychopathology, while a discussion of genetic, social, developmental, and personality variables in schizophrenia is beyond the scope of this book. Brain mechanisms may be ultimately responsible for abnormal behaviour, but there is no doubt that they represent only the final common pathway for a large number of influences, from cultural down to biochemical. The neurochemists and psychobiologists do not have the field to themselves; the eventual explanation of the disorder will result from a coordination of all levels of investigation.

Depression

Around 5 per cent of men and 10 per cent of women will, in their lifetime, suffer a single or recurring depressive attack severe enough for them to seek therapeutic help. The symptoms of depression are, much more so than schizophrenia, recognizable by sufferers and non-sufferers alike. Most of us have been 'down', even if only for a while. Table 12.4 lists a representative sample of clinical symptoms.

The classification of the depressive disorders is still subject to

Table 12.4   Symptoms of depression

Unipolar depression:	Insomnia, loss of appetite, decreased ability to experience pleasure, reduced energy, passivity, difficulties in concentrating, feelings of pessimism, guilt, and suicide
Bipolar depression (manic-depression):	Depressive phases as above, interspersed with periods of one week or more of overactivity, decreased need for sleep, 'pressure' of ideas. At extremes, ideas become delusional and hallucinations may occur, producing a manic-depressive *psychosis*

some confusion, though less so than schizophrenia (see Kendell, 1976, for a full review).

The aim of a classification into subtypes is to link aetiology (origins) and symptomatology with treatment and prognosis, and the depressions (or 'affective disorders') have been relatively amenable to this approach. Although there is still some dispute on the precise nature of the difference between endogenous (or psychotic) and reactive (or neurotic) depressions, there is complete agreement on the existence of a unipolar and bipolar form of the disorder. The former appears as single or recurrent episodes of depression, while the latter ('manic-depressive illness') presents as single or recurrent episodes alongside bouts of mania or hypomania (Akiskal and McKinney, 1975). Besides differing symptomatically, and in terms of genetic loading, unipolar and bipolar depressions may also be distinguished in terms of the most effective pharmacological treatment, and possibly by the neurotransmitter metabolite methods mentioned in the previous section. But to return to the beginning. . . .

Schildkraut (1965) first suggested a neurotransmitter hypothesis for the affective disorders, emphasizing the role of the catecholamines dopamine and noradrenaline; since then, the interest in brain chemistry and depression has paralleled the work in schizophrenia in terms of methods and logic. Research has concentrated upon the pharmacology of antidepressant drugs, the use of animal models of depression, and the measurement of neurotransmitters and their metabolites in post-mortem brains and in the urine and cerebro-spinal fluid of clinically diagnosed depressives.

The catecholamine hypothesis (sometimes referred to as the 'amine hypothesis') began life as a postulated deficit in brain noradrenaline, which as Stein had demonstrated the role of noradrenergic pathways in the 'reward' system, would explain the anhedonia (loss of the normal reaction to reinforcement) found in depression. This, of course, is precisely analogous to the argument used by Stein to attribute schizophrenia to a central noradrenaline deficiency. Does this match the known effects of anti-depressant drugs?

The monoamines (i.e. the catecholamines dopamine and noradrenaline, and the indoleamine serotonin) are chemically closely related, in that they are all broken down after synaptic action by the enzyme monoamine oxidase. Of the two major groups of anti-depressant drugs, the first, the monoamine oxidase inhibitors (MAOIs), act, as their name implies, by inhibiting this enzyme and allowing the accumulation of monoamines in the brain. The second group, the tricyclic anti-depressants, are thought to act by blocking the re-uptake of noradrenaline and serotonin into their respective pre-synaptic terminals after action at the post-synpatic receptor; this would make more of the transmitter available at the synapse, and effectively prolong its action. The simplest conclusion is that both classes of drugs increase the action of noradrenaline and serotonin in the brain, and this has led to the equally simple hypothesis that depression represents a deficiency in noradrenergic and/or serotonergic pathways.

Before considering the animal and metabolite studies relevant to this hypothesis, two other modes of physical intervention should be mentioned. Lithium has been used successfully in the treatment of bipolar manic-depressive illness; it has no consistent action on brain neurotransmitters, and is thought to work via a non-specific action on the neuronal cell membrane. It cannot as yet be incorporated into our neurochemical hypothesis. Before drug therapy emerged, electro-convulsive therapy (ECT) was the treatment of choice for depression, and is still in wide use. As a massive neurological trauma it would be unexpected if ECT therapeutic effects were correlated with changes in any one neurotransmitter system, and this seems to be the case; Abrams *et al.* (1976), measuring CSF levels of various metabolites, found no consistent variations with frequency of ECT.

Monoamine oxidase inhibitors and tricyclic anti-depressants seem to act by increasing monoamine levels in the brain, particularly noradrenaline and serotonin. This would imply that decreasing monamine levels should be the basis of depression, and this has been the stimulus for animal models. Unfortunately, and inevitably, we here come up against the problem of identifying in animals behaviour homologous with human depression.

It was pointed out that, given the essentially cognitive nature of its symptomatology, schizophrenia was not a feasible subject for animal modelling. In contrast, depressive behaviour has as a large component 'psychomotor retardation'; general inertia of thought and behaviour, with a noticeable slowing of motor responses. This latter symptom is obviously identifiable in animals.

Drugs which deplete monoamines in general (e.g. reserpine), or catecholamines in particular (e.g. α-methyl-para-tyrosine; α-mpt), can be given to animals, and they do produce something resembling psychomotor retardation. Unfortunately, so do tranquillizers like the barbiturates, and neuroleptics such as chlorpromazine – the problem is to distinguish between a genuine psychomotor retardation and behavioural sedation. It is always easier to eliminate responses completely than to produce specific behavioural changes.

Reserpine and α-mpt do not consistently produce depression on the infrequent occasions they are given to humans (for a general review, see Luchins, 1976), and some drugs which increase catecholamine levels in the brain, such as amphetamines, are not effective as clinical anti-depressants. The therapeutic actions of MAOIs and the tricyclics also take a few days to develop, which suggests that they may not be due to the drug's initial and dominant pharmacological effect; the effective agent may be a metabolite of the drug, or a gradual shift in neurotransmitter balances.

Studies on neurotransmitter metabolites have been slightly

more illuminating with regard to depression than to schizophrenia. Although several critical reveiws consider the evidence for or against neurotransmitter hypotheses of depressive disorders ambiguous and controversial (Luchins, 1976; Baldessarini, 1975; Shopsin *et al.*, 1973), others are cautiously positive (Murphy *et al.*, 1978; Van Praag, 1977a). The major metabolite of serotonin is 5-hydroxy-indole-acetic acid (5-HIAA), and of noradrenaline 3-methoxy-4-hydroxy-phenylglycol (MHPG). Many studies have been made on levels of 5-HIAA and MHPG in the cerebro-spinal fluid (CSF) and urine of depressed patients, and it is quite clear that no systematic variation in these metabolites is found across subjects. It is equally clear that significantly lower levels have been identified in some depressives, and have led to the suggestion that these and other biochemical measures may be useful in reclassifying depression.

The decrease in urinary MHPG found in some subjects (Mendels *et al.*, 1976) has been used by Schildkraut (1978) to define three sub-groups of depressives. Lower levels were found in manic-depression and in depressions associated with schizophrenia, and normal levels observed in unipolar non-endogenous depressions.

Following this empirical approach, the presence of lowered urinary MHPG has also been used as a relatively precise indicator for drug therapy (Goodwin *et al.*, 1978). These workers suggest that lowered MHPG defines a 'noradrenaline-deficient' depression best treated with a tricyclic anti-depressant which has a greater effect on NA levels than on serotonin, e.g. imipramine; high or normal levels define a 'serotonin-deficient' depression, and indicate treatment with a tricyclic which has a greater effect on serotonin levels, e.g. amitriptyline.

The emphasis on noradrenaline and serotonin has been a consistent feature of research on the neurochemistry of depression, and receives further support from Van Praag (1977a). By studying the accumulation of 5-HIAA in the CSF of patients on anti-depressant medication and using his own rather idiosyncratic classification Van Praag identifies two sub-types of endogenous depression: one is 'serotonin-deficient' and the other is 'noradrenaline-deficient'. Confirmation is by the therapeutic response to drugs, and he emphasizes the empirical nature of the enterprise by showing that the two are symptomatically indistinguishable. The similarity between Van Praag's position and that of Goodwin *et al.* is obvious, and the two approaches represent good examples of how research into the neurochemical bases of psychopathology has developed. From the original use of clinical psychiatric diagnosis and classification, we now have the beginnings of a purely pragmatic approach centring on the studies of biochemistry and drug response in the individual patient. As the background is provided by neurochemical hypotheses of brain function in psychopathology, hypotheses which are subject to experimental testing, such pragmatism may ultimately be more fruitful in terms both of treatment and of theory. However, schizophrenia and depression are heterogeneous disorders, and possibly no single approach, be it neurochemical, psychological, or sociological, will ever be sufficient.

The noradrenaline/serotonin involvement in depressive disorders is better established than that of dopamine in schizophrenia, although this depends more on the range of evidence than on any one particularly convincing finding. The data from peripheral measures of urinary and CSF metabolites are very valuable, but even these are subject to some constraints. It is not known precisely what proportion of any peripheral metabolite represents activity of a brain neurotransmitter pathway. CSF studies would appear to be that much more relevant, although the contribution of spinal pathways should not be underestimated.

The data are also correlational, introducing the problem of cause and effect. The previous section mentioned the possible correlation between the reduction in CSF HVA found occasionally in schizophrenics and simple motor activity, rather than with the specific psychopathology. Even if a systematic change in a metabolite level does correlate with a given psychopathology, the effective relationship between them would still be unclear; perhaps the primary malfunction in depression leads, as a secondary effect or epiphenomenon, to a change in serotonin activity. For both depression and schizophrenia, the driving force behind the 'amine hypothesis' remains the known pharmacological actions of neuroleptic and anti-depressant drugs.

Anxiety

The study of the neurochemistry of anxiety states has not followed the same pattern as for schizophrenia and depression. Anxiety, as a psychiatric condition, has not the same profound personal and social consequences, although, for the individual concerned, it can be a debilitating condition. The symptoms are outlined in Table 12.5.

Table 12.5   Symptoms of simple anxiety

Feelings of unease, apprehension, and danger with no obvious precipitant. Experience of helplessness. Panic attacks. Increases in physical tension leading to tremor and bodily weakness. Increased peripheral physiological arousal, with pallor, fainting, palpitations, increased heart-rate and blood pressure. Vomiting. Insomnia.

'Anxiety' states occur in association with many other conditions, including depression, obsessive–compulsive disorders, and phobias, and have been used to define an 'anxious' personality (Gray, 1982).

The pressure for research into anxiety states has come not from the institutionalization of patients, but from the massive increase over the last twenty years in the prescribing of and dependence upon anti-anxiety drugs in the 'normal' population. If you have personal experience of any prescribed psychoactive drug, it will probably be one of the benzodiazepine anti-anxiety agents, or one of the other anti-anxiety drugs (also known as minor tranquillizers) such as a barbiturate.

The two most commonly encountered benzodiazepines are chlordiazepoxide (trade name Librium) and diazepam (Valium), while the non-prescription drug with similar effect is alcohol.

The minor tranquillizers can have significant therapeutic actions in chronically anxious patients. Librium and Valium are the drugs of first choice in view of their relative lack of side-effects and physically addictive properties compared with barbiturates or alcohol. Whether the minor tranquillizers have a common neurochemical substrate is uncertain; barbiturates and alcohol have a very wide range of pharmacological actions involving virtually all neurotransmitter systems, while research on the benzodiazepines is in a particularly dynamic phase, as will be shown.

Any discussion of anxiety states must acknowledge the major involvement of autonomic and endocrine systems, providing a picture of pathological peripheral arousal associated with a central affective state of fear and foreboding.

For the moment we return to a feature held in common by brain research into anxiety, schizophrenia, and depression, which is their catalysis by the work of Larry Stein on electrical self-stimulation in the rat.

In his original formulation, Stein conceived of a noradrenergic reward pathway reciprocally balanced against a cholinergic punishment pathway; increasing activity in one had the same effect as reducing activity in the other, which explained the rewarding value of avoiding punishment, i.e. reducing activity in the punishment pathway. His extrapolation of the model to schizophrenia and depression emphasized the role of the reward system while paying little attention to the punishment pathways. Then, early, in the 1970s (Wise *et al.*, 1973), Stein and his group focused on anxiety states and their possible association with the punishment system. They suggested that the transmitter for the system was serotonin rather than acetylcholine (this fundamental switch was not, unfortunately, discussed), and that the benzodiazepines achieved their anti-anxiety actions by reducing serotonin turnover in the brain. This would reduce activity in the punishment pathway, rendering the patient less susceptible to the negatively reinforcing stimuli of everyday life.

Such a view of the behavioural effects of the benzodiazepines meshes in with some data from animal experiments; when rats bar-pressing to avoid electric footshock are given, e.g., chlordiazepoxide, performance deteriorates as though the animals' sensitivity to the punishing effects of the shock has been

reduced. The Geller–Seifter conflict procedure is also sensitive
to anti-anxiety drugs. This operant schedule has three components: reward, in which bar-presses receive a food pellet; time
out, in which bar-presses have no consequence; and conflict, in
which bar-presses produce a food pellet and a mild footshock.
Control rats, being quite sensible, press vigorously in the
reward component, and less so during time out, and suppress
responding completely during conflict. Benzodiazepines massively and specifically increase conflict responding (e.g.
Hodges and Green, 1984), and there is a significant correlation
between the effectiveness of benzodiazepines in increasing conflict responding and their anti-anxiety potency in humans.
Thus this particular schedule seems an impressively valid
animal model of human anxiety, as drug effects are predictable
and the behaviour itself has analogies with the human experience of high arousal and 'fear'.

The drugs appear to reduce the subject's sensitivity to the
punishing or aversive consequences of behaviour; it can be
reasonably suggested that 'fear' or 'anxiety' mediate responding in aversive situations, and so the effect of anti-anxiety drugs
may be to lessen fear or anxiety in animals as well as people.
Anecdotal evidence of the release from social constraints induced by alcohol supports the conclusion that anti-anxiety
agents lead to behaviour that is normally inhibited.

A primary action on the mechanisms of behavioural inhibition would help to localize drug effects within the brain.
Chapter 6 described the possible role of the hippocampus in the
control of response inhibition, and Gray (1982) has broadened
this idea out and produced a comprehensive model of the brain
mechanisms of anxiety. In a landmark text, he puts forward the
Behavioural Inhibition System (BIS) as the central substrate of
anxiety. Neural activity in the BIS is what we know as anxiety,
and anti-anxiety drugs act by reducing such activity. The BIS
is responsive to various environmental stimuli – signals associated with punishment or non-reward, novel stimuli, and innate
fear stimuli. It reacts by inhibiting ongoing motor behaviour,
and increasing arousal and attention to the environment.

Anatomically the BIS centres upon the closely related limbic
structures, the septum and the hippocampus, in association

with other limbic structures and various ascending pathways. Overactivity in the BIS is experienced as anxiety. Anti-anxiety drugs reduce the activity, but may not act directly upon the septo-hippocampal complex. BIS activity is modulated by the ascending pathways, and drugs which influence one or more of these pathways may indirectly alter the state of the BIS, i.e. anxiety levels. Gray marshals a mountain of evidence for his proposed model, mostly from animal experiments, but also including human clinical data. Much of the evidence is controversial, but in attempting to integrate research from many areas into a coherent framework, Gray's work represents an approach rarely attempted by the psychobiologist.

The core of his evidence is the demonstration that the behavioural effects of anti-anxiety drugs correlate with a highly specific blocking action on the theta wave of the hippocampal EEG. As the septo-hippocampal complex and related limbic circuits are heterogeneous with respect to synaptic neurotransmitters, and hippocampal blocking is probably not a direct effect anyway, but secondary to drug-induced variations in ascending pathways, Gray's model does not specify the pharmacological basis of anti-anxiety drug action. Stein's hypothesis implicated serotonin, while there is evidence of an interaction between benzodiazepines and the neurotransmitter GABA in the brain (Hodges and Green, 1984). Then the field was radically altered by Braestrup (Squires and Braestrup, 1977), who reported evidence for the existence in the brain of receptors which were specific for benzodiazepine drugs.

This finding is of profound importance. In Chapter 3 the isolation of the opiate receptor and the subsequent discovery of enkephalin were described, and the logic behind the discovery also applies to the benzodiazepine system. If synaptic receptors are present, we must assume that they evolved for the purpose of binding a neurotransmitter; in which case there should be, in the brain, a naturally occurring neurotransmitter that binds and acts through the benzodiazepine receptor – i.e. an endogenous agent, but one which may have either an anti-anxiety effect or a pro-anxiety (anxiogenic) effect, as we do not know the *natural* function of the benzodiazepine receptor.

Neurotransmitters are stored in and released from the

pre-synaptic terminal; after release they diffuse across the synaptic gap and act on the post-synaptic receptors. If the logic is valid, then, at some point, the neuronal terminals containing the endogenous neurotransmitter should be isolated; normally, after release, the transmitter will act on the post-synaptic benzodiazepine receptors and modify activity in the post-synaptic neuron. As this neuron might be a serotonin, noradrenaline, dopamine, acetylcholine, etc. releasing neuron, it is easy to visualize how anti-anxiety agents, whether endogenous or applied (Librium or Valium), could interact with other neurotransmitters.

Recent evidence provides more detail of this interaction. The benzodiazepine receptor exists in close combination with GABA receptors, and the effects of anti-anxiety drugs appear to be mediated by this post-synaptic receptor complex (Gallager, 1978). Chlordiazepoxide, for instance, would bind to the benzodiazepine receptor, which would have the secondary consequence of increasing GABA transmission. As GABA is an inhibitory transmitter, increased transmission would *decrease* neuronal activity in the post-synaptic neuron, be it serotonergic, noradrenergic, etc. Thus the final outcome of giving chlordiazepoxide would be to decrease neurotransmission in various neuronal systems. Whether the effect is limited to one specific system is as yet unclear. In addition, the endogenous agent has not yet been identified, although there are several promising candidates (for a general review of this area, see, e.g., Haefely, 1985).

Quite what the purpose of the endogenous system is cannot be defined as yet. 'Anxiety' has a peculiarly human ring to it, but benzodiazepine receptors have been identified across the vertebrate animal kingdom. Interestingly, they are not found in invertebrates, and are relatively sparse in primitive vertebrates (Nielsen *et al.*, 1978), suggesting that they are a recent evolutionary development. Animal work shows that the behavioural effects of anti-anxiety drugs are best seen in conditions of fear, frustration, or punishment, conditions which presumably exist throughout the animal kingdom (as operationally defined, of course; we cannot know if the subjective experience of fear or anxiety exist in, for instance, the hagfish).

If the endogenous neurotransmitter mimics the drug, then behaviour in these conditions will be disinhibited when the system is activated. It is possible to conceive of situations where responding, even in the presence of increased punishment, would be more adaptive than not responding. However, the links between perception, cognition, fear, and anxiety, are complex, and at the neurochemical level entirely unknown. Realistic attempts to describe the role of the endogenous anti-anxiety system in normal behaviour must wait until the system itself has been fully traced.

This review of current approaches to the neurochemistry of anxiety illustrates an alternative strategy to those already discussed. Instead of post-mortem studies and analysis of urinary and CSF metabolites, there is an integrating behavioural concept ('behavioural inhibition') and drug-specific receptors. But there are significant individual differences in coping responses to stress and anxiety, and in the reaction to drugs. Whether these individual differences are reflected in central neurochemistry will probably need to be studied using the more traditional methods referred to above, and already of established value in the study of schizophrenia and depression.

References

Abrams, R., Essman, W.B., Taylor, M.A., and Fink, M. (1976). Concentrations of 5-hydroxyindoleacetic acid, homovanillic acid, and tryptophan in the cerebro-spinal fluid of depressed patients before and after ECT. *Biological Psychiatry*, *11*, 85–90.

Adam, K., and Oswald, I. (1977). Sleep is for tissue restoration. *Journal of the Royal College of Physicians*, *11*, 376–88.

Adametz, J.H. (1959) Rate of recovery of function in cats with rostral reticular lesions. *Journal of Neurosurgery*, *16*, 85–98.

Adams, D.B. (1979). Brain mechanisms for offense, defense, and submission. *Behavioral and Brain Sciences*, *2*, 201–41.

Ahlskog, J.E., and Hoebel, B.G. (1973). Overeating and obesity from damage to a noradrenergic system in the brain. *Science*, *182*, 166–9.

Aitken, P.P. (1970). Fear levels and rat's open-field activity and defecation. *Psychonomic Science*, *19*, 275–6.

Akelaitis, A.J. (1940). A study of gnosis, praxis and language following partial and complete section of the corpus callosum. *Transactions of the American Neurological Association*, *66*, 182–5.

Akiskal, H.S., and McKinney, W.T. (1975). Overview of recent research in depression. *Archives of General Psychiatry*, *32*, 285–305.

Allison, T., and Cicchetti, D.V. (1976). Sleep in mammals: ecological and constitutional correlates. *Science*, *194*, 732–4.

Amaral, D.G., and Sinnamon, H.M. (1977). The locus coeruleus: neurobiology of a central noradrenergic nucleus. *Progress in Neurobiology*, *9*, 147–96.

Anand, B.K., and Brobeck, J.R. (1951). Hypothalamic control of food intake in rats and cats. *Yale Journal of Biological Medicine*, *24*, 123–40.

Anderson, G.H., Leprohon, C., Chambers, J.W., and Coscina, D.V. (1979). Intact regulation of protein intake during the development of hypothalamic or genetic obesity in rats. *Physiology and Behavior*, *23*, 751–5.

Andersson, B. (1978). Regulation of water intake. *Physiological Reviews*, *58*, 582–603.

Annett, M. (1978). Genetic and nongenetic influences on handedness. *Behavior Genetics*, *8*, 227–49.

Annett, M. (1980). Handedness. In M.A. Jeeves (ed.), *Psychology Survey No. 3*. London: George Allen & Unwin.

Annett, M. (1984). *Left, Right, Hand and Brain: The Right Shift Theory*. London: Erlbaum.

Aprison, M.H., and Hingtgen, J.N. (1972). Serotonin and behavior: a brief summary. *Federation Proceedings*, *31*, 121–9.

Aravich, P.F., and Beltt, B.M. (1982). Perifornical fiber system mediates VMH electrically-induced suppression of feeding. *Physiology and Behavior, 29*, 195–200.

Archer, J. (1973). Tests for emotionality in rats and mice: a review. *Animal Behaviour, 21*, 205–35.

Avis, H.H. (1974). The neuropharmacology of aggression: a critical review *Psychological Bulletin, 81*, 47–63.

Ax, A.F. (1953). Physiological differentiation of emotional states. *Psychosomatic Medicine, 15*, 433–42.

Bacopoulos, N.C., Spokes, E.G., Bird, E.D., and Roth, R.H. (1979). Antipsychotic drug action in schizophrenic patients: effect on cortical dopamine metabolism after long-term treatment. *Science, 205*, 1405–7.

Baez, L.A., Ahlskog, J.E., and Randall, P.K. (1977). Body weight and regulatory deficits following unilateral nigrostriatal lesions. *Brain Research, 132*, 467–76.

Bagshaw, M.H., and Benzies, S. (1968). Multiple measures of the orienting reaction and their dissociation after amygdalectomy in monkeys. *Experimental Neurology, 20*, 175–87.

Baker, H.F., Bloxham, C., Crow, T.J., Davies, H., Ferrier, I.N., Johnstone, E.C., Parry, R.P., Ridley, R.M., Taylor, G.R., and Tyrrell, D.A.J. (1983). The viral hypothesis of schizophrenia: some experimental approaches. In J. Mendlewicz and H.M. Van Praag (eds), *Advances in Biological Psychiatry*, Vol. 12. Basel: S. Karger.

Balasubramanian, V., and Ramamurthi, B. (1970). Stereotaxic amygdalotomy in behaviour disorders. *Confinia Neurologica, 32*, 367–73.

Baldessarini, R.J. (1975). The basis of amine hypotheses in affective disorders. *Archives of General Psychiatry, 32*, 1087–93.

Bandler, R.J. (1970). Cholinergic synapses in the lateral hypothalamus for the control of predatory aggression in the rat. *Brain Research, 20*, 409–24.

Bandler, R.J. (1971). Direct chemical stimulation of the thalamus: effects on aggressive behavior in the rat. *Brain Research, 26*, 81–93.

Bard, P. (1928). Diencephalic mechanism for the expression of rage with special reference to the sympathetic nervous system. *American Journal of Physiology, 84*, 490–515.

Bard, P., and Mountcastle, V.B. (1947). Some forebrain mechanisms involved in the expression of rage with special reference to suppression of angry behavior. *Research Publications of the Association for Research into Nervous and Mental Disease, 27*, 362–404.

Barondes, S.H. (1970). Cerebral protein synthesis inhibitors block long-term memory. *International Review of Neurobiology, 12*, 177–205.

Batini, C., Moruzzi, G., Palestrini, M., Rossi, G.F., and Zanchetti, A. (1959). Effects of complete pontine transections on the sleep–wakefulness rhythm: the midpontine pretrigeminal preparation. *Archives of Italian Biology, 97*, 1–12.

Belluzzi, J.D., and Stein, L. (1977). Enkephalin may mediate euphoria and drive–reduction reward. *Nature, 266*, 556–8.

Berger, H. (1929). Über das Elektrenkephalogramm des Menschen. *Archiv für Psychiatrie und Nervenkrankheiten, 87*, 527–70.

Berlin. C.I., and Cullen, J.K., Jr. (1977). Acoustic problems in dichotic listening tasks. In S.J. Segalowitz and F.A. Gruber (eds), *Language Development and Neurological Theory*. New York: Academic Press.

Berman, R.F., Kesner, R.P., and Partlow, L.M. (1978). Passive avoidance impairment in rats following cycloheximide injection into the amygdala. *Brain Research, 158,* 171–88.

Berntson, G.G., Hughes, H.C., and Beattie, M.S. (1976). A comparison of hypothalamically induced biting attack with natural predatory behavior in the cat. *Journal of Comparative and Physiological Psychology, 90,* 167–78.

Berntson, G.G., and Leibowitz, S.F. (1973). Biting attack in cats: evidence for central muscarinic mediation. *Brain Research, 51,* 366–70.

Bever, T.G., and Chiarello, R.J. (1974). Cerebral dominance in musicians and non musicians. *Science, 185,* 137–9.

Bird, E.D., Spokes, E.G.S., and Iversen, L.L. (1979). Increased dopamine concentrations in limbic areas of brain from patients dying with schizophrenia. *Brain, 102,* 347–60.

Blakemore, C., and Mitchell, D.E. (1973). Environmental modification of the visual cortex and the neural basis of learning and memory. *Nature, 241,* 467–8.

Blanchard, R.J., and Blanchard, D.C. (1977). Aggressive behavior in the rat. *Behavioral Biology, 21,* 197–224.

Blanchard, R.J., Kelley, M.J., and Blanchard, D.C. (1974). Defensive reactions and exploratory behaviour in rats. *Journal of Comparative and Physiological Psychology, 87,* 1129–33.

Bland, R.C., and Orn, H. (1979). Schizophrenia: diagnostic criteria and outcome. *British Journal of Psychiatry, 134,* 34–8.

Bland, R.C., and Orn, H. (1980). Schizophrenia: Schneider's first-rank symptoms and outcome. *British Journal of Psychiatry, 137,* 63–8.

Blass, E.M., and Hall, W.G. (1976). Drinking termination: interactions among hydrational, orogastric, and behavioral controls in rats. *Psychological Review, 83,* 356–74.

Blinkov, S.M., and Glezer, I.I. (1968). *The Human Brain in Figures and Tables: A Quantitative Handbook*. New York: Basic Books.

Bogen, J.E., and Vogel, P.J. (1962). Cerebral commissurotomy in man: preliminary case report. *Bulletin of the Los Angeles Neurological Society, 27,* 169–72.

Bolles, R.C. (1967). *Theory of Motivation*. New York: Harper & Row.

Borison, R.L., and Diamond, B.I. (1978). A new animal model for schizophrenia. *Biological Psychiatry, 13,* 217–25.

Bowers, M.B. (1974). Central dopamine turnover in schizophrenic syndromes. *Archives of General Psychiatry, 31,* 50–4.

Bradshaw, J.L., and Nettleton, N.C. (1981). The nature of hemispheric specialization. *Behavioral and Brain Sciences, 4,* 51–91.

Bradshaw, J.L., and Sherlock, D. (1982). Bugs and faces in the two visual fields: the analytic/holistic processing dichotomy and task sequencing. *Cortex, 18,* 211–26.

Brady, J.V., Porter, R.W., Conrad, D.G., and Mason, J.W. (1958).

Avoidance behavior and the development of gastroduodenal ulcers. *Journal of the Experimental Analysis of Behavior, 1,* 69–72.

Braestrup, C., and Squires, R.F. (1978). Brain specific benzodiazepine receptors. *British Journal of Psychiatry, 133,* 249–60.

Bremer, F. (1937). L'activité cérébrale au cours du sommeil et de la narcose: contribution a l'étude du mécanisme du sommeil. *Bulletin de l'Académie Royale de Médecine Belgique, 4,* 68–86.

Bremer, F. (1977). Cerebral hypnogenic centers. *Annals of Neurology, 2,* 1–6.

Broadbent, D.E. (1971). *Decision and Stress.* London: Academic Press.

Broca, P. (1861). Remarques sur le siège de la faculté du langage articulé suivées d'une observation d'aphémie. *Bulletin de la Société Anatomique* (Paris), *6,* 330–57.

Brodmann, K. (1909). *Vergleichende Lokalisationlehre der Grosshirnrinde in ihren Prinzipien dargestellt auf Grund des Zellenbaues.* Leipzig: J.A. Barth.

Bruce, C. (1982). Face recognition by monkeys: absence of an inversion effect. *Neuropsychologia, 20,* 515–21.

Bryden, M.P. (1973). Perceptual asymmetry in vision: relation to handedness, eyedness, and speech lateralization. *Cortex, 9,* 418–35.

Bryden, M.P., Ley, R.G., and Sugarman, J.H. (1982). A left-ear advantage for identifying the emotional quality of tonal sequences. *Neuropsychologia, 20,* 83–7.

Burki, H.R., Eichenberger, E., and Sayer, A.C. (1975). Clozapine and the dopamine hypothesis of schizophrenia, a critical appraisal. *Pharmakopsychiatrica, 8,* 115–21.

Butler, S.R. (1979). Interhemispheric transfer of visual information via the corpus callosum and anterior commissure in the monkey. In I. Steele-Russell, M.W van Hof, and G. Berlucchi (eds), *Structure and Function of the Cerebral Commissures.* London: Macmillan.

Butters, N., and Cermak, L.S. (1974). Some comments on Warrington and Baddeley's report of normal short-term memory in amnesic patients. *Neuropsychologia, 12,* 283–5.

Cannon, W.B. (1929). *Bodily Changes in Pain, Hunger, Fear and Rage.* New York: Appleton.

Cannon, W.B., and Washburn, A.L. (1912). An explanation of hunger. *American Journal of Physiology, 29,* 441–54.

Carey, S., and Diamond, R. (1977). From piecemeal to configurational representation of faces. *Science, 195,* 312–14.

Carli, G., Malliani, A., and Zanchetti, A. (1963). Midbrain course of descending pathways mediating sham rage behavior. *Experimental Neurology, 7,* 210–23.

Carlsson, A. (1978). Does dopamine have a role in schizophrenia? *Biological Psychiatry, 13,* 3–21.

Carlton, P.L. (1969). Brain-acetylcholine and inhibition. In J.T. Tapp (ed.), *Reinforcement and Behavior.* New York: Academic Press.

Carmon, A. (1978). Spatial and temporal factors in visual perception of patients with unilateral cerebral lesions. In M. Kinsbourne (ed.), *Asymmetrical Functions of the Brain.* Cambridge: Cambridge University Press.

Carpenter, M.B. (1978). *Core Text of Neuroanatomy.* 2nd edn. Baltimore: Williams & Wilkins.

Carroll, D., and O'Callaghan, M.A.J. (1983). Psychosurgery and brain-behavior relationships in animals. In G.C.L. Davey (ed.), *Animal Models of Human Behavior.* Chichester: Wiley.

Castellucci, V.F., and Kandel, E.R. (1974). A quantal analysis of the synaptic depression underlying habituation of the gill-withdrawal reflex in Aplysia. *Proceedings of the National Academy of Sciences of the United States, 71,* 5004–8.

Castellucci, V., and Kandel, E. (1976). An invertebrate system for the cellular study of habituation and sensitization. In T.J. Tighe and R.N. Leaton (eds), *Habituation: Perspectives from Child Development, Animal Behaviour and Neurophysiology.* New Jersey: Erlbaum.

Cermak, L.S. (1976). The encoding capacity of a patient with amnesia due to encephalitis. *Neuropsychologia, 14,* 311–26.

Cermak, L.S., Butters, N., and Moreines, J. (1974). Some analyses of the verbal encoding deficit of alcoholic Korsakoff patients. *Brain and Language, 1,* 141–50.

Chapouthier, G. (1973). Behavioral studies of the molecular basis of memory. In J.A. Deutsch (ed.), *The Physiological Basis of Memory.* New York: Academic Press.

Chapouthier, G. (1983). Protein synthesis and memory. In J.A Deutsch (ed.), *The Physiological Basis of Memory.* New York: Academic Press.

Chi, J.G., Dooling, E.C., and Gilles, F.H. (1977). Left–right asymmetries of the temporal speech areas of the human fetus. *Archives of Neurology, 34,* 346–8.

Chorover, S.L. (1976). The pacification of the brain: from phrenology to psychosurgery. In T.P. Morley (ed.), *Current Controversies in Neurosurgery.* Philadelphia: W.B. Saunders.

Chorover, S.L., and Schiller, P.H. (1965). Short term retrograde amnesia in rats. *Journal of Comparative and Physiological Psychology, 59,* 73–8.

Clark, T.K. (1979). The locus coeruleus in behavior regulation: evidence for behavior-specific versus general involvement. *Behavioral and Neural Biology, 25,* 271–300.

Cleland, B.G., and Levick, W.R. (1974). Properties of rarely encountered types of ganglion cells in the cat's retina and an overall classification. *Journal of Physiology, 240,* 457.

Collins, R.L. (1975). When left-handed mice live in right-handed worlds. *Science, 187,* 181–9.

Corsellis, J.A.N. (1979). On the transmission of dementia. *British Journal of Psychiatry, 134,* 553–9.

Crow, T.J. (1973). Catecholamine-containing neurones and electrical self-stimulation: 2. A theoretical interpretation and some psychiatric implications. *Psychological Medicine, 3,* 66–73.

Crow, T.J. (1980). Molecular pathology of schizophrenia: more than one disease process? *British Medical Journal, 280,* 66–8.

Crow, T.J. (1984) A re-evaluation of the viral hypothesis. *British Journal of Psychiatry, 145,* 243–53.

Czeisler, C.A., Weitzman, E.D., Moore-Ede, M.C., Zimmerman, J.C., and Knauer, R.S. (1980). Human sleep: its duration and organization depend on its circadian phase. *Science, 210*, 1264–7.

Davis, J.M., and Garver, D.L. (1978). Neuroleptics: clinical use in psychiatry. In L.L. Iversen, S.D. Iversen, and S.H. Snyder (eds). *Handbook of Psychopharmacology*. Vol. 10, *Neuroleptics and Schizophrenia*. New York: Plenum.

Davis, M. (1972). Differential retention of sensitization and habituation of the startle response in the rat. *Journal of Comparative and Physiological Psychology, 78*, 260–7.

Davis, M. (1974a). Signal-to-noise ratio as a predictor of startle amplitude and habituation in the rat. *Journal of Comparative and Physiological Psychology, 86*, 812–25.

Davis, M. (1974b). Sensitization of the rat startle response by noise. *Journal of Comparative and Physiological Psychology, 87*, 571–81.

Davis, M., and Wagner, A.R. (1969). Habituation of the startle response under incremental sequence of stimulus intensities. *Journal of Comparative and Physiological Psychology, 67*, 486–92.

Davison, K., and Bagley, C.R. (1969). Schizophrenia-like psychoses associated with organic disorders of the central nervous system: a review of the literature. *British Journal of Psychiatry*, Special Publication No. 4, 113–84.

DeCastro, J.M., Paullin, S.K., and De Lugas, G.M. (1978). Insulin and glucagon as determinants of body weight set point and microregulation in rats. *Journal of Comparative and Physiological Psychology, 92*, 571–9.

Dement, W., Holman, R.B., and Guilleminault, C. (1976). Neurochemical and neuropharmacological foundations of the sleep disorders. *Psychopharmacology Communications, 2*, 77–90.

Denenberg, V.H. (1981). Hemispheric laterality in animals and the effects of early experience. *Behavioral and Brain Sciences, 4*, 1–49.

De Wied, D. (1976). Pituitary adrenal system hormones and behaviour. *Symposium on Developments in Endocrinology*. Organon International, Oss, The Netherlands.

De Wied, D. (1977). Peptides and behavior. *Life Sciences, 20*, 195–204.

Dimond, S.J., Farrington, L., and Johnson, P. (1976). Differing emotional response from right and left hemispheres. *Nature, 261*, 690–2.

Donovan, B.T. (1970). *Mammalian Neuroendocrinology*. London: McGraw-Hill.

Douglas, R.J. (1966). Cues for spontaneous alternation. *Journal of Comparative and Physiological Psychology, 62*, 171–83.

Douglas, R.J. (1967). The hippocampus and behavior. *Psychological Bulletin, 67*, 416–42.

Douglas, R.J. (1975). The development of hippocampal function: implications for theory and for therapy. In R.L. Isaacson and K.H. Pribram (eds), *The Hippocampus*, Vol. 2. New York: Academic Press.

Eccles, J.C., Fatt, P., and Koketsu, K. (1954). Cholinergic and inhibitory synapses in a pathway from motor-axon collaterals to motor neurones. *Journal of Physiology* (London), *216*, 524–62.

Eichelman, B.S., Jr., and Thoa, N.B. (1973). The aggressive monoamines. *Biological Psychiatry*, 6, 143–64.

Eichenbaum, H.B. (1975). Localization of memory by regional brain protein inhibition. *Dissertation Abstracts International*, 36, 1495.

Ekman, P., Levenson, R.W., and Friesen, W.V. (1983). Autonomic nervous system activity distinguishes among emotions. *Science*, 221, 1208–10.

Fairweather, H. (1982). Sex differences: little reason for females to play midfield. In J.G. Beaumont (ed.), *Divided Visual Field Studies of Cerebral Organization*. London: Academic Press.

Farel, P.B., Glanzman, D.L., and Thompson, R.F. (1973). Habituation of a monosynaptic response in vertebrate central nervous system: lateral column–motorneuron pathway in isolated frog spinal cord. *Journal of Neurophysiology*, 36, 1117–30.

Feighner, J.P., Robins, F., Guze, J.B., Woodruff, R.A., Winokur, G., and Munoz, R. (1972). Diagnostic criteria for use in psychiatric research. *Archives of General Psychiatry*, 26, 57–63.

Feldman, S., and Waller, H. (1962). Dissociation of electrocortical activation and behavioral arousal. *Nature*, 196, 1320–2.

Fisher, A.E. and Coury, J.N. (1962). Cholinergic tracing of a central neural circuit underlying the thirst drive. *Science*, 138, 691–3.

Fitzsimons, J.T. (1972). Thirst. *Physiological Reviews*, 52, 468–561.

Flor-Henry, P., Fromm-Auch, D., and Schopflocher, D. (1983). Neuropsychological dimensions in psychopathology. In P. Flor-Henry and J. Gruzelier (eds), *Laterality and Psychopathology*. Amsterdam: Elsevier.

Flor-Henry, P., and Gruzelier, J. (eds) (1983). *Laterality and Psychopathology*. Amsterdam: Elsevier.

Flynn, J.P. (1976). Neural basis of threat and attack. In R.G. Grenell and S. Gabay (eds), *Biological Foundations of Psychiatry*. New York: Raven Press.

Flynn, J.P., Edwards, S.B., and Bandler, R.J. (1971). Changes in sensory and motor systems during centrally-elicited attack. *Behavioral Science*, 16, 1–19.

Folkard, S. (1977). Time of day effects in school children's immediate and delayed recall of meaningful material. *British Journal of Psychology*, 68, 45–50,

Fowler, H. (1965). *Curiosity and Exploratory Behaviour*. New York: Macmillan.

Frankenhaeuser, M. (1975). Experimental approaches to the study of catecholamines and emotion. In L. Levi (ed.), *Emotions – Their Parameters and Measurement*. New York: Raven Press.

Frankenhaeuser, M. (1983). The sympathetic-adrenal and pituitary-adrenal response to challenge: comparison between the sexes. In T.M. Dembroski, T.H. Schmidt, and G. Blümchen (eds), *Behavioral Bases of Coronary Heart Disease*. Basel: S. Karger.

Frankenhaeuser, M., Dunne, E., and Lundberg, U. (1976). Sex differences in sympathetic-adrenal medullary reactions induced by different stressors. *Psychopharmacology*, 47, 1–5.

Frankenhaeuser, M., Lundberg, U., and Forsman, L. (1980a). Note on arousing Type-A persons by depriving them of work. *Journal of Psychosomatic Research*, 24, 45–7.

Frankenhaeuser, M., Lundberg, U., and Forsman, L. (1980b). Dissociation between sympathetic-adrenal and pituitary-adrenal responses to an achievement situation characterized by high controllability: comparison between Type A and Type B males and females. *Biological Psychology, 10,* 79–91.

Frankenhaeuser, M., Rauste-Von Wright, M., Collins, A., von Wright, J., Sedvall, G., and Swahn, C.G. (1978). Sex differences in psychoneuroendocrine reactions to examination stress. *Psychosomatic Medicine, 40,* 334–43.

Freeman, W. (1971). Frontal lobotomy in early schizophrenia: long follow-up in 415 cases. *British Journal of Psychiatry, 119,* 621–4.

Freud, S. (1955). *The Interpretation of Dreams.* New York: Basic Books.

Fulton, J.F., and Jacobsen, C.F. (1935). The functions of the frontal lobes; a comparative study in monkeys, chimpanzees and man. *Abstracts from the 2nd International Neurological Congress.* London.

Funkenstein, D.H. (1956). Norepinephrine-like and epinephrine-like substances in relation to human behavior. *Journal of Mental Diseases, 124,* 58–68.

Gainotti, G. (1972). Emotional behaviour and hemispheric side of lesion. *Cortex, 8,* 41–55.

Galaburda, A.M., LeMay, M., Kemper, T.L., and Geschwind, N. (1978). Right–left asymmetries in the brain. *Science, 199,* 852–6.

Galin, D. (1974). Implications for psychiatry of left and right cerebral specialization. *Archives of General Psychiatry, 31,* 572–83.

Gallager, D.W. (1978). Benzodiazepines: potentiation of a GABA inhibitory response in the dorsal raphé nucleus. *European Journal of Pharmacology, 49,* 133–43.

Gallistel, C.R. (1973). Self-stimulation: the neurophysiology of reward and motivation. In J.A. Deutsch (ed.), *The Physiological Basis of Memory.* New York: Academic Press.

Gazzaniga, M.S. (1983). Right hemisphere language following brain bisection: 20-year perspective. *American Psychologist, 38,* 525–37.

Gazzaniga, M.S., Bogen, J.E., and Sperry, R.W. (1962). Some functional effects of sectioning the cerebral commissures in man. *Proceedings of the National Academy of Sciences of the United States of America, 48,* 1765–9.

Gellhorn, E., and Loufbourrow, G.N. (1963). *Emotions and Emotional Disorders: A Neurophysiological Study.* New York: Harper & Row.

German, D.C., and Bowden, D.M. (1974). Catecholamine systems as the neural substrate for intra-cranial self-stimulation: a hypothesis. *Brain Research, 73,* 381–419.

Geschwind, N., and Levitsky, W. (1968). Human brain: left–right asymmetries in temporal speech region. *Science, 161,* 186–7.

Geyer, M.A., Puerto, A., Menkes, D.B., Segal, D.S., and Mandell, A.J. (1976). Behavioural studies following lesions of the mesolimbic and mesostriatal serotonergic pathways. *Brain Research, 106,* 256–70.

Gibbs, J., Young, R.C., and Smith, G.P. (1972). Effect of gut hormones on feeding behaviour in the rat. *Federation Proceedings, 31,* 397.

Gillin, J.C., Buchsbaum, M.S., and Jacobs, L.S. (1974). Partial REM sleep deprivation, schizophrenia, and field articulation. *Archives of General Psychiatry, 30,* 653–62.

Glass, A.S., Gazzaniga, M.S., and Premack, D. (1973). Artificial language training in global aphasics. *Neuropsychologia,* 11, 95–104.

Glick, S.D., Jerussi, T.P., and Zimmerberg, B. (1977). Behavioural and neuropharmacological correlates of nigrostriatal asymmetry in rats. In S. Harnad, R.W. Doty, L. Goldstein, J. Jaynes, and G. Krauthamer (eds), *Lateralization in the Nervous System.* London: Academic Press.

Glick, Z. (1982). Inverse relationship between brown fat thermogenesis and meal size: the thermostatic control of food intake revisited. *Physiology and Behavior, 29,* 1137–40.

Glosser, G., Butters, N., and Samuels, I. (1976). Failures in information processing in patients with Korsakoff's syndrome. *Neuropsychologia, 14,* 327–34.

Gold, P.E., and King, R.A. (1974). Retrograde amnesia: storage failure versus retrieval failure. *Psychological Review, 81,* 465–9.

Gold, R.M. (1973). Hypothalamic obesity: the myth of the ventromedial nucleus. *Science, 182,* 488–90.

Goldstein, D., Fink, D., and Mettee, D.R. (1972). Cognition of arousal and actual arousal as determinants of emotion. *Journal of Personality and Social Psychology, 21,* 41–51.

Goldstein, M. (1974). Brain research and violent behavior. *Archives of Neurology, 30,* 1–35.

Goodwin, F.K., Cowdry, R.W., and Webster, M.H. (1978). Predictors of drug response in the affective disorders: toward an integrated approach. In M.A. Lipton, A. DiMascio, and K.F. Killam (eds), *Psychopharmacology: A Generation of Progress.* New York: Raven Press.

Gray, J.A. (1982). *The Neuropsychology of Anxiety.* Oxford: Oxford University Press.

Green. S. (1983). Animal models in schizophrenia research. In G.C.L. Davey (ed.), *Animal Models of Human Behavior.* Chichester: Wiley.

Gregg. V.H. (1986). *Introduction to Human Memory.* London: Routledge & Kegan Paul.

Grossman, S.P. (1960). Eating or drinking elicited by direct adrenergic or cholinergic stimulation of the hypothalamus. *Science, 132,* 301–2.

Grossman, S.P. (1967). *A Textbook of Physiological Psychology.* New York: Wiley.

Grossman, S.P. (1972). Neurophysiologic aspects: extra-hypothalamic factors in the regulation of food intake. *Advances in Psychosomatic Medicine, 7,* 49–72.

Groves, P.M., and Lynch, G.S. (1972). Mechanisms of habituation in the brain stem. *Psychological Review, 79,* 237–44.

Groves, P.M., and Thompson, R.F. (1970). Habituation: a dual-process theory. *Psychological Review, 77,* 419–50.

Gruzelier, J.H. (1978). Propranolol and the neuropsychophysiology of schizophrenia: implications for the drug's central mechanisms of action. In E. Roberts and L. Amacher (eds), *Propranolol and Schizophrenia.* New York: Raven Press.

Gruzelier, J. (1983). Disparate syndromes in psychosis delineated by the direction of electrodermal response lateral asymmetry. In P. Flor-Henry and J. Gruzelier (eds), *Laterality and Psychopathology*. Amsterdam: Elsevier.

Gruzelier, J., and Flor-Henry, P. (eds) (1979). *Hemispheric Asymmetries of Function in Psychopathology*. Amsterdam: Elsevier.

Gruzelier, J.H., and Venables, P.H. (1974). Bimodality and lateral asymmetry of skin conductance orienting activity in schizophrenics. *Biological Psychiatry, 8*, 55–73.

Haefely, W. (1985). The biological basis of benzodiazepine actions. In D.E. Smith and D.R. Wesson (eds), *The Benzodiazepines – Current Standards for Medical Practice*. Lancaster: MTP Press.

Halliday, M.S. (1966). Exploration and fear in the rat. *Symposia of the Zoological Society of London*, No. 18, 45–59.

Hardyck, C., and Petrinovich, L.F. (1977). Left-handedness. *Psychological Bulletin, 84*, 385–404.

Harnad, S., Doty, R.W., Goldstein, L., Jaynes, J., and Krauthamer, G. (eds) (1977). *Lateralization in the Nervous System*. London: Academic Press.

Harris, J.D. (1943). Habituatory response decrement in the intact organism. *Psychological Bulletin, 40*, 385–422.

Harris, M., and Coltheart, M. (1986). *Language Processing in Children and Adults*. London: Routledge & Kegan Paul.

Harris, V.A., and Katkin, E.S. (1975). Primary and secondary emotional behaviour: an analysis of the role of autonomic feedback on affect, arousal and attribution. *Psychological Bulletin, 82*, 904–16.

Heath, R.G. (1976). Correlation of brain function with emotional behaviour. *Biological Psychiatry, 11*, 463–80.

Heath, R.G. (1977). Modulation of emotion with a brain pacemaker *Journal of Nervous and Mental Disease, 165*, 300–17.

Hebb, D.O. (1949). *The Organization of Behavior*. New York: Wiley.

Hebb, D.O. (1958). *A Textbook of Psychology*. Philadelphia: W.B. Saunders.

Hebben, N., Corkin, S., Eichenbaum, H., and Shedlack, K. (1985). Diminished ability to interpret and report internal states after bilateral medial temporal resection: Case H.M. *Behavioral Neuroscience, 99*, 1031–9.

Hemsley, D.R. (1977). What have cognitive deficits to do with schizophrenic symptoms? *British Journal of Psychiatry, 130*, 167–73.

Henkin, R.I. (1975). Effects of ACTH, adrenocorticosteroids and thyroid hormone on sensory function. In W.E. Stumpf and L.D. Grant (eds), *Anatomical Neuroendocrinology*. Basel: S. Karger.

Henkin, R.I., Patten, B.M., Re, P.K., and Bronzert, D.A. (1975). A syndrome of acute zinc loss. *Archives of Neurology, 32*, 745–51.

Hennessey, J.W., King, M.G., McClure, T.A., and Levine, S. (1977). Uncertainty, as defined by the contingency between environmental events, and the adrenocortical response of the rat to electric shock. *Journal of Comparative and Physiological Psychology, 91*, 1447–60.

Herberg, L.J., Stephens, D.N., and Franklin, K.B. (1976). Catecholamines and self-stimulation: evidence suggesting reinforcing role for noradrenaline and a motivating role for dopamine. *Pharmacology, Biochemistry and Behavior, 4*, 575–82.

Hernandez-Peon, R., and Chavez-Ibarra, G. (1963). Sleep induced by localized electrical or chemical stimulation of the forebrain. *Electroencephalography and Clinical Neurophysiology*, Suppl. 24, 188–98.

Hess, W.R. (1954). *Diencephalon: Autonomic and Extrapyramidal Functions.* London: Heinemann.

Hetherington, A.W., and Ranson, S.W. (1942). The relation of various hypothalamic lesions to adiposity in the rat. *Journal of Comparative Neurology*, 76, 475–99.

Hewes, G.W. (1973). Primate communication and the gestural origin of language. *Current Anthropology*, 14, 5–24.

Hirschman, R.D. (1975). Cross-modal effects of anticipatory bogus heart-rate feedback in a negative emotional context. *Journal of Personality and Social Psychology*, 31, 13–19.

Hodges, H., and Green, S. (1984). Evidence for the involvement of brain GABA and serotonin systems in the anti-conflict activity of chlordiazepoxide in rats. *Behavioral and Neural Biology*, 40, 127–54.

Hodos, W., and Campbell, R.G. (1969). Scala Naturae: why there is no theory in comparative psychology. *Psychological Review*, 76, 337–50.

Holloway, F.A., and Wansley, R.A. (1973). Multiple retention deficits at periodic intervals after passive avoidance learning. *Science*, 180, 208–10.

Horel, J.A. (1978). The neuroanatomy of amnesia: a critique of the hippocampal memory hypothesis. *Brain*, 101, 403–45.

Horne, J.A. (1978). A review of the biological effects of total sleep deprivation in man. *Biological Psychology*, 7, 55–102.

Horne, J.A. (1979). Restitution and human sleep: a critical review. *Physiological Psychology*, 7, 115–25.

Hornykiewicz, O. (1978). Psychological implications of dopamine and dopamine antagonists: a critical evaluation of current evidence. *Neuroscience*, 3, 773–83.

Hornykiewicz, O. (1982). Brain catecholamines in schizophrenia – a good case for noradrenaline. *Nature*, 299, 484–6.

Hubel, D.H., and Wiesel, T.N. (1959). Receptive fields of single neurones in the cat's striate cortex. *Journal of Physiology*, 148, 574–91.

Hubel, D.H., and Wiesel, T.N. (1979). Brain mechanisms of vision. *Scientific American*, 241, 130–44.

Hughes, J. (1975). Isolation of an endogenous compound from the brain with properties similar to morphine. *Brain Research*, 88, 295–308.

Hull, C.L. (1943). *Principles of Behavior*. New York: Appleton-Century-Crofts.

Hunsperger, R.W. (1956). Affectreaktionen auf elektrische Reizung im Hirnstamm der Katze. *Helvetica Physiologica et Pharmacologica Acta*, 14, 70–92.

Hunter, J., and Jasper, H. (1949). Effect of thalamic stimulation in unanaesthetized animals. *Electroencephalography and Clinical Neurophysiology*, 1, 305–24.

Huppert, F.A. (1981). Memory in split-brain patients: a comparison with organic amnesic syndromes. *Cortex*, 17, 303–12.

Huppert, F.A., and Piercey, M. (1978). Dissociation between learning and remembering in organic amnesia. *Nature*, 275, 317–18.

Huppert, F.A., and Piercey, M. (1979). Normal and abnormal forgetting in organic amnesia: effects of locus of lesion. *Cortex, 15,* 385–90.

Hyden, H., and Egyhazi, E. (1962). Nuclear RNA changes in nerve cells during a learning experiment in rats. *Proceedings of the National Academy of Sciences, 48,* 1366–72.

Inglis, J., Ruckman, M., Lawson, J.S., MacLean, A.W., and Monga, T.N. (1982). Sex differences in the cognitive effects of unilateral brain damage. *Cortex, 18,* 257–76.

Iversen, S.D. (1977). Striatal function and stereotyped behaviour. In A.R. Cools, A.H.M. Lohman, and J.H.L. Van Den Bercken (eds), *Psychobiology of the Striatum.* Amsterdam: North Holland.

Iversen, S.D., and Iversen, L.L. (1981). *Behavioral Pharmacology.* 2nd edn. Oxford: Oxford University Press.

Jacobs, B.L. (1976). An animal behavior model for studying central serotonergic synapses. *Life Sciences, 19,* 777–86.

James, W. (1884). What is an emotion? *Mind, 19.* 188–205.

Janowsky, D.S., El-Yousef, M.K., Davis, J.M., and Sekerke, H.J. (1972). Cholinergic antagonism of methylphenidate-induced stereotyped behavior. *Psychopharmacologia, 27,* 295–303.

Jerison, H.J. (1973). *Evolution of the Brain and Intelligence.* New York: Academic Press.

Jernigan, T.L., Zatz, L.M., Moses, J.A., Jr., and Berger, P.A. (1982). Computed tomography in schizophrenics and normal volunteers. I. Fluid volume. *Archives of General Psychiatry, 39,* 765–70.

Johnson, P. (1977). Dichotically stimulated ear differences in musicians and nonmusicians. *Cortex, 13,* 385–9.

Johnstone, E.C., Crow, T.J., Frith, C.D., Husband, J., and Kreel, L. (1976). Cerebral ventricular size and cognitive impairment in chronic schizophrenia. *Lancet, II,* 924–6.

Jouvet, M. (1969). Biogenic amines and the states of sleep. *Science, 163,* 32–40.

Jouvet, M. (1972). The role of monoamines and acetylcholine-containing neurons in the regulation of the sleep-waking cycle. *Ergebnisse der Physiologie, 64,* 166–307.

Kanai, T., and Szerb, J.C. (1965). Mesencephalic reticular activating system and cortical acetylcholine output. *Nature, 205,* 80–2.

Kandel, E.R., and Schwartz, J.H. (eds) (1985). *Principles of Neural Science.* 2nd ed. New York: Elsevier.

Kapatos, G., and Gold, R.M. (1973). Evidence for ascending noradrenergic mediation of hypothalamic hyperphagia. *Pharmacology, Biochemistry and Behavior, 1,* 81–7.

Keesey, R.E., and Powley, T.L. (1975). Hypothalamic regulation of body weight. *American Scientist, 63,* 558–65.

Kelly, D. (1973). Therapeutic outcome in limbic leucotomy in psychiatric patients. *Psychiatrica, Neurologica, Neurochirurgica* (Amst.), *76,* 353–63.

Kelly, D.H.W., Richardson, A., and Mitchell-Heggs, N. (1973a). Stereotactic limbic leucotomy: neurophysiological aspects and operative technique. *British Journal of Psychiatry, 123,* 133–40.

Kelly, D.H.W., Richardson, A., Mitchell-Heggs, N., Greenup, J., Chen, C., and Hafner, R.J. (1973b). Stereotactic limbic leucotomy: a preliminary report c n forty patients. *British Journal of Psychiatry, 123*, 141–8.

Kendell, R.E. (1976). The classification of depressions: a review of contemporary confusion. *British Journal of Psychiatry, 129*, 15–28.

Kendell, R.E. (1981). The present status of electroconvulsive therapy. *British Journal of Psychiatry, 139*, 265–83.

Kertesz, A. (ed.) (1983) *Localization in Neuropsychology*. New York: Academic Press.

Kiloh, L.G., Gye, R.S., Rushworth, R.G., Bell, D.S., and White, R.T. (1974). Stereotactic amygdaloidotomy for aggressive behavior. *Journal of Neurology, Neurosurgery, and Psychiatry, 37*, 437–44.

Kimble, D.P. (1968). Hippocampus and internal inhibition. *Psychological Bulletin, 70*, 285–95.

Kimura, D. (1961). Cerebral dominance and the perception of verbal stimuli. *Canadian Journal of Psychology, 13*, 166–71.

Kimura, D. (1977). Acquisition of a motor skill after left hemisphere damage. *Brain, 100*, 527–42.

Kimura, D. (1979). Neuromotor mechanisms in the evolution of human communication. In H.D. Steklis and M.J. Raleigh (eds), *Neurobiology of Social Communication in Primates*. New York: Academic Press.

King, B.M., Carpenter, R.G., Stamoutsos, B.A., Frohman, L.A., and Grossman, S.P. (1978). Hyperphagia and obesity following ventromedial hypothalamic lesions in rats with sub-diaphragmatic vagotomy. *Physiology and Behavior, 20*, 643–51.

King, F.A., and Meyer, P.M. (1958). Effects of amygdaloid lesions upon septal hyper-emotionality in the rat. *Science, 128*, 655–6.

Klein, D.F., and Davis, J.M. (1969). *Diagnosis and Drug Treatment of Psychiatric Disorders*. Baltimore: Williams & Wilkins.

Kling, A., Lancaster, J., and Benitone, J. (1970). Amygdalectomy in the free-ranging vervet (Cercopithecus aethiops). *Journal of Psychiatric Research, 7*, 191–9.

Kluver, H., and Bucy, P. (1939). Preliminary analysis of functions of the temporal lobes in monkeys. *Archives of Neurology and Psychiatry, 42*, 979–1000.

Kosterlitz, H.W. and Hughes, J. (1977). Peptides with morphine-like action in the brain. *British Journal of Psychiatry, 130*, 298–304.

Kostowski, W. (1971). The effects of some drugs affecting 5-HT on electrocortical synchronization following low-frequency stimulation of the brain. *Brain Research, 31*, 151–7.

Kuffler, S.W. (1953). Discharge patterns and functional organization of mammalian retina. *Journal of Neurophysiology, 16*, 37–68.

Kulkosky, P.J., Breckenridge, C., Krinsky, R., and Woods, S.C. (1976). Satiety elicited by the C-terminal octapeptide of cholecystokinin-pancreozymin in normal and VMH-lesioned rats. *Behavioral Biology, 18*, 227–34.

Lacoste-Utamsing, C., and Holloway, R.L. (1982). Sexual dimorphism in the human corpus callosum. *Science, 216*, 1431–2.

Landfield, P.W., McGaugh, J.L., and Tusa, R.J. (1972). Theta rhythm: temporal correlate of memory storage processes in the rat. *Science, 175,* 87–9.

Lazarus, R.S. (1984). On the primacy of cognition. *American Psychologist, 39,* 124–9.

LeDoux, J.E. (1982). Neuroevolutionary mechanisms of cerebral asymmetry in man. *Brain, Behavior, and Evolution, 20,* 196–12.

LeDoux, J.E., Risse, G.L., Springer, S.P., Wilson, D.H., and Gazzaniga, M.S. (1977). Cognition and commissurotomy. *Brain, 100,* 87–104.

LeDoux, J.E., Wilson, D.H., and Gazzaniga, M.S. (1977). A divided mind: observations on the conscious properties of the separated hemispheres. *Annals of Neurology, 2,* 417–24.

Leehey, S., Carey, S., Diamond, R., and Cahn, A. (1978), Upright and inverted faces: the right hemisphere knows the difference. *Cortex, 14,* 411–19.

Leibowitz, S.F. (1970). Hypothalamic β-adrenergic 'satiety' system antagonizes an α-adrenergic 'hunger' system in the rat. *Nature,* 226, 963–4.

Le Magnen, J. (1972). Regulation of food intake. *Advances in Psychosomatic Medicine, 7,* 73–90.

LeMay, M. (1976). Morphological cerebral asymmetries of modern man, fossil man and non-human primates. *Annals of the New York Academy of Sciences, 280,* 349–66.

LeMay, M., and Culebras, A. (1972). Human brain-morphologic differences in the hemispheres demonstrable by carotid arteriography. *New England Journal of Medicine, 287,* 168–70.

Leon, G., and Roth, L. (1977). Obesity: psychological causes, correlations, and speculations. *Psychological Bulletin, 84,* 117–39.

Lettvin, J.Y., Maturana, H.R., McCulloch, W.S., and Pitts, W.H. (1959). What the frog's eye tells the frog's brain. *Proceedings of the Institute of Radio Engineers, 47,* 1940–51.

LeVay, S., Wiesel, T.N., and Hubel, D.H. (1980). The development of ocular dominance columns in normal and visually deprived monkeys. *Journal of Comparative Neurology, 191,* 1–51.

Levick, W.R. (1967). Receptive fields and trigger features of ganglion cells in the visual streak of the rabbit's retina. *Journal of Physiology, 188,* 285–307.

Levy, J. (1969). Possible basis for the evolution of lateral specialization of the human brain. *Nature, 224,* 614–15.

Levy, J., and Levy, J.M. (1978). Human lateralization from head to foot: sex-related factors. *Science, 200,* 1291–2.

Levy, J., and Nagylaki, T. (1972). A model for the genetics of handedness. *Genetics, 72,* 117–28.

Levy, J., and Reid, M. (1978). Variations in cerebral organization as a function of handedness, hand posture in writing, and sex. *Journal of Experimental Psychology: General, 107,* 119–44.

Levy, J., and Trevarthen, C. (1977). Perceptual, semantic and phonetic aspects of elementary language processes in split-brain patients. *Brain, 100,* 105–18.

Lewis, P.R., and Shute, C.C.D. (1967). The cholinergic limbic system: projections to hippocampal formation, medial cortex, nuclei of the ascending cholinergic reticular system, and the subfornical organ and supra-optic crest. *Brain, 90*, 521–39.

Ley, R.G., and Bryden, M.P. (1979). Hemispheric differences in processing emotions and faces. *Brain and Language, 7*, 127–38.

Lindsley, D.B., Bowden, J., and Magoun, H.W. (1949). Effect upon EEG of acute injury to the brain stem activating system. *Electroencephalography and Clinical Neurophysiology, 1*, 475–86.

Lindsley, D.B., Schreiner, L.H., Knowles, W.B., and Magoun, H.W. (1950). Behavioral and EEG changes following brain stem lesions in the cat. *Electroencephalography and Clinical Neurophysiology, 2*, 483–98.

Lindvall, O., and Bjorklund, A. (1974). The organization of the ascending catecholamine neuron systems in the rat brain as revealed by the glyoxylic acid fluorescence method. *Acta Physiologica Scandinavica*, Suppl. 412, 1–48.

Lishman, W.A., and McMeekan, E.R.L. (1977). Handedness in relation to direction and degree of cerebral dominance for language. *Cortex, 13*, 30–43.

Loewi, O., and Navratil, E. (1926). Ueber humorale Uebertragbarkeit der Herzennervenwirkung. X. Ueber das Schicksal des Vagusstoffes. *Pfluegers Archiv Gesamte Physiologie, 214*, 678–88.

Lorenz, D.N., and Goldman, S.A. (1982). Vagal mediation of the cholecystokinin satiety effect in rats. *Physiology and Behavior, 29*, 599–604.

Lucas, E.A., and Sterman, M.B. (1975). The effect of forebrain lesions upon the polycyclic sleep–wake cycle and sleep–wake patterns in the cat. *Experimental Neurology, 46*, 368–88.

Luchins, D. (1976). Biogenic amines and affective disorders: a critical analysis. *International Pharmacopsychiatry, 11*, 135–49.

Lynch, S., and Yarnell, P.R. (1973). Retrograde amnesia: delayed forgetting after concussion. *American Journal of Psychology, 86*, 643–5.

McClelland, D.C. (1961). *The Achieving Society*. Princeton. NJ: Van Nostrand.

Maccoby, E.E., and Jacklin, L.N. (1975). *The Psychology of Sex Differences*. London: Oxford University Press.

McDougall, W. (1932). *The Energies of Men: A Study of the Fundamentals of Dynamic Psychology*. London: Methuen.

McEntee, W.J., Biber, M.P., Perl, D.P., and Benson, D.F. (1976). Diencephalic amnesia: a reappraisal. *Journal of Neurology, Neurosurgery, and Psychiatry, 39*, 436–41.

McEwen, B.S., and Weiss, J.M. (1970). The uptake and action of corticosterone: regional and subcellular studies on rat brain. In D. De Wied and J.A.W. Weijnen (eds), *Progress in Brain Research*. Vol. 32, *Pituitary, Adrenal and the Brain*. Amsterdam: Elsevier.

McGaugh, J.L., and Dawson, R.G. (1971). Modification of memory storage processes. In W.K. Honig and P.H.R. James (eds), *Animal Memory*. New York: Academic Press.

McGeer, P.L., Eccles, J.C., and McGeer, E.G. (1978). *Molecular Neurobiology of the Mammalian Brain*. New York: Plenum.

McGlone, J. (1980). Sex differences in human brain asymmetry: a critical survey. *Behavioral and Brain Sciences*, *3*, 215–27.

MacKay, A.V.P., Iversen, L.L., Rosser, M., Spokes, E., Bird, E., Arregui, A., Creese, I., and Snyder, S.H. (1982). Increased brain dopamine and dopamine receptors in schizophrenia. *Archives of General Psychiatry*, *39*, 991–7.

McKeever, W.F., and Hoff, A.L. (1982). Familial sinistrality, sex and laterality differences in naming and lexical decision latencies of right-handers. *Brain and Language*, *17*, 225–39.

McKeever, W.F. and Van Deventer, A.D. (1977). Visual and auditory language processing asymmetries: influence of handedness, familial sinistrality, and sex. *Cortex*, *13*, 225–41.

McKeever, W.F., and Van Deventer, A.D. (1980). Inverted handwriting position, language laterality, and the Levy–Nagylaki genetic model of handedness and cerebral organization. *Neuropyschologia*, *18*, 99–102.

MacLean, P.D. (1949). Psychosomatic disease and the 'visceral brain': recent developments bearing on the Papez theory of emotion. *Psychosomatic Medicine*, *11*, 338–53.

Mahut, H., Moss, M. and Zola-Morgan, S. (1981). Retention deficits after combined amygdalo-hippocampal and selective hippocampal resections in the monkey. *Neuropsychologia*, *19*, 201–25.

Maranon, G. (1924). Contribution à l'étude de l'action émotive de l'adrénaline. *Revue Française d'Endrocrinologie*, *2*, 301–325.

Mark, V.H., and Ervin, F.R. (eds) (1970). *Violence and the Brain*. New York: Harper & Row.

Marshall, G.D., and Zimbardo, P.G. (1979). Affective consequences of inadequately explained physiological arousal. *Journal of Personality and Social Psychology*, *37*, 970–88.

Marshall, J.F., Richardson, J.S., and Teitelbaum, P. (1974). Nigrostriatal bundle damage and the lateral hypothalamic syndrome. *Journal of Comparative and Physiological Psychology*, *87*, 808–30.

Marshall, J.F., and Teitelbaum, P. (1974). Further analysis of sensory inattention following lateral hypothalamic damage in rats. *Journal of Comparative and Physiological Psychology*, *86*, 375–95.

Martin, I., and Venables, P.H. (1980). *Techniques in Psychophysiology*. Chichester: Wiley.

Martin, J.R., and Novin, D. (1977). Decreased feeding in rats following hepatic-portal infusion of glucagon. *Physiology and Behavior*, *19*, 461–6.

Marzi, C.A., Brizzolara, D., Rizzolatti, G., Umilta, C., and Berlucchi, G. (1974). Left hemisphere superiority for the recognition of well known faces. *Brain Research*, *66*, 358–9.

Marzi, C.A., and Berlucchi, G. (1977). Right visual field superiority for accuracy of recognition of famous faces in normals. *Neuropsychologia*, *15*, 751–6.

Maslach, C. (1979). Negative emotional biasing of unexplained arousal. *Journal of Personality and Social Psychology*, *37*, 953–69.

Maslow, A.H. (1970). *Motivation and Personality*. New York: Harper & Row.

Mason, J.W. (1968). A review of psychoendocrine research on the pituitary-adrenal cortical system. *Psychosomatic Medicine, 30*, 576–607.

Mason, S.T., and Fibiger, H.C. (1978). 6-OHDA lesions of the dorsal noradrenergic bundle alters extinction of passive avoidance. *Brain Research, 152*, 209–14.

Mason, S.T., and Iversen, S.D. (1977). An investigation of the role of cortical and cerebellar noradrenaline in associative motor learning in the rat. *Brain Research, 134*, 513–27.

Masserman, J.H. (1941). Is the hypothalamus a center of emotion? *Psychosomatic Medicine, 3*, 3–25.

Matthysse, S. (1974). Schizophrenia: relationships to dopamine transmission, motor control and feature extraction. In F.O. Schmitt and F.G. Worden (eds), *Neurosciences: Third Study Program*. Cambridge, Mass.: MIT Press.

Mattis, S., Kovner, R., and Goldmeier, E. (1978). Different patterns of mnemonic deficits in two organic amnestic syndromes. *Brain and Language, 6*, 179–81.

Mayer-Gross, W., Slater, E., and Roth, M. (1977). *Clinical Psychiatry*. London: Baillière Tindall.

Meddis, R. (1977). *The Sleep Instinct*. London: Routledge & Kegan Paul.

Meddis, R. (1979). The evolution and function of sleep. In D.A. Oakley and H.C. Plotkin (eds), *Brain, Behavior and Evolution*. London: Methuen.

Mellor, C.S. (1970). First rank symptoms of schizophrenia. *British Journal of Psychiatry, 117*, 15–23.

Mellor, C.S. (1982). The present status of first rank symptoms. *British Journal of Psychiatry, 140*, 423–4.

Melzack, R., and Wall, P.D. (1965). Pain mechanisms: a new theory. *Science, 150*, 971–9.

Mendels, J., Stern, S., and Frazer, A. (1976). Biochemistry of depression. *Diseases of the Nervous System, 37*, 3–9.

Mesulam, M.M., Van Hoesen, G.W., Pandya, D.N., and Geschwind, N. (1977). Limbic and sensory connections of the inferior parietal lobule (area PG) in the rhesus monkey: a study with a new method of horseradish peroxidase histochemistry. *Brain Research, 136*, 393–414.

Miller, R.R., and Kraus, J.N. (1977). Somatic and autonomic indexes of recovery from electroconvulsive shock-induced amnesia in rats. *Journal of Comparative and Physiological Psychology, 91*, 434–42.

Miller, R.R., and Springer, A.D. (1973). Amnesia, consolidation, and retrieval. *Psychological Review, 80*, 69–79.

Mills, L., and Rollman, G.B. (1979). Left hemisphere selectivity for processing duration in normal subjects. *Brain and Language, 7*, 320–35.

Milner, B. (1971). Interhemispheric differences in the localization of psychological processes in man. *British Medical Bulletin, 27*, 272–7.

Mishkin, M. (1978). Memory in monkeys severely impaired by combined but not separate removal of amygdala and hippocampus. *Nature, 273*, 297–8.

Mogenson, G.J., and Phillips, A.G. (1976). Motivation: a psychological construct in search of a physiological substrate. In J.M. Sprague and A.N. Epstein (eds), *Progress in Psychobiology and Physiological Psychology*, Vol. 6. New York: Academic Press.

Moniz, E. (1936). *Tentatives Opératoires dans le Traitement de Certaines Psychoses.* Paris: Masson.

Monnier, M., Dudler, L., Gachter, R., Maier, P.F., Tobler, H.J. and Schoenenberger, G.A. (1977). The delta sleep-inducing peptide (DSIP): comparative properties of the original and synthetic nonapetide. *Experientia*, 33/34, 548–52.

Morgan, C.T. (1965). *Physiological Psychology.* New York: McGraw-Hill.

Morgane, P.J., and Stern, W.C. (1974). Chemical anatomy of brain circuits in relation to sleep and wakefulness. In E. Weitzmann (ed.), *Advances in Sleep Research*, Vol. 1. New York: Spectrum.

Morgane, P.J., Stern, W.C., and Bronzino, J.D. (1977). Experimental studies of sleep in animals. In R.D. Myers (ed.), *Methods in Psychobiology*, Vol. 3. New York: Academic Press.

Morton, J. (1985). The problem with amnesia: the problem with human memory. *Cognitive Neuropsychology*, 2, 281–90.

Moruzzi, G. (1964). Reticular influences on the EEG. *Electroencephalography and Clinical Neurophysiology*, 16, 2–17.

Moruzzi, G., and Magoun, H.W. (1949). Brain stem reticular formation and activation of the EEG. *Electroencephalography and Clinical Neurophysiology*, 1, 455–73.

Moscovitch, M. (1976). On interpreting data regarding the linguistic competence and performance of the right hemisphere: a reply to Selnes. *Brain and Language*, 3, 590–9.

Moyer, K.E. (1968). Kinds of aggression and their physiological basis. *Communications in Behavioral Biology*, 2, 65–87.

Mueller, K., and Hsiao, S. (1979). Consistency of cholecystokinin satiety effect across deprivation levels and motivational states. *Physiology and Behavior*, 22, 809–15.

Mulas, A., Crabai, F., and Pepeu, G. (1970). The influence of repeated experience on the effects of scopolamine and of amphetamine on exploratory behavior in the rat. *Pharmacological Research Communications*, 2, 169–76.

Murphy, D.L., Campbell, I., and Costa, J.L. (1978). Current status of the indoleamine hypothesis of the affective disorders. In M.A. Lipton, A. DiMascio, and K.F. Killam (eds), *Psychopharmacology: A Generation of Progress.* New York: Raven Press.

Musten, B., Peace, D., and Anderson, G.H. (1974). Food intake regulation in the weanling rat; self-selection of protein and energy. *Journal of Nutrition*, 104, 563–72.

Myers, R.E. (1956). Functions of the corpus callosum in interocular transfer. *Brain*, 79, 358.

Natale, M., Gur, R.E., and Gur, R.C. (1983). Hemispheric asymmetries in processing emotional expressions. *Neuropsychologia*, 21, 555–65.

Nauta, W.J.H. (1946). Hypothalamic regulation of sleep in rats: an experimental study. *Journal of Neurophysiology*, 9, 285–316.

Nebes, R.D. (1971). Handedness and the perception of whole–part relationship. *Cortex*, 7, 350–6.

Nielsen, M., Braestrup, C., and Squires, R.F. (1978). Evidence for a late evolutionary appearance of brain specific benzodiazepine receptors: an investigation of 18 vertebrate and 5 invertebrate species. *Brain Research, 141*, 342–6.

Nisbett, R.E. (1972). Hunger, obesity and the ventromedial hypothalamus. *Psychological Review*, 79, 433–53.

Nottebohm, F. (1977). Asymmetries in neural control of vocalization in the canary. In S. Harnad, R.W. Doty, L. Goldstein, J. Jaynes, and G. Krauthamer (eds), *Lateralization in the Nervous System*. London: Academic Press.

Oakley, D.A. (1979). Instrumental reversal learning and subsequent fixed ratio performance on simple and go/no-go schedules in neodecorticate rabbits. *Physiological Psychology*, 7, 29–42.

Ojemann, G.A. (1983). Brain organization for language from the perspective of electrical stimulation mapping. *Behavioural and Brain Sciences*, 6, 189–230.

Oke, A., Keller, R., Mefford, I., and Adams, R.N. (1978). Lateralization of norepinephrine in human thalamus. *Science, 200*, 1411–13.

O'Keefe, J., and Nadel, L. (1978). *The Hippocampus as a Cognitive Map*. Oxford: Clarendon Press.

Olds, J., and Milner, P. (1954). Positive reinforcement produced by electrical stimulation of septal area and other regions of rat brain. *Journal of Comparative and Physiological Psychology*, 47, 419–27.

Olds, J., and Olds, M. (1965). Drive, rewards and the brain. In T.M. Newcombe (ed.), *New Directions in Psychology II*, New York: Holt, Rinehart & Winston.

Olton, D.S. (1976). Spatial memory, *Scientific American, 236*, 82–98.

Olton, D.S. (1979). Mazes, maps and memory. *American Psychologist, 34*, 583–96.

Olton, D.S., Becker, J.T., and Handelmann, G.E. (1980). Hippocampal function: working memory or cognitive mapping? *Physiological Psychology, 8*, 239–46.

Opsahl, C.A., and Powley, T.L. (1974). Failure of vagotomy to reverse obesity in the genetically obese Zucker rat. *American Journal of Physiology, 226*, 34–8.

Ornstein, R. (1977). *Psychology of Consciousness*. 2nd edn, New York: Harcourt Brace Jovanovich.

Oscar-Berman, M., and Zola-Morgan, S.M. (1980a). Comparative neuropsychology and Korsakoff's syndrome. I-Spatial and visual reversal learning. *Neuropsychologia, 18*, 499–512.

Oscar-Berman, M., and Zola-Morgan, S.M. (1980b). Comparative neuropsychology and Korsakoff's syndrome. II – Two-choice visual discrimination learning. *Neuropsychologia, 18*, 513–26.

Oswald, I. (1976). The function of sleep. *Postgraduate Medical Journal, 52*, 15–18.

Oswald, I. (1980). *Sleep*. 4th edn. Harmondsworth, Middx: Penguin Books.

Overman, W.H., and Doty, R.W. (1982). Hemispheric specialization displayed by man but not macaques for analysis of faces. *Neuropsychologia*, *20*, 113–28.

Overton, D.A. (1966). State-dependent learning produced by depressant and atropine-like drugs. *Psychopharmacologia*, *10*, 6–31.

Papez, J.W. (1937). A proposed mechanism of emotion. *Archives of Neurology and Psychiatry* (Chicago), *38*, 725–43.

Pappenheimer, J.R., Koski, G., Fencl, V., Karnovsky, M.L., and Krueger, J. (1975). Extraction of sleep-promoting Factor S from cerebrospinal fluid and from brains of sleep-deprived animals. *Journal of Neurophysiology*, *38*, 1299–1311.

Passingham, R. (1982). *The Human Primate*. Oxford: Freeman.

Penfield, W., and Mathieson, G. (1974). Memory: autopsy findings and comments on the role of the hippocampus in experiential recall. *Archives of Neurology*, *31*, 145–54.

Pepeu, G. (1972). Cholinergic neurotransmission in the central nervous system. *Archives internationale de Pharmacodynamie et de Thérapie*, Suppl. to Vol. 196, 229–243.

Perrett, D.I., Rolls, E.T., and Caan, W. (1982). Visual neurones responsive to faces in the monkey temporal cortex. *Experimental Brain Research*, *47*, 329–42.

Petersen, M.R., Beecher, M.D., Zoloth, S.R., Moody, D., and Stebbins, W.L. (1978). Neural lateralization of species-specific vocalizations by Japanese macaques (Macaca fuscata). *Science*, *202*, 324–7.

Pettigrew, J.D., and Freeman, R.D. (1973). Visual experience without lines: effect on developing cortical neurons. *Science*, *182*, 599–600.

Pirozzolo, F.J., and Rayner, K. (1977). Hemispheric specialisation in reading and word recognition. *Brain and Language*, *4*, 248–61.

Pi-Sunyer, X., Kissileff, H.R., Thornton, J., and Smith, G.P. (1982). C-Terminal octapeptide of cholecystokinin decreases food intake in obese men. *Physiology and Behavior*, *29*, 627–30.

Plutchik, R. (1980). *Emotion: A Psychoevolutionary Synthesis.*, New York: Harper & Row.

Powley, T.L. (1977). The ventromedial hypothalamic syndrome, satiety, and a cephalic phase hypothesis. *Psychological Review*, *84*, 89–126.

Powley, T.L., and Opsahl, C.A. (1974). Ventromedial hypothalamic obesity abolished by subdiaphragmatic vagotomy. *American Journal of Physiology*, *226*, 25–33.

Ramm, P. (1979). The locus coeruleus, catecholamines, and REM sleep: a critical review. *Behavioral and Neural Biology*, *25*, 415–48.

Randrup, A., and Munkvad, I. (1970). Biochemical, anatomical and psychological investigations of stereotyped behavior induced by amphetamines. In E. Costa and S. Garattini (eds), *Amphetamines and Related Compounds*. New York: Raven Press.

Rasmussen, T., and Milner, B. (1977). The role of early left-brain injury in determining lateralization of cerebral speech functions. *Annals of the New York Academy of Sciences*, *299*, 355–69.

Rauste-Von Wright, M. Von Wright, J., and Frankenhaeuser, M. (1981). Relationships between sex-related psychological chararcteristics during adolescence and catecholamine excretion during achievement stress. *Psychophysiology, 18*, 362–70.

Rezek, M., Kroeger, E.A., Lesiuk, H., Havlicek, V., and Novin, D. (1977). Cerebral and hepatic glucoreceptors: assessment of their role in food intake control by the uptake of 3H-2 Deoxy-D-Glucose. *Physiology and Behavior, 18*, 679–83.

Riccio, D.C., Mactutus, C.F., Hinderliter, C.F., and McCutcheon, K. (1979). Severity of amnesia and the effectiveness of reactivation treatment: evidence for a retrieval process. *Physiological Psychology, 7*, 59–63.

Riccio, D.C., and Richardson, R. (1984). The status of memory following experimentally induced amnesias: gone, but not forgotten. *Physiological Psychology, 12*, 59–72.

Rigter, H., and Van Riezen, H. (1975). Anti-amnesic effect of ACTH 4–10: its independence of the nature of the amnesic agent and the behavioral test. *Physiology and Behavior, 14*, 563–6.

Robertshaw, S., and Sheldon, M. (1976). Laterality effects in judgement of the identity and position of letters: a signal detection analysis. *Quarterly Journal of Experimental Psychology, 28*, 115–21.

Robinson, R.G., Kubos, K.L., Starr, L.B., Rao, K., and Price, T.R. (1984). Mood disorders in stroke patients: importance of location of lesion. *Brain, 107*, 81–93.

Rockel, A.J., Hiorns, R.W., and Powell, T.P.S. (1980). The basic uniformity of structure of the neocortex. *Brain, 103*, 221–244.

Rodin, J. (1975). Effects of obesity and set point on taste responsiveness and ingestion in humans. *Journal of Comparative and Physiological Psychology, 89*, 1003–9.

Roger, A., Rossi, G.F., and Zirondoli, A. (1956). Le rôle des nerfs craniens dans le maintien de l'état vigile de la préparation 'encéphale isolé'. *Electroencephalography and Clinical Neurophysiology, 8*, 1–13.

Roland, P.E. (1984). Metabolic measurements of the working frontal cortex in man. *Trends in Neuroscience, 7*, 430–5.

Rolls, B.J., Rowe, E.A., and Rolls, E.T. (1982) How sensory properties of foods affect human feeding behavior. *Physiology and Behavior, 29*, 409–17.

Rothwell, N.J., and Stock, M.J. (1979). A role for brown adipose tissue in diet-induced thermogenesis. *Nature, 281*, 31–5.

Roueché, B. (1977). All I could do was stand in the woods. *New Yorker, September 12*, 97–117.

Rubens, A.B., Mahowald, M.W., and Hutton, J.T. (1976). Asymmetry of the lateral sylvian fissures in man. *Neurology, 26*, 620–4.

Russell, P.A. (1973). Relationships between exploratory behaviour and fear: a review. *British Journal of Psychology, 64*, 417–33.

Sackheim, H.H., Gur, R.C., and Sauly, M.C. (1978). Emotions are expressed more intensely on the left side of the face. *Science, 202*, 434–6.

Safer, M.A. (1981). Sex and hemisphere differences in access to codes for processing emotional expressions and faces. *Journal of Experimental Psychology: General, 110*, 86–100.

Schachter, S., and Singer, J.E. (1962). Cognitive, social, and physiological determinants of emotional state. *Psychological Review*, *69*, 379–99.

Schachter, S., and Singer, J.E. (1979). Comments on the Maslach and Marshall/Zimbardo experiments. *Journal of Personality and Social Psychology*, *37*, 989–95.

Schachter, S., and Wheeler, L. (1962). Epinephrine, chlorpromazine, and amusement. *Journal of Abnormal and Social Psychology*, *65*, 121–8.

Schallert, T., and Whishaw, I.Q. (1978). Two types of aphagia and two types of sensorimotor impairment after lateral hypothalamic lesions: observations in normal weight, dieted, and fattened rats. *Journal of Comparative and Physiological Psychology*, *92*, 720–41.

Schildkraut, J.J. (1965). The catecholamine hypothesis of affective disorders: a review of supporting evidence. *American Journal of Psychiatry*, *122*, 509–22.

Schildkraut, J.J. (1978). Current status of the catecholamine hypothesis of affective disorders. In M.A. Lipton, A. Di Mascio, and K.F. Killam (eds), *Psychopharmacology: A Generation of Progress*. New York: Raven Press.

Schmajuk, N.A. (1984). Psychological theories of hippocampal function. *Physiological Psychology*, *12*, 166–83.

Schneider, A.M. (1976). Two faces of memory consolidation: storage of instrumental and classical conditioning. In D. Deutsch and J.A. Deutsch (eds), *Short-Term Memory*. New York: Academic Press.

Sclafani, A. (1976). Appetite and hunger in experimental obesity syndromes. In D. Novin, W. Wyrwicka, and G. Bray (eds), *Hunger: Basic Mechanisms and Clinical Implications*. New York: Raven Press.

Sclafani, A., and Springer, D. (1976). Dietary obesity in adult rats: similarities to hypothalamic and human obesity syndromes. *Physiology and Behavior*, *17*, 461–71.

Scott, J.P. (1958). *Aggression*. Chicago: University of Chicago Press.

Scoville, W.B. (1954). The limbic lobe in man. *Journal of Neurosurgery*, *11*, 64–6.

Scoville, W.B., and Milner, B. (1957). Loss of recent memory after bilateral hippocampal lesions. *Journal of Neurology, Neurosurgery, and Psychiatry*, *20*, 11–21.

Seltzer, B., and Benson, D.F. (1974). The temporal pattern of retrograde amnesia in Korsakoff's disease. *Neurology*, Minneapolis, *24*, 527–30.

Selye, H. (1950). *Stress*. Montreal: Acta.

Sergent, J. (1983). Unified response to bilateral hemispheric stimulation by a split-brain patient. *Nature*, *305*, 800–2.

Shanon, B. (1980). Lateralization effects in musical decision tasks. *Neuropsychologia*, *18*, 21–31.

Shopsin, B., Wilk, S., Gershon, S., Davis, K., and Suhl, M. (1973). An assessment of norepinephrine metabolism in affective disorders. *Archives of General Psychiatry*, *28*, 230–3.

Shute, C.C.D., and Lewis, P.R. (1967). The ascending cholinergic reticular system: neocortical, olfactory and subcortical projections. *Brain*, *90*, 497–520.

Shuttlesworth, D., Neill, D., and Ellen, P. (1984). The place of physiological psychology in neuroscience. *Physiological Psychology*, *12*, 3–7.

Siddle, D.A.T. (1978). Effects of changes in verbal stimulus meaning on autonomic components of the orienting response. *Psychophysiology*, *15*, 284.

Sidman, M., Mason, J.W., Brady, J.V., and Thach, J. (1962). Quantitative relations between avoidance behaviour and pituitary-adrenal cortical activity. *Journal of the Experimental Analysis of Behavior*, *5*, 353–62.

Siegel, A., Edinger, H., and Koo, A. (1977). Suppression of attack behavior in the cat by the prefrontal cortex: role of the mediodorsal thalamic nucleus. *Brain Research*, *127*, 185–90.

Simantov, R., Goodman, R., Aposhian, D., and Snyder, S.H. (1976). Phylogenetic distribution of a morphine-like peptide 'enkephalin'. *Brain Research*, *111*, 204–11.

Simon, E.J. (1976). The opiate receptors. *Neurochemical Research*, *1*, 3–28.

Sloviter, R.S, Drust, E.G., and Connor, J.D. (1978). Specificity of a rat behavioral model for serotonin receptor activation. *Journal of Pharmacology and Experimental Therapeutics*, *206*, 339–47.

Small, I.F., Heimburger, R.F., Small, J.G., Milstein, V., and Moore D.F. (1977). Follow-up of stereotaxic amygdalotomy for seizure and behavior disorders. *Biological Psychiatry*, *12*, 401–11.

Smith, A., and Burkland, C.W. (1966). Dominant hemispherectomy. *Science*, *153*, 1280–2.

Smith, A., and Sugar, O. (1975). Development of above normal language and intelligence 21 years after left hemispherectomy. *Neurology*, *25*, 813–18.

Smith, D.E., King, M.B., and Hoebel, B.G. (1970). Lateral hypothalamic control of killing: evidence for a cholinoceptive mechanism. *Science*, *167*, 900–1.

Sokolov, E.N. (1963). Higher nervous functions: the orienting reflex. *Annual Review of Physiology*, *25*, 545–80.

Sokolov, E.N. (1975). The orienting reflex. In E.N. Sokolov and O.S. Vinogradova (eds), *Neuronal Mechanisms of the Orienting Reflex*. New York: Wiley.

Spear, N. (1973). Retrieval of memory in animals. *Psychological Review*, *80*, 163–94.

Sperry, R.W. (1961). Cerebral organization and behavior. *Science*, *133*, 1749–57.

Sperry, R.W. (1967). The great cerebral commissure. In *Psychobiology: Readings from Scientific American*. London: Freeman.

Sperry, R.W. (1982). Some effects of disconnecting the cerebral hemispheres. *Science*, *217*, 1223–6.

Sperry, R.W., Zaidel, E., and Zaidel, D. (1979). Self-recognition and social awareness in the deconnected minor hemisphere. *Neuropsychologia*, *17*, 153–66.

Springer, A.D. (1975). Vulnerability of skeletal and autonomic manifestations of memory in the rat to electroconvulsive shock. *Journal of Comparative and Physiological Psychology*, *88*, 890–903.

Springer, S.P., and Deutsch, G. (1981). *Left Brain, Right Brain*. San Francisco: Freeman.

Squire, L.R. (1980). Specifying the defect in human anmesia: storage, retrieval and semantics. *Neuropsychologia*, *18*, 368–72.

Squire, L.R. (1982). Comparisons between forms of amnesia: some deficits are unique to Korsakoff's syndrome. *Journal of Experimental Psychology: Learning, Memory, and Cognition, 8*, 560–71.

Squire, L.R., Nadel, L., and Slater, P.C. (1981). Anterograde amnesia and memory for temporal order. *Neuropsychologia, 19*, 141–5.

Squires, R.F., and Braestrup, C. (1977). Benzodiazepine receptors in rat brain. *Nature, 266*, 732–4.

Stein, L. (1968). Chemistry of reward and punishment. In D.H. Efron (ed.), *Psychopharmacology, A Review of Progress: 1957–1967*. Washington: U.S. Government Printing Office.

Stein, L., and Wise, C. (1971). Possible etiology of schizophrenia: progressive damage to the noradrenergic reward system by 6-hydroxydopamine. *Science, 171*, 1032–6.

Stephan, F.K., and Kovacevic, N.S. (1978). Multiple retention deficit in passive avoidance in rats is eliminated by suprachiasmatic lesions. *Behavioral Biology, 22*, 456–62.

Sterman, M.B., and Clemente, C.D. (1962). Forebrain inhibitory mechanisms: sleep patterns induced by basal forebrain stimulation in the behaving cat. *Experimental Neurology, 6*, 103–17.

Stern, E., Parmelee, A.H., and Harris, M.A. (1973). Sleep state periodicity in prematures and young infants. *Developmental Psychobiology, 6*, 357–65.

Stern, W.C., and Morgane, P.J. (1974). Theoretical view of REM sleep function: maintenance of catecholamine systems in the central nervous system. *Behavioral Biology, 11*, 1–32.

Stevens, J. (1977). Striatal function and schizophrenias. In A.R. Cools, A.H.M. Lohman, and J.H.L. van den Bercken (eds), *Psychobiology of the Striatum*. Amsterdam: North Holland.

Stevens, J.R. (1973). An anatomy of schizophrenia? *Archives of General Psychiatry, 29*, 177–89.

Strauss, E., and Wada, J. (1983). Lateral preferences and cerebral speech dominance. *Cortex, 19*, 165–77.

Stumpf, W.E. (1975). The brain: an endocrine gland and hormone target. In W.E. Stumpf and L.D. Grant (eds), *Anatomical Neuroendocrinology*. Basel: S. Karger.

Swadlow, H.A., and Waxman, S.G. (1979). Ultrastructure and conduction properties of visual callosal axons of the rabbit. In I. Steele-Russell, M.W. van Hof, and G. Berlucchi (eds), *Structure and Function of the Cerebral Commissures*. London: Macmillan.

Swanson, L.W. (1976). The locus coeruleus: a cytoarchitecture, golgi, and immunohistochemical study in the albino rat. *Brain Research, 110*, 39–56.

Szasz, T.S. (1976) Schizophrenia: the sacred symbol of psychiatry. *British Journal of Psychiatry, 129*, 308–16.

Tapley, S.M., and Bryden, M.P. (1983). Handwriting position and hemispheric asymmetry in right-handers. *Neuropsychologia, 21*, 129–38.

Tapp, J.T. (1969). Activity, reactivity and the behaviour-directing properties of stimuli. In J.T. Tapp (ed.), *Reinforcement and Behavior*. New York: Academic Press.

Taylor, M., and Abrams, R. (1983). Cerebral hemisphere dysfunction in the major psychoses. In P. Flor-Henry and J. Gruzelier (eds), *Laterality and Psychopathology*. Amsterdam: Elsevier.

Teuber, H.L., Milner, B., and Vaughan, H.G., Jr. (1968). Persistent anterograde amnesia after stab wound of the basal brain. *Neuropsychologia*, *6*, 267–82.

Thompson, R. (1974). Localization of the 'maze memory system' in the white rat. *Physiological Psychology*, *2*, 1–17.

Thompson, R. (1978). Localization of a 'passive avoidance memory system' in the white rat. *Physiological Psychology*, *6*, 263–71.

Thompson, R., Arabie, G.J., and Sisk, G.B. (1976). Localization of the 'incline plane discrimination memory system' in the white rat. *Physiological Psychology*, *4*, 311–24.

Thompson, R.F. (1967). *Foundations of Physiological Psychology*. New York: Harper & Row.

Thompson, R.F., Berger, T.W., Berry, S.D., Hoehler, F.K., Kettner, R.E., and Weisz, D.J. (1980). Hippocampal substrate of classical conditioning. *Physiological Psychology*, *8*, 262–79.

Thompson, R.F. and Spencer, W.A. (1966). Habituation: a model phenomenon for the study of neuronal substrates of behavior. *Psychological Review*, *73*, 16–43.

Tolman, E.C. (1932). *Purposive Behavior in Animals and Men*. New York: Appleton-Century-Crofts.

Torrey, E.F., and Petersen, M.R. (1974). Schizophrenia and the limbic system. *Lancet*, *II*, 942–6.

Tulving, E. (1974). Cue-dependent forgetting. *American Scientist*, *62*, 74–82.

Ungar, G. (1974). Molecular coding of memory. *Life Sciences*, *14*, 595–604.

Ungar, G., Desiderio, D.M., and Parr, W. (1972). Isolation, identification, and synthesis of a specific-behavior-inducing brain peptide. *Nature*, *238*, 198–202.

Ungerleider, L.G., and Mishkin, M. (1982). Two cortical visual systems. In D.J. Ingle, M.A. Goodale, and R.J.W. Mansfield (eds), *Analysis of Visual Behavior*. Cambridge, Mass.: MIT Press.

Ungerstedt, U. (1971a). Aphagia and adipsia after 6-hydroxydopamine induced degeneration of the nigrostriatal dopamine system. *Acta Physiologica Scandinavica*, Suppl. 367, 95–122.

Ungerstedt, U. (1971b). Striatal dopamine release after amphetamine or nerve degeneration revealed by rotational behavior. *Acta Physiologica Scandinavica*, Suppl. 367, 49.

Ungerstedt, U. (1971c). Sterotaxic mapping of the monoamine pathways in the rat brain. *Acta Physiologica Scandinavica*, Suppl. 367, 1–48.

Valenstein, E.S. (1967). Selection of nutritive and non-nutritive solutions under different conditions of need. *Journal of Comparative and Physiological Psychology*, *63*, 429–33.

Valenstein, E.S. (1973). *Brain Control*. New York: Wiley.

Valenstein, E.S., Cox, V.C., and Kakolewski, J.W. (1970). Re-examination of the role of the hypothalamus in motivation. *Psychological Review*, *77*, 16–31.

Valins, S. (1966). Cognitive effects of false heart-rate feedback. *Journal of Personality and Social Psychology*, *4*, 400–8.

Van Praag, H.M. (1977a). New evidence of serotonin-deficient depressions. *Neuropsychobiology*, *3*, 56–63.

Van Praag, H.M. (1977b). The significance of dopamine for the mode of action of neuroleptics and the pathogenesis of schizophrenia. *British Journal of Psychiatry*, *130*, 463–74.

Van Toller, C. (1979). *The Nervous Body*. Chichester: Wiley.

Van Wagenen, W.P., and Herren, R.Y. (1940). Surgical division of commissural pathways in the corpus callosum: relation to spread of an epileptic attack. *Archives of Neurology and Psychiatry*, *44*, 740–59.

Venables, P.H. (1983). Cerebral mechanisms, autonomic responsiveness, and attention in schizophrenia. *Nebraska Symposium on Motivation*, *31*, 47–91.

Victor, M., Adams, R.D., and Collins, G.H. (1971). *The Wernicke–Korsakoff Syndrome*. Philadelphia: F.A. Davis.

Vinogradova, O.S. (1975). The hippocampus and the orienting reflex. In E.N. Sokolov and O.S. Vinogradova (eds), *Neuronal Mechanisms of the Orienting Reflex*. New York, Wiley.

Vogel, G.W. (1975). A review of REM sleep deprivation. *Archives of General Psychiatry*, *32*, 749–61.

Von Euler, U.S. (1967). Adrenal medullary secretion and its neural control. In L. Martini and W.F. Ganong (eds), *Neuroendocrinology*, Vol. 2. New York: Academic Press.

Wada, J.A., Clarke, R., and Hamm, A. (1975). Cerebral hemisphere asymmetry in humans: cortical speech zones in 100 adult and 100 infant brains. *Archives of Neurology*, *32*, 239–46.

Wagner, A.R. (1976). Priming in STM: an information-processing mechanism for self-generated or retrieval-generated depression in performance. In T.J. Tighe and R.N. Leaton (eds), *Habituation*. New Jersey: Erlbaum.

Wagner, A.R. and Pfautz, P.L. (1978). A bowed serial-position function in habituation of sequential stimuli. *Animal Learning and Behavior*, *6*, 395–400.

Walker, S.F. (1980). Lateralization of functions in the vertebrate brain. *British Journal of Psychology*, *71*, 329–67.

Walker, S.F. (1981). Necessary asymmetries in bilaterally symmetrical brains. *Speculations in Science and Technology*, *4*, 575–8.

Walker, S. (1983). *Animal Thought*. London: Routledge & Kegan Paul.

Walsh, K.W. (1978). *Neuropsychology*. Edinburgh: Churchill Livingstone.

Wampler, R.S., and Snowdon, C.T. (1979). Development of VMH obesity in vagotomized rats. *Physiology and Behavior*, *22*, 85–93.

Warburton, D.M. (1977). Stimulus selection and behavioral inhibition. In L.L. Iversen, S.D. Iversen, and S.H. Snyder (eds), *Handbook of Psychopharmacology*. Vol. 8, *Drugs, Neurotransmitters and Behavior*. New York: Plenum.

Warrington, E.K. (1975). The selective impairment of semantic memory. *Quarterly Journal of Experimental Psychology*, *27*, 635–57.

Warrington, E.K., and Sanders, H.L. (1971). The fate of old memories. *Quarterly Journal of Experimental Psychology*, *23*, 132–42.

Warrington, E.K., and Weiskrantz, L. (1970). Amnesic syndrome: consolidation or retrieval? *Nature, 288*, 628–30.

Warrington, E.K., and Weiskrantz, L. (1974). The effect of prior learning on subsequent retention in amnesic patients. *Neuropsychologia, 12*, 419–28.

Weingarten, H.P. (1982). Diet palatability modulates sham feeding in VMH-lesion and normal rats: implications for finickiness and evaluation of sham-feeding data. *Journal of Comparative and Physiological Psychology, 96*, 223–33.

Weiss, J.M. (1972). Influence of psychological variables on stress-induced pathology. In J. Knight and R. Porter (eds), *Physiology, Emotion and Psychosomatic Illness*. Amsterdam: Elsevier.

Welker, W.I. (1959). Escape, exploratory and food-seeking responses of rats in a novel situation. *Journal of Comparative and Physiological Psychology, 52*, 106–11.

Wernicke, C. (1874). *Der aphasische Symptomenkomplex*. Breslau: Cohn und Weigert.

Wester, K. (1971). Habituation to electrical stimulation of the thalamus in unanesthetized cats. *Electroencephalography and Clinical Neurophysiology, 30*, 52–61.

Wheatley, M.D. (1944). The hypothalamus and affective behavior in cats: a study of the effects of experimental lesions with anatomic correlations. *Archives of Neurology and Psychiatry, 52*, 296–316.

Whimbey, A.E., and Denenberg, V.H. (1967). Two independent behavioral dimensions in open-field performance. *Journal of Comparative and Physiological Psychology, 63*, 500–4.

Whitlow, J.W. (1975). Short-term memory in habituation and dishabituation. *Journal of Experimental Psychology: Animal Behavior Processes, 1*, 189–206.

Wimersma Greidanus, T.B. van (1977). Effects of MSH and related peptides on avoidance behavior in rats. *Frontiers in Hormone Research, 4*, 129–39.

Wise, C.D., Baden, M.M., and Stein, L. (1974). Post-mortem measurement of enzymes in human brain: evidence of a central noradrenergic deficit in schizophrenia. *Journal of Psychiatric Research, 11*, 185–98.

Wise, C.D., Berger, B.D., and Stein, L. (1973). Evidence of α-noradrenergic reward receptors and serotonergic punishment receptors in the rat brain. *Biological Psychiatry, 6*, 3–21.

Wise, C.D., and Stein, L. (1975). Reply to Wyatt *et al. Science, 187*, 370.

Wise, R.A. (1978). Catecholamine theories of reward: a critical review. *Brain Research, 152*, 215–47.

Witelson, S.F. (1976). Sex and the single hemisphere: specialization of the right hemisphere for spatial processing. *Science, 193*, 425–7.

Witelson, S.F. (1983). The corpus callosum is larger in left handers. *Abstract No. 269.5*, Society for Neuroscience Meeting, Boston.

Witelson, S.F., and Pallie, W. (1973). Left hemisphere specialization for language in the newborn: neuroanatomical evidence of asymmetry. *Brain, 96*, 641–6.

Wolff, J.R., and Zaborszky, L. (1979). On the normal arrangement of fibres and terminals and limits of plasticity in the callosal system of the rat. In I.S. Russell, W.M. van Hof, and G. Berlucchi (eds), *Structure and Function of the Cerebral Commissures*. London: Macmillan.

Wollberg, Z., and Newman, J.D. (1972). Auditory cortex of squirrel monkey: response patterns of single cells to species-specific vocalizations. *Science, 175*, 212–14.

Wyatt, R.J., Schwartz, M.A., Erdelyi, E., and Barchas, J.D. (1975). Dopamine-β-hydroxylase activity in brains of chronic schizophrenic patients. *Science, 187*, 368–70.

Yakovlev, P.I., and Lecours, A. (1967). The myelogenetic cycles of regional maturation of the brain. In A. Minkowski (ed.), *Regional Development of the Brain in Early Life*. London: Blackwell.

Yarnell, P.R., and Lynch, S. (1979). Retrograde memory immediately after concussion. *Lancet, I*, 863–5.

Zaidel, D., and Sperry, R.W. (1974). Memory impairment after commissurotomy in man. *Brain, 97*, 263–72.

Zaidel, E. (1983). A response to Gazzaniga: language in the right hemisphere, convergent perspectives. *American Psychologist, 38*, 542–6.

Zaidel, E., and Peters, A.M. (1981). Phonological encoding and ideographic reading by the disconnected right hemisphere: two case studies. *Brain and Language, 14*, 205–34.

Zajonc, R.B. (1984). On the primacy of affect. *American Psychologist, 39*, 117–23.

Zatorre, R.J. (1979). Recognition of dichotic melodies by musicians and non-musicians. *Neuropsychologia, 17*, 607–17.

Zeigler, H.P. (1975). Trigeminal deafferentation and hunger in the pigeon (Columba livia). *Journal of Comparative and Physiological Psychology, 89*, 827–44.

Zeigler, H.P., and Karten, H.J. (1974). Central trigeminal structures and the lateral hypothalamic syndrome in the rat. *Science, 186*, 636–8.

Zepelin, H., and Rechtschaffen, A. (1974). Mammalian sleep, longevity and energy metabolism. *Brain and Behavioral Evolution, 10*, 425–70.

Zola-Morgan, S., and Squire, L.R. (1985). Medial temporal lesions in monkeys impair memory on tests sensitive to human amnesia. *Behavioral Neuroscience, 99*, 22–34.

Subject index

Selected author index